GOD'S
NEW ISRAEL

Edited by
CONRAD CHERRY
Pennsylvania State University

GOD'S
NEW ISRAEL

Religious
Interpretations
of
American Destiny

PRENTICE-HALL, INC.,
Englewood Cliffs, New Jersey

Library of Congress Catalog Card Number: 70-143585

Printed in the United States of America

C 13-357343-5
P 13-357335-4

Current Printing (last digit):

10 9 8 7 6 5 4 3

PRENTICE-HALL INTERNATIONAL, INC., *London*
PRENTICE-HALL OF AUSTRALIA, PTY. LTD., *Sydney*
PRENTICE-HALL OF CANADA, LTD., *Toronto*
PRENTICE-HALL OF INDIA PRIVATE LIMITED, *New Delhi*
PRENTICE-HALL OF JAPAN, INC., *Tokyo*

Americans have tended to find their religious faith in various forms of belief about their own existence as a people.

Max Lerner, *America as a Civilization*

It has been often remarked that the people of the United States come nearer to a parallel with Ancient Israel, than any other nation upon the globe. Hence OUR AMERICAN ISRAEL is a term frequently used; and common consent allows it apt and proper.

Abiel Abbot, *Thanksgiving Sermon,* 1799

Preface

Wee shall finde that the God of Israell is among
us . . . when hee shall make us a prayse and glory,
that men shall say of succeeding plantacions: the lord
make it like that of New England: for wee must
Consider that wee shall be as a Citty upon a Hill, the
eies of all people are uppon us.

John Winthrop, 1630

These words of expectation, composed by the first governor of
the Massachusetts Bay Colony, express a conviction that has exerted a
shaping influence on the American mind. They are words that anticipate
the future glory of New England; in time, such words and the conviction
they convey would embrace the United States. Throughout their history
Americans have been possessed by an acute sense of divine election. They
have fancied themselves a New Israel, a people chosen for the awesome
responsibility of serving as a light to the nations, a city set upon a hill.
This preponderating self-image, in its original form as well as in its
myriad mutations, has served as both a stimulus of creative American
energy and a source of American self-righteousness. It has long been, in
other words, the essence of America's motivating mythology.

The purpose of this book of readings is to trace the theme of American destiny under God through major developments in American history.
Most of the documents are from the pens of religious and political leaders, though there are selections also from two poets and a journalist. In
any case, the influence of all the spokesmen extended well beyond their
specific "professions." American religious and political literature alone
is so saturated with the theme that a full selection of documents bearing
significantly on the subject would fill several volumes. The spokesmen
who have been selected for inclusion here reflect the attitudes and aspirations of their day (even if, in some cases, they are critics of their *zeitgeist*).
Above all, they preserve the basic continuity of the theme but also bring
to light the variations on it that have arisen as Americans have undertaken to define the call of their destiny in different ways.

The book is neither a history of American religious denominations nor a history of American theology. It is, rather, a history of Americans chief religious perspective on themselves as a people. It is a treatment of the central belief in America's national faith, in her civil religion. The large majority of the clergymen whose views are represented here are Protestant because the first well-delineated versions of American destiny were Protestant and because the basic convictions of the national religion were blended with a generalized Protestantism during the nineteenth century. Some of the nation's most distinguished theologians do speak within these pages, but the selections from their writings are not discursive, doctrinal treatises. The theologians' insights into the theme of American destiny are cast, like those of the other spokesmen, in a popular vein for lay consumption.

The presupposition underlying this volume is that any vital myth does not hide in the hinterland of a "realm of ideas" but impinges upon the life of a people as a spring of their action. To give serious attention to the myth of American destiny in its various forms is to heed the concrete courses of action that are excited by it and that in turn affect it. The introductions to the seven parts of this book note the shifts in the myth occasioned by changing historical circumstances and indicate the links between the myth and the events it inspires and vindicates. More extensive discussion of the historical settings and, in some cases, of the mythology itself may be found in the references cited in the notes and suggested readings.

Contents

GOD'S
NEW ISRAEL

Introduction

The belief that America has been providentially chosen for a special destiny has deep roots in the American past, and it is by no means a belief that has been given up in this secular age. It is at the heart of the attempt by contemporary Americans to understand their nation's responsibility at home and abroad. It is a conviction that manifests itself most vividly in occasions of public worship when American citizens meet to share common religious sentiments. Below are descriptions of two such religious ceremonies. The first is set within the intimacy of a small rural community; the second is set in a metropolis and reaches millions of persons through television. Despite differences in setting, style, and ideology, both are American sacred ceremonies which have in common a ritualistic form and a symbolic structure. Both are celebrations of a national religious faith. Both focus on the conviction that America has been called to a special task by God.

I: TWO AMERICAN SACRED CEREMONIES

Boalsburg, a town of approximately 800 people in central Pennsylvania, proudly announces from its billboards its claim to historical significance:

Boalsburg
An American Village
Birthplace of Memorial Day

In the spring of every year, when American patriots gather at cemeteries, town halls, shrines, and churches to celebrate Memorial Day the citizens of Boalsburg and vicinity remind themselves that their ancestors brought forth an event that has become a national holiday.[1] Memorial Day is, as

---

[1] Boalsburg did meet a disappointment in 1966 when President Johnson and both houses of Congress officially recognized Waterloo, New York, as

1

W. Lloyd Warner has observed, "both sacred and secular, it is a holy day as well as a holiday and is accordingly celebrated."[2] Along with Thanksgiving Day and the perhaps less explicitly religious observances of the Fourth of July and the birthdays of Washington and Lincoln, Memorial Day is part of an American ceremonial calendar. It is a day of pleasure and relaxation for most Americans, but it is also—particularly for the towns and small cities of the northeastern United States—a sacred day when the war dead are mourned, the spirit of redemptive sacrifice is extolled, and pledges to American ideals are renewed.

In Boalsburg and the surrounding communities elaborate preparations precede the day itself. During the week or two prior to May 30th, students in the public elementary schools construct flag displays which are pictured in the local newspapers. Graves of the war dead are decorated by families and patriotic organizations. The Veterans of Foreign Wars and the American Legion of the area hold meetings to plan for the holy day and services to commemorate their dead. As the day nears, merchants and residents put up American flags, and newspaper editorials encourage patriotic observance and sometimes lament languid patriotic zeal in the community. On the Sunday before Memorial Day, churches feature sermons on the virtue of human sacrifice for God and country, and veterans and their families gather at the Twenty-Eighth Division Memorial Shrine in Boalsburg to hear messages on the same theme. The climax of the celebration occurs, however, at the end of Memorial Day when all the patriotic groups and celebrants converge at the cemeteries to bring their ceremonies to a collective conclusion.

At 6 P.M. on May 30th, 1967, the crowd gathered on Church Street in Boalsburg to watch a brief parade made up of a high school band, color guards of the VFW and the Legion, fire trucks, and Girl Scouts and Brownies bearing wreaths of flowers. The crowd followed the march two blocks to the cemetery behind Zion Lutheran Church. As people found their places in front of the speakers' platform the Girl Scouts placed their flowers on the soldiers' graves and a drill team fired a rifle salute. For over a hundred yards behind the crowd stretched the cemetery containing stones marking those fallen in American wars. The grave of Amos Meyers was there, the private who was killed on the last day of the battle of Gettysburg at the age of twenty-three and whose mother decorated his

---

the birthplace of the Memorial Day observance. The old-timers, leaders of patriotic organizations, and the press in Boalsburg insist, however, that this was simply a miscarriage of justice: whereas Waterloo's claim rests on the original decoration of soldiers' graves there on May 5, 1866, the first grave decorations in Boalsburg occurred almost two years earlier.

[2] W. Lloyd Warner, *American Life: Dream and Reality* (Chicago: University of Chicago Press, 1953), p. 1.

grave on that first Memorial Day in 1864. The minister of Zion Lutheran Church offered an invocation, and the district representative to the state legislature in Harrisburg rose to give the address.

It was a typical Memorial Day message that lifted up images the people anticipated on this occasion. The nation's and community's war dead were honored as the speaker symbolically united the ethnic and religious groups. He called upon his hearers to remember on this day the sacrificed dead—the Smiths and Steins killed in Vietnam, the Maloneys and Rossis who fell in the Pacific islands, the Heidlers and Lozoskis who made the "supreme sacrifice" in the battle of Meuse-Argonne. And only if the living of the community pledge themselves to the principles for which these men died—democratic freedom and the defense of freedom against tyranny and oppression around the world—will these blood sacrifices not have been in vain. The sacrifices are the sanctification of America's "divine mission" of preserving and dispensing freedom.

Since the spirit of protest against United States involvement in Vietnam was very much in the air in the spring of 1967, several Memorial Day speakers attempted to draw a distinction between democratic freedom and certain types of dissent. "Those who practice civil disobedience," said a Legionnaire at a town a few miles from Boalsburg, "must expect to suffer the penalties provided for violating our laws. It is not an exercise of free expression to burn a draft card, nor to desecrate the flag of the United States."

The Memorial Day celebration is an American sacred ceremony, a religious ritual, a modern cult of the dead. Although it shares the theme of redemptive sacrifice with Christianity and other religions, and although its devotees would insist that the God called upon is the same as the God of Judaism and Christianity, the Memorial Day rite is a civic service that unites Protestants, Catholics, and Jews beyond their sectarian differences. Lloyd Warner has described the essential function of the rite:

> Each man's church provides him and those of his faith with a
> set of beliefs and a way of acting to face these problems [of our own,
> our friends' and all men's death]; but his church and those of other
> men do not equip him with a common set of social beliefs and rituals
> which permit him to unite with all his fellows to confront this com-
> mon and most feared of all his enemies. The Memorial Day rite and
> other subsidiary rituals connected with it form a cult which partially
> satisfies this need for common action on a common problem. It dra-
> matically expresses the sentiments of unity of all the living among
> themselves, of all the living to all the dead, and of all the living and
> dead as a group to the gods.[3]

3 Ibid., p. 24.

Joined with the unifying and existential problem-solving function of the cult is the conviction repeatedly expressed by the speakers that this nation has the providentially bestowed responsibility of acting as guardian and preserver of freedom. American soldiers have presented themselves as sacrifices on the altar of history that America's God-given task of rescuing oppressed peoples might not fail, that she may continue to be a beacon of freedom to all the world, that the sacred principles contained in the Declaration of Independence and the Constitution might remain untarnished.

There are, of course, large segments of American society that would feel little or no affinity with the Memorial Day ceremony. Many citizens in our larger cities, in fact, have never witnessed the celebration of Memorial Day as a sacred event. These portions of our society are doubtless inclined to dismiss the celebration as a vestige of village tribalism. Those who are personally acquainted with the ceremony as a sacred event may be offended by the Legionnaire superpatriotism, frequently involved in the rite, which calls down the blessing of God on all-things-American simply because they are American, and which defends "American freedoms" while at the same time undermining the personal freedom of dissent from and criticism of particular national commitments. Yet Memorial Day remains a holy day for those rural and small-town Americans who have been largely bypassed by the effects of urbanization, and it continues to be taken with special seriousness by those who have been to war and those who have sent their sons to war. Memorial Day is not America's only sacred ceremony, however, and is not the only way Americans as citizens attempt to cope with death. In her funerals for great men, especially her political leaders, America has created another religious ceremony that meets anxiety over death in a corporate way and that transcends sectarian religious differences. The funeral for Senator Robert F. Kennedy was one such ceremony.

After Senator Kennedy's death on June 6, 1968, hundreds of thousands of Americans waited outside St. Patrick's Cathedral in New York City to pay their last respects, and millions of citizens who could not take their places in those long lines were able to assume a kind of presence their through their television sets. By way of television they witnessed the funeral on Saturday, followed the funeral train at its points of passage to Washington, and grieved with the family at the burial. Once again in the 1960s Americans participated in a ceremony honoring a leader who had been stopped by an act of destructive violence. In the funeral Robert Kennedy was vested with a meaning that derived from his "American dream" or his vision of American destiny. The funeral was another sacred ceremony in which the dilemma of death was met corporately, religious differences were transcended, and death was construed in terms of

America's destiny under God. The day of the funeral, unlike Memorial Day, was altogether a holy day, devoid of mixture with a holiday spirit. And because of the suddenness and circumstances of Kennedy's death, the intensity of emotion permeating the funeral was undoubtedly much greater than that of the Memorial Day ceremony. Nevertheless, many of the same themes, symbols, and invocations were present.

Senator Kennedy's funeral was obviously a religious affair; it was "religious" in the sense in which most Americans think of that term since it had the trappings of one of the traditional Western religious communities. It was, after all, a Roman Catholic funeral mass. It was at the same time a civil-religious ceremony that appealed to Americans regardless of their denominational persuasions. The occasion was one in which the Catholic doctrines of hope, resurrection, and heavenly reward for a life well-lived were drawn upon as resources of comfort by a mourning Kennedy family and other Christians. It was also an occasion when the Kennedys and numerous other Americans found a degree of comfort in the conviction that Robert Kennedy had met his death in the midst of an endeavor to secure freedom for all Americans and thereby fulfill that portion of America's destiny.

The funeral liturgy affirmed in the face of death, "For those who have been faithful all the way, life is not ended but merely changed. And when this earthly abode dissolves, an eternal dwelling place awaits them in Heaven." Senator Edward Kennedy, quoting from and commenting on a speech by his brother, offered a different kind of affirmation:

> "Our future may lie beyond our vision, but it is not completely beyond our control. It is the shaping impulse of America that neither faith nor nature nor the irresistible tides of history, but the work of our own hands, matched to reason and principle, will determine our destiny. There is pride in that, even arrogance, but there is also experience and truth. In any event, it is the only way we can live."
> This is the way he lived.[4]

Those words invited their hearers to a hope and a sense of social responsibility in a way that the promise of an "eternal dwelling place" alone could not.

In his eulogy Archbishop Terence J. Cooke also sensed the national religious meaning of the occasion and of Robert Kennedy's life and death. To be sure, the message was sensitive to the deep personal loss that the Kennedy family had sustained and appropriately commented on Robert Kennedy as devoted husband, father, and son. The liturgy's reference to

---

[4] From a transcript of the eulogy furnished by the office of Senator Edward Kennedy.

eternal life after death was cited at the beginning and at the end of the eulogy, providing the frame for the substance of the address. The greater part of Archbishop Cooke's eulogy, however, was a placing of Robert Kennedy in the context of an American dream and was a challenge to Americans to prevent the waste of Kennedy's life by fulfilling that dream.

Although Robert Kennedy could have chosen a much less arduous manner of life, the archbishop said, it was because he was driven by the ideal of building "a better world for his fellow man" that he accepted the demanding challenge of public service. "We admire the ability to identify so that Negro people spoke of him as 'one of ours'. We admire his vision in confronting the problems of poverty and civil rights." It was a dream that he had for America that evoked this admiration and enlisted his followers: "the dream of an America purged of prejudice, assuring freedom for all her citizens, a land of truly equal opportunity." The proper response to this man's tragic death, therefore, is to occupy ourselves with his dream of America's destiny. "Our sense of shame and discouragement tears alone will not wash away. Somehow, by the grace of God, and with the strength that still lies deep within the soul of America, we must find the courage to take up again the laborious work to which Senator Kennedy devoted all his energies: the building of a great and honorable nation. Especially in this hour, we must keep faith with America and her destiny and we must not forsake our trust in one another." Participation in America's historic destiny is the socially responsible way to meet Senator Kennedy's death. "We have always believed in our national destiny marked by unity in lofty ideals. We believe that our country came into existence to secure the blessings of freedom, equality, and peace for ourselves and those who will come after us."[5]

In this funeral Americans joined in a sacred ceremony, the scope of which crossed denominational religious boundaries. Many citizens had participated in another such ceremony only a few weeks earlier at the funeral for Dr. Martin Luther King, Jr., and in still another only a few short years earlier at the funeral for President John F. Kennedy. American history is, in fact, replete with leaders who have been canonized in the national consciousness as exemplars of American ideals and as particular bearers of America's destiny under God. When those leaders have met their deaths they have become, in the national memory as well as in the ceremonies and speeches that surround their deaths, martyrs for the American cause, even in some cases redeemers.[6]

---

[5] From a transcript of the eulogy provided by the office of Archbishop Cooke.

[6] The most obvious example of the process is Lincoln. Since Lincoln's assassination occurred on Good Friday, hundreds of speakers on the following Sunday ("Black Easter") were quick to note that assassination day was also crucifixion day. Said one: "Jesus Christ died for the world: Abraham

There are, of course, differences between the two sacred ceremonies considered here, differences of content as well as emotional climate. The human "freedom" for which the supreme sacrifice has been made and which constitutes the essence of American destiny does not, for example, have the same meaning or call for the same kind of response in the two ceremonies. In the Memorial Day celebration it means the freedom of all peoples of the world to share in American democratic principles, a freedom that Americans are obligated to safeguard. In the Kennedy funeral, "freedom" stands for the civil right of all American citizens to enjoy full and equal participation in their society. Despite such important differences, the two ceremonies have in common a symbolic, thematic, and ritualistic structure. Both are cults of the dead in which the living are united with one another, the living are united with the dead, and all are united with God and what are believed to be his purposes in history. Both ceremonies stress the belief that God has in store—has always had in store—for this nation a special destiny for which the supreme sacrifice has been made and to the fulfillment of which all Americans must dedicate themselves. And both rites are able to unite Americans beyond their religious divisions.

In the early part of the twentieth century the French sociologist Emile Durkheim observed that it is ritual that causes a religious man's faith to come alive, that quickens and sustains his religious belief. "In fact," Durkheim wrote, "whoever has really practiced a religion knows very well that it is the cult which gives rise to [the] impressions of joy, of interior peace, of serenity, of enthusiasm which are, for the believer, an experimental proof of his beliefs." Durkheim also noted that society itself (in addition to specifically "religious" groups within society) employs ritual to reaffirm its common sentiments:

> There can be no society which does not feel the need of upholding and reaffirming at regular intervals the collective sentiments and the collective ideas which make its unity and its personality. Now this moral remaking cannot be achieved except by the means of reunions, assemblies and meetings where the individuals, being closely united to one another, reaffirm in common their common sentiments; hence come ceremonies which do not differ from regular religious ceremonies, either in their object, the results which they produce, or the processes employed to attain these results.[7]

Lincoln died for his country." Cf. the apotheosizing of Jefferson who died on Independence Day, discussed in Merrill D. Peterson, *The Jefferson Image in the American Mind* (New York: Oxford University Press, Inc., 1960), pp. 3ff.

[7] Emile Durkheim, *The Elementary Forms of the Religious Life*, trans. J. W. Swain (New York: The Free Press, 1965), pp. 464, 474–75.

Memorial Day and Robert Kennedy's funeral are only two of the many rituals (all of which are not, of course, rituals for the dead) in which Americans "reaffirm in common their common sentiments." They are ritualistic ceremonies that appeal to their participants as American citizens, elevate American leaders to the status of heroes or martyrs, and celebrate what are held to be American ideals.

The sentiment that is continually reaffirmed by these sacred ceremonies is the conviction that America is a nation called to a special destiny by God. A consideration of the character and shape of the national religion to which this conviction belongs is prerequisite to understanding the development of the theme of this book.

II: THE AMERICAN CIVIL RELIGION

It has become a commonplace to refer to radical pluralism as the cardinal mark of religion in America. The setttlement of this land by peoples of different—often antagonistic—churchly orientations and the influx of numerous European religious groups during periods of heavy immigration meant that Americans eventually had to learn to live with other Americans of diverse religious traditions. The disestablishment of religion by federal and state constitutions meant that no one religion was favored by the laws of the land and that religious organizations in this country had to become altogether "voluntaristic." Every American religion must recruit and hold its members through methods of persuasion rather than coercion, relying upon the free consent of the people rather than upon the arm of the state.

The truth of this portrait of the American religious development has often obscured the other truth, however, that most Americans have come to share a common religion. The plurality of religious sects and denominations and the often misunderstood "separation of church and state" have by no means altered the fact that Americans participate in and celebrate a civil religion. In the words of the sociologist Robert Bellah, "there actually exists alongside of and rather clearly differentiated from the churches an elaborate and well-institutionalized civil religion in America."[8] Although this civil religion is not established by the laws of the land, it is supported and perpetuated by the mores and folk practices of American society. It finds ritual expression in public occasions like the two sacred ceremonies discussed above.

Bellah takes John F. Kennedy's inaugural address as an example of the verbalization of the civil religion and as a clue to the way in which

[8] Robert N. Bellah, "Civil Religion in America," *Daedalus,* Winter 1967, p. 1.

the civil religion may be differentiated from the religious denominations of this country. Kennedy began and closed his address with references to God and God's relation to American tasks and principles. In the opening statement he said,

> I have sworn before you and Almighty God the same solemn oath our forebears prescribed nearly a century and three quarters ago.
>
> The world is very different now. For man holds in his mortal hands the power to abolish all forms of human poverty and to abolish all forms of human life. And yet the same revolutionary beliefs for which our forebears fought are still at issue around the globe—the belief that the rights of man come not from the generosity of the state but from the hand of God.

Kennedy's closing statement reflects the recurrent conviction in American sacred ceremonies:

> Finally, whether you are citizens of America or of the world, ask of us the same high standards of strength and sacrifice that we shall ask of you. With a good conscience our only sure reward, with history the final judge of our deeds, let us go forth to lead the land we love, asking His blessing and His help, but knowing that here on earth God's work must truly be our own.

As Bellah points out, similar God-references appear in all the inaugural addresses with the exception of Washington's second and "are almost invariably to be found in the pronouncements of American presidents on solemn occasions, though usually not in the working messages that the president sends to Congress on various concrete issues." To the cynic who would insist that the invocations of God are merely ritualistic expresssions that a president must use to get votes or to gain the support of pious people, Bellah replies, "What people say on solemn occasions need not be taken at face value, but it is often indicative of deep-seated values and commitments that are not made explicit in the course of everyday life."[9] Commenting on the rhetoric of a different public ceremony, Alan Trachtenberg offers a similar judgment: ". . . speeches might be dismissed as highly conventional and insincere. Sincerity, however, is not a necessary qualification for cultural significance; surely the conventions of language themselves suggest predispositions among Americans to react in certain ways at certain times."[10]

[9] Ibid., p. 2.
[10] Alan Trachtenberg, *Brooklyn Bridge: Fact and Symbol* (New York: Oxford University Press, Inc., 1965), p. 117.

It is significant that Kennedy did not refer to Jesus Christ, to the Roman Catholic church, or to any specifically Catholic doctrine. This does not mean that on this occasion President Kennedy ceased to be a Catholic; it does mean that the particular doctrines of his Catholic faith were inappropriate to the public occasion. It indicates that the religious point of view he was propounding was not to be confused with his Catholicism. His religious language was aimed altogether toward the American as a citizen. He mentioned the fact that his oath of office was made before both the people and Almighty God. "In American political theory," Bellah comments, "sovereignty rests, of course, with the people, but implicitly, and often explicitly, the ultimate sovereignty has been attributed to God." Kennedy reinforced this appeal to an ultimate authority when he said, "the rights of man come not from the generosity of the state but from the hand of God." Again, in Bellah's words, "the rights of man are more basic than any political structure and provide a point of revolutionary leverage from which any state structure may be radically altered." Finally, in his statement that "here on earth God's work must truly be our own," Kennedy gave voice to the continuous theme in American history that it is this nation's destiny—for Kennedy, in conjunction with "the citizens of the world"—to carry out God's will on earth. Kennedy's inaugural address recalls the God-references in the Declaration of Independence: the mention of the "Laws of Nature and of Nature's God" that entitle any people to independence; the statement that all men "are endowed by their Creator with certain inalienable Rights"; the appeal to "the Supreme Judge of the world for the rectitude of our intentions"; and the urging of "a firm reliance on the protection of divine Providence."[11]

The Declaration of Independence, the inaugural addresses of presidents, the celebration of American sacred ceremonies indicate that the disestablishment of the church hardly meant that the American political sphere was denied a religious dimension. In fact, that dimension so permeates the political, educational and social life of America that it constitutes a civil religion that cannot be identified with Protestantism, Catholicism, or Judaism as such. Americans may be participants in *both* the religious dimension of their civil life *and* one of the traditional Western religions. The American church historian Sidney Mead is so convinced of the presence of this civil religion at the very foundations of American life and of its potential catholicity that he has said, "just as the ideal of America has been that 'of moulding many peoples into the visible image of the citizen,' so it was implied that the religious ideal was that of melding the many diverse sectarianisms into one cosmopolitan religion."[12]

---

[11] Bellah, "Civil Religion," pp. 4–6.
[12] Sidney E. Mead, "The 'Nation With the Soul of a Church,'" *Church History*, Sept. 1967, p. 263.

The sacred ceremonies and Kennedy's inaugural provide some clues to the beliefs that make up the civil religion. This nation's destiny under God, the guarantee of human rights by the hand of God, the need for sacrifice and martyrdom for the fulfillment of the nation's destiny—all these are parts of the belief structure of the civil religion. When dealing with any religion, however—be it Christianity, Buddhism, or the American civil religion—it is a highly questionable practice to detail beliefs in isolation from their historical settings. In some cases a religion's reformulation of a belief—in responding to the problems, or in absorbing the spirit, of a given milieu—involves little more than a shift in phraseology. In other instances, however, changes in expression reflect changes in the very substance of the belief. The readings in this book are concerned with the central, continuous belief around which other convictions in the civil religion cluster. The readings also portray the changes—some of them quite drastic—that have occurred in the formulation of the belief. At this point the contours of the general religious context in which that belief is set should emerge in a sketch of three features of the American civil religion: (1) the sources of its beliefs and symbols, (2) its institutions, (3) the relation between the civil religion and other religions in this country.

1. *The Sources of the Beliefs and Symbols of the Civil Religion*

The deepest source lies in the Old and New Testaments, but the more immediate source is the history of America or certain events of that history which have been judged revelatory. In the ceremonies of the civil religion the images of God's deliverance of and demands upon his chosen people and the rebirth that can issue from sacrificial death are definitely biblical images. But they are given immediacy by being translated into events of American history. God's demands upon his chosen people became demands upon America at this particular juncture of her history. Rebirth through sacrificial death becomes the rebirth of the nation through the sacrifices of her war dead and martyrs. Biblical events serve as the archetypes, but *the immediate events of revelation*—those paradigmatic events by which the celebrants of the civil religion interpret the meaning of their national life and the purposes of God in history—*are events in the American experience*.[13] As will be apparent in many of the selections in this anthology, two chief revelatory events for the civil religion are the American Revolution (joined with the entire constitutional period) and the American Civil War. The first was a moment when God delivered the colonies from Pharaoh Britain and the "evils" of the Old

---

[13] Cf. Bellah, "Civil Religion," p. 18.

World, revealed the purposes of the nation, and adopted the Young Republic as an example and instrument of freedom and republican government for the rest of the world. The Civil War was the nation's first real "time of testing" when God tried the permanence of the Union or, in some interpretations, brought judgment upon his wayward people. Documents like the Declaration of Independence and the Gettysburg Address function as scriptures that interpret these events and hence preserve the traditions of the civil religion. Washington becomes both Moses and Joshua, both the deliverer of the American people out of bondage and the leader of the chosen people into the Promised Land of independence. Lincoln assumes the role of a Christ figure in the national memory: one who tragically dedicated himself to the destiny of a united nation and whose death summed up the sacrifices that redeemed the nation for that destiny.[14]

Other events, persons, and documents in American history have taken on sacred meaning, but these are sufficient to point to the way in which that history most immediately supplies the civil religion with its symbolic material. It is somewhat misleading, therefore, to refer to the civil or national religion as a "common denominator" faith, as if it were formed by reducing Christianity and Judaism to their bare essentials. The belief structure is primarily constituted by the inflow of a history that *Americans as Americans* hold in common. Although the national religion borrows heavily from the Jewish and Christian religions, it is not the borrowed elements but the American experience itself that creates the commonality of the civil faith. "The Lord hath more light yet to break forth out of his Holy Word" was a declaration of John Robinson, pastor of the settlers of Plymouth in 1620 while they were still exiles at Leyden. It is also a statement that catches the spirit of the American civil religion which supposes that the light of God's revelation continually breaks forth in crucial events of American history.

2. *The Institutional Framework of the Civil Religion.*

Clearly the foremost institution is the nation itself, with the public school serving as an important subinstitution. Churches and synagogues have also provided a haven for the myths, symbols, and ceremonies of the civil religion.

John E. Smylie has convincingly argued that the nation gradually assumed the traditional role of the church for most Americans. As these shores were inundated by a host of diverse religious organizations and as

---

[14] On American heroes and hero cults see Dixon Wecter, *The Hero in America* (New York: Charles Scribner's Sons, 1941).

our laws made clear that no one religious denomination could operate as a national religion, the word "church" made sense to Americans only in the plural. Every church became for the citizens of this land "a voluntary society, perhaps the most important among others, but hardly the organ through which God made his ultimate historical demands and offered his fullest earthly rewards." Lacking special endorsement by the state, the American churches gave up the functions normally associated with the universal church. But where the churches moved out, the nation moved in. "Gradually in America the nation emerged as the primary agent of God's meaningful activity in history. Hence Americans bestowed on it a catholicity of destiny similar to that which theology attributes to the universal church." Early colonial groups believed that their own church covenants were vehicles of God's action in history, but eventually the Declaration of Independence, the Constitution and the Bill of Rights became the covenants that bound together the people of the nation and secured to them God's blessing, protection and call to historic mission.[15]

The public schools of this country have played an inestimable role both in advancing the traditions of the civil religion and in undergirding the religious function of the nation. They have provided the place of instruction (often, admittedly, the place of unexamined propaganda) in the "sacred history" of the civil religion. To be sure, until recent efforts at redirection the public schools were unabashedly Protestant in their prayers, morning devotions, and general religious orientation. But they were also the depositories and purveyors of the events and documents of the civil religion. The Supreme Court rulings forbidding devotional Bible reading and prayer are more an effort to disentangle the practices and beliefs of the diverse American religions (including, according to the Court, the "religion of secularism") from those of the civil religion than an attempt to put an end to the civil religion in the schools. In the texts and classrooms students are still instructed in the basic documents of the civil religion (including their references to God and providence), the religion's heroes and martyrs are still celebrated on their birthdays and on Memorial Day, the American ceremonial calendar is still observed. Furthermore, the public schools have long encouraged their teachers to awaken in their pupils something very similar to what John Dewey called the "common faith," a faith consisting basically of the ideals supportive of American democracy and a type of humanism. A commission of the National Education Association in 1951 named such things as "the supreme importance of the individual personality," "common consent," "brotherhood," and "the pursuit of happiness" as items of a common faith

---

[15] John Edwin Smylie, "National Ethos and the Church," *Theology Today*, Oct. 1963, pp. 313–17.

worthy of being taught in the schools and as "the values which made America great."[16]

Although the civil religion has its own ceremonies, scriptures, events of revelation, and institutions, it has also found immeasurable support from the American churches. The Americanization of the churches and synagogues has been so well documented that it only needs mentioning here. To a great extent the churches of this land have come to abide by the suggestion of the Founding Fathers that the different religious groups should not only exist for the sake of their own beliefs and practices but should also assume responsibility for maintenance of the public order, the dissemination of the essential religious beliefs (for example, the existence of a Deity, the governance of the world by his providence, the reward of virtue and the punishment of crime), and the promotion of the public welfare. The presence of the American flag in the churches, the celebration of national events by religious groups, the frequent mixing of biblical and "sacred" American history in sermons are some of the obvious signs that the national religion has found a home in the American churches. The obvious signs are often misleading, however, for the history of the relationship between the national religion and the denominations has been complex.

3. The Relation Between the Civil Religion and Other Religions in America.

At least three modes of this relationship have turned up in the American experience.

Robert Bellah notes one mode when he uses Kennedy's inaugural address as an indication that the civil religion "exists alongside of" and is "rather clearly differentiated from the churches." In this address as well as in the two sacred ceremonies discussed above, sectarian religious beliefs do not intrude; in fact, religious differences are transcended to the plane of a national faith made up of images and beliefs that Americans hold in common. The religious references do have their deepest source in the biblical tradition of the churches, but they are so woven into the fabric of national history that they lose any potentially sectarian color. In this relationship, therefore, the national religion and the denominations remain quite distinct. An American may be a Methodist, a Conservative Jew, or a Roman Catholic and at the same time participate in the civil religion— without insisting that the civil religion be expressed in specifically Methodist, Jewish, or Catholic terms.

---

[16] See Robert Michaelsen, "The Public Schools and 'America's Two Religions,'" *A Journal of Church and State*, Autumn 1966, pp. 380–400.

Although this type of relationship has had its defenders in American history from Jefferson and Franklin to Lincoln to Dewey, only recently has it become a vital option in America. Only after Protestantism lost its powerful grip on the public life of the nation did the civil religion begin to dislodge itself from Protestant articulation and custody. During the nineteenth century and well into the twentieth, leading spokesmen for the civil religion couched its beliefs in terms that were unmistakably Protestant. It took such factors as the impact of non-Protestant immigrants, a Supreme Court determined to de-Protestantize the public schools, and a pluralization of values in many regions of American life through modern means of communication to break through this confusion of Protestantism and the religion of America. "Not until the modern period," as Franklin Littell has said, "when Catholics and Jews and others have come into full and unabashed participation in the public life of the nation, as symbolized by the 1960 election, has the old Protestant culture-religion been frontally challenged."[17]

A second kind of relationship between the civil religion and other religions, therefore, has a long historical precedent, though that precedent is in the process of being broken. It is marked by a rather thorough blending of a generalized Protestantism with the national religion. The Protestantism is "generalized" in that it is nondenominational. Its representatives tend to define America as a "Christian civilization," but their Christianity is seldom big enough to include Roman Catholicism.

Lyman Beecher, that colorful and influential Congregational minister of the nineteenth century, was quite a man of his time when he mixed his Protestantism and his civil religion in about equal doses. Beecher's Protestantism was generalized in the sense that he was extremely capable of glossing over theological differences in somewhat typical nineteenth-century American Protestant fashion, but also, as Sidney Mead has remarked, because "Protestantism had become for him a principle of high generality which, he thought, permeated and was being incarnated in the democratic institutions of the Republic."[18] Despite the generality of his Protestantism, however, like so many other nineteenth-century Protestants, Beecher could find no room in his civil faith for Roman Catholics. His popular and oft-delivered address, "A Plea for the West", took up that central theme in the civil religion: "America is, in the providence of God, destined to lead the way in the moral and political emancipation of the world." Beecher anchored the theme to what he considered "equally plain," namely "that the religious and political destiny of our nation is

[17] Franklin H. Littell, "The Churches and the Body Politic," *Daedalus*, Winter 1967, p. 33.
[18] Mead, "Soul of a Church," p. 280.

to be decided in the West." Beecher drew upon a lively vision of the West as he encouraged easterners to pour their resources into educational and religious enterprises on the frontier, but he gave his plea urgency by warning that the West had to be educated and made religious before it was completely inundated by European immigrants who would wreck democratic principles with a "Catholic system" that is "adverse to liberty." Such a peremptory exclusion of Catholics from the religious and political nucleus of the nation has been transcended in contemporary American life, but its ideological source (the confusion of Protestantism with the religion of the nation) has not yet been completely destroyed.

Finally, the civil religion and other religions in America have existed in a relationship of tension. The most obvious instances of the tension appear in those sects, like the Jehovah's Witnesses, that spurn patriotic symbols, reject American sacred ceremonies, and refuse to allow the nation to function for them as a "church." But clergy and scholars within the Christian and Jewish mainstream have also insisted that a tension exists between their own traditions and the American "culture faith."

During the 1950s and early 1960s a flood of criticism flowed from the pens of Protestants, Catholics, and Jews who were convinced that the Americanization of their faiths resulted in a banal, watered-down version of their potent Judeo-Christian heritage. Charges against the "American Shinto," that vague "religion in general" which is the heart of the "American way of life," ranged from claims of its sentimental piosity and theological naiveté to indictments of its idolatrous worship of American values and narrow-minded nationalism. Much was made of the way in which God and religion were *used* in our culture by politicians, clergymen, popularizers of religion, and businessmen for their own higher ends: for the support of particular national tasks, for the swelling of church membership rolls, for gaining "peace of mind" in a troubled world, for achieving success in a society of capitalistic competition. Professor Will Herberg summed up the reasons for his condemnation of the civil religion:

> ... civic religion has always meant the sanctification of the society and culture of which it is the reflection, and that is one of the reasons why Jewish-Christian faith has always regarded such religion as incurably idolatrous. Civic religion is a religion which validates culture and society, without in any sense bringing them under judgment. . . .
>
> The burden of this criticism of American religion from the point of view of Jewish-Christian faith is that contemporary religion is so naively, so innocently *man-centered*. Not God, but man—man in his individual and corporate being—is the beginning and end of the spiritual system of much present-day American religiosity. . . .

God is conceived as man's "omnipotent servant," faith as a sure-fire device to get what we want.[19]

There have been some who have replied to the critics of the civil religion. Sidney Mead has written, "The 'American religion,' contrary to Will Herberg's much popularized misunderstanding, is *not* 'the American way of life' as we know and experience it, any more than the Christian faith *is* the way of life that ordinary professing 'Christians' commonly exemplify in their everyday activities."[20] Along the same line Robert Bellah insists that the critics "take as criteria the best in their own religious tradition and as typical the worst in the tradition of the civil religion," conveniently overlooking the fact that spokesmen for the civil religion have often drawn upon a vivid belief in a transcendent God who cannot be reduced to human designs, in order to censure American society.[21] Abraham Lincoln, for example, who identified with no particular denomination, was able to perform this "prophetic" role for the civil religion during the sectional crisis (see Part IV). And one is reminded of John Kennedy's use of the idea of "the rights of man from the hand of God" as a revolutionary lever. Mead and Bellah seem to be after a distinction between *religious nationalism* and *national religion*. Religious nationalism implies a corporate attitude of unconditional reverence for the nation and for its pretended or real goals. National religion, on the other hand, suggests a national attitude of reverence for a transcendent sovereign authority whose designs cannot be identified one-to-one with the designs of the nation. In the latter case America can function as a "church" or as an inclusive institution whose ideals and goals bind a people together under a sovereign God. When those ideals or goals themselves usurp the transcendent authority, or when the nation's every move receives uncritical religious endorsement, the national religion slips into the idolatry of religious nationalism.[22] Many readings in this book will

---

[19] Will Herberg, *Protestant-Catholic-Jew* (Garden City, N.Y.: Doubleday & Company, Inc., Anchor Books, 1960), p. 263, 268. Similar criticisms are abundant, but see especially Martin E. Marty, *The New Shape of American Religion* (New York: Harper & Row, Publishers, 1959); A. Roy Eckardt, "The New Look in American Piety," *Christian Century*, Nov. 17, 1954; Peter Berger, *The Noise of Solemn Assemblies* (Garden City, N.Y.: Doubleday & Company, Inc., 1961).

[20] Mead, "Soul of a Church," pp. 274–75.

[21] Bellah, "Civil Religion," p. 12.

[22] For this formulation of the distinction I am indebted to my colleague Professor John R. Whitney in his unpublished paper, "Civil Religion in the Philippines." Cf. his "Commentary on 'Civil Religion in America,'" in *The Religious Situation: 1968,* ed. Donald R. Cutler (Boston: Beacon Press, 1968), pp. 365–81.

show that the sense of national destiny has frequently led Americans to make the passage from national religion to religious nationalism. Other readings will demonstrate, however, that Americans have often recoiled from the passage and have understood the deluding temptations of the path.

This much must be said on behalf of the critics of the American civil religion: their indictment of the utilitarian distortions of religion (which reached their peak in the 1950s) has been very much to the point. However much they have identified the whole of the civil religion with its worst side, they have portrayed the idolatry involved when the civil religion sanctifies, without question, the values or goals of American society. To that extent, when other American religions exist in a relation of tension with the civil religion, the tension can point up the distortions of the latter.

The accumulated tradition of the civil religion by no means guarantees that it will persist as a vital religious orientation in American life, for it faces serious problems in the modern world.

Much of the symbolism of the civil religion, for instance, has lost its clarity and specificity. Words such as freedom, democracy, providence, and (especially) God which recur in the celebrations of the national faith seem to lack uniform meaning for contemporary Americans. This problem of language is not so much a case of the death of the symbols themselves as it is a matter of the symbols becoming ambiguous. In fact, the ambiguity seems to increase the symbols' capacity to conjure up, like words of Black Magic, diverse and potent images. As W. H. Auden has put the matter, "words like Communism, Capitalism, Imperialism, Peace, Freedom, Democracy, have ceased to be words the meaning of which can be inquired into and discussed, and have become right or wrong noises to which the response is as involuntary as a knee reflex."[23]

When the civil religion's central symbol, God, becomes ambiguous but retains its evocative powers, the resultant problem is much more serious than a mere problem of language. If that symbol does not refer clearly to a transcendent reality that brings all nations to judgment, the national religion is more than a little inclined to ignore the narrowness and evil within the nation. Reinhold Niebuhr's understanding of the Jewish-Christian God as one "who laughs at human pretensions without being hostile to human aspirations" can exercise a powerful check on chauvinism without destroying the national spirit. When a transcendent

---

[23] From an excerpt of Auden's speech made upon acceptance of the 1967 Medal for Literature of the National Book Committee, *The Washington Post Book World*, Dec. 24, 1967, p. 8.

perspective of that kind is lacking, the lost causes and less than virtuous aspirations of a people are hidden under a cloak of self-righteousness. Americans have more than once been blinded to their vices by their pretensions to virtue (as well as by their real virtues). As Sidney Mead has so aptly put it, while Americans have consistently viewed themselves as the bearers of a special destiny under God, "God, like Alice's Cheshire Cat, has sometimes threatened gradually to disappear altogether or, at most, to remain only as a disembodied and sentimental smile."[24] In theological terms the God who smiles innocuously on American undertakings is a sentimental Deity whose wrath has ceased to burn toward national sins. In more secular terms the American people have failed to measure themselves by their own highest national ideals. (See Part VII.)

The civil religion, like any religion which becomes an established part of a culture, is always in danger of sanctifying the virtues of a society while ignoring its vices. Although the danger is not characteristic of the contemporary scene alone, America's present position as a great world power intensifies the peril. Americans have long lived under the conviction that their nation always comes to the defense of other countries for the sake of "free institutions" and "democratic governments." Can we admit, rhetoric to the contrary notwithstanding, that we have also rushed to the aid of military dictatorships (as in South Vietnam) when we believe such action will serve our own national interests? The powerful *and clear* symbolizing of a transcendent reality is a religious assurance that such pretensions and shortcomings of the nation will be brought to light.

The civil religion faces another dilemma. How inclusive can that religion become without losing its identity? For the sake of a healthy openness it is called upon to embrace a plurality of values and standpoints both within the nation and in the world at large. Within the national boundaries, however, it has found no way of embracing agnostic or atheistic elements. Perhaps it is absurd to expect a civil *religion* to include these elements within its own fold. But as a *civil* religion, it definitely has a responsibility to these components of the national life. Since the civil religion is so intimate a part of American society, it is capable of obstructing the full participation of Americans in the nation's public life. When it performs that function it fails to support the democratic principle that no person or group of persons shall be disadvantaged by either their religious or their nonreligious beliefs. "We have had a Catholic president; it is conceivable that we could have a Jewish one. But could we have an agnostic president? Could a man with conscientious scruples about using the word *God* the way Kennedy and Johnson have used it be

---

[24] Sidney E. Mead, *The Lively Experiment* (New York: Harper & Row, Publishers, 1963), p. 152.

elected chief magistrate of our country?"[25] One may expect that the further pluralization of American society will permit a positive answer to that question; in the meantime Americans must wrestle with the issue of how inclusive American public life really is when it is informed by the present attitudes of the civil religion.

A more urgent aspect of this same dilemma turns on whether the civil religion will truly encompass the black American, the poor, the American Indian, and all those other citizens who have been excluded from a white, affluent mainstream. The civil religion certainly has the resources for meeting this problem in its doctrine of the rights of all men, and its spokesmen have not neglected civil rights when articulating the theme of "America's destiny under God." Solutions to this paramount problem will not come easily, however, inasmuch as the social issues which have increasingly divided Americans since the end of World War II portend a loss of corporate identity, a loss of what Durkheim called "collective religious sentiments." The civil religion is not simply the heir of this dilemma; it has been one of its chief creators as well. Surely, for example, the revelatory events of the civil religion have been drawn too exclusively from the history of white America. Time will tell whether the national faith will include in its revelatory traditions Negro and American Indian history and "saints." Martin Luther King, Jr., and Nathan Wright, Jr., have indicated at least the possibility of this course of action in their vision of American blacks as a redemptive remnant for the whole of American society (see Part VII).

Finally, the question of the possible inclusiveness of the civil religion has international implications. In the midst of a twentieth-century quest for world order and understanding, a *national* civil religion—one that draws its traditions from a national history and institutionalizes itself in a nation—seems terribly provincial. Does not the civil religion tighten the hold of national prejudices on the American mind? Although the civil religion need not play this deleterious role, that has been its overwhelming tendency. Although the ideals and goals of the civil religion need not exclude connection with what John Kennedy called the ideals and goals of the "citizens of the world," Americans, like citizens of other nations, are apt to confine their visions within the limits of national self-interest. Since the end of the First World War, statements of leading American clergymen and church councils (traditionally strong supporters of the civil religion) indicate the hesitancy on the part of church leaders to commit themselves to the United States as the decisive locus of God's action in history. The theological rediscovery of the sin that infects all nations, the apotheosis of racism and extreme nationalism in Nazi Germany, and an ecumenical movement that attempts to cross both religious and cultural

25 Bellah, "Civil Religion," p. 15.

barriers have convinced these clergymen that any acceptable religion must have much wider institutional boundaries than those of the United States.[26] There is no evidence, however, that the reservations and protests of church leaders have seriously weakened the appeal of the national religion to the masses of American society. In fact, in a world that continues to be somewhat nervously balanced by national power blocks, it is perhaps hoping for too much to expect most Americans to give up the religious endorsement of their national tasks. Still, two improvements of the American civil religion do seem to be within the realm of immediate possibility: it could begin to incorporate international or transnational symbols and creeds into its framework, and it could take the position that it is only *one* of a host of more or less acceptable civil religions in the world.

III: AMERICAN DESTINY UNDER GOD

Beheld from the angle of governing myths and symbols, the history of the American civil religion is a history of the conviction that the American people are God's New Israel, his newly chosen people. The belief that America has been elected by God for a special destiny in the world is the focus of American sacred ceremonies, the inaugural addresses of our presidents, the sacred scriptures of the civil religion. It has become so pervasive a motif in the national life that the word "belief" does not really capture the dynamic role that it has played for the American people. It has long since passed into "the realm of motivational myths."[27] It is a myth in the sense that it provides a religious outlook on history and its purpose, and by finding a place in the feelings and choices as well as in the ideas of the people, it can move them to action. When a spokesman for the civil religion appeals to this myth, therefore, he not only strikes a responsive chord in his auditors, for if he dramatizes his subject, he may elicit a commitment.

A sense of providential calling is not, of course, an exclusive possession of the American people. Other nations have been sustained by the belief that God or Fate or historical circumstance has elected them to a preeminent role in history. The sentiment is probably as old as nationalism itself;[28] at any rate, it has furnished other nations and groups of people with a sense of purpose as they have developed their corporate ideals

---

[26] This shift on the part of the clergy is delineated by John E. Smylie in his doctoral dissertation, "Protestant Clergymen and America's World Role, 1865–1900" (Princeton Theological Seminary, 1959), pp. 569–81.

[27] The phrase is Sidney Mead's in his discussion of the motif, *The Lively Experiment*, p. 75.

[28] Russel B. Nye, *This Almost Chosen People* (East Lansing: Michigan State University Press, 1966), pp. 164–65.

and their historical tasks. The fact that the conviction is not uniquely American, however, by no means derogates from its importance in the American experience. It has sustained the American people from the colonial period to the present, and it has taken on a distinctively American appearance as it has both motivated and vindicated American projects. It has been such a powerful myth for the nation that it has decisively shaped our foreign relations as well as our own internal developments. "It needs to be taken into account if we are to understand the American willingness to help, the passion to build and reform, and how these virtues get mixed up with America's complacency and, at times, her insufferable self-righteousness."[29]

It would, of course, be highly misleading to assume that this pervasive and continuous theme of American destiny has received uniform interpretation throughout American history. The various challenges that have faced the American people—the settlement of a wilderness frontier, the formation of a republic, the fighting of wars, the preservation of peace—have evoked different interpretations of America's high calling. And occasionally within the same period of history, with respect to the same challenge, Americans have been deeply divided over the meaning of the national mission. The following documents and their introductions are concerned with these variations on the one theme of American destiny under God. It is well to note beforehand, however, that there have been two basic versions when the theme has been applied to the relation between America and other peoples.

America has been regarded either as a "light to the nations" which by force of example will positively influence other peoples and perhaps draw them to an American haven of freedom, or as a chosen people with an obligation actively to win others to American principles and to safeguard those principles around the world. The first pattern is what Clinton Rossiter has called the "true American Mission" and the "finest expression of American nationalism":

> It assumes that God, at the proper stage in the march of history, called forth certain hardy souls from the old and privilege-ridden nations; that He carried these precious few to a new world and presented them and their descendents with an environment ideally suited to the development of a free society; and that in bestowing His grace He also bestowed a peculiar responsibility for the success of popular institutions. Were the Americans to fail in their experiment in self-government, they would fail not only themselves, but all men wanting or deserving to be free.[30]

[29] Gordon Harland, "Religious Faith and the National Task," *Religion in the Public Domain,* eds. Conrad Cherry and John Fenton (University Park, Pa.: Center for Continuing Liberal Education, 1966), p. 45.

[30] Clinton Rossiter, "The American Mission," *The American Scholar,* 20 (1950–51), 19–20.

This view of American destiny had its classic expression during the Revolution and the constitutional period, but it had been nursed by the Puritans of Massachusetts Bay and has appeared repeatedly in the course of American history. According to the second version, Americans have presupposed that their divine election involves more than being an example for the rest of the world. They have believed that this nation is called to spread abroad the fundamental principles stated in the Bill of Rights, to preserve democratic government around the world, and to protect free men wherever and whenever their freedoms are threatened. Such assumptions undergirded the foreign-mission enterprises of the American churches during the late nineteenth and early twentieth centuries, and they have stimulated and vindicated American participation in foreign wars.

The second version of American destiny has had its unlovely manifestations: a muscular imperialism that cloaks American self-interest with platitudes about saving the world for democracy, a racist myth that justifies American actions abroad because of "Anglo-Saxon superiority," etc. But the first version contains within it the seeds of an extreme isolationism that would preclude the nation's responsibility for the international welfare. Again Clinton Rossiter's remarks are appropriate when he says that America's mission understood as example

> can serve as a cloak for the revival of the most short-sighted, ethnocentric stamp of isolationism, but only if internationally-minded Americans permit it to be stolen from their keeping. The American Mission, a view of national destiny neither vulgar nor imperialistic, can certainly be squared with a healthy attitude of international cooperation.[31]

The key word here is "cooperation", which means that if the avoidance of isolationism is not to result in some form of imperialism, America must free herself from the messianic illusions which have led her to insist that she is the Savior of the world. International cooperation requires an openness to alternatives and compromise, something which is altogether foreign to messianic absolutism.

All of the contemporary problems facing the civil religion come to a head in the myth of American destiny under God. The ambiguity of the God symbolism tends to render the direction of American destiny indistinct; and an attitude of international cooperation balks at any nation's assumption that it has a higher destiny than any other nation. Above all, the belief in America as God's New Israel has come to support America's arrogant self-righteousness. It has been all too easy for Americans to convince themselves that they have been chosen to be a free and powerful

31 Ibid., p. 27.

people not because God or the circumstances of history choose in mysterious ways but because they *deserve* election. The blessings of success, wealth, and power are readily taken as signs of their having merited a special place in history. Much of this smug self-satisfaction doubtless stems from the fact that America has never tasted the bitter dregs of tragic defeat. "As a civilization," Max Lerner has said, "America has never had to meet the great test of apparently irretrievable failure. Except for the Civil War, its history has been without sharp breaks, and even the Civil War was (in the phrase of Allan Nevins) an 'ordeal of union' rather than a break in history." The relative smoothness of America's movement from the past into the future sets her apart from other civilizations. "America as a civilization has been far removed from the great type-enactment of the Christian story, or the disasters of Jewish history or of the Asiatic empires: it has not suffered, died, been reborn. The weight it bears as it faces its destiny is the weight not of history but of institutions. Its great tests are still to come."[32]

It may be, however, that America's tests are already upon her and that her historical resources for dealing with the tragic dimensions of life simply have not been mined. The most recent crises both at home and abroad have cast dark clouds of doubt over the unbroken American success story. These crises may force Americans to recover the largely ignored components of frustration, failure, and defeat in the national experience —components discernible, for example, in the history of the South and in the history of the black American.[33] But to make this suggestion is to anticipate the concluding part of this book. A grasp of the recent threats to the mythology of American destiny requires, first of all, an understanding of the rich, complex history of that mythology.

[32] Max Lerner, *America as a Civilization* (New York: Simon and Schuster, Inc., 1957), p. 948.
[33] See C. Vann Woodward, *The Burden of Southern History* (New York: Random House, Inc., Vintage Books, 1960), pp. 3–25; and Vincent Harding, "The Uses of the Afro-American Past," in *The Religious Situation: 1969*, ed. Donald R. Cutler (Boston: Beacon Press, 1969), pp. 829–40.

part one

THE COLONIAL ERRAND INTO THE WILDERNESS

The rudiments of the theme of American destiny under God emerged in the English colonization of the New World. The new nation that was to appear would inherit from the thirteen colonies an English language, legal system, and set of social customs, all appropriately adapted to the American environment. It would fall heir also to a religious view of history that had developed in the mother country. By the time they launched their colonial enterprises in the seventeenth century, Englishmen had been taught from childhood that the course of human history is directed by God's overruling providence and that God's redemptive efforts centered on England and English Christianity. These assumptions about history were frequently joined with the millennialist belief that God and his chosen English saints were actively defeating the powers of Satan, the first major victory being the Protestant Reformation.[1] The establishment

---

[1] As Winthrop S. Hudson notes, this perspective on history was greatly influenced by the writings of John Foxe, whose *Book of Martyrs* was officially placed in every cathedral church in 1571 and later came to occupy a place second only to the Bible in Protestant homes. Winthrop S. Hudson, *Religion in America* (New York: Charles Scribner's Sons, 1965), p. 19. On Foxe see William Haller, *The Elect Nation: The Meaning and Relevance of Foxe's Book of Martyrs* (New York: Harper & Row, Publishers, 1963). On millennialism see Ernest Lee Tuveson, *Redeemer Nation: The Idea of America's Millennial Role* (Chicago: University of Chicago Press, 1968), pp. 1–30.

of colonies, therefore, was scarcely considered an ordinary undertaking. Many Englishmen saw it as an opportunity to extend the influence of their civilization through which God was working for the redemption of mankind. For others colonization was a chance to bring England to her senses by achieving on new soil what they had not been able to do at home. The Quaker William Penn was moved to announce that his "holy experiment" in religious toleration was meant to be God's own "example to the nations." The letters of the Jesuit father Andrew White claimed that the settlement of Maryland was continuously presided over by the providence of God and that the "first and most important design" of the colony was "sowing the seeds of religion and piety."

Religion was by no means the only, or even the dominant, motive for the settlement of most of the colonies. A religious view of history, however, did furnish a framework of self-understanding for colonists and stockholders who were impelled by a variety of motives. In the early literature of Virginia, for example, an admitted economic motive was interwoven with a historical perspective in which the providence of God loomed large. John Rolfe, whose method of cultivating a sweet leaf of tobacco was instrumental in establishing Virginia's staple crop, wrote that the migration to Virginia was a venture of "a peculiar people, marked and chosen by the finger of God" to possess the land. Alexander Whitaker, a clergyman of the Church of England who arrived at Jamestown with Sir Thomas Dale in 1611 and helped Dale found the town of Henrico, explicated the religious meaning of the Virginia planting but not without reference to economics. Whitaker's *Good Newes From Virginia* was sent to the Virginia Company, which directed it into publication in 1613. In that sermon he enumerated the religious reasons why an Englishman should maintain a financial interest in Virginia. God's deliverance of Sir Thomas Gates and the survivors of the *Sea Venture* which wrecked on Bermuda and His saving of the colony from famine were signs of providential blessing on the enterprise. As a Christian nation England was obligated to answer God's call to convert the heathen Indians to the Christian faith and civilized customs. England was being challenged to defend her reputation among the nations as a charitable and persevering people. Though counseling patience and condemning a usurious spirit, Whitaker frankly appealed to the economic motive, placing it in his religious framework: "fortie years were expired, before Israel could plant in Canaan, and yet God had called them by the word of his mouth, had led them himselfe by a high hand. Yet may you boldly looke for a shorter time of reward."

The most self-conscious pursuit of destiny under God in the New World was enacted by the Puritans of Massachusetts Bay, and the most articulate colonial spokesman for the theme of American destiny were the

Puritans. Ecclesiastical and civic leaders in New England conceived of America as a place where a Protestant Reformation of church and society could be completed—a task that had not been carried out in England and Europe. They envisioned their journey to these shores less as an escape from religious persecution than as a positive mission for the construction of a model Christian society. They were on an "errand into the wilderness"; their purpose was to build a holy commonwealth in which the people were covenanted together by their public profession of religious faith and were covenanted with God by their pledge to erect a Christian society. Their government also shared in this covenant since one of the roles of government was to protect their Congregational form of church polity and safeguard their religion against dissident groups. The original errand, however, was more than a mission for the Puritans themselves. They believed that, like Israel of old, they had been singled out by God to be an example for the nations (especially for England). With their charter and company in America, the Puritans could in effect construct a republic independent of an English crown that had not allowed them the freedom of their experiment at home. Nevertheless, they insisted that they were Englishmen on an English errand: their godly commonwealth was to be a New England that would serve as a working model for Old England. If they succeeded in their errand, they would mark a turning point in history, for their commonwealth would be imitated by the nations. If they failed, they would fail not only themselves but their God and the very course of history.

The sense of destiny in the New World pervaded Puritan literature. John Winthrop, first governor of the Bay Colony, gave the theme one of its earliest and most pointed expressions. Winthrop's *Model of Christian Charity*, written aboard the flagship *Arbella* as it led the Puritan expedition toward the Promised Land, briefly spelled out the terms of the Puritan covenant (terms founded on a divinely ordained social order in which "some must be rich, some poore") and captured both the anticipation and the dread that arose in the heart of Puritan New Israel as she struck a covenant with Jehovah.

Beginning around 1650 much Puritan literature was replete with lamentations over the failure of New England to measure up to her divine calling. Sermons before the General Assembly at election time became particularly mournful as the clergy bewailed the decline of godliness among the people. Numerous signs of decay were cited: conflict among church members and between pastors and laity, the appearance of heretics, violations of Sabbath observance, impious children. And since the Puritan was extremely capable of discerning the hand of God in most any natural or historical event, the jeremiads warned that New England's crop failures, Indian wars, droughts, and epidemics were the judgment of a thoroughly provoked God upon his wayward people. It seemed that Winthrop's worst fears aboard the *Arbella* had come true: "if our hearts shall turne away soe that wee will not obey, but shall be seduced and worshipp . . . other Gods, our pleasures, and proffitts, and serve them; it is propounded unto us this day, wee shall surely perishe out of the good Land." Behind this sense of apostasy regarding the internal task of New England hovered the even greater frustration over the failure of New England to become a model for the nations. In fact, it was probably this frustration that led the clergy to look for signs of a broken covenant in the first place. The root of the problem was, quite simply, that England refused to look upon the Holy Commonwealth as her model. Even the Puritan brethren back home, living under improved conditions of religious toleration, became critical of the American Puritans' harsh treatment of dissenting religious groups. In Perry Miller's apt metaphor, the American Puritans must have felt something like the actor with the dramatic role of the century who rehearsed his lines, took a deep breath, and strode onto the stage only to find the theater empty and no spotlight working.[2]

Michael Wigglesworth, usually judged one of three major poets in seventeenth-century America, laments the state of the Puritan New Israel in his *God's Controversy with New England*. A graduate of Harvard, Wigglesworth enjoyed considerable influence as both a minister and a physician in Malden, Massachusetts, but his verse rather than his sermons or medical practice exerted the greatest impact on Puritan New England. Within a year after the publication of his poetic account of Judgment Day, *Day of Doom* (1662), all eighteen hundred copies of the work had been sold. The first edition alone, therefore, had a distribution of one copy to every thirty-five people in Massachusetts.[3] *God's Controversy* did not attain the renown of *Day of Doom*, but it was widely read and was quoted and imitated by other Puritan proclaimers of God's wrath. Like most other lamentations of the period, *God's Controversy* contrasts the vision, zeal, and sacrifices of the original settlers with the shortsightedness, sloth, and materialism of a later generation of New Englanders. Although the judgment of God thunders forth in the poem in the form of warnings and punishments, the hope is still held out that New England may renew her covenant with God if she will but repent of her sinful ways.

[2] Perry Miller, *Errand into the Wilderness* (Cambridge, Mass.: Harvard University Press, Belknap Press, 1956), pp. 12–13.

[3] Richard Crowder, *No Featherbed to Heaven: A Biography of Michael Wigglesworth, 1631–1705* (East Lansing: Michigan State University Press, 1962), p. 121.

There is no evidence that New Englanders were as morally bankrupt as the preachers of doom intimated, but as the years passed there was a waning of the ardor with which the Puritans pursued their errand into the wilderness. As later generations became more interested in their growing economic prosperity than in their spiritual state, there was a cooling of religious zeal and a corresponding diminution of the vision of America's destiny under God. Furthermore, the establishment of a tightly knit holy commonwealth in the wilderness suffered a series of disappointments. After 1650 there was a decline in the growth rate of church membership and in the ratio of church members to the population, Massachusetts eventually lost her charter (1684), dissenting groups (Quakers and Baptists) made inroads into the Puritan Zion. Yet the hope that God had something special in store for New England was never completely abandoned. Therefore, when the revivals of the Great Awakening deluged the colonies in the 1740s, there occurred not only an upsurge of religious vitality but also a revivification of the view of the New World as the place where God was breaking forth new light for the world at large. Jonathan Edwards, the foremost theologian of the eighteenth century and a formidable defender of the Great Awakening, stated a widely held conviction that the revivals might very well mark the beginning of God's religious renewal of all mankind. It appeared to Edwards that America's opportunity to become a "city upon a hill" had returned to her through the movement of God's Spirit in the Awakening. In his *Thoughts Concerning the Present Revival of Religion* (1742), Edwards engaged in a typological interpretation of Scripture and world history to describe the likelihood that his age would be the time when the Kingdom of God would spread from America—and especially from the shores of New England.

Many eighteenth-century men, including Edwards, found their enthusiasm for the Awakening checked by some of the results of the revivals: heated theological controversies, the division of denominations into prorevivalist and antirevivalist factions, uncontrolled emotionalism. Yet, as H. Richard Niebuhr has said, the religious awakening was roughly simultaneous with America's "awakening to national self-consciousness."[4] Despite the Great Awakening's divisive influence upon Protestant denominations and the Protestant religious consciousness, it played an important cohesive role in the colonies. It crossed class and geographical boundaries (the revivals were well received by city dwellers as well as by rural folk, by highly educated as well as by uneducated) and generated a common religious interest. Above all, it aroused anew the sense of American destiny

---

[4] H. Richard Niebuhr, *The Kingdom of God in America* (New York: Harper & Row, Publishers, 1959), p. 126.

under God, thus contributing to an emerging feeling of American unity and preparing the way for a new nation's bid for a crucial historical mission.

SUGGESTED READING

Boorstin, Daniel J. *The Americans: The Colonial Experience*. New York: Random House, Inc., Vintage Books, 1964.

Gaustad, Edwin S. *The Great Awakening in New England*. Gloucester, Mass: Peter Smith, 1965.

Miller, Perry. *Errand into the Wilderness*. Cambridge, Mass.: Harvard University Press, Belknap Press, 1956.

Morgan, Edmund S. *The Puritan Dilemma: The Story of John Winthrop*. Boston: Little, Brown and Company, 1958.

———. *Visible Saints; The History of a Puritan Idea*. New York: New York University Press, 1963.

Williams, George H. *Wilderness and Paradise in Christian Thought*. New York: Harper & Row, Publishers, 1962.

Wright, Louis B. *Religion and Empire: The Alliance between Piety and Commerce in English Expansion, 1558–1625*. New York: Octagon Books, Inc., 1965.

ALEXANDER WHITAKER

Good Newes From Virginia

[sent to]
The Right Worshipful
Sir Thomas Smith, Knight, Treasurer of
the English Colonie in Virginia

Ecclesiastes 11.1. *"Cast thy bread upon*
the waters: for after many
daies thou shalt finde it."

.   .   .   .

. . . let me turne your eyes, my brethren of England, to behold the
waters of *Virginia*: where you may behold a fit subject for the exercise of
your Liberalitie, persons enough on whom you may cast away your Bread,
and yet not without hope, after many daies to finde it. Yea, I will not
feare to affirme unto you, that those men whom God hath made able any
way to be helpfull to this Plantation, and made knowne unto them the
necessities of our wants, are bound in conscience by vertue of this precept,
to lay their helping hands to it, either with their purse, persons, or prayers,
so farre forth as God hath made them fit for it. For it is evident that our
wise God hath bestowed no gift upon any man, for their private use, but
for the good of other men, whom God shall offer to their Liberalitie.

Wherefore, since God hath opened the doore of *Virginia*, to our
countrey of England, wee are to thinke that God hath, as it were, by word
of mouth called us in, to bestow our severall Charity on them. And that
this may the better appeare, we have many reasons to encourage us to bee
Liberall minded and open-handed toward them.

From Alexander Whitaker, *Good Newes from Virginia* (London, 1613),
pp. 21–35, 44. [In this and other selections from colonial American literature, I have altered the text slightly (e.g., by substituting *u* for *v*, adding
and eliminating some punctuation marks, expanding abbreviations, breaking up long paragraphs), but I have sought to preserve the early American
flavor by retaining the original form when it does not seem to obscure the
meaning for the modern reader.—EDITOR]

First, if we consider the almost miraculous beginning, and continu-ance of this plantation, we must needs confesse that God hath opened this passage unto us, and led us by the hand unto this work. For the Marriners that were sent hither first to discover this Bay of Chaesapeac, found it onely by the meere directions of Gods providence: for I heard one of them confesse, that even then, when they were entred within the mouth of the Bay, they deemed the place they sought for to have beene many degrees further. The finding was not so strange, but the continuance and upholding of it hath bin most wonderful. I may fitly compare it to the growth of an Infant, which hath been afflicted from his birth with some grievous sicknes, that many times no hope of life hath remained, and yet it liveth still. Againe, if there were nothing else to encourage us, yet this one thing may stirre us up to go on chearefully with it: that the Divell is a capitall enemy against it, and continually seeketh which way to hinder the prosperitie and good proceedings of it. Yea, hath heretofore so farre prevailed, by his Instruments, the covetous hearts of many back-sliding Adventurers at home, and also by his servants here: some striving for superioritie, others by murmurings, mutinies, & plaine treasons; & others by fornication, prophanenes, idlenes, and such monstrous sinnes; that he had almost thrust us out of this kingdome, and had indeed quitted this Land of us, if God had not then (as one awaked out of sleepe) stood up and sent us meanes of great helpe, when we needed most, and expected least reliefe. The saving of those two honorable Knights, Sir Thomas Gates and Sir George Somers, with Captaine Newport and the rest of the Adventurers in the Sea Venture, as also their happy deliverance out of those unhabited and unfrequented (because feared) Islands of the Barmudaes, could proceed from none other, but the singular providence of God. If this worthie Governour, Sir Thomas Gates, had bin hindred but one weeke longer, it might be feared that the famine, which had by that time devoured the most of our countrimen heere, would have con-sumed the rest. And when hee considering that his weake meanes was not able to restore, or sustaine the burthen of such wofull distresses, had shipped the few remaining for England, and had forsaken with Hannibals sighes, the first builded James-Towne: upon the sudden newes met him, of the comming in of that Honorable Lord La war, with a fresh supplie. Whereupon he presently returned to the Towne he had so lately forsaken. Since, when this English Colony hath taken better root; and as a spread-ing herbe, whose top hath bin often cropped off, renewes her growth, and spreads her selfe more gloriously, than before. So this Plantation, which the divell hath so often troden downe, is by the miraculous blessing of God revived, and daily groweth to more happy and more hopefull suc-cesse. I have shut up many things in few words, and have alleadged this onely to prove unto us, that the finger of God hath been the onely true worker heere; that God first shewed us the place, God first called us hither, and here God by his speciall providence hath maintained us. Wherefore, by him let us be encouraged to lay our helping hands to this good work (yea Gods work) with all the strength of our abilitie.

Secondly, let the miserable condition of these naked slaves of the divell move you to compassion toward them. They acknowledge that there is a great good God, but know him not, having the eyes of their understanding as yet blinded: wherefore they serve the divell for feare, after a most base manner, sacrificing sometimes (as I have heere heard) their owne Children to him. I have sent one Image of their god to the Counsell in England, which is painted upon one side of a toad-stoole, much like unto a deformed monster. Their priests (whom they call *Quiokosoughs*) are no other but such as our English Witches are. They live naked in bodie, as if their shame of their sinne deserved no covering: Their names are as naked as their bodie: they esteeme it a vertue to lie, deceive and steale as their master the divell teacheth them. Much more might be said of their miserable condition, but I refer the particular narration of these things to some other season. If this bee their life, what thinke you shall become of them after death? but to be partakers with the divell and his angels in hell for evermore. Wherefore, my brethren, put on the bowels of compassion, and let the lamentable estate of these miserable people enter in your consideration: One God created us, they have reasonable soules and intellectuall faculties as well as wee; we all have Adam for our common parent: yea, by nature the condition of us both is all one, the servants of sinne and slaves of the divell. Oh remember (I beseech you) what was the state of England before the Gospell was preached in our Countrey? How much better were we then, and concerning our soules health, than these now are? Let the word of the Lord sound out that It may be heard in these parts; and let your faith which is toward God spread it selfe abroad, and shew forth the charitable fruits of it in these barren parts of the world: "And let him know that he which hath converted a sinner from going a stray out of his way, shall save a soule from death, and hide a multitude of sinnes."

But if any of us should misdoubt that this barbarous people is uncapable of such heavenly mysteries, let such men know that they are farre mistaken in the nature of these men, for besides the promise of God, which is without respect of persons, made as well to unwise men after the flesh, as to the wise, etc. let us not thinke that these men are so simple as some have supposed them: for they are of bodie lustie, strong, and very nimble: they are a very understanding generation, quicke of apprehension, suddaine in their dispatches, subtile in their dealings, exquisite in their inventions, and industrious in their labour. I suppose the world hath no better marke-men with their bow and arrowes than they be; they will kill birds flying, fishes swimming, and beasts running: they shoote also with mervailous strength, they shot one of our men being unarmed quite through the bodie, and nailed both his armes to his bodie with one arrow: one of their Children also, about the age of 12 or 13 years, killed a bird with his arrow in my sight. The service of their God is answerable to their life, being performed with great feare and attention, and many strange dumb shewes used in the same, stretching forth their limbes and straining their bodie, much like to the counterfeit women in England who faine themselves bewitched, or possessed of some evill spirit.

They stand in great awe of their *Quiokosoughs* or Priests, which are a generation of vipers even of Sathans owne brood. The manner of their life is much like to the popish Hermits of our age; for they live alone in the woods, in houses sequestred from the common course of men, neither may any man bee suffered to come into their house or to speake with them, but when this Priest doth call him. He taketh no care for his victuals, for all such kinde of things both bread and water, etc. are brought unto a place neere unto his cottage and there are left, which hee fetcheth for his proper neede. If they would have raine, or have lost any thing, they have their recourse to him, who conjureth for them, and many times prevaileth. If they be sicke, he is their Physition, if they bee wounded he sucketh them. At his command they make warre and peace, neither doe they any thing of moment without him. I will not bee teadious in these strange Narrations, when I have more perfectly entered into their secrets, you shall know all.

Finally, there is a civill governement amongst them which they strictly observe, and shew thereby that the law of Nature dwelleth in them: for they have a rude kinde of Common-wealth, and rough governement, wherein they both honour and obey their Kings, Parents, and Governours, both greater and lesse, they observe the limits of their owne possessions, and incroach not upon their neighbours dwellings. Murther is a capitall crime scarce heard of among them: adultery is most severely punished, and so are their other offences. These unnurtured grounds of reason in them, may serve to incourage us: to instruct them in the knowledge of the true God, the rewarder of all righteousnesse, not doubting but that he that was powerfull to save us by his word, when we were nothing, wil be mercifull also to these sonnes of Adam in his appointed time, in whom there bee remaining so many footsteps of Gods image.

Wherefore you wealthy men of this world, whose bellies God hath filled with his hidden Treasure: trust not in uncertain riches, neither cast your eyes upon them; for riches taketh her to her wings as an Eagle, and flieth into Heaven. But "bee rich in good works ready to distribute or communicate." How shamefully doe the most of you either miserably detaine, or wickedlie mispend Gods goods, whereof hee made you his stewards? The Covetous person seekes to hide his talent from the good of others and himselfe, honouring it as his God, which should be his servant. The Prodigall men of our land make hast to fling away Gods treasures, as a greevious burthen which they desire to be eased of. Some make no scruple at it, to spend yearely an hundred pounds, two, three, five hundred, and much more about dogs, haukes and hounds and such sports; which will not give five hundred pence to the releefe of Gods poore members. Others will not care to lose two or three thousand pound in a night, at Cards and Dice, and yet suffer poore Lazarus to perish in their streets for want of their Charitable Almes. Yea divers will hyer gardens at great rents, and build stately houses for their whoores, which have no compassion on the Fatherlesse and widdowes. How much better were it for these men to remember the afflictions of Joseph, to extend the bowels of their compassion to the poore, the fatherles, afflicted and the like, than to mispend that which they must give a straite account of at the day of judgement? Are not these miserable people heere better than hawks, hounds, whores, and the like? O you that spend so much on them, thinke it no dishonour to your persons, no impoverishing to your state, to bestow somewhat to the raising up of Christs kingdome, and maintenance of so holy and heavenly an action as this is, God of his goodnesse that hath given you abilitie to performe it, make you willing to help it forward with the best of your power.

"For after many daies thou shalt find it." Hitherto have we spoken of the commandement and the severall branches of the same: Now followes the reason of this Commandement which the Holy Ghost useth heere to stir us up unto liberality, which is taken from the reward which wee shall have of our well-doing, "for after many daies thou shalt find it." The some of which reason is, that though God doe not presently reward our well doing, but doe defer the requitall of it for many daies, yet thy good works shall not perish, but God at the appointed time, shall abundantly recompence thy liberality. Out of this reason wee may gather two notable conclusions touching the reward of liberality. First wee may conclude from hence, that God doth not alwaies give a present reward to the good works; he doth for the most part defer his rewards manie daies, sometimes many yeares, yea sometimes even till death it selfe, when hee will never cease to reward us according to our works, with unspeakeable joyes of blessed immortality. And the wisdome of God doth thus defer his rewards for most singular reasons. For if God should presently reward good works, who then would not be a prodigall giver, who then would bee a faithful giver? For when a man is certaine of present gaine he will not spare to give abundantly, because he seeth an exceeding profit ready to be put into his hands for so doing: and this would stirre up the most covetous wretch in the world to be liberall, gaping out of meere covetousnesse, after an overplus of reward. Wherefore God hath made the time and condition of his rewards doubtfull, that we might not bee covetous of the benefit: but that he might exercise our faith, and teach us with patience of hope to expect the appointed time of his reward. The principall point of perfect charity is, that wee give in faith, whose true nature is to depend upon God for the good successe of our almes, "for Faith is the ground of things that are hoped for, & the evidence of things that are not seene": now if we should have the reward of good works in the view of our eies, and ready as it were to be put into our hands, what place would then be left for practise of faith whose object is unseene, whose hopes bee of afterwards? ...

Let then your liberall minds (you honourable and charitable Adventurers of Virginia) be stirred up to cast your almes on the waters of Virginia, without hope of present profit. The base affections of the Usurer will not looke for the overplus of encrease, untill the covenanted time of his loane be expired. The husbandman casting his seed into the earth, waiteth upon God until Harvest for a fruitful crop: verily he that beleeveth doth not make haste. Be not over hastie with God: God will not yet reward you, that he may make you more famous in the world, that the world may see your zeale, and beare witnesse to the patience of your faith, not to greedie haste of covetous desires. The worke is honourable, and now more than ever, sustained by most honorable men. O let us not then be weary of well-doing: fortie yeares were expired, before *Israel* could plant in Canaan, and yet God had called them by the word of his mouth, had led them himselfe by an high hand. Yet may you boldly looke for a shorter time of reward. The returnes which you have from the East Indies, though they be exceeding rich, yet is the adventure doubtfull, the expence chargeable, and ·the expectation of returne, of three yeares continuance.

Let me advise you to be as liberall in adventure hither, and I dare affirme, that by Gods assistance, your profitable returnes shall be of more certainty, and much shorter expectation. Remember, I beseech you, how many lives were lost, how many yeares were spent, what discouragements, what great losses the Adventurers of Spaine and Portugale suffered and under-went, before they could be setled in the West Indies, or receive any profitable returne from thence: and now behold what rich loads, what profitable returnes are yearely shipped from thence. Shall our Nation, hitherto famous for noble attempts, and the honorable finishing of what they have undertaken, be now taxed for inconstancie, and blamed by the enemies of our protestation, for uncharitablenesse? Yea, shall we be a scorne among Princes, and a laughing stocke among our neighbour Nations, for basely leaving what we honorably began; yea, for beginning a Discoverie, whose riches other men shall gather, so soone as wee have forsaken it? Awake you true hearted English men, you servants of Jesus Christ, remember that the Plantation is Gods, and the reward your Countries. Wherefore, aime not at your present privat gaine, but let the glory of God, whose Kingdome you now plant, & good of your Countrey, whose wealth you seeke, so farre prevaile with you, that you respect not a present returne of gaine for this yeare or two: but that you would more liberally supplie for a little space, this your Christian worke, which you so charitably began. As for those spirits of slander, whom the Divell hath stirred up to speak evill of this good Land, and to weaken the hands of our brethren, lest they should go forward, and pull Satan out of his Dominions. Let them take heed, lest the punishment of Shammua and his nine companions, the faithlesse searchers of the Land of Canaan, do befall them: and that they never live to taste of the commodities of this good Land.

But lest I may seeme to exhort you to an unprofitable Liberalitie, or to argue God of forgetfulnes to those that serve him faithfully: heare now what a comfortable promise of reward God hath made unto us in these words: which is, "That after many dayes we shall find." If God should have commanded us to cast away without finding, some discouragement there might have been to our weake nature; but since God hath assuredly promised us, that we shall find in the end, who will not obey the command? who will not be Liberall. God hath been alwayes found true in his word, most faithfull in his promises. If God do promise Abraham that his seed shall inherit the Land of Canaan: Abrahams posteritie shall after many daies in the appointed time be planted peaceably in the land of Canaan. If God promise Salomon wisdome and riches: Salomon shall be wiser and richer than any Prince of the earth. If God promiseth that he will give his only Sonne, that whosoever beleeveth in him shall not perish, but have life everlasting: his Sonne Jesus Christ shal be borne into the world at the appointed time, and undergoe the weight of Gods wrath for redemption of beleevers. Shall God then faithfully performe all his promises in so great matters, and be unfaithfull in lesser matters: oh let no such base conceit of the Almightie enter into our minds, as to thinke that he that spared not his owne Sonne, to performe his promises to us, will be so unmindfull of us in so small a thing. . . .

Wherefore you (right wise and noble Adventurers of Virginia) whose hearts God hath stirred up to build him a Temple, to make him an house, to conquer a Kingdome for him here: be not discouraged with those many lamentable assaults that the divell hath made against us: he now rageth most, because he knoweth his kingdome is to have a short end. Goe forward boldly, and remember that you fight under the banner of Jesus Christ, that you plant his Kingdome, who hath already broken the Serpents head: God may deferre his temporall reward for a season, but be assured that in the end you shall find riches and honour in this world, and blessed immortality in the world to come. And you my brethren my fellow labourers, send up your earnest prayers to God for his Church in Virginia, that since his harvest heere is great, but the labourers few, hee would thrust forth labourers into his harvest; and pray also for mee that the ministration of his Gospell may be powerfull and effectuall by me to the salvation of many, and advancement of the kingdome of Jesus Christ, to whom with the Father and the holy Spirit, bee all honour and glorie for evermore, Amen.

JOHN WINTHROP

A Modell
Of
Christian Charity

Written
On Boarde the Arrabella,
On the Attlantick Ocean.
Anno 1630

. . . .

CHRISTIAN CHARITIE

A Modell Hereof

God Almightie in his most holy and wise providence hath soe disposed of the Condicion of mankinde, as in all times some must be rich, some poore, some highe and eminent in power and dignitie; others meane and in subjeccion.

The Reason Hereof

1. Reason: *First,* to hold conformity with the rest of his workes, being delighted to shewe forthe the glory of his wisdome in the variety and differance of the Creatures and the glory of his power, in ordering all these differences for the preservacion and good of the whole; and the glory of his greatnes that as it is the glory of princes to have many officers, soe this great King will have many Stewards, counting himselfe more honoured in dispenceing his guifts to man by man, than if hee did it by his owne immediate hand.

From *Winthrop Papers,* vol. II (The Massachusetts Historical Society, 1931), pp. 282–84, 292–95.

2. Reason: *Secondly*, That he might have the more occasion to manifest the worke of his Spirit: first, upon the wicked in moderateing and
restraineing them: soe that the riche and mighty should not eate upp the
poore, nor the poore and dispised rise upp against their superiours and
shake off thiere yoake; secondly in the regenerate in exerciseing his graces
in them, as in the greate ones, their love, mercy, gentlenes, temperance,
etc., in the poore and inferiour sorte, theire faithe, patience, obedience,
etc.

3. Reason: *Thirdly*, That every man might have need of other, and
from hence they might be all knitt more nearly together in the Bond of
brotherly affeccion: from hence it appeares plainely that noe man is made
more honourable than another or more wealthy etc., out of any perticuler
and singuler respect to himselfe but for the glory of his Creator and the
Common good of the Creature, Man; Therefore God still reserves the
propperty of these guifts to himselfe as Ezek: 16.17. he there calls wealthe
his gold and his silver, etc. Prov: 3.9 he claimes theire service as his due,
honour the Lord with thy riches, etc. All men being thus (by divine providence) rancked into two sortes, riche and poore; under the first, are comprehended all such as are able to live comfortably by theire owne meanes
duely improved; and all others are poore according to the former distribution. There are two rules whereby wee are to walke one towards another:
JUSTICE and MERCY. These are allwayes distinquished in theire Act
and in theire object, yet may they both concurre in the same Subject in
eache respect; as sometimes there may be an occasion of shewing mercy to
a rich man, in some sudden danger of distresse, and allsoe doeing of meere
Justice to a poor man in regard of some perticuler contract, etc. There is
likewise a double Lawe by which wee are regulated in our conversacion
one towardes another: in both the former respects, the lawe of nature and
the lawe of grace, or the morrall lawe or the lawe of the gospell, to omitt
the rule of Justice as not propperly belonging to this purpose otherwise
than it may fall into consideraction in some perticuler Cases: By the first
of these lawes man as he was enabled soe withall [is] commaunded to love
his neighbour as himselfe. Upon this ground stands all the precepts of the
morrall lawe, which concernes our dealings with men. To apply this to
the works of mercy this lawe requires two things: first, that every man
afford his help to another in every want or distress. Secondly, That hee
performe this out of the same affeccion which makes him carefull of his
owne good according to that of our Saviour, Math: [7.12] Whatsoever ye
would that men should doe to you. This was practised by Abraham and
Lott in entertaineing the Angells and the old man of Gibea.

The Lawe of Grace or the Gospell hath some differance from the
former as in these respects: first, the lawe of nature was given to man in
the estate of innocency; this of the gospell in the estate of regeneracy.
Secondly, the former propounds one man to another, as the same fleshe

and Image of god; this as a brother in Christ allsoe, and in the Communion of the same spirit and soe teacheth us to put a difference betweene
Christians and others. Doe good to all, especially to the household of
faith; upon this ground the Israelites were to putt a difference betweene
the brethren of such as were strangers though not of the Canaanites.
Thirdly, the Lawe of nature could give noe rules for dealeing with enemies, for all are to be considered as friends in the estate of innocency, but
the Gospell commands love to an enemy. Proofe: If thine Enemie hunger
feede him; Love your Enemies, doe good to them that hate you, Math:
5.44.

This Lawe of the Gospell propoundes likewise a difference of seasons
and occasions. There is a time when a Christian must sell all and give to
the poore, as they did in the Apostles times. There is a tyme allsoe when
a Christian (though they give not all yet) must give beyond theire abillity,
as they of Macedonia. Cor: 2.6. Likewise community of perills calls for
extraordinary liberallity and soe doth Community in some speciall service
for the Churche. Lastly, when there is noe other meanes whereby our
Christian brother may be relieved in this distresse, wee must help him
beyond our ability, rather than tempt God, in putting him upon help by
miraculous or extraordinary meanes.

. . . .

It rests now to make some applicacion of this discourse by the present designe which gave the occasion of writeing of it. Herein are four
things to be propounded: first, the persons; secondly, the worke; thirdly,
the end; fourthly, the meanes.

1. For the persons, wee are a Company professing our selves fellow
members of Christ, in which respect onely though wee were absent from
eache other many miles, and had our imploymentes as farre distant, yet
wee ought to account our selves knitt together by this bond of love, and
live in the exercise of it, if wee would have comforte of our being in
Christ. This was notorious in the practise of the Christians in former
times, as is testified of the Waldenses from the mouth of one of the adversaries Aeneas Sylvius, mutuo [solent amare] penè antequam norint. They
use to love any of theire own religion even before they were acquainted
with them.

2. For the worke wee have in hand, it is by a mutuall consent
through a speciall overruleing providence, and a more than an ordinary
approbation of the Churches of Christ to seeke out a place of Cohabita-
tion and Consorteshipp under a due forme of Government both civill and
ecclesiasticall. In such cases as this the care of the publique must oversway
all private respects, by which not onely conscience, but meare Civill pol-
licy doth binde us; for it is a true rule that perticuler estates cannott sub-
sist in the ruine of the publique.

3. The end is to improve our lives, to doe more service to the Lord,

the comforte and encrease of the body of Christe whereof wee are members, that our selves and posterity may be the better preserved from the
Common corrupcions of this evill world, to serve the Lord and worke out
our Salvacion under the power and purity of his holy Ordinances.

4. For the meanes whereby this must bee effected, they are twofold,
a Conformity with the worke and end wee aime at; these wee see are
extraordinary, therefore wee must not content our selves with usuall ordinary meanes. Whatsoever wee did or ought to have done when wee lived
in England, the same must wee doe and more allsoe where wee goe: That
which the most in theire Churches mainteine as a truthe in profession
onely, wee must bring into familiar and constant practice, as in this duty
of love wee must love brotherly without dissimulation, wee must love one
another with a pure hearte fervently, wee must beare one anothers bur-
thens, wee must not looke onely on our owne things but allsoe on the
things of our brethren, neither must wee think that the lord will beare
with such faileings at our hands as hee dothe from those among whome
wee have lived.

. . . .

Thus stands the cause betweene God and us. Wee are entered into
Covenant with him for this worke, wee have taken out a Commission, the
Lord hath given us leave to draw our owne Articles, wee have professed
to enterprise these Accions upon these and these ends, wee have hereupon
besought him of favour and blessing: Now if the Lord shall please to
heare us, and bring us in peace to the place wee desire, then hath hee
ratified this Covenant and sealed our Commission [and] will expect a
strickt performance of the Articles contained in it, but if wee shall neglect
the observacion of these Articles which are the ends wee have propounded, and dissembling with our God, shall fall to embrace this present
world and prosecute our carnall intencions seekeing greate things for
our selves and our posterity, the Lord will surely breake out in wrathe
against us, be revenged of such a perjured people and make us knowe the
price of the breache of such a Covenant.

Now the onely way to avoyde this shipwracke and to provide for our
posterity is to followe the Counsell of Micah, to doe Justly, to love mercy,
to walke humbly with our God. For this end, wee must be knitt together
in this worke as one man, wee must entertaine each other in brotherly
Affeccion, wee must be willing to abridge our selves of our superfluities,
for the supply of others necessities, wee must uphold a familiar Commerce together in all meeknes, gentlenes, patience and liberallity, wee
must delight in each other, make others Condicions our owne, rejoyce
together, mourne together, labour and suffer together, allwayes haveing
before our eyes our Commission and Community in the worke, our Community as members of the same body, soe shall wee keepe the unitie of

the spirit in the bond of peace, the Lord will be our God and delight to dwell among us as his owne people and will commaund a blessing upon us in all our wayes, soe that wee shall see much more of his wisdome, power, goodnes and truthe than formerly wee have beene acquainted with. Wee shall finde that the God of Israell is among us, when tenn of us shall be able to resist a thousand of our enemies, when hee shall make us a prayse and glory, that men shall say of succeeding plantacions: the lord make it like that of New England: for wee must Consider that wee shall be as a Citty upon a Hill, the eies of all people are uppon us; soe that if wee shall deale falsely with our god in this worke wee have undertaken and soe cause him to withdrawe his present help from us, wee shall shame the faces of many of gods worthy servants, and cause theire prayers to be turned into Cursses upon us till wee be consumed out of the good land whither wee are goeing: And to shutt upp this discourse with that exhortacion of Moses, that faithfull servant of the Lord in his last farewell to Israell, Deut. 30. Beloved there is now sett before us life, and good, deathe and evill in that wee are Commaunded this day to love the Lord our God, and to love one another, to walke in his wayes and to keepe his Commaundements and his Ordinance, and his lawes, and the Articles of our Covenant with him that wee may live and be multiplied, and that the Lord our God may blesse us in the land whither we goe to possesse it: But if our heartes shall turne away soe that wee will not obey, but shall be seduced and worship . . . other Gods, our pleasures, and proffitts, and serve them; it is propounded unto us this day, wee shall surely perishe out of the good Land whither wee passe over this vast Sea to possesse it;

> Therefore lett us choose life,
> that wee, and our Seede,
> may live; by obeyeing his
> voyce, and cleaveing to him,
> for hee is our life,.and
> our prosperity.

MICHAEL WIGGLESWORTH

God's Controversy
With New England

Written in the time of the great drought Anno 1662

. . . .

Beyond the great Atlantick flood
  There is a region vast,
A country where no English foot
  In former ages past:
A waste and howling wilderness,   5
  Where none inhabited
But hellish fiends, and brutish men
  That Devils worshiped.

This region was in darkness plac't
  Far off from heavens light,   10
Amidst the shaddows of grim death
  And of eternal night.
For there the Sun of righteousness
  Had never made to shine
The light of his sweet countenance,   15
  And grace which is divine:

Until the time drew nigh wherein
  The glorious Lord of hostes
Was pleasd to lead his armies forth
  Into those forrein coastes.   20
At whose approach the darkness sad
  Soon vanished away,
And all the shaddows of the night
  Were turned to lightsome day.

From *Proceedings of the Massachusetts Historical Society,* vol. XII (1871–1873), pp. 83–93.

The dark and dismal western woods   25
   (The Devils den whilere)
Beheld such glorious gospel-shine,
   As none beheld more cleare.
Where sathan had his scepter sway'd
   For many generations,   30
The King of Kings set up his throne
   To rule amongst the nations.

The stubborn he in pieces brake,
   Like vessels made of clay:
And those that sought his peoples hurt   35
   He turned to decay.
Those curst Amalekites, that first
   Lift up their hand on high
To fight against Gods Israel,
   Were ruin'd fearfully.   40

Thy terrours on the Heathen folk,
   O Great Jehovah, fell:
The fame of thy great acts, o Lord,
   Did all the nations quell.
Some hid themselves for fear of thee   45
   In forrests wide & great:
Some to thy people croutching came,
   For favour to entreat.

Some were desirous to be taught
   The knowledge of thy wayes,   50
And being taught, did soon accord
   Therein to spend their dayes.
Thus were the fierce & barbarous
   Brought to civility,
And those that liv'd like beasts (or worse)   55
   To live religiously.

O happiest of dayes wherein
   The blind received sight,
And those that had no eyes before
   Were made to see the light!   60
The wilderness hereat rejoyc't,
   The woods for joy did sing,
The vallys & the little hills
   Thy praises ecchoing.

Here was the hiding place, which thou,   65
  Jehovah, didst provide
For thy redeemed ones, and where
  Thou didst thy jewels hide
In per'lous times, and saddest dayes
  Of sack-cloth and of blood,   70
When th' overflowing scourge did pass
  Through Europe, like a flood.

While almost all the world beside
  Lay weltring in their gore:
We, only we, enjoyd such peace   75
  As none enjoyd before.
No forrein foeman did us fray,
  Nor threat'ned us with warrs:
We had no enemyes at home,
  Nor no domestick jarrs.   80

The Lord had made (such was his grace)
  For us a Covenant
Both with the men, and with the beasts,
  That in this desert haunt:
So that through places wilde and waste   85
  A single man, disarm'd,
Might journey many hundred miles,
  And not at all be harm'd.

Amidst the solitary woods
  Poor travellers might sleep   90
As free from danger as at home,
  Though no man watch did keep.
Thus were we priviledg'd with peace,
  Beyond what others were.
Truth, Mercy, Peace, with Righteousness,   95
  Took up their dwelling here.

Our Governor was of our selves,
  And all his Bretheren,
For wisdom & true piety,
  Select, & chosen men.   100
Who, Ruling in ye fear of God,
  The righteous cause maintained,
And all injurious violence,
  And wickedness, restrained.

Our temp'rall blessings did abound: 105
  But spirituall good things

Much more abounded, to the praise
  Of that great King of Kings.
Gods throne was here set up; here was
  His tabernacle pight: 110
This was the place, and these the folk
  In whom he took delight.

Our morning starrs shone all day long:
  Their beams gave forth such light,
As did the noon-day sun abash,   115
  And 's glory dazle quite.
Our day continued many yeers,
  And had no night at all:
Yea many thought the light would last,
  And be perpetuall.   120

Such, o New-England, was thy first,
  Such was thy best estate:
But, Loe! a strange and suddain change
  My courage did amate.
The brightest of our morning starrs   125
  Did wholly disappeare:
And those that tarried behind
  With sack-cloth covered were.

Moreover, I beheld & saw
  Our welkin overkest,   130
And dismal clouds for sun-shine late
  O'respread from east to west.
The air became tempestuous;
  The wilderness gan quake:
And from above with awfull voice   135
  Th' Almighty thundring spake.

Are these the men that erst at my command
  Forsook their ancient seats and native soile,
To follow me into a desart land,
  Contemning all the travell and the toile,   140
Whose love was such to purest ordinances
  As made them set at nought their fair inheritances?

Are these the men that prized libertee
  To walk with God according to their light,
To be as good as he would have them bee,   145
  To serve and worship him with all their might,
Before the pleasures which a fruitfull field,
  And country flowing-full of all good things, could yield,

Are these the folk whom from the brittish Iles,
  Through the stern billows of the watry main,   150
I safely led so many thousand miles,
  As if their journey had been through a plain?
Whom having from all enemies protected,
  And through so many deaths and dangers well directed,

I brought and planted on the western shore,   155
  Where nought but bruits and salvage wights did swarm
(Untaught, untrain'd, untam'd by vertue's lore)
  That sought their blood, yet could not do them harm?
My fury's flaile them thresht, my fatall broom
  Did sweep them hence, to make my people elbow-room.   160

Are these the men whose gates with peace I crown'd,
  To whom for bulwarks I salvation gave,
Whilst all things else with rattling tumults sound,
  And mortall frayes send thousands to the grave?
Whilest their own brethren bloody hands embrewed   165
  In brothers blood, and fields with carcases bestrewed?

Is this the people blest with bounteous store,
  By land and sea full richly clad and fed,
Whom plenty's self stands waiting still before,
  And powreth out their cups well tempered?   170
For whose dear sake an howling wildernes
  I lately turned into a fruitfull paradeis?

Are these the people in whose hemisphere
  Such bright-beam'd, glist' ring, sun-like starrs I placed,
As by their influence did all things cheere,   175
  As by their light blind ignorance defaced,
As errours into lurking holes did fray,
  As turn'd the late dark night into a lightsome day?

Are these the folk to whom I milked out
  And sweetnes stream'd from consolations brest;   180
Whose soules I fed and strengthened throughout
  With finest spirituall food most finely drest?
On whom I rained living bread from Heaven,
  Withouten Errour's bane, or Superstition's leaven?

With whom I made a Covenant of peace,   185
  And unto whom I did most firmly plight
My faithfulness, If whilst I live I cease
  To be their Guide, their God, their full delight;

Since them with cords of love to me I drew,
 Enwrapping in my grace such as should them ensew. 190

Are these the men, that now mine eyes behold,
 Concerning whom I thought, and whilome spake,
First Heaven shall pass away together scrold,
 Ere they my lawes and righteous wayes forsake,
Or that they slack to runn their heavenly race? 195
 Are these the same? or are some others come in place?

If these be they, how is it that I find
 In stead of holiness Carnality,
In stead of heavenly frames an Earthly mind,
 For burning zeal luke-warm Indifferency, 200
For flaming love, key-cold Dead-heartedness,
 For temperance (in meat, and drinke, and cloaths) excess?

Whence cometh it, that Pride, and Luxurie
 Debate, Deceit, Contention, and Strife,
False-dealing, Covetousness, Hypocrisie 205
 (With such like Crimes) amongst them are so rife,
That one of them doth over-reach another?
 And that an honest man can hardly trust his Brother?

How is it, that Security, and Sloth,
 Amongst the best are Common to be found? 210
That grosser sins, in stead of Graces growth,
 Amongst the many more and more abound?
I hate dissembling shews of Holiness.
 Or practise as you talk, or never more profess.

Judge not, vain world, that all are hypocrites 215
 That do profess more holiness then thou:
All foster not dissembling, guilefull sprites,
 Nor love their lusts, though very many do.
Some sin through want of care and constant watch,
 Some with the sick converse, till they the sickness catch. 220

Some, that maintain a reall root of grace,
 Are overgrown with many noysome weeds,
Whose heart, that those no longer may take place,
 The benefit of due correction needs.
And such as these however gone astray 225
 I shall by stripes reduce into a better way.

Moreover some there be that still retain
 Their ancient vigour and sincerity;

Whom both their own, and others sins, constrain
  To sigh, and mourn, and weep, and wail, & cry: 230
And for their sakes I have forborn to powre
  My wrath upon Revolters to this present houre.

To praying Saints I always have respect,
  And tender love, and pittifull regard:
Nor will I now in any wise neglect   235
  Their love and faithfull service to reward;
Although I deal with others for their folly,
  And turn their mirth to tears that have been too jolly.

For thinke not, O Backsliders, in your heart,
  That I shall still your evill manners beare: 240
Your sinns me press as sheaves do load a cart,
  And therefore I will plague you for this geare
Except you seriously, and soon, repent,
  Ile not delay your pain and heavy punishment.

And who be those themselves that yonder shew?   245
  The seed of such as name my dreadfull Name!
On whom whilere compassions skirt I threw
  Whilest in their blood they were, to hide their shame!
Whom my preventing love did neer me take!
  Whom for mine own I mark't, lest they should me forsake!   250

I look't that such as these to vertue's Lore
  (Though none but they) would have Enclin'd their ear:
That they at least mine image should have bore,
  And sanctify'd my name with awfull fear.
Let pagan's Brats pursue their lusts, whose meed   255
  Is Death: For christians children are an holy seed.

But hear O Heavens! Let Earth amazed stand;
  Ye Mountaines melt, and Hills come flowing down:
Let horror seize upon both Sea and Land;
  Let Natures self be cast into a stown.   260
I children nourisht, nurtur'd and upheld:
  But they against a tender father have rebell'd.

What could have been by me performed more?
  Or wherein fell I short of your desire?
Had you but askt, I would have op't my store,   265
  And given what lawfull wishes could require.
For all this bounteous cost I lookt to see
  Heaven-reaching-hearts, & thoughts, Meekness, Humility.

But lo, a sensuall Heart all void of grace,
   An Iron neck, a proud presumptuous Hand;   270
A self-conceited, stiff, stout, stubborn Race,
   That fears no threats, submitts to no command:
Self-will'd, perverse, such as can beare no yoke;
   A Generation even ripe for vengeance stroke.

Such were that Carnall Brood of Israelites   275
   That Josua and the Elders did ensue,
Who growing like the cursed Cananites
   Upon themselves my heavy judgements drew.
Such also was that fleshly Generation,
   Whom I o'rewhelm'd by waters deadly inundation.   280

They darker light, and lesser meanes misused;
   They had not such Examples them to warn:
You clearer Rules, and Precepts, have abused,
   And dreadfull monuments of others harm.
My gospels glorious light you do not prize: 285
   My Gospels endless, boundless grace you clean despize.

My painfull messengers you disrespect,
   Who toile and sweat and sweale themselves away,
Yet nought at all with you can take effect,
   Who hurrie headlong to your own decay.   290
In vain the Founder melts, and taketh pains:
   Bellows and Lead's consum'd, but still your dross remains.

What should I do with such a stiff-neckt race?
   How shall I ease me of such Foes as they?
What shall befall despizers of my Grace?   295
   I'le surely beare their candle-stick away,
And Lamps put out. Their glorious noon-day light
   I'le quickly turn into a dark Egyptian night.

Oft have I charg'd you by my ministers
   To gird your selves with sack cloth, and repent.   300
Oft have I warned you by my messengers;
   That so you might my wrathfull ire prevent:
But who among you hath this warning taken?
   Who hath his crooked wayes, & wicked works forsaken?

Yea many grow to more and more excess;   305
   More light and loose, more Carnall and prophane.
The sins of Sodom, Pride, and Wantonness,
   Among the multitude spring up amain.

Are these the fruits of Pious Education,
   To run with greater speed and Courage to Damnation?   310

If here and there some two, or three, shall steere
   A wiser course, then their Companions do,
You make a mock of such; and scoff, and jeere
   Becaus they will not be so bad as you.
Such is the Generation that succeeds   315
   The men, whose eyes have seen my great & awful deeds.

Now therefore hearken and encline your ear,
   In judgement I will henceforth with you plead;
And if by that you will not learn to fear,
   But still go on a sensuall life to lead: 320
I'le strike at once an All-Consuming stroke;
   Nor cries nor tears shall then my fierce intent revoke.

Thus ceast his Dreadful-threatning voice
   The High & lofty-One.
The Heavens stood still Appal'd thereat;   325
   The Earth beneath did groane:
Soon after I beheld and saw
   A mortall dart come flying:
I lookt again, & quickly saw
   Some fainting, others dying.   330

The Heavens more began to lowre,
   The welkin Blacker grew:
And all things seemed to forebode
   Sad changes to ensew.
From that day forward hath the Lord   335
   Apparently contended
With us in Anger, and in Wrath:
   But we have not amended.

Our healthfull dayes are at an end,
   And sicknesses come on   340
From yeer to yeer, becaus our hearts
   Away from God are gone.
New-England, where for many yeers
   You scarcely heard a cough,
And where Physicians had no work,   345
   Now finds them work enough.

Now colds and coughs, Rhewms, and sore-throats,
   Do more & more abound:

Now Agues sore & Feavers strong
   In every place are found.   350
How many houses have we seen
   Last Autumn, and this spring,
Wherein the healthful were too few
   To help the languishing.

One wave another followeth,   355
   And one disease begins
Before another cease, becaus
   We turn not from our sins.
We stopp our ear against reproof,
   And hearken not to God: 360
God stops his ear against our prayer,
   And takes not off his rod.

Our fruitful seasons have been turnd
   Of late to barrenness,
Sometimes through great & parching drought,   365
   Sometimes through rain's excess.
Yea now the pastures & corn fields
   For want of rain do languish:
The cattell mourn, & hearts of men
   Are fill'd with fear & anguish.   370

The clouds are often gathered,
   As if we should have rain:
But for our great unworthiness
   Are scattered again.
We pray & fast, & make fair shewes,   375
   As if we meant to turn:
But whilst we turn not, God goes on
   Our field, & fruits to burn.

And burnt are all things in such sort,
   That nothing now appears,   380
But what may wound our hearts with grief,
   And draw foorth floods of teares.
All things a famine do presage
   In that extremity,
As if both men, and also beasts,   385
   Should soon be done to dy.

This O New-England hast thou got
   By riot, & excess:

This hast thou brought upon thy self
    By pride & wantonness.   390
Thus must thy worldlyness be whipt.
    They, that too much do crave,
Provoke the Lord to take away
    Such blessings as they have.

We have been also threatened   395
    With worser things then these:
And God can bring them on us still,
    To morrow if he please.
For if his mercy be abus'd,
    Which holpe us at our need   400
And mov'd his heart to pitty us,
    We shall be plagu'd indeed.

Beware, O sinful Land, beware;
    And do not think it strange
That sorer judgements are at hand,   405
    Unless thou quickly change.
Or God, or thou, must quickly change;
    Or else thou art undon:
Wrath cannot cease, if sin remain,
    Where judgement is begun.   410

Ah dear New England! dearest land to me;
    Which unto God hast hitherto been dear,
And mayst be still more dear than formerlie,
    If to his voice thou wilt incline thine ear.

Consider wel & wisely what the rod,   415
    Wherewith thou art from yeer to yeer chastized,
Instructeth thee. Repent, & turn to God,
    Who wil not have his nurture be despized.

Thou still hast in thee many praying saints,
    Of great account, and precious with the Lord,   420
Who dayly powre out unto him their plaints,
    And strive to please him both in deed & word.

Cheer on, sweet souls, my heart is with you all,
    And shall be with you, maugre Sathan's might:
And whereso'ere this body be a Thrall,   425
    Still in New-England shall be my delight.

JONATHAN EDWARDS

The Latter-Day Glory
Is Probably
To Begin In America

It is not unlikely that this work of God's Spirit [i.e. the religious revival], so extraordinary and wonderful, is the dawning, or at least a prelude of that glorious work of God, so often foretold in scripture, which, in the progress and issue of it, shall renew the world of mankind. If we consider how long since the things foretold as what should precede this great event, have been accomplished; and how long this event has been expected by the church of God, and thought to be nigh by the most eminent men of God, in the church; and withal consider what the state of things now is, and has for a considerable time been, in the church of God, and the world of mankind; we cannot reasonably think otherwise, than that the beginning of this great work of God must be near. And there are many things that make it probable that this work will begin in America. —It is signified that it shall begin in some very remote part of the world, with which other parts have no communication but by navigation, in Isa. lx. 9. "Surely the isles shall wait for me, and the ships of Tarshish first, to bring my sons from far." It is exceeding manifest that this chapter is a prophecy of the prosperity of the church, in its most glorious state on earth, in the latter days; and I cannot think that any thing else can be here intended but America by the isles that are far off, from whence the first-born sons of that glorious day shall be brought. Indeed, by *the isles*, in prophecies of gospel-times, is very often meant Europe. It is so in prophecies of that great spreading of the gospel that should be soon after Christ's time, because it was far separated from that part of the world where the church of God had till then been, by the sea. But this prophecy cannot have respect to the conversion of Europe, in the time of that great work of God, in the primitive ages of the Christian

From Jonathan Edwards, "Some Thoughts Concerning the Present Revival of Religion in New England," *The Works of President Edwards,* IV (New York: S. Converse, 1830), 128–33.

church; for it was not fulfilled then. The isles and ships of Tarshish, thus understood, did not wait for God first; that glorious work did not begin in Europe, but in Jerusalem, and had for a considerable time been very wonderfully carried on in Asia, before it reached Europe. And as it is not *that* work of God which is chiefly intended in this chapter, but some more glorious work that should be in the latter ages of the Christian church; therefore, some other part of the world is here intended by the isles, that should be, as Europe then was, far separated from that part of the world where the church had before been, and with which it can have no communication but by the ships of Tarshish. And what is chiefly intended is not the British isles, nor any isles near the other continent; they are spoken of as at a great distance from that part of the world where the church had till then been. This prophecy therefore seems plainly to point out America, as the first-fruits of that glorious day.

God has made as it were two worlds here below, two great habitable continents, far separated one from the other: The latter is as it were now but newly created; it has been, till of late, wholly the possession of Satan, the church of God having never been in it, as it has been in the other continent, from the beginning of the world. This new world is probably now discovered, that the new and most glorious state of God's church on earth might commence there; that God might in it begin a new world in a spiritual respect, when he creates the *new heavens* and *new earth*.

God has already put that honour upon the other continent, that Christ was born there literally, and there made the "purchase of redemption." So, as Providence observes a kind of equal distribution of things, it is not unlikely that the great spiritual birth of Christ, and the most glorious "application of redemption," is to begin in this. The elder sister brought forth Judah, of whom Christ came, and so she was the mother of Christ; but the younger sister, after long barrenness, brought forth Joseph and Benjamin, the beloved children, Joseph who had the most glorious apparel, the coat of many colours; who was separated from his brethren, and was exalted to great glory out of a dark dungeon—who fed and saved the world when ready to perish with famine, and was as a fruitful bough by a well, whose branches ran over the wall, and was blessed with all manner of blessings and precious things of heaven and earth, through the good-will of him that dwelt in the bush—was, as by the horns of an unicorn, to push the people together to the ends of the earth, i.e. conquer the world. See Gen. xlix. 2, etc. and Deut. xxxiii. 13, etc. And Benjamin, whose mess was five times so great as that of any of his brethren, and to whom Joseph, that type of Christ, gave wealth and raiment far beyond all the rest, Gen. xlv. 22.

The other continent hath slain Christ, and has from age to age shed the blood of the saints and martyrs of Jesus, and has often been as it were, deluged with the church's blood. —God has, therefore, probably reserved the honour of building the glorious temple to the daughter that has not shed so much blood, when those times of the peace, prosperity and glory of the church, typified by the reign of Solomon, shall commence.

The Gentiles first received the true religion from the Jews: God's church of ancient times had been among them, and Christ was of them. But, that there may be a kind of equality in the dispositions of Providence, God has so ordered it, that when the Jews come to be admitted to the benefits of the evangelical dispensation, and to receive their highest privileges of all, they should receive the gospel from the Gentiles. Though Christ was of them, yet they have been guilty of crucifying him; it is therefore the will of God, that the Jews should not have the honour of communicating the blessings of the kingdom of God in its most glorious state to the Gentiles; but on the contrary, they shall receive the gospel in the beginning of that glorious day from the Gentiles. In some analogy to this, I apprehend, God's dealings will be with the two continents. America has received the true religion of the old continent; the church of ancient time has been there, and Christ is from thence. But that there may be an equality, and inasmuch as that Continent has crucified Christ, they shall not have the honour of communicating religion in its most glorious state to us, but we to them.

The old continent has been the source and original of mankind in several respects. The first parents of mankind dwelt there; and there dwelt Noah and his sons; there the second Adam was born, and crucified, and raised again: And it is probably that, in some measure to balance these things, the most glorious renovation of the world shall originate from the new continent, and the church of God in that respect be from hence. And so it is probable that will come to pass in spirituals, which has taken place in temporals, with respect to America: that whereas, till of late, the world was supplied with its silver, and gold, and earthly treasures from the old continent, now it is supplied chiefly from the new; so the course of things in spiritual respects will be in like manner turned. —And it is worthy to be noted, that America was discovered about the time of the reformation, or but little before: Which reformation was the first thing that God did towards the glorious renovation of the world after it had sunk into the depths of darkness and ruin, under the great anti-christian apostacy. So that, as soon as this new world stands forth in view, God presently goes about doing some great thing in order to make way for the introduction of the church's latter-day glory—which is to have its first seat in, and is to take its rise from that new world.

It is agreeable to God's manner, when he accomplishes any glorious work in the world, in order to introduce a new and more excellent state of his church, to begin where no foundation had been already laid, that the power of God might be the more conspicuous; that the work might appear to be entirely God's, and be more manifestly a creation out of nothing: agreeable to Hos. i. 10. "And it shall come to pass, that in the place where it was said unto them, Ye are not my people, there it shall be said unto them, Ye are the sons of the living God." When God is about to turn the earth into a paradise, he does not begin his work where there is some good growth already, but in the wilderness, where nothing grows, and nothing is to be seen but dry sand and barren rocks; that the light may shine out of darkness, the world be replenished from emptiness, and the earth watered by springs from a droughty desert: agreeable to many prophecies of scripture, as Isa. xxxii. 15. "Until the spirit be poured from on high, and the wilderness become a fruitful field." And chap. xli. 18, 19. "I will open rivers in high places, and fountains in the midst of the valleys: I will make the wilderness a pool of water, and the dry land springs of water. I will plant in the wilderness the cedar, the shittah-tree, and the myrtle, and the oil-tree: I will set in the desert, the fir-tree, and the pine, and the box-tree together." And chap. xliii. 20. "I will give waters in the wilderness, and rivers in the desert, to give drink to my people, my chosen." And many other parallel scriptures might be mentioned. Now as when God is about to do some great work for his church, his manner is to begin at the lower end; so, when he is about to renew the whole habitable earth, it is probable that he will begin in this utmost, meanest, youngest and weakest part of it, where the church of God has been planted last of all; and so the first shall be last, and the last first; and that will be fulfilled in an eminent manner in Isa. xxiv. 19. "From the uttermost part of the earth have we heard songs, even glory to the righteous."

There are several things that seem to me to argue, that the sun of righteousness, the sun of the new heavens and new earth, when he rises— and "comes forth as the bridegroom" of his church, "rejoicing as a strong man to run his race, having his going forth from the end of heaven, and his circuit to the end of it, that nothing may be hid from the light and heat of it," shall rise in the west, contrary to the course of things in the old heavens and earth. The movements of Providence shall in that day be so wonderfully altered in many respects, that God will as it were change the course of nature, in answer to the prayers of his church; as he caused the sun to go from the west to the east, when he promised to do such great things for his church; a deliverance out of the hand of the king of Assyria, is often used by the prophet Isaiah, as a type of the glorious deliverance of the church from her enemies in the latter-days. The resurrection as it were of Hezekiah, the king and captain of the church (as he is called, 2 Kings xx. 5) is given as an earnest of the church's resurrection and salvation, Isa. xxxviii. 6, and is a type of the resurrection of Christ.

At the same time there is a resurrection of the sun, or coming back and rising again from the west, whither it had gone down; which is also a type of the sun of righteousness. The sun was brought back ten degrees; which probably brought it to the meridian. The sun of righteousness has long been going down from east to west; and probably when the time comes of the church's deliverance from her enemies, so often typified by the Assyrians, the light will rise in the west, till it shines through the world like the sun in its meridian brightness.

The same seems also to be represented by the course of the waters of the sanctuary, Ezek. xlvii. which was from west to east; which waters undoubtedly represented the Holy Spirit, in the progress of his saving influences, in the latter ages of the world; for it is manifest, that the whole of those last chapters of Ezekiel treat concerning the glorious state of the church at that time. And if we may suppose that this glorious work of God shall begin in any part of America, I think, if we consider the circumstances of the settlement of New England, it must needs appear the most likely, of all American colonies, to be the place whence this work shall principally take its rise. And, if these things be so, it gives us more abundant reason to hope that what is now seen in America, and especially in New England, may prove the dawn of that glorious day; and the very uncommon and wonderful circumstances and events of this work, seem to me strongly to argue that God intends it as the beginning or forerunner of something vastly great.

part two

REVOLUTION, CONSTITUTION, AND A NEW NATION'S DESTINY

Although the Great Awakening brought about a renewal of the idea that the New World was the Promised Land, the birth of the republic lent special credence to the idea. The birth pangs of the Revolutionary War both announced the coming of independence and awakened the colonists to a new errand into the wilderness. Victory was interpreted as both a hard-earned opportunity for American self-determination and a proof of God's blessing on American tasks. The achievement of constitutional government was seen as the first step in a bold experiment that would assure basic human freedoms; it was also understood as a serious effort to erect an American model for the Old World. God's New Israel was transformed into a republic; her colonial destiny became a national destiny.

Protestant clergy were instrumental in rallying support for the revolutionary cause, and their success was due in great part to their ability to arouse in the people a sense of American destiny under God. There were clergy and laymen in practically every denomination who either remained neutral or favored the British side, but as a whole the churches supported the Revolution. The strongest advocacy came from Congregationalists, Presbyterians, and Baptists. Aggressive missionary activity on the part of the Anglican Society for the Propagation of the Gospel angered many a non-Anglican colonist, and the attempt of the S.P.G. to convince the British government to establish an episcopate in America raised colonial fears to a pitch. For those of Puritan background, an Anglican bishop

61

symbolized both political and religious tyranny. The more positive religious base for revolution resided in a Puritan political ideology that stressed man's *primary* loyalty to God rather than king and described government as the result of a compact which, when broken, required adjustment even to the point of rebellion.

More colonists were prepared for armed resistance by the clergy's Sunday and election sermons and weekly lectures than by the books and pamphlets of a Locke or a Paine. Rural communities seldom exposed to the latest newspapers and books received from their clergymen instruction in the meaning of covenantal government and the "inalienable rights" of man. Of more immediate import was the "preaching up" of the Revolution itself on Sundays, fast days, and times of military recruitment. Curiously, such sermons were often cast in the form of the lamentation or jeremiad which had become a major part of the Puritan homiletical arsenal. Now, however, the jeremiad was bent to a most practical purpose. The sins of God's New Israel were examined so that she might repent and gird herself with holiness for the defeat of her enemy. The minister's lamentation was paralleled by successive recommendations of the Continental Congress that days of "publick humiliation, fasting, and prayer" be observed by the thirteen colonies in order to "confess and deplore our many sins" and implore God to "turn from his wrath." Both sermon and congressional recommendation constituted a call to action. "What carried the ranks of militia and citizens," Perry Miller has written, "was the universal persuasion that they, by administering to themselves a spiritual purge, acquired the energies God had always, in the manner of the Old Testament, been ready to impart to His repentant children. Their first responsibility was not to shoot redcoats but to cleanse themselves; only thereafter to take aim."[1]

Nicholas Street, graduate of Yale and pastor of East Haven (Congregational) Church, supported the Revolution by preaching on political topics and actively raising men, money, and goods for the Continental army.[2] Street's jeremiad, *The American States Acting Over the Part of the Children of Israel in the Wilderness*, was typical of the time. It insisted that the agonies of war had befallen the colonies because of their sins and warned against letting the injustices and cruelties of Pharaoh Britain obscure the wickedness of American Israel. Only after God's chosen people had been "humbled and reformed" would they be delivered from British bondage, make their way through the Red Sea of armed conflict and the wilderness of indecision, and reach the Promised Land of independence.

[1] Perry Miller, "From the Covenant to the Revival," *The Shaping of American Religion,* ed. James W. Smith and A. Leland Jamison (Princeton, N.J.: Princeton University Press, 1961), p. 333.
[2] See Harry K. Eversull, *The Evolution of an Old New England Church* (East Haven, Conn.: Tuttle, Morehouse & Taylor, 1924), pp. 57–86.

The end of the Revolutionary War offered American orators an occasion to rejoice in victory, praise God for the triumph, and look ahead with confidence to the destiny beckoning an independent people. Although public exultations usually avoided undisguised self-righteousness (the claim was often made that God had granted the colonies victory despite their unworthiness), there was little doubt in any patriot's mind that victory had come because the revolutionary *cause* (freedom) was just. Exhilaration quickly gave way to apprehension as Americans faced postwar poverty and the confusion resulting from government by confederation. Nevertheless, the conviction that God had given in the victory a sure sign of his approval of the new nation was firmly planted in the American mind. This conviction would, on more than one occasion, prompt the nation to confuse the justice of her grand cause with the righteousness of her every move.

When Governor Trumbull asked his friend Ezra Stiles, president of Yale, to preach the Connecticut election sermon in 1783, Stiles was offered a chance to give full vent to current American optimism and let his imagination wander over the opportunities awaiting "God's American Israel." The sermon, *The United States Elevated to Glory and Honor*, was lengthy, running over one hundred pages in its printed form. As Stiles addressed the body of state representatives, his words actually stretched toward a much wider audience. "He was talking over their heads," Edmund Morgan has judged, "to the world that lay three thousand miles over the water. America, he was saying, had not merely conquered George III; America had conquered monarchy. America was the future of Europe. In the coming years, as American ships carried the flag around the globe, the power of freedom would everywhere become apparent."[3] America's destiny was disclosed: she was to be the pinnacle of liberty, "both civil and religious," and Stiles found ample evidence that she had already begun to realize that glorious historical role. Particularly striking was Stiles's paean to George Washington: Washington was portrayed as God's anointed and a paragon of virtue. Following the Revolution, praises of Washington reached such heights (he was compared most often with Moses, Gideon, and Joshua, but occasionally also with Jesus Christ) that a number of clergy warned against apotheosizing the general.[4] Clearly, Washington became the first "saint" in the American civil religion.

The formulation of a constitution encouraged further definition of

---

3 Edmund S. Morgan, *The Gentle Puritan. A Life of Ezra Stiles, 1727–1795* (New Haven, Conn.: Yale University Press, 1962), pp. 454–55.

4 James H. Smylie, "American Clergymen and the Constitution of the United States of America, 1781–1796" (Th.D. dissertation, Princeton Theological Seminary, 1958), pp. 342–52. Regarding the impact of Washington on American oratory see William A. Bryan, *George Washington in American Literature, 1775–1865* (New York: Columbia University Press, 1952), pp. 51–85.

American destiny. The Constitutional Convention was preacherless, though eight of the state ratifying conventions had clerical representatives; it was also prayerless, despite Ben Franklin's suggestion that the sessions be opened with prayer to overcome "partial interests." The Convention's product, however, by no means lacked religious support and grounding. Reformed or Calvinist theories of government, for example, had long preferred a "mixed state" containing a system of checks and balances to guard against every man's tendency to pursue his own self-interests. A view of the nature of man and government deeply rooted in New England religion was expressed by John Witherspoon—Presbyterian clergyman, delegate to the Continental Congress, signer of the Declaration of Independence, president of the College of New Jersey, member of the New Jersey ratifying convention:

> Pure democracy cannot subsist long, nor be carried far into the departments of state—it is very subject to caprice and the madness of popular rage. . . . Hence it appears, that every good form of government must be complex, so that the one principle may check the other. It is of consequence to have as much virtue among the particular members of a community as possible; but it is folly to expect that a state should be upheld by integrity in all who have a share in managing it. They must be so balanced, that when every one draws to his own interest or inclination, there may be an overpoise upon the whole.[5]

When the Constitution went to the states for debate and ratification, defenders of the document were quick to depict its significance in terms of American destiny. New Hampshire, which had the honor of being the ninth state to ratify the Constitution and hence put it into effect on June 21, 1788, included as a member of its ratifying convention Samuel Langdon, a New England Congregational minister and the president of Harvard from 1774 until 1780. In an election sermon before the General Court of New Hampshire on June 5, 1788, Langdon urged ratification and drew parallels between the laws of Israel and the federal Constitution. The sermon, *The Republic of the Israelites An Example to the American States*, detailed evidences of God's providence in the events of American history and prescribed ways to "make a wise improvement" of what God had granted the New Israel. The states were to secure the human liberties fought for in the Revolution with the establishment of and adherence to a sound federal Constitution. Thereby the states could claim their destiny under God and "RISE! RISE to fame among all nations." Like many other New England ministers at this time, Langdon did not feel that the Constitution excluded the need for state government to preserve

---

[5] John Witherspoon, "Lectures on Moral Philosophy," *Works*, III (Philadelphia: William W. Woodward, 1802), 435.

and support the Christian religion. And although Langdon insisted in his election sermon that the Christian religion "is confined to no particular nation, sect, or denomination," there is little doubt that he believed his own brand of Protestantism to be that religion's purest form. During the constitutional period, citizens were divided over the question whether the states should support a "religious establishment"; and although the tendency clearly was toward complete disestablishment, it was not until 1833 (in Massachusetts) that the last vestige of religious establishment was abolished in the states.

The American Founding Fathers were as vigorous in their pronouncements on America's providential destiny as any clergyman. Benjamin Franklin, Thomas Jefferson, and John Adams—all of whose "rationalist" ideas on religion were later to be severely criticized by those of more traditional religious leanings—were never so rationalistic or Deistic that they envisioned God as a watchmaker who simply wound up the universe and then let events take their course. Their God was intimately involved in the events of American history. Divine providence was the force that moved the United States to liberty; eventually providence would, through the example of the United States, direct the world to the same end. In a diary entry for February, 1765, Adams wrote, "I always consider the settlement of America with reverence and wonder, as the opening of a grand scene and design in Providence for the illumination of the ignorant, and the emancipation of the slavish part of mankind all over the earth."[6] Franklin and Jefferson preferred the image of Israel's exodus from Egypt and eventual arrival in Canaan as the best representation of the American struggle for freedom. On July 4, 1776, Congress directed Franklin, Jefferson, and Adams to design a seal for the United States. Franklin proposed a portrayal of "Moses lifting his hand and the Red Sea dividing, with Pharaoh in his chariot being overwhelmed by the waters, and with a motto in great popular favor at the time, 'Rebellion to tyrants is obedience to God.'" Jefferson suggested "a representation of the children of Israel in the wilderness, led by a cloud by day and a pillar of fire by night."[7]

No one spoke more deliberately or persistently of the American Israel's destiny than Thomas Jefferson. He was later to conclude his second inaugural address with an image similar to the one he suggested for the seal: "I shall need . . . the favor of that Being in whose hands we are, who led our fathers, as Israel of old, from their native land and planted them in a country flowing with all the necessaries and comforts of life." According to Jefferson, America was to act as a model democratic

---

6 Quoted in Ernest Lee Tuveson, *Redeemer Nation: The Idea of America's Millennial Role* (Chicago: University of Chicago Press, 1968), p. 25.
7 Irving L. Thomson, "Great Seal of the United States," *Encyclopedia Americana*, XIII (1967), 362.

republic, thereby serving as "the world's best hope." "A just and solid republican government maintained here," he wrote to John Dickinson in 1801, "will be a standing monument and example for the aim and imitation of the people of other countries."[8] Geographically separated from the tyrannies and corruptions of Europe, America could perform her experiment in self-government unmolested by outside forces and outmoded traditions. In that way she would become the hope and example for all freedom-loving men. The major themes in Jefferson's version of American destiny were presented in his first inaugural address.

"Jeffersonian isolationism expressed an essentially cosmopolitan spirit," Daniel Boorstin has said.[9] It was for the sake of all men that America was to isolate herself and perform her experiment in republican democracy. Yet the Jeffersonian view of American destiny also contained the seeds of American self-righteousness. Believing that she had escaped the wickedness of the Old World and the guilt of the past, God's New Israel would find it all too easy to ignore her vices and all too difficult to admit a loss of innocence.

SUGGESTED READING

Baldwin, Alice M. *The New England Clergy and the American Revolution.* Durham, N.C.: Duke University Press, 1928.

Boorstin, Daniel J. *The Lost World of Thomas Jefferson.* Boston: Beacon Press, 1948.

Bridenbaugh, Carl. *Mitre and Sceptre: Transatlantic Faiths, Ideas, Personalities, and Politics, 1689–1775.* New York: Oxford University Press, Inc., 1962.

Cousins, Norman, ed. *In God We Trust: The Religious Beliefs and Ideas of the American Founding Fathers.* New York: Harper & Row, Publishers, 1958.

Heimert, Alan. *Religion and the American Mind: From the Great Awakening to the Revolution.* Cambridge: Harvard University Press, 1966.

Hudson, Winthrop S. "Theological Convictions and Democratic Government," *Theology Today,* X (July 1953), 230–39.

Mead, Sidney E. "American Protestantism During the Revolutionary Epoch" and "Thomas Jefferson's 'Fair Experiment'—Religious Freedom," Chaps. 3 and 4, *The Lively Experiment.* New York: Harper & Row, Publishers, 1963.

Miller, Perry, "From the Covenant to the Revival," in *The Shaping of American Religion,* edited by James W. Smith and A. Leland Jamison. Princeton, N.J.: Princeton University Press, 1961, pp. 322–68.

[8] A. E. Bergh, ed., *The Writings of Thomas Jefferson,* X (Washington, D.C.: The Thomas Jefferson Memorial Association, 1907), 217.
[9] Daniel J. Boorstin, *The Lost World of Thomas Jefferson* (Boston: Beacon Press, 1948), p. 229.

NICHOLAS STREET

The American States Acting Over the Part Of The Children Of Israel In The Wilderness And Thereby Impeding Their Entrance Into Canaan's Rest

Deuteronomy viii. 2. *"And thou shalt remember all the way which the Lord thy GOD led thee these forty years in the wilderness, to humble thee, and to prove thee, to know what was in thine heart, whether thou wouldest keep his commandments or no."*

The history of the children of Israel in Egypt, their sufferings and oppression under the tyrant Pharaoh, their remarkable deliverance by the hand of Moses out of that state of bondage and oppression, and their trials and murmurings in the wilderness, is well known by those who have been conversant with their bibles, and have attended to those important lessons contained in the five Books of Moses. But why God thus dealt with that people, perhaps has not been duly attended to by those that have made conscience of reading the sacred story. But the text tells us, that it was to humble them, and to prove them, that they might know what was in their hearts, and whether they would keep his commandments, or no. All the events which befel them in the way; the miraculous protections, deliverances, provisions and instructions which God gave them, and withal, the frequent and severe punishments which were inflicted for their disobedience, was to discover to themselves and others, all that infidelity, inconstancy, hypocrisy, apostacy, rebellion and perverseness which lay hid in their hearts; the discovery of which was of singular

A sermon preached at East Haven, Connecticut, April, 1777. (New Haven: Thomas and Samuel Green, 1777), pp. 3–25, 27–34.

use both to them, and to the church of God in all succeeding ages. For as Watts has it,

> There, as in a glass our hearts may see,
> How fickle and how false they be.

God, by them, designed to let after generations know what was in their hearts. But it is not generally known and believed till it comes to the trial; and then it is found that we are prone to act over the same stupid vile part that the children of Israel did in the wilderness, under the most instructive and speaking providences that ever obtained in the world. . . .

I. I am to show that the hearts of the children of men are naturally the same from generation to generation. This is so plain a point that I need not stand long for the proof of it, tho' it may be profitable to illustrate it by some examples. "For of one blood God made all nations of men that dwell upon the face of the earth," Acts 17.26.   And this blood is under one common attainder by guilt; "for by one man's disobedience many were made sinners," says the apostle, Rom. 5.19. And the apostle speaking of the natural state of the heart says, that "it is enmity against God, not subject to his law, neither indeed can be," Rom. 8.7. And our Savior testifieth that "out of the heart of man proceed evil thoughts, murders, adulteries, fornication, thefts, covetousness, wickedness, deceit, lasciviousness, an evil eye, blasphemy, pride, foolishness. All these things come from within and defile the man." Mark 7.21, 22, 23. And we find this radical evil of the heart early breaking forth and exemplifying itself in the lives of all the generations of men that have been upon the earth, from Adam our primogenitor to the present race of men that inhabit the earth. . . .

Tho' we have all the wickedness of the world to teach us what there is in our hearts, and our daily experience to instruct us, yet we do not learn the depths of wickedness that lodge in that cavern, till a suitable temptation draws it forth into exercise. The children of Israel were not aware ('tis like) of the hundredth part of the wickedness that lay lurking in their hearts, while they were in Egypt in their cruel state of bondage to Pharaoh. They were doubtless ready then to think, that if they could once get free from that state of vassalage, that they would serve the Lord with chearfulness, and that none of his commandments should be grievous. But when they came to the trial, they found unbelief, distrust of God and of his tender care of them, springing up in the midst of the most extraordinary manifestations of God's power and goodness on their behalf that ever were made to a people. And tho' they had been lately delivered from the severest bondage and oppression, yet they were as impatient under trials, and as ready to murmur at any difficulties in their way, as tho' they had newly come out of the most prosperous state. Now if any one had told them while in their cruel state of bondage, that such were their hearts, they would not have believed them, 'tis like. Therefore God led them those forty years in the wilderness to humble and prove them, that they might know what was in their hearts, as 'tis said in the text. And tho' when we read their history, we are ready to be moved with indignation towards them; yet we are acting over at this day the same stupid part with them in the wilderness.

We in this land are, as it were, led out of Egypt by the hand of Moses. And now we are in the wilderness, i.e. in a state of trouble and difficulty, Egyptians pursuing us, to overtake us and reduce us. There is the Red Sea before us, I speak metaphorically, a sea of blood in your prospect before you, perhaps. And when you apprehend this in your imaginations, are you not ready to murmur against Moses and Aaron that led you out of Egypt, and to say with the people of Israel, "It had been better for us to serve the Egyptians, than that we should die in the wilderness." Exod. 14.12. And tho' God has been pleased to work marvellously for us at times as he did for them; yet if any new difficulty arises, and if things don't go on so prosperously as at other times, how soon does our faith fail us, and we begin to murmur against Moses and Aaron, and wish ourselves back again in Egypt, where we had some comforts of life, which we are now deprived of? not considering that we chose our leaders, and that in obtaining any deliverance there are great troubles and difficulties generally attending it; neither considering that our ill successes are owing to the sins of the people, as was the case of the people of Israel in the wilderness. We find them ten times as ready to find fault with their leaders, and to ascribe their misfortunes to them, as to recoil in upon themselves, and to say, What have we done? tho' it was owing entirely to them that they were not delivered. And thus we in this land are murmuring and complaining of our difficulties and ill successes at times, thinking our leaders to blame, and the like, not considering at the same time that we are practising those vices that have a natural tendency to destroy us, besides the just judgments of Heaven which they tend to draw down upon us as a people. . . . And when we are favoured with a little success, we are apt to be elated in our minds like the children of Israel after the overthrow of the Egyptians in the red sea, and then with them to rejoice, and to encourage ourselves in the cause in which we are engaged; then we can trust, as we imagine, in God, and hope for his salvation and deliverance. But let the scale turn a little against us, our confidence begins to fail, and we grow distrustful of God and his providence, and begin to murmur and repine.

> Thus the faithless Jews forgot
> The dreadful wonders God had wrought,
> Then they provoke him to his face,
> Nor fear his power, nor trust his grace.
>
> —WATTS

Thus we are acting over the like sins with the children of Israel in the wilderness, under the conduct of Moses and Aaron, who was leading them out of a state of bondage into a land of liberty and plenty in Canaan. Again, we are ready to marvel at the unreasonable vileness and cruelty of the British tyrant and his ministry, in endeavouring to oppress, enslave and destroy these American States, who have been some of his most peaceable and profitable subjects. And yet we find the same wicked temper and disposition operating in Pharaoh king of Egypt above 3000 years ago. . . . When Israel began to increase in Egypt, the king said, "Come on, let us deal wisely with them lest they multiply; and it comes to pass when there falleth out any war, they join unto our enemies and fight against us, and so get them out of the land." Therefore they did set over them task-masters to afflict them with their burdens; they made them to serve with rigour, and they made their lives bitter with hard bondage, etc. And afterwards they laid the burthen heavier, allowing them no straw, and yet requiring the full tale of brick. Exod. 5.6–11. And when they endeavoured to make their escape from this cruel and oppressive tyrant, Pharaoh pursued after Israel with a great army unto the Red Sea. Exod. 14.7–10. So that the British tyrant is only acting over the same wicked and cruel part, that Pharaoh king of Egypt acted towards the children of Israel above 3000 years ago.

But some may be ready to wonder, that since we are gone off from Great-Britain, and have declared ourselves independent States, and insist upon standing by ourselves, that they don't let us alone, especially as they have pretended that we are but of little consequence to Great-Britain. But we find the same disposition in the adversaries of Judah and Benjamin, who troubled them in building, and hired counsellors against them to frustrate their purposes. Afterwards Rehum the chancellor wrote to the king, The Jews are building the rebellious and bad city. If this city be builded, and the walls set up again, say they, then they will not pay toll, tribute, etc. and so thou shalt endamage the revenue of the kings. Now because we have maintenance from the king's palace, and it was not meet for us to see the king's dishonour, etc. this city is a rebellious city, and hurtful to kings; and that they have moved sedition within the same of old. If this city be built, by this means thou shalt have no portion on this side the river, and so they hasted to Jerusalem to stay the work by force. Ezra 4, from the beginning to the 24th verse. Now this was a right Tory letter and conduct; and Sanballat's behaviour towards those that encouraged the work of building the city was just like that of the tories towards those that would build up these American States. See Neh. 2.19. "But when Sanballat the Horonite and Tobiah the servant, the Ammonite, heard it, they laughed us to scorn, and despised us, and said, 'What is this thing that ye do? Will ye rebel against the king?' " Thus there were some men then as well as in these days, that seemed to look upon it as a greater crime to oppose the king in his most arbitrary measures, than to violate the law of the realm and of their God. "And when Sanballat and others heard that the walls of Jerusalem were made up, they were very wroth, and conspired all of them together to come and fight against Jerusalem, and to hinder it." Neh. 4.7, 8.

And Great-Britain is now acting over just the same part towards us in these American States, endeavouring to prevent our building ourselves up into Free, Independent States. So that the temper and disposition of the world has been much the same throughout all generations. Great men are generally proud, ambitious and aspiring, disdainful of inferiors, and apt to resent the least indignities. We see this in Haman, an aspiring courtier, who when he saw that Mordecai bowed not nor did him reverence, was full of wrath; wherefore Haman sought to destroy all the Jews that were throughout the whole kingdom of Ahasuerus. And Haman said unto the king, " 'There is a certain people scattered abroad, and dispersed among the people in all the provinces of thy kingdom, and their laws are diverse from all people, neither keep they the king's laws; therefore it is not for the king's profit to suffer them. Let it please the king that it may be written that they may be destroyed; and I will pay ten thousand talents of silver to the hands of those that have the charge of the business, to bring it into the king's treasuries.' " And the king grants his desire. Esth. 3.5–11. And the British ministry have been acting over the same wicked, mischievous plot against the American States, as Haman did against the Jews, and we have reason to hope that they will meet with the like fate. But what I mention these instances for, is to let you see that the wickedness of man has been much the same throughout all ages . . . we see that our complaints and trials at this day are nothing new. People have been oppressed under the colour of law, as we are by the British ministry; and have been most cruelly oppressed and insulted by those that have been in power; and have been derided and laughed at by their enemies in their most afflicted state.

II. God frequently brings his own people into a state of peculiar trials, to discover to them and others what there is in their hearts. Thus God tempted Abraham, when he put him upon offering up his son Isaac, Gen. 22.2, 3 (i.e.) tried him with that peculiar trial, that he might discover to himself and others, what there was in his heart; whether he would keep God's commandments or no, however trying or self-denying they might be. And the issue discovered to himself and to others the firmness and fixedness of his principles to the glory of God and his own comfort and satisfaction. For the trial proved his sincerity in the cause of God, and that he would keep his commandments under the most trying circumstances of obedience, that nothing should deter him from the service of his God, tho' his best beloved son, as a sacrifice, should be the test of his obedience. Thus nobly did the faith and obedience of this Father of the faithful display itself under the exercise of peculiar trials... and as God is thus pleased to bring his own people into a state of peculiar trials for the discovery of their virtues, so likewise for the discovery of their vices, that they and others may see what corruption there still remains in their hearts unmortified and unsubdued. Thus good Hezekiah was tried with a prosperous scene to discover what was in his heart. God gave him a remarkable victory over the Assyrians and granted him miraculous restoration from a dangerous sickness, and not only so, but God gave him peculiar honour by an embassy from the great and potent king of Babylon; all which probably raised in him too high an opinion of himself, as if these things were done, if not by his power, yet at least for his piety and virtues. So that instead of walking humbly with God, and giving the glory of all entirely to him, he took the honour to himself, and vain-gloriously shewed his riches and precious treasures to the Babylonish ambassadors. 2 Kings 20.13....

And so a suitable temptation will frequently draw forth such corruptions into exercise, as persons before were not aware of being in their hearts. This we see in a striking light in Hazael, whom the prophet informed how wicked and cruel he would be when he came to be king, viz. that he would burn their strong holds, and slay their young men with the sword, dash their children, and rip up their women with child, etc. Hazael when he came to hear the descripton was shocked at it, and resented the thought, as you see from his reply. 2 Kings 8.13. "And Hazael said, 'But what is thy servant a dog, that he should do this great thing?' " And yet we find, as a worthy author observes upon this passage, that the dog did it. He could not conceive that there was such cruelty and barbarity in his heart as to practise such inhumanity as the prophet pointed out. But when he came to the trial, and was made king, and felt the pleasing power of having the world under him, as it were, then pride, insolence, and a tyrannical disposition sprung up in his heart, like noxious and baleful weeds in an overfattened soil, to the destruction of the design of regal dignity, whereby he became a curse and destroyer of his people, rather than a minister of God for good unto them. But he was not aware, it seems, when the prophet told him that he should be king of Syria, that he should ever be left to practise such inhumanity and barbarity as afterwards he was guilty of.

Neither is it probable that George the third, when he first came to the throne of Great-Britain, and swore to govern according to the good and wholesome laws of the realm, and issued that proclamation for the suppression of immoralities, would in a few years by a royal edict butcher a great number of his best subjects for not submitting to his arbitrary mandates. Doubtless when he first came to the throne, if it had been suggested to him, that he would have practised all that tyranny, cruelty, and oppression which he has not long since gone into with regard to the American States, he would have been greatly ready to have replied in indignation with Hazael, "Is thy servant a dog that he should do this great thing?" But we find he has done it to our grievous wounding, and to his dishonour and bloody guilt! He that should have been our father and protector has become the bloody murderer of thousands of his best subjects! And tho' this seems harsh to assert with regard to one whom we have heretofore addressed with the kind and honorary epithet of a gracious sovereign, yet I now boldly assert him to be a cruel tyrant, who seeks to govern us without law, without reason, or the sacred dictates of revelation; impiously declaring that he has a right to give us laws binding in all cases whatsoever. If such a prince is not a tyrant, then I know not who deserves the name! But he is only with that dog Hazael, acting out the cruelty of his heart and that of his bloody court. The seven abominations that have lain hid there, have now come forth like the locusts from the bottomless pit upon this land to distress and annoy it; burning and laying waste populous towns that were erected without any of his expence or patronage; carrying fire and sword among those who have been his most peaceable and faithful subjects; ravishing the women where the armies have marched; exercising the greatest inhumanity and barbarity towards their prisoners; freezing and starving them to death. And all this done by British troops, who used to be famed for their humanity and generosity to prisoners! Who would have thought that such savage cruelty had been in their hearts? But the trial has brought it out to the disgrace of the British tyrant and his bloody troops. Some are disposed, 'tis true, to talk much of the mercy and mildness of British government, to encourage people to submit to their lawless claims; but I am never disposed to look to that power for mercy, that is devoid of justice, but forever reject the cruel wretch, who for the sake of a lawless domination would sacrifice almost one quarter of the globe to his resentment. I think the trial has discovered what is in the heart of British administration, and I never desire to be again connected with that government, which instead of speaking peace to us, and to our seed, threatens death and destruction to us and our posterity.

But as the trial has discovered what is in the heart of British administration, so likewise the peculiar situation that the American States have been in has tried what is in our hearts. As *The American Crisis* observes,

"These are the times that try men's souls;" and many things are discovered in the trial, which otherwise might have lain concealed in the heart. Tho' as our Savior observes, "Out of the abundance of the heart the mouth speaketh"; yet some will conceal what is within, till a proper temptation draw it forth. The contest has been whether we should submit to the arbitrary, oppressive claims of British administration, or maintain our own rights and repel force by force. Vastly the greatest majority has been for the latter; and the general will is always said to be of the nature of a law. A small part of the States have opposed the general will, and have openly taken part with British administration. Others have been more reserved, and have waited to see which is the safest side, in order to determine their conduct. These are men of no principle, only to save themselves, which is the most sordid of all; for they will be on this side or the other, just as the scale is like to turn for or against the country. Now these are trying times to sift men out, that they and others may know what is in their hearts; whether they will sell their country and their God for a little worldly pelf; or whether they will make a noble sacrifice of all their worldly goods, and even bleed and die for their dear country and dear bought privileges. Many have done it already, and many more seem ready to do it, whose names ought to be honoured and held dear in the annals of the American States, so long as there are any to remember their deeds. But this will not be the fame of all that had their birth and education in this noble land! No, it will be said to the eternal disgrace of some, that instead of standing for the precious land of their nativity and its dear bought privileges, that they vilely betrayed it; and with Esau they sold their birth-right for a mess of pottage; that they turned their sword, which should have been drawn in the defence of their country, against the father that begat them, and against the tender bowels of the mother that bare them, and the loving brothers and sisters that solaced them, and all the dear friends and neighbours that used to aid and assist them.

Oh, this is an image too horrid and shocking to look to! I turn from it as a picture too monstrous to behold! and turn to one of a more diminutive size, tho' not much less despicable than the former. And that is such as aim not to use the sword upon either side, but aim to take a part upon that side that will best secure their darling interest. Their souls are so immersed in silver and gold that they would fall into that scale which would weigh down with the most penny weight! These are they that make gold their hope, and the fine gold their confidence, and deny the God that is above, as Job elegantly expresses it. Job 31.24. . . . Such persons trust that their money and interest will secure them from distresses and troubles, and therefore greedily procure it, and then are ready to join with that party which they think are like to conquer; not considering that the events of war are altogether uncertain, and that that side which appears the most promising at present may be in a few days the most gloomy and threatening. 'Tis not worth while under the most promising prospects to say with David, "My mountain stands so strong that I shall not be moved." For God may hide his face as he did from him, and then with him we shall soon be troubled. But then we should always act upon principle, and be uniform in our conduct, committing our cause to God, who sits in the throne judging righteously, and can save and deliver with few or with many. But some people have no notion about trusting in God; they rise and fall just like a ship at anchor with the ebbing and flowing tide. And these trying times are designed to shew us what is in our hearts; whether we will trust in him at all times, and adhere to the cause which we profess to believe to be right in dark and gloomy days, as well as in those that are more fair and prosperous.

It is no great matter for men to trust in God when every thing looks fair and prosperous; they then deceive themselves, thinking they trust in God, whereas they trust in the fair prospect that is before them. But this is the trial of our sincerity, when every thing looks dark and gloomy, according to human prospects, then to commit our cause to God and trust in him for a favourable issue. This is truly trusting in God. And these shifting scenes of adverse and prosperous appearances are designed to humble us and prove us, that we may know what is in our hearts. There is a variety of temptations arising from our particular state and circumstances, to draw out what there is in our hearts. There are many things to try us whether we are of a public spirit; whether we regard our country, our liberties and privileges more than our own private pelf. And some we shall find shrinking back from the public cause, avoiding all occasions in which the public calls for assistance, while others less able must bear the weight of the public weal or let it sink. Others are tried as to their humanity and benevolence, whether they will assist others with the necessary supports of life, when they can do it, at a reasonable lay. And here, alas! we find the trial betraying what is in the hearts of many, given a wicked, oppressive disposition, refusing to part with their provision at that high price allowed and stated by the legislature of the state; waiting, it seems, to take the advantage of people's necessities, to get a more exorbitant price. This is a wickedness prevailing in the country which we should not have imagined to have been in their hearts had not the trial brought it forth. And God is trying us and proving us by all the variety of his dispensations, that we may know what is in our hearts, and whether we will keep his commandments or no; whether the sabbath-profaner will become a sabbath sanctifier; whether the profane swearer will bridle his tongue, and leave off his profaneness; whether the wanton and intemperate will become chaste and sober; and whether people will reform their ways, mortify their corruptions, and become new creatures. The land have sadly corrupted their way; religion has been losing ground for many years; and all manner of vice and profaneness has become rampant in the land. And God is visiting us for these things with general judgments; and 'tis likely God will keep us in this wilderness of trouble to humble us and prove us, that we may see our errors, and know that God has a righteous controversy with us at this day.

We are apt to think that our cause is so righteous with regard to Great-Britain, that I fear we are ready to forget our unrighteousness towards God. And while we are endeavouring to get rid of the unreasonable commands of an earthly sovereign, I fear we forget to obey the most reasonable commands of the rightful Sovereign of the Universe. Let us look upon the ground on which we stand; consider our guilt and danger, and be humble for our sins, and under all the tokens of God's displeasure against us on the account of our sins, repent and reform whatever is amiss in the midst of us, that we may be prepared for a deliverance out of our troubles; that being delivered out of the hands of our enemies, we may serve God without fear in righteousness and true holiness all the days of our lives.

III. People when they are proved and tried, generally shew what they are. A suitable trial generally shews what people are, whether virtuous or vicious; if they are of a virtuous disposition, a suitable trial will generally bring out their virtues to public view; and if vicious, their vices.

We have been ready to look upon ourselves as a virtuous people in this land, to be sure in comparison with Great-Britain, and so to encourage ourselves that we should not be vanquished on account of our virtues. But the trial discovers that there is not so much virtue in the land as we were ready to imagine. There is a vast deal of wickedness brought out to public view in this day of trial. Many we find will betray their dear bought country for a little worldly pelf, preferring their present interest, ease and advantage, to all the liberties and privileges of their future posterity. And many who aim not to betray their country are so mercenary that they would imbark on that side that they think would best serve their interest, without regard to the righteousness of the cause. And others who profess to be zealous in the cause of their country are so fond of making a fortune, as we say, or of advancing their interest, that they become blind to the bleeding wounds of their country, and deaf to the cries of the poor and needy; and will not reach forth the helping hand to their distresses, unless with the iron hand of oppression to extort an exorbitant sum for their relief. Indeed the trial shews that there is but little of a public spirit prevailing amongst people in general at this day. The bigger part seem exceedingly selfish, striving for the highest price for every article that they have to part with; and if they think there is a prospect of its arriving to a more extravagant price thro' the exigencies of the country, they will withhold it from the needy, tho' "the stone should cry out of the wall, and the beam out of the timber should answer it." Hab. 2.11. . . . If this disposition had not appeared upon the trial, we should have been self-righteous and trusted in ourselves; and have been ready to have thought if we had any successes, this was owing to our being more righteous than Great-Britain, and so arrogated the glory to ourselves. . . .

But then oppression is not the only sin that our trials have brought forth to view, but the sins of treachery, falsehood and deceit have crept out in one place and another thro' the land, in divers persons who would betray its sacred cause into the hands of tyranny and oppression. And others under the notion of being high sons of liberty will act without law and above law, and so encourage and promote universal tyranny under the notion of a plenitude of liberty. For to govern without law is tyranny: for law is the guardian of liberty, securing a people in their rights and liberties; and whosoever endeavours to set law aside or to supersede it, so far endeavours to destroy the liberties of his country, and so far to promote a tyrannical government. And yet the trying situation of the country has discovered some to be of this complexion; and however high they may think themselves for liberty, they are throwing down the very bulwark that secures it. But the trial discovers another sort of people, who tho' they are not for going against law, yet they are not for putting the law in execution, which enervates government and renders the law of no force. And such, however well meaning they may have been, have inadvertently fallen into an opinion that has proved very hurtful to the country. For the relaxation of the laws has encouraged some to act out themselves to the disadvantage of the country. The civil sword has not been a terror to evil doers as heretofore, and a praise and protection to such as do well. And the debtor has shewn the dishonesty of his heart in refusing to pay his honest dues, because courts of judicature have not been kept up in times back, to oblige him to do this justice; and men have hereby been defrauded of their honest dues. And this is not the greatest evil; for this has laid the foundation for the most of that oppression that there is in the midst of us. For the country finding themselves not obliged to part with their monies, feel not the necessity of parting with their provision, and so withhold it from the consumer till an extortionate price draws it out of their hands . . . so that it appears that we have much less public virtue in the country than we were aware of, many being disposed to take the advantage of the distresses of their country, not caring who sinks if they can but swim. . . .

Thus the god of this world blinds the eyes of men. If they were not deluded by the devil and the deceitfulness of their own wicked hearts, they could no more think themselves conscientious and friends to their country, than the thief and the high-way man; for oppression is as much spoken against in Scripture as the forementioned vices, and has as direct a tendency to ruin the country. For these things the wrath of God cometh upon the children of disobedience. And when there is the oppression of the poor, and the sighing of the needy in the midst of us, we can't expect any other, but God will arise to judgment and make his plagues dreadful upon this land. We have been ready to wonder that British troops should be so oppressive and cruel to our people; but it has been observed by some worthy divines, that God is wont to punish people frequently with such a kind of punishment as bespeaks the nature of their crimes. And our Saviour tells us that such measure as you mete, shall be measured to you again. Mat. 7.2. And we have reason to believe that God thus permits us to be oppressed by the British troops, as a righteous correction for the oppressive disposition that prevails in this land. . . .

But besides, the trial has brought out many other vices, which we should have hoped were not so predominant in the land, if the trial had not discovered them. To instance a few: the little regard that is shewn to the sabbath by the soldiery and others, who look upon themselves a little at liberty from the restraints of human laws; and that profaneness that there is in our armies, raised from the midst of us for the defence of our dear land, as well as against people at home, at a time in which the land is involved in the greatest distresses that ever it knew and when there has been the most express prohibitions against profane swearing, issued from the highest authority in America . . . a strange spirit of falsehood has gone forth into the land, so that it is very difficult to ascertain facts of the most interesting nature as to our military operations, bespeaking the want of a spirit of integrity and uprightness in the land. All which forebode ill concerning us as a people. For if public virtue fails and people grow vicious and profane, selfish and oppressive under the sorest judgments and calamities, we have reason to fear the worst; that God will multiply our distresses and increase his judgments, till we are brought to a repentance and reformation. We see that God kept the children of Israel in the wilderness for many years after he had delivered them from the hand of Pharaoh, on the account of their wickedness. He led them so long in the wilderness to humble and prove them that they might know what there was in their hearts; and one trial after another brought it out. And so our trials in this wilderness state are bringing out our corruptions one after another, that we and others may know what there is in our hearts; what pride, what selfishness, what covetousness, what ingratitude, rebellion, impatience and distrust of God and his providence, all these come flowing forth from the midst of us under our trials, in as conspicuous a manner as they did from the children of Israel in the wilderness. Which if it had not been for our trials, that have discovered them, we should not have imagined to have been in such a privileged, gospelized land as this.

IV. The discovering to a people their errors and wickedness is designed to humble and reform them. This is spoken of as being the express end and design of bringing the children of Israel into the wilderness, and leading them there forty years. It was to humble them and prove them, that they might know what there was in their hearts, and whether they would keep his commandments or no. God did it not merely to bring out such a deformed character to view, as they exhibit under their trials; but that being brought forth, they might see their own wickedness and deformity, and be humbled and repent of this their great wickedness and reform their lives, by keeping his commandments for the future. And this is the end and design of God in bringing us into this wilderness of trouble and confusion, that we may know what there is in our hearts, that being brought out to public view, we and others may see what a wicked people we are, and that we may be deeply humbled and abased before God on the same account, repent and reform. 'Tis not because God delights in bringing such a deformed character to view. No, for it is more odious and irksome to him, for he hateth all the workers of iniquity, and he is "of purer eyes than to behold evil, and cannot look on iniquity." Hab. 1.13. A vicious character is like a noisom stench in his nostrils; and therefore when God brings such a character into view, it is that we may be humbled under it, repent and reform. Therefore let us be sollicitous to get a clear view of our manifold guilt, and to be deeply humbled on the account of our own sins, and the manifold high handed abominations that are daily committed in this distinguished land of light and liberty: That there is so much of a disposition in the midst of us to oppress one another, while the land is wading in blood to oppose and resist this wickedness in British administration. Oh, let us see the deformity of this vice thro' the bloody spectacles of those parliamentary acts, that declare that they have a right to tax the American States, and to give laws to us in all cases whatsoever; and in consequence of such a claim have sent their bloody troops to butcher us, till we are reduced to such a cruel yoke of tyranny and oppression. Methinks this shocking scene of oppression is enough to give you to see the deformity of this vice, and to make you flee from it as a monster that devours without pity! And if you do not see it in this horrid picture, look into hell—and there see Dives roaring in the fire of hell for a drop of water to cool his tormented tongue, for denying the crumbs that he had to spare from his own table to a poor, perishing Lazarus! . . . Every sin is of a destructive, deadly nature; and if sin was thus seen and viewed, it would not be so difficult to dissuade people from it. But they view it thro' the devil's spectacles, which makes it to appear more delighting and contenting than ever it is found to be; and he blinds their minds as to the deformity and destructive nature of it, so that he may lead them blindfold down to eternal perdition. Therefore we had need take much pains to bring sinners to a just view of their sins; for till then they will not be humbled for them, nor repent and reform.

And hence it is that God brings people into some trying situation to bring their wickedness out to view, that they may know what there is in their hearts and be humbled for it; and the trials that we have been under in this land have brought out a vast deal of wickedness which we should not have been aware of, if the trial had not betrayed it. And what is the end of this discovery? Why to humble us, to bring us to repentance and a general reformation. Let us then be sensible of the ends of Divine Providence in permitting such wickedness to break out in the midst of us. It is to humble us and to give us to see that we have no cause to trust in ourselves—in our own righteousness, which we are very prone to, that disclaiming all confidence in ourselves, we may trust in him who raiseth the dead—and who will have mercy on whom he will have mercy.

Several useful inferences might be made from this subject, but I shall confine myself to one, with which I shall conclude the discourse.

Seeing it as we have heard, that the wickedness of man has been much the same thro' all generations, hence we may infer that every generation may rationally expect the like punishments and calamities that have been inflicted upon generations back. The history of the world is nothing scarcely but a history of the wickedness and miseries of it. Take the sacred history from the fall of man till Christ's appearance on earth, till his crucifixion, resurrection and ascension to glory, and even from the mission of the Holy Ghost till the completion of the sacred canon, and what do we find but the wickedness of man acted forth in a variety of shapes, together with the just judgments of God pursuing it with a variety of calamities thro' life, till death swallows them up in one undistinguished ruin! This is the general melancholy account of the human race as fallen! Then have we reason to look upon it as strange that we see and feel the like distresses and calamities with the world that has gone before us? Surely no. When we read in sacred or profane history of the unnatural wars that have arisen among those of the same nation, people and language, we are ready to be shock'd at the horrid scene, and to marvel at the outrage, cruelty and devastation that they will make of one another in such a contest! But if God did not restrain the wrath and wickedness of mankind, they would always be acting over the horrid scene, biting and devouring one another!

And the wickedness of the British nation, I mean of the governing part of them, has arrived to that pitch, that they are disposed to act over all that wickedness, cruelty and oppression that Pharaoh and the other cruel tyrants of the earth have been disposed to practise towards those in their power. Witness the cruel and unnatural war that they have levied against us; burning and laying waste many noble towns with a savage barbarity and wantonness of rage; abusing the prisoners that have fallen into their hands, with worse than savage barbarity! freezing and starving them to death with a relentless cruelty! so that the cries of those poor oppressed prisoners have entered, I trust, into the ears of the Lord of Sabbaoth, and that he has arisen to avenge their blood upon those inhumane butchers, who have come above 3000 miles to destroy their neighbours that are more righteous than they! This is the nation that heretofore has been famed for their humanity and generosity to their enemies, especially when prisoners, that have now sunk into such a degree of cruelty and barbarism that they can abuse them after they have sur-rendered, cane them, strip them of their clothing, and then drive them like a flock of sheep into prison, and there freeze and starve them to death! Oh how is the nation fallen and debased by the most sordid wickedness and inhumanity! and from once being famed for christianity, their conduct would disgrace the most barbarous nation on earth! Thus the wickedness of the human heart, without the restraints of divine grace, will act out a part not much inferior in vileness to that of infernals!

But then tho' I thus inveigh against the cruelty and wickedness of British administration and their sordid troops, yet I would by no means intimate that we are innocent and free from wickedness. No, God has a righteous controversy with us in this land; and our iniquities have arrived to that aggravated height, that they have called for these sore calamities that we feel! And the British nation are the rod of God's anger to scourge and chastise us for our sins, as the Assyrian monarch was to God's people of old. See Isa. 10.5, 6, 7. "Oh Assyrian, the rod of mine anger, and the staff in their hand is mine indignation! I will send him against an hypo-critical nation, and against the people of my wrath will I give him a charge to take the spoil, and to take the prey and to tread them down as the mire of the streets; howbeit, he meaneth not so, neither doth his heart think so, but it is in his heart to destroy and cut off nations not a few," etc. Tho' this haughty tyrant had no design of executing God's will and the glory of his justice in punishing an hypocritical people, but only to enlarge his own empire and satisfy his own lusts by sacrificing multi-tudes of people to his own ambition and covetousness; yet God meant to use him as a rod and the instrument of his anger to chastise and correct his sinful, degenerate, backsliding people. And we have reason to think (let the designs of the British tyrant be what they will) that God designs him as the rod of his anger to correct us for the foul sins and abomina-tions of this highly privileged land! Therefore let us be humble, kiss the rod and accept the punishment of our sins—repent and turn to God by an universal reformation—that God may be intreated for the land, spare his heritage, and not give it up to a reproach but restore to us our liberties as at the first, and our privileges as at the beginning.

EZRA STILES

The United States Elevated
To Glory And Honour

Deuteronomy XXVI. 19. *"And to make thee high above all*
nations which he hath made,
in praise, and in name,
and in honour;
and that thou mayest be
an holy people unto
the Lord thy God."

Taught by the omniscient Deity, Moses foresaw and predicted the
capital events relative to Israel, through the successive changes of depression and glory, until their final elevation to the first dignity and eminence
among the empires of the world. These events have been so ordered as to
become a display of retribution and sovereignty; for while the good and
evil, hitherto felt by this people, have been dispensed in the way of exact
national retribution, their ultimate glory and honour will be of the divine
sovereignty, with a "not for your sakes, do I this, saith the Lord, be it
known unto you—but for mine holy name's sake."

However it may be doubted whether political Communities are
rewarded and punished in this world only; and whether the prosperity
and decline of other Empires have corresponded with their moral state, as
to virtue and vice: Yet the history of the Hebrew theocracy shews that the
secular welfare of God's ancient people depended upon their virtue, their
religion, their observance of that holy covenant which Israel entered into
with God on the plains at the foot of Nebo on the other side Jordan. Here
Moses, the man of God, assembled three millions of people, the number
of the United States, recapitulated and gave them a second publication of
the sacred jural institute, delivered thirty-eight years before, with the most
awful solemnity at Mount Sinai. A Law dictated with sovereign authority

A sermon preached before Governor Jonathan Trumbull and the General
Assembly of the State of Connecticut, convened at Hartford at the Anni-
versary Election, May 8th, 1783. Second edition (Worcester, Mass.: Isaiah
Thomas, 1785), pp. 5–9, 58–75, 88–92, 95–98.

by the Most High to a people, a world, a universe, becomes of invincible force and obligation without any reference to the consent of the governed. It is obligatory for three reasons, *viz.* its original justice and unerring equity, the omnipotent Authority by which it is enforced, and the sanctions of rewards and punishments. But in the case of Israel, he condescended to a mutual covenant; and by the hand of Moses led his people to avouch the Lord Jehovah to be their God, and in the most publick and explicit manner voluntarily to engage and covenant with God to keep and obey his Law. Thereupon this great prophet, whom God has raised up for so solemn a transaction, declared in the name of the Lord that the Most High avouched, acknowledged and took them for a peculiar people to himself; promising to be their God and Protector, and upon their obedience to make them prosperous and happy. Deut. xxix. 10 & 14. Chap. xxx. 9 & 19. He forsaw indeed their rejection of God and predicted the judicial chastisement of apostacy, a chastisement involving the righteous with the wicked. But as well to comfort and support the righteous in every age, and under every calamity, as to make his power known among all nations, God determined that a remnant should be saved. Whence Moses and the Prophets by divine direction interspersed their writings with promises that, when the ends of God's moral government should be answered in a series of national punishments, inflicted for a succession of ages, he would by his irresistible power and sovereign grace subdue the hearts of his people to a free, willing, joyful obedience; turn their captivity—recover and gather them "from all the nations whither the Lord had scattered them in his fierce anger—bring them into the land which their fathers possessed—and multiply them above their fathers—and rejoice over them for good, as he rejoiced over" their fathers. Deut. xxx. 3 [–9]. Then the words of Moses, hitherto accomplished but in part, will be literally fulfilled; when this branch of the posterity of Abraham shall be nationally collected, and become a very distinguished and glorious people under the Great Messiah the Prince of Peace. He will then make them "high above all nations which he hath made in praise, and in name, and in honour," and they shall become "a holy people unto the Lord" their God.

I shall enlarge no further upon the primary sense and literal accomplishments of this and numerous other prophecies respecting both Jews and Gentiles, in the latter day glory of the church. For I have assumed the text only as introductory to a discourse upon the political welfare of God's American Israel, and as allusively prophetick of the future prosperity and splendour of the United States.

. . . .

Already does the new constellation of the United States begin to realize this glory. It has already risen to an acknowledged sovereignty among the republicks and kingdoms of the world. And we have reason to hope, and I believe to expect, that God has still greater blessings in store for this vine which his own right hand hath planted, to make us "high among the nations in praise, and in name, and in honour." The reasons are very numerous, weighty, and conclusive.

In our civil constitutions, those impediments are removed which obstruct the progress of society towards perfection: Such, for instance, as respect the tenure of estates, and arbitrary government. The vassalage of dependent tenures, the tokens of ancient conquests by Goths and Tartars, still remain all over Asia and Europe. In this respect, as well as others, the world begins to open its eyes. One grand experiment in particular has lately been made. The present Empress of Russia, by granting lands in freehold in her vast wilderness of Volkouskile, together with religious liberty, has allured and already draughted from Poland and Germany a colonization of six hundred thousand souls in six years only, from 1762 to 1768.

Liberty, civil and religious, has sweet and attractive charms. The enjoyment of this, with property, has filled the English settlers in America with a most amazing spirit, which has operated, and still will operate, with great energy. Never before has the experiment been so effectually tried, of every man's reaping the fruits of his labour and feeling his share in the aggregate system of power. The ancient republicks did not stand on the people at large; and therefore no example or precedent can be taken from them. Even men of arbitrary principles will be obliged, if they would figure in these states, to assume the patriot so long that they will at length become charmed with the sweets of liberty.

Our degree of population is such as to give us reason to expect that this will become a great people. It is probable that within a century from our independence the sun will shine on fifty million of inhabitants in the United States. This will be a great, a very great nation, nearly equal to half Europe. Already has our colonization extended down the Ohio and to Koskaseah on the Mississippi. And if the present ratio of increase should be rather diminished in some of the elder settlements, yet an accelerated multiplication will attend our general propagation and overspread the whole territory westward for ages. So that before the Millennium, the English settlements in America may become more numerous millions than that greatest dominion on earth, the Chinese empire. Should this prove a future fact, how applicable would be the text, when the Lord shall have made his American Israel "high above all nations which he hath made," in numbers, "and in praise, and in name, and in honour!"

I am sensible some will consider these as visionary Utopian ideas. And so they would have judged had they lived in the apostolick age and been told that by the time of Constantine the empire would have become christian. As visionary that the twenty thousand souls which first settled New-England should be multiplied to near a million in a century and a half. As visionary that the Ottoman empire must fall by the Russian. As visionary to the Catholicks is the certain downfall of the Pontificate. As Utopian would it have been to the loyalists, at the battle of Lexington, that in less than eight years the independence and sovereignty of the United States should be acknowledged by four European sovereignties, one of which should be Britain herself. How wonderful the revolutions, the events of Providence! We live in an Age of Wonders. We have lived an age in a few years. We have seen more wonders accomplished in eight years than are usually unfolded in a century.

God be thanked, we have lived to see peace restored to this bleeding land, at least a general cessation of hostilities among the belligerent powers. And, on this occasion, does it not become us to reflect how wonderful, how gracious, how glorious has been the good hand of our God upon us in carrying us through so tremendous a warfare! We have sustained a force brought against us which might have made any empire on earth to tremble—and yet our bow has abode in strength; and having obtained help of God, we continue unto this day. Forced unto the last solemn appeal, America watched for the first blood: this was shed by Britons on the 19th of April, 1775; which instantly sprung an army of 20,000 into spontaneous existence, with the enterprizing and daring resolution of entering Boston and forcibly disburdening it of its bloody legions. Every patriot trembled until we had proved our armour, until it could be seen whether this hasty concourse was susceptible of exercitual arrangement and could face the enemy with firmness. They early gave us the decided proof of this, in the memorable battle of Bunker-Hill. We were satisfied. This instantly convinced us, and for the first time convinced Britons themselves, that Americans both would and could fight with great effect. Whereupon Congress put at the head of this spirited army the only man on whom the eyes of all Israel were placed. Posterity, I apprehend, and the world itself, inconsiderate and incredulous as they may be of the dominion of heaven, will yet do so much justice to the divine moral government as to acknowledge that this American Joshua was raised up by God and divinely formed by a peculiar influence of the Sovereign of the Universe for the great work of leading the armies of this American Joseph (now separated from his brethren) and conducting this people through the severe, the arduous conflict, to Liberty and Independence. Surprizing was it with what instant celerity men ascended and rose into generals and officers of every subordination; formed chiefly by the preparatory discipline of only the preceding year, 1774; when the ardour and spirit of military discipline was by heaven, and without concert, sent through the continent like lighting. Surprizing was it how soon the army was organized, took its formation, and rose into a firm system and impregnable arrangement.

To think of withstanding and encountering Britain by land was bold, and much more bold and daring by sea; yet we immediately began a navy and built ships of war with an unexampled expedition. It is presumed never was a 35 gun ship before built quicker than that well built and noble ship the *Raleigh*, which was finished from the keel and equipt for sea in a few months. Soon had we got, though small, a very gallant initial navy, which fought gallantly; and wanted nothing but numbers of ships for successful operations against that superior naval force before which we fell. We have, however, exhibited proof to posterity and the world that a powerful navy may be originated, built and equipped for service in a much shorter period than was before imagined. The British navy has been many centuries growing; and France, Holland, the Baltick powers, or any of the powers of this age, in twenty years may build navies of equal magnitude, if necessary for dominion, commerce, or ornament.

A variety of success and defeat hath attended our warfare both by sea and land. In our lowest and most dangerous estate in 1776 and 1777, we sustained ourselves against the British army of sixty thousand troops commanded by Howe, Burgoyne, Kniphausen, and Clinton, and other the ablest generals Britain could procure throughout Europe, with a naval force of 22,000 seamen in above eighty British men of war. These generals we sent home one after another, conquered, defeated, and convinced of the impossibility of subduing America. While oppressed by the heavy weight of this combined force, heaven inspired us with resolution to cut the Gordian knot when the die was cast irrevocably in the glorious act of INDEPENDENCE. This was sealed and confirmed by God Almighty in the victory of General Washington at Trenton, and in the surprizing movement and battle of Princeton; by which astonishing effort of generalship, General Howe, and the whole British army, in elated confidence and in open-mouthed march for Philadelphia, was instantly stopt, remanded back, and cooped up for a shivering winter in the little borough of Brunswick. Thus God "turned the battle to the gate"; and this gave a "finishing to the foundation" of the American republick. This with the Burgoynade at Saratoga by General Gates, and the glorious victory over the Earl of Cornwallis in Virgina, together with the memorable victory of Eutaw springs, and the triumphant recovery of the southern states by General Greene, are among the most heroick acts and brilliant atchievements which have decided the fate of America. And who does not see the indubitable interposition and energetick influence of Divine Providence in these great and illustrious events? Who but a Washington, inspired by heaven, could have struck out the great movement and manoeuvre of Princeton? To whom but the Ruler of the winds shall we ascribe it that the British reinforcement, in the summer of 1777, was delayed on the ocean three months by contrary winds, until it was too late for the conflagrating General Clinton to raise the siege of Saratoga? What but a providential miracle detected the conspiracy of Arnold, even in the critical moment of the execution of that infernal plot, in which the body of the American army, then at West-Point, with his Excellency General Washington himself, were to have been rendered into the hands of the enemy! Doubtless inspired by the Supreme Illuminator of great minds were the joint councils of a Washington and a Rochambeau, in that grand effort of generalship with which they deceived and astonished a Clinton and eluded his vigilance in their transit by New-York and rapid marches for Virginia. Was it not of God that both the navy and army should enter the Chesapeak at the same time? Who but God could have ordained the critical arrival of the Gallick fleet, so as to prevent and defeat the British and assist and co-operate with the combined armies in the siege and reduction of York-Town? Should we not ever admire and ascribe to a supreme energy the wise and firm generalship displayed by General Greene, when (leaving the active, roving Cornwallis to pursue his helter-skelter ill-fated march into Virginia) he coolly and steadily went onwards and deliberately, judiciously, and heroically recovered the Carolinas and the southern states?

How rare have been the defections and apostacies of our capital characters, though tempted with all the charms of Gold, Titles, and Nobility? Whence is it that so few of our army have deserted to the enemy? Whence that our brave sailors have chosen the horrours of prison ships and death, rather than to fight against their country? Whence that men of every rank have so generally felt and spoken alike, as if the cords of life struck unison through the continent? What but a miracle has preserved the UNION OF THE STATES, the PURITY OF CONGRESS, and the unshaken PATRIOTISM OF EVERY GENERAL ASSEMBLY? It is God who has raised up for us a great and powerful ALLY, an ally which sent us a chosen army and a naval force; who sent us a Rochambeau and a Chatelleux, and other characters of the first military merit and eminence, to fight side by side with a Washington and a Lincoln, and the intrepid Americans, in the siege and battle of York-Town. It is God who so ordered the balancing interests of nations as to produce an irresistible motive in the European maritime powers to take our part. Hence the recognition of our independence by Spain and Holland, as well as France. Britain ought to have forseen that it must have given joy to surrounding nations, tired and wearied out with the insolence and haughtiness of her domineering flag, a flag which spreads terrour through the oceans of the terraqueous globe, to behold the era when their forces should have arrived to such maturity and strength that a junction of national navies would produce an aggregate force, adequate to the humiliation of Britain and her gallant and lofty navy. Nor could they resist the operation of this motive, prompting them to assist in the cutting off a member, with which the growing aggrandisment and power of Britain were connected; as thus she would be disarmed of terrour, and they should be at rest. If Britain doth not learn wisdom by these events and disclaim the sovereignty of the ocean, the junction of national navies will settle the point for her in less than half a century. So wonderfully does Divine Providence order the time and coincidence of the publick national motives, co-operating in effecting great publick events and revolutions.

But the time would fail me to recount the wonder working Providence of God in the events of this war. Let these serve as a specimen and lead us to hope that God will not forsake this people, for whom he has done such marvellous things (whereof we are glad and rejoice this day) having at length brought us to the dawn of Peace. O peace! thou welcome guest! all hail, thou heavenly visitant! calm the tumult of nations, and wave thy balmy wing to perpetuity over this region of liberty. Let there be a tranquil period for the unmolested accomplishment of the *Magnalia Dei*, the great events in God's moral government, designed from eternal ages to be displayed in these ends of the earth.

And here I beg leave to congratulate my country upon the termination of this cruel and unnatural war, the cessation of hostilities, and the prospect of peace. May this great event excite and elevate our first, our highest acknowledgments to the SOVEREIGN MONARCH of Universal Nature, to the Supreme Disposer and Controller of all Events; let our pious, sincere and devout gratitude ascend in one general effusion of heart-felt praise and hallelujah, in one united cloud of incense, even the incense of universal joy and thanksgiving to God, from the collective body of the United States.

And while we render our supreme honours to the Most High, the God of armies, let us recollect with affectionate honour the bold and brave sons of freedom, who willingly offered themselves and bled in the defence of their country. Our fellow-citizens, the Officers and Soldiers of the Patriot Army, who, with the Manlys, the Joneses, and other gallant commanders and brave seamen of the American navy, have heroically fought the war by sea and by land, merit of their once bleeding but now triumphant country, Laurels, Crowns, Rewards, and the highest honours. Never was the possession of arms used with more glory, or in a better cause, since the days of Joshua the son of Nun. O WASHINGTON! how do I love thy name! how have I often adored and blessed thy God for creating and forming thee the great ornament of human kind! upheld and protected by the Omnipotent, by the Lord of Hosts, thou hast been sustained and carried through one of the most arduous and most important wars in all history. The world and posterity will, with admiration, contemplate thy deliberate, cool, and stable judgment, thy virtues, thy valour and heroick atchievements, as far surpassing those of Cyrus, whom the world loved and adored. The sound of thy fame shall go out into all the earth, and extend to distant ages. Thou has convinced the world of the Beauty of Virtue—for in thee this Beauty shines with distinguished lustre. Those who would not recognize any beauty in virtue in the world beside will yet reverence it in thee. There is a glory in thy disinterested benevolence, which the greatest characters would purchase, if possible, at the expence of worlds, and which may excite indeed their emulation, but cannot be felt by the venal great—who think every thing, even virtue, and true glory, may be bought and sold, and trace our every action to motives terminating in self.

> "Find virtue local, all relation scorn,
> See all in self, and but for self be born."

But thou, O Washington, forgottest thyself, when thou lovedst thy bleeding country. Not all the gold of Ophir, nor a world filled with rubies and diamonds could effect or purchase the sublime and noble feelings of thine heart in that single, self-moved act when thou renouncedst the Rewards of Generalship and heroically tookest upon thyself the dangerous as well as arduous office of our Generalissimo—and this at a solemn moment when thou didst deliberately cast the die for the dubious, the very dubious alternative of a gibbet or a Triumphal Arch. But beloved, enshielded and blessed by the great Melchizedeck, the King of Righteousness as well as peace, thou hast triumphed gloriously. Such has been thy military wisdom in the struggles of this arduous conflict, such a noble rectitude, amiableness and mansuetude of thy character, something is there so singularly glorious and venerable thrown by heaven about thee that not only does thy country love thee, but our very enemies stop the madness of their fire in full volley, stop the illiberality of their slander at thy name, as if rebuked from heaven with a "touch not mine anointed, and do my HERO no harm." Thy fame is of sweeter perfume than Arabian spices in the gardens of Persia. A Baron de Steuben shall waft its fragrance to the Monarch of Prussia; a Marquis de la Fayette shall waft it to a far greater Monarch and diffuse thy renown throughout Europe; listening angels shall catch the odour, waft it to heaven, and perfume the universe!

And now that our warfare is ended, do thou, O man of God, greatly beloved of the Most High, permit a humble minister of the blessed Jesus, who, though at a distance, has vigilantly accompanied thee through every stage of thy military progress, has watched thine every movement and danger with an heart-felt anxiety and solicitude; and who, with the most sincere and fervent wishes for thy safety and success, has not ceased day nor night to pray for thee and to commend thee and thy army to God—condescend to permit him to express his most cordial congratulations, and to share in the triumphs of thy bosom on this great and joyous occasion. We thank the Lord of Hosts that has given his servant to see his desire upon his enemies, and peace on Israel. And when thou shalt now at length retire from the fatigues of nine laborious campaigns to the tranquil enjoyment, to the sweetness and serenity of domestick life, may you never meet the fate of that ornament of arms and of humanity, the great Belisarius; but may a crown of universal reverence and honour of thy saved country, rest and flourish upon the head of its Veteran General and glorious Defender; until, by the divine Jesus, whom thou hast loved and adored, and of whose holy religion thou art not ashamed, thou shalt be translated from a world of war to a world of peace, liberty, and eternal triumph.

. . . .

This great American revolution, this recent political phenomenon of a new sovereignty arising among the sovereign powers of the earth, will be attended to and contemplated by all nations. Navigation will carry the American flag around the globe itself and display the Thirteen Stripes and New Constellation at Bengal and Canton on the Indus and Ganges, on the Whang-ho and the Yang-tse-kiang; and with commerce will import the wisdom and literature of the east. That prophecy of Daniel is now literally fulfilling—there shall be an universal travelling "too and fro, and knowledge shall be increased." This knowledge will be brought home and treasured up in America: and being here digested and carried to the highest perfection, may reblaze back from America to Europe, Asia and Africa, and illumine the world with TRUTH and LIBERTY.

That great Civilian, Dr. John Adams, the learned and illustrious American Ambassadour, observes thus, "But the great designs of Providence must be accomplished;—great indeed! The progress of society will be accelerated by centuries by this revolution. The Emperour of Germany is adopting, as fast as he can, American Ideas of toleration and religious liberty: And it will become the fashionable system of Europe very soon. Light spreads from the day-spring in the west; and may it shine more and more until the perfect day."—So spreading may be the spirit for the restoration and recovery of long lost national rights, that even the Cortes of Spain may re-exist and resume their ancient splendour, authority, and control of royalty. The same principles of wisdom and enlightened politicks may establish rectitude in publick government throughout the world.

The most ample religious liberty will also probably obtain among all nations. Benevolence and religious lenity is increasing among the nations. The Reformed in France, who were formerly oppressed with heavy persecution, at present enjoy a good degree of religious liberty, though by silent indulgence only. A re-establishment of the edict of Nantz would honour the Grand Monarch by doing publick justice to a large body of his best and most loyal subjects. The Emperour of Germany, last year, published an imperial decree granting liberty for the free and unmolested exercise of the protestant religion within the Austrian territories and denominations. The Inquisition has been, in effect, this year suppressed in Spain, where the King, by an edict of 3d of November, 1782, proclaimed liberty for inhabitants of all religions: And by a happily conceived plan for literary reformation, the Aurora of science will speedily blaze into meridian splendour in that kingdom. An emulation for liberty and science is enkindled among the nations and will doubtless produce something very liberal and glorious in this age of science, this period of the empire of reason.

The United States will embosom all the religious sects or denominations in Christendom. Here they may all enjoy their whole respective systems of worship and church government, complete. . . .

Little would Civilians have thought ages ago that the world should ever look to America for models of government and polity. Little did they think of finding this most perfect polity among the poor outcasts, the contemptible people of New-England, and particularly in the long despised civil polity of Connecticut; a polity conceived by the sagacity and wisdom of a Winthrop, a Wyllys, a Ludlow, Haynes, Hopkins, Hooker, and the other first settlers of Hartford, in 1636. And while Europe and Asia may hereafter learn that the most liberal principles of law and civil polity are to be found on this side of the Atlantick, they may also find the true religion here depurated from the rust and corruption of ages, and learn from us to reform and restore the church to its primitive purity. It will be long before the ecclesiastical pride of the splendid European hierarchies can submit to learn wisdom from those whom they have been inured to look upon with sovereign contempt. But candid and liberal disquisition will sooner or later have a great effect. Removed from the embarrassments of corrupt systems, and the dignities and blinding opulence connected with them, the unfettered mind can think with a noble enlargement, and with an unbounded freedom go wherever the light of truth directs. Here will be no bloody tribunals, no cardinals inquisitors-general, to bend the human mind, forcibly to control the understanding, and put out the light of reason, the candle of the Lord, in man; to force an innocent Galileo to renounce truths demonstrable as the light of day. Religion may here receive its last, most liberal, and impartial examination. Religious liberty is peculiarly friendly to fair and generous disquisition. Here deism will have its full chance; nor need libertines more to complain of being overcome by any weapons but the gentle, the powerful ones of argument and truth. Revelation will be found to stand the test to the ten thousandth examination.

There are three coetaneous events to take place whose fruition is certain from prophecy, the annihilation of the Pontificate, the reassembling of the Jews, and the fulness of the Gentiles. That liberal and candid disquisition of Christianity, which will most assuredly take place in America, will prepare Europe for the first event, with which the other will be connected, when, especially on the return of the twelve tribes to the Holy Land, there will burst forth a degree of evidence hitherto unperceived and of efficacy to convert a world. More than three quarters of mankind yet remain heathen. Heaven put a stop to the propagation of Christianity when the church became corrupted with the adoration of numerous deities and images, because this would have been only exchanging an old for a new idolatry. Nor is Christendom now larger than it was nine centuries ago. The promising prospects of the *Propaganda fide* at Rome are coming to nothing: and it may be of the divine destiny that all other attempts for gospelizing the nations of the earth shall prove fruitless, until the present Christendom itself be recovered to the primitive purity and simplicity. At which time, instead of the Babel confusion of contradicting missionaries, all will harmoniously concur in speaking one language, one holy faith, one apostolick religion to an unconverted world. At this period, and in effecting this great event, we have reason to think that the United States may be of no small influence and consideration. It was of the Lord to send Joseph into Egypt, to save much people, and to shew forth his praise. It is of the Lord that "a woman clothed with the sun, and the moon under her feet," and upon "her head a crown of twelve stars," (not to say thirteen) should "flee into the wilderness, where she hath a place prepared of God" (Rev. xii. 1 & 6), and where she might be the repository of Wisdom, and "keep the commandments of God, and have the testimony of Jesus." It may have been of the Lord that Christianity is to be found in such great purity in this church exiled into the wilderness of America; and that its purest body should be evidently advancing forward, by an augmented natural increase and spiritual edification, into a singular superiority—with the ultimate subserviency to the glory of God, in converting the world.

.   .   .   .

SAMUEL LANGDON

The Republic Of The Israelites An Example To The American States

Deuteronomy IV. 5–8.

> *"Behold, I have taught you statutes and judgments, even as the Lord my God commanded me, that ye should do so in the land whither ye go to possess it. Keep therefore and do them; for this is your wisdom and your understanding in the sight of the nations, who shall hear all these statutes, and say, surely this great nation is a wise and understanding people: for what nation is there so great, which hath God so nigh unto them as the Lord our God is in all things that we call upon him for? and what nation is there so great, which hath statutes and judgments so righteous as all this law which I set before you this day?"*

Here Moses recommends to Israel the strict observance of all the laws which he had delivered to them by God's command, relating both to their civil polity and religion, as the sure way to raise their reputation high among all nations as a wise and understanding people; because no other nation was blessed with such excellent national laws, or the advantage of applying to the oracle of the living God, and praying to him in all difficulties with assurance that all their requests would be answered.

As to every thing excellent in their constitution of government, except what was peculiar to them as a nation separated to God from the

A sermon preached at Concord, New Hampshire, before the General Court at the Annual Election, June 5, 1788. (Exeter, N. H.: Lamson and Ranlet, 1788), pp. 6–15, 17–19, 29–43, 45–48.

rest of mankind, the Israelites may be considered as a pattern to the world in all ages; and from them we may learn what will exalt our character, and what will depress and bring us to ruin.

Let us therefore look over their constitution and laws, enquire into their practice, and observe how their prosperity and fame depended on their strict observance of the divine commands both as to their government and religion.

They had both a civil and military establishment under divine direction, and a complete body of judicial laws drawn up and delivered to them by Moses in God's name. They had also a form of religious worship by the same authority, minutely prescribed, designed to preserve among them the knowledge of the great Creator of the Universe, and teach them to love and serve him, while idolatry prevailed through the rest of the world. And this religion contained not only a public ritual, but a perfect, though very concise, system of morals, comprehended in ten commands, which require the perfection of godliness, benevolence, and rectitude of conduct.

When first the Israelites came out from the bondage of Egypt, they were a multitude without any other order than what had been kept up, very feebly, under the ancient patriarchal authority. They were suddenly collected into a body under the conduct of Moses, without any proper national or military regulation. Yet in the short space of about three months after they had passed the red sea, they were reduced into such civil and military order, blended together by the advice of Jethro, as was well adapted to their circumstances in the wilderness while destitute of property. Able men were chosen out of all their tribes, and made captains and rulers of thousands, hundreds, fifties and tens: and these commanded them as military officers and acted as judges in matters of common controversy.

But the great thing wanting was a permanent constitution, which might keep the people peaceable and obedient while in the desert and after they had gained possession of the promised land. Therefore, upon the complaint of Moses that the burden of government was too heavy for him, God commanded him to bring seventy men, chosen from among the elders and officers, and present them at the tabernacle; and there he endued them with the same spirit which was in Moses, that they might bear the burden with him. Thus a Senate was evidently constituted, as necessary for the future government of the nation, under a chief commander. And as to the choice of this Senate, doubtless the people were consulted, who appear to have had a voice in all public affairs from time to time, the whole congregation being called together on all important occasions. The government therefore was a proper republic.

And beside this general establishment, every tribe had elders and a

prince according to the patriarchal order, with which Moses did not interfere; and these had an acknowledged right to meet and consult together,
and with the consent of the congregation do whatever was necessary to
preserve good order and promote the common interest of the tribe. So
that the government of each tribe was very similar to the general government. There was a President and Senate at the head of each, and the people assembled and gave their voice in all great matters: for in those ages
the people in all republics were entirely unacquainted with the way of
appointing delegates to act for them, which is a very excellent modern
improvement in the management of republics.

Moreover, to complete the establishment of civil government, courts
were to be appointed in every walled city, after their settlement in Canaan,
and elders most distinguished for wisdom and integrity were to be made
judges, ready always to sit and decide the common controversies within
their respective jurisdictions. The people had a right likewise to appoint
such other officers as they might think necessary for the more effectual
execution of justice, according to that order given in Deut. 16.18, 19. . . .
But from these courts an appeal was allowed in weighty causes to higher
courts appointed over the whole tribe, and in very great and difficult
cases to the supreme authority of the general Senate and chief magistrate.

A government, thus settled on republican principles, required laws,
without which it must have degenerated immediately into aristocracy or
absolute monarchy. But God did not leave a people, wholly unskilled in
legislation, to make laws for themselves. He took this important matter
wholly into his own hands, and beside the moral laws of the two tables,
which directed their conduct as individuals, gave them by Moses a complete code of judicial laws. They were not numerous indeed, but concise
and plain and easily applicable to almost every controversy which might
arise between man and man, and every criminal case which might require
the judgment of the court. Of these some were peculiarly adapted to their
national form, as divided into tribes and families always to be kept distinct; others were especially suited to the peculiar nature of the government as a theocracy, God himself being eminently their king and mani-
festing himself among them in a visible manner, by the cloud of glory in
the tabernacle and temple. This was the reason why blasphemy and all
obstinate disobedience to his laws were considered as high treason and
punished with death, especially idolatry, as being a crime against the
fundamental principles of the constitution. But far the greater part of the
judicial laws were founded on the plain immutable principles of reason,
justice, and social virtue, such as are always necessary for civil society.
Life and property were well guarded, and punishments were equitably
adapted to the nature of every crime. In particular, murder stands foremost among capital crimes and is defined with such precision, and so

clearly distinguished from all cases of accidental and undesigned killing, that the innocent were in no danger of punishment and the guilty could not escape. And if we still pay regard to this divine law, which is evidently founded on reason and justice, the modern distinction of manslaughter must be rejected as a popish invention, contrived and added in times when superstition reigned and claimed a power above all laws. These laws were sufficient for a nation which had but little commerce abroad, especially as the oracle of Jehovah might be consulted in all cases of a very extraordinary nature.

Let us now consider the national worship which God established among his people, on which their obedience to the moral law very much depended. For unless they paid constant reverence and homage to their God, agreeable to his nature and will, they would soon break loose from all other obligations to morality.

Now as to their ritual; however contemptible, and even ridiculous, it may seem to men whose ideas are all modern and who proudly contemn divine revelation, and notwithstanding it is now abrogated by a far more glorious revelation of grace and truth by Jesus Christ, no religious institution could be more perfectly accommodated to those early ages of the world, and the situation of the Israelites in the midst of idolaters, or better prepare the way for the truth and mercy of the gospel. In those ages the minds of men were not sufficiently cultivated to receive that religion which is spiritual and simple, detached from sensible objects, and destitute of worldly grandeur. Other nations worshipped their gods with an endless variety of superstitious rites, a multitude of costly sacrifices, and all kinds of external pomp, which they fancied would be acceptable to deities to whom they attributed the imperfections and even the worst vices of men. Their worship gratified all the senses, was accommodated to every passion and lust, and indulgent to gross immoralities; it not only captivated vulgar minds, but bound the greatest heroes, politicians, and philosophers fast in the chains of superstition. Therefore it was necessary that the worship of the true God should not be destitute of that splendour which, in those ages, struck the minds of men with awe and reverence. Without some magnificence the best religion would have appeared contemptible in the view of the world; and the Israelites themselves, dazzled with the pageantry of idols, would almost inevitably have been captivated; as, notwithstanding every guard which could be placed about them, we find the fashion of the rest of the world had surprising power over them. But the ceremonies of worship which God commanded his people to observe were not, like those of the heathen, inhuman, frantic, obscene, varied a thousand ways according to the different characters of their gods; . no, but by infinite wisdom they were calculated to promote the knowledge of the divine perfections and obedience to the laws of righteousness, and give the most encouraging hope in the goodness and mercy of God. The ritual of the Israelites was rational, sober, uniform, plainly intended to exhibit the majesty, purity, and mercy of the eternal king; to humble men before him under a continual sense of guilt; and to assure true penitents of free pardon by virtue of the appointed sacrifices, which were types of that one sacrifice which Christ has offered for the sins of the world. And to render their worship more striking, in their own view and in the eyes of the world, their tabernacle and temple, their priesthood with its ornaments, their solemn assemblies and great festivals, were decent and magnificent beyond every thing seen among the nations around.

How unexampled was this quick progress of the Israelites from abject slavery, ignorance, and almost total want of order to a national establishment perfected in all its parts far beyond all other kingdoms and States! from a mere mob to a well regulated nation, under a government and laws far superior to what any other nation could boast!

. . . .

Upon a review of what has been said, must it not appear quite unaccountable that the Israelites should so speedily attain to such an height of good policy and legislation, beyond all other nations? Are we not constrained to acknowledge an immediate interposition and direction of heaven? Had the unexperienced multitude been left to themselves to draw up a system of civil and military government for themselves, it would have been entirely beyond their abilities to comprehend so complicated a subject; they must have committed innumerable mistakes, in attempting to introduce and establish it; they would have been in danger of jarring opinions, tumults, and insurrections; and probably before the design could be effected, discouragement and confusion would have forced them to surrender into the hands of despotism. But their God provided every thing necessary for their happiness, and nothing more was left to their own wisdom than to submit to his authority and adhere strictly to his commands. By this, their reputation among the nations would have been equal to the excellency of their laws.

But now you may say, Why then were they not universally celebrated? Why did not princes and politicians from all parts of the world visit them, to learn maxims of polity from so well regulated a nation? Why did not philosophers come and enquire into that system of religion and morality which carried virtue to such an height of perfection? Surely a nation, of which all the parts were so firmly cemented, must be strong and formidable. A people who enjoyed the most rational liberty and yet were under the most voluntary and absolute subjection to authority, free from all the convulsions and revolutions which frequently arise from the raging folly of the populace, must become famous. A wise and impartial administration of justice, according to the most excellent laws, by which all were kept in perfect security and peace, could not but be admired. And the commerce of a people whose morals were governed by the best precepts, whose word might be trusted, who practised no kind of fraud, and whose behavior was always benevolent, sober, prudent, and sincere must be highly valued by the world. Whereas on the contrary, the Israelites were often weak, distressed, and generally despised and hated by all their neighbours. The plain answer to this objection is—They never adhered in practice either to the principles of their civil polity or religion, but on their practice depended the prosperity and honor of the nation. They received their law from God, but they did not keep it. They neglected their government, corrupted their religion, and grew dissolute in their morals, and in such a situation no nation under heaven can prosper.

.   .   .   .

And now, my fellow Citizens, and much honored Fathers of the State, you may be ready to ask—"To what purpose is this long detail of antiquated history on this public occasion?" I answer—Examples are better than precepts; and history is the best instructor both in polity and morals. I have presented you with the portrait of a nation, highly favoured by Heaven with civil and religious institutions, who yet, by not improving their advantages, forfeited their blessings and brought contempt and destruction on themselves. If I am not mistaken, instead of the twelve tribes of Israel, we may substitute the thirteen States of the American union and see this application plainly offering itself, *viz.* That as God in the course of his kind providence hath given you an excellent constitution of government, founded on the most rational, equitable, and liberal principles by which all that liberty is secured which a people can reasonably claim, and you are impowered to make righteous laws for promoting public order and good morals; and as he has moreover given you by his Son Jesus Christ, who is far superior to Moses, a complete revelation of his will and a perfect system of true religion, plainly delivered in the sacred writings; it will be your wisdom in the eyes of the nations, and your true interest and happiness, to conform your practice in the strictest manner to the excellent principles of your government, adhere faithfully to the doctrines and commands of the gospel, and practice every public and private virtue. By this you will increase in numbers, wealth, and power, and obtain reputation and dignity among the nations; whereas, the contrary conduct will make you poor, distressed and contemptible.

The God of heaven hath not indeed visibly displayed the glory of his majesty and power before our eyes, as he came down in the sight of Israel on the burning mount; nor has he written with his own finger the laws of our civil polity. But the signal interpositions of divine providence, in saving us from the vengeance of a powerful irritated nation from which we were unavoidably separated by their inadmissible claim of absolute parliamentary power over us; in giving us a WASHINGTON to be captain-general of our armies; in carrying us through the various distress-ing scenes of war and desolation, and making us twice triumphant over numerous armies, surrounded and captivated in the midst of their career; and finally giving us peace with a large territory and acknowledged inde-pendence; all these laid together fall little short of real miracles and an heavenly charter of liberty for these United-States. And when we reflect how wonderfully the order of these states was preserved when government was dissolved, or supported only by feeble props; with how much sobriety, wisdom, and unanimity they formed and received the diversified yet simi-lar constitutions in the different states; with what prudence, fidelity, patience, and success the Congress have managed the general government under the great disadvantages of a very imperfect and impotent confedera-tion; we cannot but acknowledge that God hath graciously patronized our cause and taken us under his special care, as he did his ancient cove-nant people.

Or we may consider the hand of God in another view. Wisdom is the gift of God, and social happiness depends on his providencial govern-ment; therefore, if these states have framed their constitutions with supe-rior wisdom and secured their natural rights and all the advantages of society with greater precaution than other nations, we may with good reason affirm that God hath given us our government; that he hath taught us good statutes and judgments, tending to make us great and respectable in the view of the world. Only one thing more remains to complete his favor toward us, which is the establishment of a general government, as happily formed as our particular constitutions, for the perfect union of these states. Without this, all that we glory in is lost; but if this should be effected, we may say with the greatest joy—"*God hath done great things for us.*" The general form of such a constitution hath already been drawn up, and presented to the people, by a convention of the wisest and most celebrated patriots in the land. Eight of the states have approved and accepted it, with full testimonies of joy. And if it passes the scrutiny of the whole, and recommends itself to be universally adopted, we shall have abundant reason to offer elevated thanksgivings to the supreme Ruler of the universe for a government completed under his direction.[1]

Now our part is to make a wise improvement of what God grants us,

---

[1] Soon after this Sermon was delivered, the Convention of the State of New Hampshire, met according to adjournment, and on the twenty first day of June accepted the proposed general Constitution of government. This being the ninth State which has acceded to this form of national Union, it will be carried into effect; and there is no reason to doubt of the speedy accession of all the other States, which are now debating on the important question. May all rejoice in the Lord, who has formed us into a nation, and honour him as our Judge, Lawgiver, and King, who hath saved us, and will save us from all enemies and fears, if we thankfully receive and rightly improve his great mercies.

and not neglect or despise our distinguishing privileges. For the best constitution, badly managed, will soon fall and be changed into anarchy or
tyranny. Without constant care of your families, you will have bad servants and your estates will be wasted. So we must pay constant attention
to the great family, if we desire to be a free and happy people.

The power in all our republics is acknowledged to originate in the
people: it is delegated by them to every magistrate and officer; and to the
people all in authority are accountable, if they deviate from their duty
and abuse their power. Even the man who may be advanced to the chief
command of these United States, according to the proposed constitution;
whose office resembles that of a king in other nations, which has always
been thought so sacred that they have had no conception of bringing a
king before the bar of justice; even he depends on the choice of the people
for his temporary and limited power and will be liable to impeachment,
trial, and disgrace for any gross misconduct. On the people, therefore, of
these United-States it depends whether wise men, or fools, good or bad
men, shall govern them; whether they shall have righteous laws, a faithful
administration of government, and permanent good order, peace, and
liberty; or, on the contrary, feel insupportable burdens and see all their
affairs run to confusion and ruin.

Therefore, I will now lift up my voice and cry aloud to the people,
to the people of this State in particular, whom I will consider as present
by their representatives and rulers, and the congregation here collected
from various towns—RISE! RISE to fame among all nations, as a wise and
understanding people! political life and death are set before you; be a
free, numerous, well ordered, and happy people! The way has been
plainly set before you; if you pursue it, your prosperity is sure; but if not,
distress and ruin will overtake you.

Preserve your government with the utmost attention and solicitude,
for it is the remarkable gift of heaven. From year to year be careful in the
choice of your representatives and all the higher powers of government.
Fix your eyes upon men of good understanding and known honesty; men
of knowledge, improved by experience; men who fear God and hate covetousness; who love truth and righteousness, and sincerely wish the public
welfare. Beware of such as are cunning rather than wise; who prefer their
own interest to every thing; whose judgment is partial or fickle; and
whom you would not willingly trust with your own private interests.
When meetings are called for the choice of your rulers, do not carelessly
neglect them or give your votes with indifference, just as any party may
persuade or a sordid treat tempt you; but act with serious deliberation
and judgment, as in a most important matter, and let the faithful of the
land serve you. Let not men openly irreligious and immoral become your
legislators; for how can you expect good laws to be made by men who

have no fear of God before their eyes, and who boldly trample on the authority of his commands? And will not the example of their impiety and immorality defeat the efficacy of the best laws which can be made in favour of religion and virtue? If the legislative body are corrupt, you will soon have bad men for Counsellors, corrupt Judges, unqualified Justices, and officers in every department who will dishonor their stations; the consequence of which will be murmurs and complaints from every quarter. Let a superior character point out the man who is to be your head, for much depends on his inspection and care of public affairs and the influence of his judgment, advice and conduct, although his power is circumscribed. In this choice therefore be always on your guard against parties and the methods taken to make interest for unworthy men, and let distinguished merit always determine your vote. And when all places in government are filled with the best men you can find, behave yourselves as good subjects: obey the laws, cheerfully submit to such taxation as the necessities of the public call for, give tribute to whom tribute is due, custom to whom custom, fear to whom fear, and honor to whom honor, as the gospel commands you. Never give countenance to turbulent men, who wish to distinguish themselves and rise to power by forming combinations and exciting insurrections against government. For this can never be the right way to redress real grievances, since you may not only prefer complaints and petitions to the court but have the very authority, which you think has been misused, in your own power and may very shortly place it in other hands. How happy was it for this state that the insurrection, attempted here two years ago, was so seasonably and with so little difficulty suppressed, when the neighbouring state was brought into such a difficult and critical situation by the distracted populace and has now scarcely recovered from that violent political paroxism.[2]

I call upon you also to support schools in all your towns, that the rising generation may not grow up in ignorance. Grudge not any expense proportionate to your abilities. It is a debt you owe to your children and that God to whom they belong, a necessary evidence of your regard for their present and future happiness and of your concern to transmit the blessings you yourselves enjoy to future generations. The human mind without early and continual cultivation grows wild and savage: knowledge must be instilled as its capacities gradually enlarge, or it cannot expand and extend its sphere of activity. Without instruction men can have no knowledge but what comes from their own observation and experience,

---

[2] [The insurrection of the "neighboring state" refers to Shays' Rebellion in Massachusetts, the most explosive of a number of relatively bloodless revolts growing out of postwar financial readjustment and representing the protest of poor farmers against heavy taxes and payment of debts.—EDITOR]

and it will be a long time before they can be acquainted even with things most necessary for the support and comfort of the present life. Leave your children untaught to read, write, cypher, etc. teach them no trade, or husbandry; let them grow up wholly without care; and they will be more fit for a savage than civil life, and whatever inheritance you may think to leave them will be of no advantage. But, on the contrary, train them up in the fear of God, in an acquaintance with his word, and all such useful knowledge as your abilities will allow, and they will soon know how to provide for themselves, perhaps may take care of their aged parents, and fill the various stations in life with honor and advantage. Look round and see the growing youth: they are to succeed in your stead; government and religion must be continued by them; from among these will shortly rise up our legislators, judges, ministers of the gospel, and officers of every rank. Can you think of this and not promote schools, academies, and colleges? Can you leave the youth uninstructed in any thing which may prepare them to act their part well in the world? Will you suffer ignorance to spread its horrid gloom over the land? An ignorant people will easily receive idolatry for their religion and must bow their necks to the tyrant's yoke, because they are incapable of using rational liberty. Will you then consign over your posterity to foolish and abominable superstitions instead of religion, and to be the slaves of despotism, when a small proportion of the produce of your labours will make them wise, free, and happy?

Will you hear me patiently a little farther, while I say one thing more of very great importance which I dare not suppress. I call upon you to preserve the knowledge of God in the land and attend to the revelation written to us from heaven. If you neglect or renounce that religion taught and commanded in the holy scriptures, think no more of freedom, peace, and happiness; the judgments of heaven will pursue you. Religion is not a vain thing for you because it is your life: it has been the glory and defence of New-England from the infancy of the settlements; let it be also our glory and protection. I mean no other religion than what is divinely prescribed, which God himself has delivered to us with equal evidence of his authority, and even superior to that given to Israel, and which he has as strictly commanded us to receive and observe. The holy scriptures are given as the only rule of our faith, worship and obedience, and if we are guided by this perfect rule, we shall keep the way of truth and righteousness and obtain the heavenly glory. We are now no more at liberty to draw up schemes of religion for ourselves according to our own deceitful reasonings and vain imaginations, or to comply with the traditions and commands of men, or fall in with the refinements of human wisdom and the fashionable sentiments of the world, than Israel was to substitute modes of serving God different from what he had expressly required. We must believe what the Son of God, who made the worlds and was sent by the Father with a proclamation of mercy to mankind, has declared to us.

He died to redeem men from the servitude of sin and reconcile them to God that they may be raised to life eternal. And he is appointed to be like a second Moses, the captain of our salvation to conduct us to heaven. To him therefore we must hearken in all things. The principal doctrines of his gospel are quite simple, plain and important. He teaches us that the commands of God reach to the inward thoughts, principles, and affections of the heart, as well as the outward conduct, and are as pure and perfect as the divine nature; that according to the laws of his moral government all men are sinners and must repent in order to obtain mercy; that remission of sins is obtained only by believing on his name and through his blood shed for us on the cross; that his disciples must receive his word and obey whatsoever he hath commanded, endeavoring to be holy in all manner of conversation and avoid all the vices and corruptions of the world; that there will be a resurrection from the dead both of the just and unjust and a day of solemn judgment, when all mankind must give an account of their conduct in this world and receive their sentence from him whom the Father hath constituted to be the judge; and that in consequence of their sentence mankind will depart into very opposite states, the wicked into everlasting punishment and the righteous into life eternal, the present visible system of nature being then dissolved in flames. In the belief of these plain truths, and that worship and obedience connected with them, the religion of christians consists. As to worship, no multiplied forms and punctilious ceremonies are prescribed, which only serve to throw a veil over the mind; no certain modes are made necessary; but we must worship God, who is a spirit, in spirit and in truth, by prayer and praise, with love and fear, hope and joy. For such worship christians are united into societies called churches and are required to assemble every Lord's day, that they may glorify God with one heart and voice and be instructed and edified by his word and the two only ordinances of baptism and the Lord's supper, which are very simple but well adapted to the nature and design of our religion.

The christian religion, therefore, is confined to no particular nation, sect, or denomination but is designed to call all men to repentance and newness of life; to encourage their hope in the mercy of God, thro' the only mediator Jesus Christ; persuade them to the most cheerful, persevering obedience; and comfort them, under all the labours and sorrows of the world and the natural dread of death, with the assurance of a glorious immortality. This religion may be believed and practised, so as to answer the main purposes of it, under the various forms in which christian churches now appear: just as the principal ends of civil government may be obtained under the various constitutions which have taken place in different nations, however one may be much more eligible than another.

. . . .

My subject hath led me into this long and earnest address to the people. But it suggests some things which may properly be addressed to this honorable Court. Will you hear me patiently, while with the utmost respect I say a few words to excite the wise reflections of your own minds.

You will consider that you assemble from time to time as fathers of the large family, which depends on you to take care of its general welfare, and that no local views ought to govern you, nor partial instructions of your constituents bind you to act contrary to the clear conviction of your own minds. You will be cautious of forming parties for any selfish purposes, and of being too hasty in determining important matters, or too slow in your proceedings when business is urgent. In order to form a wise judgment of every thing that comes before you, you are sensible of the propriety of examining things to the bottom, attending patiently to every argument on both sides, and asking conscience, rather than any friend, what ought to be done. Like frugal householders you will save all unnecessary expences and take good care of the treasury, but not suffer the faithful servants of the State to be so stinted in their reward as to discourage them from their duty. Lay no grievous burdens on the people beyond their abilities, but take the earliest, easiest, and most righteous methods to reduce and pay off the public debt, unhappily involved in all the perplexities occasioned by boundless emissions of depreciating paper notes. Be liberal, yet frugal, in grants of money, according to the exigencies of the public. Let no laws be wanting which good order and the proper administration of government and justice require; but make no law which establisheth iniquity. And may I propose it, as worthy of your consideration, whether some reformation may not be necessary as to processes in our courts of justice: whether appeals from court to court are not allowed beyond reason and equity, in the plainest cases, and of too trivial value: by which some of our courts are made mere vehicles, justice is delayed, and the law made unnecessarily expensive, tedious and vexatious; and whether some method may not be thought of to determine the judgment of causes in lower or higher courts in proportion to their value and importance. I beg leave to say one word as to religion. With respect to articles of faith or modes of worship, civil authority have no right to establish religion. The people ought to choose their own ministers and their own denominations, as our laws now permit them; but as far as religion is connected with the morals of the people and their improvement in knowledge, it becomes of great importance to the state; and legislators may well consider it as part of their concern for the public welfare to make provision that all the towns may be furnished with good teachers, that they may be impowered to make valid contracts, and that the fulfilment of such contracts should be secured against the fickle humours of men who are always ready to shift from sect to sect or make divisions in parishes that they may get free from all legal obligations to their ministers. Perhaps a little addition to the law already in force in this state might sufficiently secure the continuance of religious instruction, enlarge rather than diminish liberty of conscience, and prevent envyings, contentions, and crumbling into parties. Will you permit me now to pray in behalf of the people, that all the departments of government may be constantly filled with the wisest and best men; that his excellency the President may have the assistance of an able and faithful Council; that the administration of justice may be in the hands of judges and justices well qualified for their offices, who will not take bribes or in any manner pervert judgment; in a word, that the constitution established may in every respect be well supported by your care, and that the people may know the blessings of good government by the union of your counsels and the wisdom of your proceedings. May the Almighty King of kings always be in the midst of you, direct and assist you, impress your hearts with his fear, and grant present and future blessings in reward of your fidelity.

And now if I have delivered words of truth, agreeably to my text, and pointed out the sure way to be a prosperous and happy people, may these things sink deep into your hearts and be accompanied with the divine blessing! May the general government of these United States, when established, appear to be the best which the nations have yet known and be exalted by uncorrupted religion and morals! And may the everlasting gospel diffuse its Heavenly light and spread Righteousness, Liberty, and Peace thro' the whole world.

THOMAS JEFFERSON

First Inaugural Address

March 4, 1801

Friends and Fellow-Citizens:

Called upon to undertake the duties of the first executive office of our country, I avail myself of the presence of that portion of my fellow-citizens which is here assembled to express my grateful thanks for the favor with which they have been pleased to look toward me, to declare a sincere consciousness that the task is above my talents, and that I approach it with those anxious and awful presentiments which the greatness of the charge and the weakness of my powers so justly inspire. A rising nation, spread over a wide and fruitful land, traversing all the seas with the rich productions of their industry, engaged in commerce with nations who feel power and forget right, advancing rapidly to destinies beyond the reach of the mortal eye—when I contemplate these transcendent objects, and see the honor, the happiness, and the hopes of this beloved country committed to the issue, and the auspices of this day, I shrink from the contemplation, and humble myself before the magnitude of the undertaking. Utterly, indeed, should I despair did not the presence of many whom I here see remind me that in the other high authorities provided by our Constitution I shall find resources of wisdom, of virtue, and of zeal on which to rely under all difficulties. To you, then, gentlemen, who are charged with the sovereign functions of legislation, and to those associated with you, I look with encouragement for that guidance and support which may enable us to steer with safety the vessel in which we are all embarked amidst the conflicting elements of a troubled world.

During the contest of opinion through which we have passed the animation of discussions and of exertions has sometimes worn an aspect which might impose on strangers unused to think freely and to speak and to write what they think; but this being now decided by the voice of the nation, announced according to the rules of the Constitution, all will, of course, arrange themselves under the will of the law, and unite in com-

From *Inaugural Addresses of the Presidents of the United States* (Washington, D.C.: Government Printing Office, 1965), pp. 13–16.

mon efforts for the common good. All, too, will bear in mind this sacred principle, that though the will of the majority is in all cases to prevail, that will to be rightful must be reasonable; that the minority possesses their equal rights, which equal law must protect, and to violate would be oppression. Let us, then, fellow-citizens, unite with one heart and one mind. Let us restore to social intercourse that harmony and affection without which liberty and even life itself are but dreary things. And let us reflect that, having banished from our land that religious intolerance under which mankind so long bled and suffered, we have yet gained little if we countenance a political intolerance as despotic, as wicked, and capable of as bitter and bloody persecutions. During the throes and convulsions of the ancient world, during the agonizing spasms of infuriated man, seeking through blood and slaughter his long-lost liberty, it was not wonderful that the agitation of the billows should reach even this distant and peaceful shore; that this should be more felt and feared by some and less by others, and should divide opinions as to measures of safety. But every difference of opinion is not a difference of principle. We have called by different names brethren of the same principle. We are all Republicans, we are all Federalists. If there be any among us who would wish to dissolve this Union or to change its republican form, let them stand undisturbed as monuments of the safety with which error of opinion may be tolerated where reason is left free to combat it. I know, indeed, that some honest men fear that a republican government can not be strong, that this Government is not strong enough; but would the honest patriot, in the full tide of successful experiment, abandon a government which has so far kept us free and firm on the theoretic and visionary fear that this Government, the world's best hope, may by possibility want energy to preserve itself? I trust not. I believe this, on the contrary, the strongest Government on earth. I believe it the only one where every man, at the call of the law, would fly to the standard of the law, and would meet invasions of the public order as his own personal concern. Sometimes it is said that man can not be trusted with the government of himself. Can he, then, be trusted with the government of others? Or have we found angels in the forms of kings to govern him? Let history answer this question.

Let us, then, with courage and confidence pursue our own Federal and Republican principles, our attachment to union and representative government. Kindly separated by nature and a wide ocean from the exterminating havoc of one quarter of the globe; too high-minded to endure the degradations of the others; possessing a chosen country, with room enough for our descendants to the thousandth and thousandth generation; entertaining a due sense of our equal right to the use of our own faculties, to the acquisitions of our own industry, to honor and confidence from our fellow-citizens, resulting not from birth, but from our actions and their sense of them; enlightened by a benign religion, professed, indeed, and practiced in various forms, yet all of them inculcating honesty, truth, temperance, gratitude, and the love of man; acknowledging and adoring an overruling Providence, which by all its dispensations proves that it delights in the happiness of man here and his greater happiness hereafter—with all these blessings, what more is necessary to make us a happy and a prosperous people? Still one thing more, fellow-citizens— a wise and frugal Government, which shall restrain men from injuring one another, shall leave them otherwise free to regulate their own pursuits of industry and improvement, and shall not take from the mouth of labor the bread it has earned. This is the sum of good government, and this is necessary to close the circle of our felicities.

About to enter, fellow-citizens, on the exercise of duties which comprehend everything dear and valuable to you, it is proper you should understand what I deem the essential principles of our Government, and consequently those which ought to shape its Administration. I will compress them within the narrowest compass they will bear, stating the general principle, but not all its limitations. Equal and exact justice to all men, of whatever state or persuasion, religious or political; peace, commerce, and honest friendship with all nations, entangling alliances with none; the support of the State Governments in all their rights, as the most competent administrations for our domestic concerns and the surest bulwarks against antirepublican tendencies; the preservation of the General Government in its whole constitutional vigor, as the sheet anchor of our peace at home and safety abroad; a jealous care of the right of election by the people—a mild and safe corrective of abuses which are lopped by the sword of revolution where peaceable remedies are unprovided; absolute acquiescence in the decisions of the majority, the vital principle of republics, from which is no appeal but to force, the vital principle and immediate parent of despotism; a well-disciplined militia, our best reliance in peace and for the first moments of war, till regulars may relieve them; the supremacy of the civil over the military authority; economy in the public expense, that labor may be lightly burthened; the honest payment of our debts and sacred preservation of the public faith; encouragement of agriculture, and of commerce as its handmaid; the diffusion of information and arraignment of all abuses at the bar of the public reason; freedom of religion; freedom of the press, and freedom of person under the protection of the habeas corpus, and trial by juries impartially selected. These principles form the bright constellation which has gone before us and guided our steps through an age of revolution and reformation. The wisdom of our sages and blood of our heroes have been devoted to their attainment. They should be the creed of our political faith, the text of civic instruction, the touchstone by which to try the services of those we trust; and should we wander from them in moments of error or of alarm, let us hasten to retrace our steps and to regain the road which alone leads to peace, liberty, and safety.

I repair, then, fellow-citizens, to the post you have assigned me. With experience enough in subordinate offices to have seen the difficulties of this the greatest of all, I have learnt to expect that it will rarely fall to the lot of imperfect man to retire from this station with the reputation and the favor which bring him into it. Without pretentions to that high confidence you reposed in our first and greatest revolutionary character, whose prominent services had entitled him to the first place of faithful history, I ask so much confidence only as may give firmness and effect to the legal administration of your affairs. I shall often go wrong through defect of judgment. When right, I shall often be thought wrong by those whose positions will not command a view of the whole ground. I ask your indulgence for my own errors, which will never be intentional, and your support against the errors of others, who may condemn what they would not if seen in all its parts. The approbation implied by your suffrage is a great consolation to me for the past, and my future solicitude will be to retain the good opinion of those who have bestowed it in advance, to conciliate that of others by doing them all the good in my power, and to be instrumental to the happiness and freedom of all.

Relying, then, on the patronage of your good will, I advance with obedience to the work, ready to retire from it whenever you become sensible how much better choice it is in your power to make. And may that Infinite Power which rules the destinies of the universe lead our councils to what is best, and give them a favorable issue for your peace and prosperity.

part three

WESTWARD THE COURSE OF DESTINY

In the nineteenth century the American understanding of destiny under God was decisively shaped by westward expansion. In the preceding century a number of spokesmen had claimed that the new nation was the rightful heir to North America and had rhapsodized the challenges of the continent's western reaches. Yet extension west did not begin in earnest until Jefferson's purchase of the Louisiana Territory from Napoleon in 1803. That acquisition doubled the territory of the nation, secured navigation of the Mississippi, and invited exploration of the Far West. Other large strides in expansion were taken during the administration of James K. Polk (1845–49). As the century progressed and the westward movement increased, American eyes would strain beyond the Pacific horizon toward distant lands that might also be embraced by an American destiny.

The magnitude and rich natural resources of the western American wilderness strengthened the conviction that Americans were the chosen people. Surely this was a land intended for the new children of Israel. As Americans mastered their territories with rifle, axe, plow, school, church, and railroad, they became doubly convinced of their divine election. Other peoples had let their resources go to waste; America's mastery of nature must surely bespeak her "special character." The shift involved in this interpretation of election has been pointedly summarized by H. Richard Niebuhr: "The old idea of American Christians as a chosen people who had been called to a special task was turned into the notion of a chosen nation especially favored. . . . As the nineteenth century went on, the note of divine favoritism was increasingly sounded."[1]

Despite this pride in the land, the West evoked widely differing—even contradictory—responses from the American people. On the one hand, guidebooks for settlers, Romantic poetry, and letters from pioneers commented on the fertility of the soil and the beauty of the landscapes; on the other, the atmosphere buzzed with reports of the manifold dangers and bitter trials of the pioneer. Many Americans saw westward expansion as an opportunity for extending democratic principles; at the same time serious doubts arose whether these principles could survive in such a vast area, doubts that turned into sheer skepticism as eastern Whigs feared political dominance by the West and as slaveholding and nonslaveholding interests competed for western territories. Nineteenth-century literature treated westward expansion both as the long-awaited "passage to India" (involving the concept of empire as maritime dominion) and as the very different cultivation of the "Garden of the World" (involving an empire of agriculture). The western wilderness was looked upon in its twofold religious sense: as a "howling wilderness"—a place of demons and death, a wasteland; and as a potential Garden of Eden—a place of retreat, renewal, and refuge. A tension also existed between the West viewed as a realm of unspoiled nature, devoid of the corruptions of man and the West seen as an area inviting the improvements of civilization.[2]

However much the conflict between Nature and Civilization may have continued as a characteristic of the American mind, in actual fact Americans consistently resolved the conflict in favor of Civilization. Nineteenth-century Americans actively set about to transform Nature in the name of progress: destiny under God came to mean in large part preparing the West to receive civilized customs. During this era, "civilized customs" included the religion of evangelical Protestant Christianity. The American Home Missionary Society was founded in the hope that Protestant revivalist preaching would save the West from barbarism and would turn the western wilderness into a Garden of the Lord. Most eastern Protestants believed, however, that preaching should be complemented by education. Firmly convinced that American destiny would be

---

[1] H. Richard Niebuhr, *The Kingdom of God in America* (New York: Harper & Row, Publishers, 1959), p. 179.

[2] For these different perspectives on the West see Henry Nash Smith, *Virgin Land* (New York: Random House, Inc., Vintage Books, 1950); George H. Williams, *Wilderness and Paradise in Christian Thought* (New York: Harper & Row, Publishers, 1962); Leo Marx, *The Machine in the Garden* (New York: Oxford University Press, Inc., 1967); Perry Miller, "The Romantic Dilemma in American Nationalism and the Concept of Nature," *Harvard Theological Review*, vol. 48 (1955), pp. 239–53.

decided west of the Alleghenies, Protestant Christians directed enormous educational energies toward the area, erecting there a host of seminaries, schools, and academies. These schools modeled themselves after eastern institutions by combining patriotic instruction with religious indoctrination.

A representative spokesman for Christian education in the West was Lyman Beecher, father of Henry Ward Beecher and Harriet Beecher Stowe and famed New England clergyman who in 1832 became the first president of Lane Theological Seminary in Cincinnati. In his speech *A Plea for the West*, which he delivered in several cities in the East during a fund drive for his seminary, Beecher declared that the United States was "destined to lead the way in the moral and political emancipation of the world" and that many of the resources for that destiny lay in the West. If the West were not given the benefits of Christian education, however, it would not adequately absorb the spirit of democracy, and America would fail to assume her redemptive role in history. The last portion of Beecher's speech, which dwelt *ad nauseam* on his (and many of his contemporaries') fears of the West being overrun by Catholic European immigrants who were unfamiliar with democratic responsibilities, is not included in the following selection. But Beecher's nativist fears are implicit in his references to "feudal institutions" in the early part of the address.

The term "Manifest Destiny," which became a popular slogan in the nineteenth century, provides a key to an important transformation of the belief in America's destiny. "Manifest Destiny," as Albert Weinberg has put it, "expressed a dogma of supreme self-assurance and ambition—that America's incorporation of all adjacent lands was the virtually inevitable fulfillment of a moral mission delegated to the nation by Providence itself." The principal justification for the dogma was a theory of "geographical predestination," or the claim that "nature or the natural order of things destined natural boundaries for nations in general and the United States, the nation of special destiny, in particular."[3] Manifest Destiny was abroad as a concept in America before it became a slogan, but its popularization as a watchword of expansionism occurred in the 1840s, greatly aided by the writings of the journalist John L. O'Sullivan. In the midst of negotiations between England and America over how the Oregon Territory was to be divided (a treaty finally granted American sovereignty up to the 49th parallel despite Polk's earlier assertion that the American title up to latitude 54°40′ N was "clear and unquestionable"), O'Sullivan brushed aside all legal questions with the claim that the whole territory belonged to the United States by virtue of her Manifest Destiny.

[3] Albert K. Weinberg, *Manifest Destiny* (Gloucester, Mass.: Peter Smith, 1958), pp. 1–2, 43.

One of O'Sullivan's editorials, "The True Title", contained an argument frequently resorted to by nineteenth-century expansionists: The United States is entitled to new territories because of her successful experiment in "liberty and federative self-government," because of her natural right to growth and expansion, because she will utilize her territories beneficently, and because the "God of nature and of nations has marked" adjacent areas "for our own."

The doctrine of Manifest Destiny did not in fact unify the nation or generate a common nationalistic sentiment; on the contrary, it signaled an emergence of sectionalism, a vigorous defense of states' rights, and a western regionalism.[4] Nevertheless, the rhetoric employed on behalf of the doctrine was nationalistic in cast, and the view of destiny under God expressed by that rhetoric transformed the nation's understanding of itself. American destiny became "manifest"; thereby it departed in a significant way from the biblical (and early American) portrayal of the destiny of a chosen people. The traditional doctrine of election held that the ultimate reason for God's choosing Israel was hidden in the mystery of the divine will. According to the exponents of Manifest Destiny, God's New Israel was elected for clear or *manifest* reasons—because of her superior form of government, her geographical location, her beneficence. The mystery of divine transcendence dissolved. As Albert Weinberg observes, in this "anthropocentric theology, in which God himself served chiefly as a Providence watchful for mankind and human values, the American approached perilously close to changing the traditional dogma, that man exists *ad majorem gloriam Dei*, into the heresy that God exists *ad majorem gloriam hominis*."[5]

A vision of American destiny in the West caught the imagination of the literati as well as the politicians, of poets as well as journalists. The writer who gave the vision its loftiest poetic expression was Walt Whitman. Although he resided on the Atlantic seaboard and had not even traveled west of the Mississippi when he wrote his principal poetry, Whitman celebrated the westward movement in a number of his poems. One of his best-known works, "Pioneers! O Pioneers," depicted the transfer of historical destiny from the Old World to the western pioneers who were the creators of a "newer, mightier world." But it was Whitman's poem of 1871, "Passage to India," that most fully revealed his impressions of the significance of westward expansion.

Whitman himself said that "Passage to India" conveyed "what, from the first . . . more or less lurks in my writings, underneath every page,

4 See Frederick Merk, *Manifest Destiny and Mission in American History* (New York: Alfred A. Knopf, Inc., 1963), pp. 57–60.
5 Weinberg, *Destiny*, p. 128.

every line, every where." The poem was inspired by three technological achievements: the completion of the Suez Canal, the spanning of the American continent by the Pacific Railroad, and the laying of the Atlantic submarine cable. Whitman felt that by virtue of these events the separate parts of the world had been linked, Columbus's voyage had been completed, and the once inscrutable purpose of human history had been made manifest:

> Lo, soul, seest thou not God's purpose from the first?
> The earth to be spann'd, connected by network . . .
> The lands to be welded together.

Addressing his passive companion, the soul, the poet represented "India" as the geographic East, the distant past, and the area of "primal thought" where man could recover his Edenic innocence and live in harmony with Nature. The discovery of America and the extension of the nation by the "mighty railroad" were, therefore, portions of a great destiny under God that were central to the entire human drama:

> thou born America
> For purpose vast, man's long probation fill'd,
> Thou rondure of the world at last accomplish'd.[6]

True, Whitman's "Passage to India" articulated a deep American hope that a link might be found with the exotic East and explicated a widely held belief that American history would fulfill human history as a whole. But nineteenth-century versions of American destiny were seldom as cosmopolitan or romantic as Whitman's. Especially during the closing years of the century, when the doctrine of Manifest Destiny was resurrected to justify American imperialism, jingoistic fever ran high and belief in American destiny under God became a muscular nationalism.

The ideology of American imperialism took root long before its clear surfacing during the Spanish-American War and the Philippine acquisition. The early prophets of empire seldom appealed to economic aggrandizement in urging American actions overseas. The appeal was more often to the missionary obligations accruing to a superior American Civilization. Josiah Strong, in his best seller of 1885, *Our Country*, elucidated these obligations. Strong insisted that the future of man devolved

---

6 My remarks on "Passage to India" rely chiefly on three sources: the critical notes of Gay Wilson Allen and Charles T. Davis, *Walt Whitman's Poems* (New York: New York University Press, 1955), pp. 242–48; Alan Trachtenberg, *Brooklyn Bridge*, pp. 16–17; and Smith, *Virgin Land*, pp. 47–51.

upon Anglo-Saxons, since they had developed the two related ideas of civil liberty and "a pure spiritual Christianity." And because the American branch of the Anglo-Saxon race had perfected these two ideas, on America especially did the destiny of man depend. "Thus," wrote Strong, "while on this continent God is training the Anglo-Saxon race for its mission, a complemental work has been in progress in the great world beyond. God has two hands. Not only is he preparing in our civilization the die with which to stamp the nations, but, by what Southey called the 'timing of Providence,' he is preparing mankind to receive our impress." Like most Americans of the period, Strong used the word "race" not in any strictly biological sense but as a loose reference to ethnic origins and cultural characteristics. And most could have added with Strong, "I do not imagine that the Anglo-Saxon is any dearer to God than a Mongolian or an African. My plea is not, Save America for America's sake, but, Save America for the world's sake." Nevertheless, this kind of nationalistic "racism" provided a rationalization for American overseas expansion; it also provided an impetus for Christian foreign missions.[7]

The cry for American destiny west of the Pacific shores grew shrill during the Philippine crisis. An eloquent spokesman for American imperialism during the crisis was the junior senator from Indiana, Albert J. Beveridge. Returning from a tour of the Philippines and the Far East, Beveridge delivered a senate speech in January, 1900, that described the wealth of the archipelago, the importance of the area for United States trade, the indolence of the natives and their current incapacity for self-government, and the way in which American opposition to the war in the Philippines was "the chief factor in prolonging it." Beveridge concluded with the assertion that God prepared the "English-speaking and Teutonic peoples" to be "the master organizers of the world to establish system where chaos reigns," that "God marked the American people as His chosen nation to finally lead in the regeneration of the world."[8]

Beveridge amplified his view of American destiny in his Republican campaign speech of 1900, "The Star of Empire." That speech took its title and its point of departure from a stanza in Bishop George Berkeley's eighteenth-century "Verses on the Prospect of Planting Arts and Learning in America":

---

[7] On Strong see Ernest Lee Tuveson, *Redeemer Nation: The Idea of America's Millennial Role* (Chicago: University of Chicago Press, 1968), pp. 165–68. On Christian missionary expansion see Kenneth M. MacKenzie, *The Robe and the Sword* (Washington, D.C.: Public Affairs Press, 1961). Cf. John Edwin Smylie, "Protestant Clergymen and America's World Role, 1865–1900" (Th.D. dissertation, Princeton Theological Seminary, 1959).
[8] *Congressional Record*, XXXIII (Washington, D.C.: Government Printing Office, 1900), 711.

Westward the Course of Empire takes its Way;
The four first Acts already past,
A fifth shall close the Drama with the Day;
Times noblest Offspring is the last.

Neither Beveridge nor many other nineteenth-century Americans whose fancies were captured by this stanza bothered to notice that Berkeley, out of disgust for England and Europe, was suggesting America as a refuge for the arts and that he did not really expect the Golden Age in the New World to radiate to other parts of the globe. The stanza was simply utilized, out of context, as a poetic endorsement of America's mission to spread her civilization westward. Beveridge's "Star of Empire" speech portrayed America's insular acquisitions as the fulfillment of the mission of a divinely anointed nation to civilize savage, degenerate peoples. And Beveridge felt no compunction at mixing a defense of national interests with the call of a "high and holy destiny" to "civilize the world."

The spirit of Beveridge's imperialism certainly did not grip all the American people. The Treaty of Paris which ended the war with Spain and acquired the Philippine Islands for America passed the Senate only after a long and bitter debate and with one vote above the necessary two-thirds majority. Anti-imperialist sentiment was shared by such respected Americans as Senator George F. Hoar of Massachusetts, presidential aspirant William Jennings Bryan, academicians William James and William Graham Sumner, clergyman Henry Van Dyke, steelmaster Andrew Carnegie, and many others.[9] Furthermore, as Nevins and Commager have said, "Time was to prove that the overseas responsibilities which the United States assumed were in part merely temporary and that at heart the nation remained nonimperialistic. As the years passed, it chose to reduce its overseas holdings, not to enlarge them."[10] Nevertheless America had begun by the turn of the century to recognize herself as a great world power, and if she was prepared to reduce her holdings abroad, she was by no means ready to relinquish her influence or to check serious efforts to sow the seeds of her "civilization." The twentieth century would furnish many opportunities for the American Israel to construe her destiny as a mission to promote and preserve American ideas and institutions abroad. And she would not always, with Beveridge's candor, acknowledge her own self-interests in the mission.

[9] See Robert L. Beisner, *Twelve Against Empire: The Anti-Imperialists, 1898–1900* (New York: McGraw-Hill Book Company, 1968).
[10] Allan Nevins and Henry Steele Commager, *A Pocket History of the United States* (New York: Washington Square Press, 1967), p. 366.

SUGGESTED READING

Bodo, John R. *The Protestant Clergy and Public Issues, 1812–1848.* Princeton, N.J.: Princeton University Press, 1954.

Burns, Edward M. *The American Idea of Mission.* New Brunswick, N.J.: Rutgers University Press, 1957.

Ekirch, Arthur A. *The Idea of Progress in America, 1815–1860.* New York: Columbia University Press, 1944.

Hofstadter, Richard. "Manifest Destiny and the Philippines," in *America in Crisis,* edited by Daniel Aaron. New York: Alfred A. Knopf, 1952.

Merk, Frederick. *Manifest Destiny and Mission in American History.* New York: Alfred A. Knopf, Inc., 1963.

Smith, Henry Nash. *Virgin Land: The American West as Symbol and Myth.* New York: Random House, Inc., Vintage Books, 1950.

Ward, John William. *Andrew Jackson: Symbol for an Age.* New York: Oxford University Press, Inc.,1962.

Weinberg, Albert K. *Manifest Destiny, A Study of Nationalist Expansionism in American History.* Gloucester, Mass.: Peter Smith, 1958.

LYMAN BEECHER

A Plea For The West

Isaiah lxvi, 8   *Who hath heard such a thing?*
who hath seen such things?
Shall the earth be made to bring
forth in one day?
or shall a nation be born at once?
for as soon as Zion travailed,
she brought forth her children.

Ever since the era of modern missions, sceptical men have ridiculed the efforts of the church to evangelize the world, and predicted their failure. "What," say they, "do these Jews build,—if a fox do but go up upon the wall, it will fall. The world can never be converted to Christianity by the power of man." And full well do we know it, and most deeply do we feel it, and in all our supplications for aid, most emphatically do we confess our utter impotency; and could no power but the power of man be enlisted, it would be indeed of all experiments the most ridiculous and hopeless. But because man cannot convert the world to Christianity, cannot God do it? Has he not promised to do it, and selected his instruments, and commanded his people to be fellow workers with him? And hath he said, and shall he not do it?

Instead of its being a work of difficulty and dilatory movement, when the time to favor Zion comes, it shall outrun all past analogies of moral causes, as if seed-time and harvest should meet on the same field, or a nation should instantly rush up from barbarism to civilization.

But as all great eras of prosperity to the church have been aided by the civil condition of the world, and accomplished by the regular operation of moral causes, I consider the text as a prediction of the rapid and universal extension of civil and religious liberty, introductory to the triumphs of universal Christianity. It is certain that the glorious things spoken of the church and of the world, as affected by her prosperity, cannot come to pass under the existing civil organization of the nations. Such a state of society as is predicted to pervade the earth, cannot exist under

From Lyman Beecher, *A Plea for the West,* Second edition (Cincinnati: Truman and Smith, 1835), pp. 7–40.

an arbitrary despotism, and the predominance of feudal institutions and usages. Of course, it is predicted that revolutions and distress of nations will precede the introduction of the peaceful reign of Jesus Christ on the earth. The mountains shall be exalted—and he shall "overturn, and overturn, and overturn, till he whose right it is, shall reign King of nations—King of saints."

It was the opinion of Edwards, that the millennium would commence in America. When I first encountered this opinion, I thought it chimerical; but all providential developments since, and all the existing signs of the times, lend corroboration to it. But if it is by the march of revolution and civil liberty, that the way of the Lord is to be prepared, where shall the central energy be found, and from what nation shall the renovating power go forth? What nation is blessed with such experimental knowledge of free institutions, with such facilities and resources of communication, obstructed by so few obstacles, as our own? There is not a nation upon earth which, in fifty years, can by all possible reformation place itself in circumstances so favorable as our own for the free, unembarrassed applications of physical effort and pecuniary and moral power to evangelize the world.

But if this nation is, in the providence of God, destined to lead the way in the moral and political emancipation of the world, it is time she understood her high calling, and were harnessed for the work. For mighty causes, like floods from distant mountains, are rushing with accumulating power, to their consummation of good or evil, and soon our character and destiny will be stereotyped forever.

It is equally plain that the religious and political destiny of our nation is to be decided in the West. There is the territory, and there soon will be the population, the wealth, and the political power. The Atlantic commerce and manufactures may confer always some peculiar advantages on the East. But the West is destined to be the great central power of the nation, and under heaven, must affect powerfully the cause of free institutions and the liberty of the world.

The West is a young empire of mind, and power, and wealth, and free institutions, rushing up to a giant manhood, with a rapidity and a power never before witnessed below the sun. And if she carries with her the elements of her preservation, the experiment will be glorious—the joy of the nation—the joy of the whole earth, as she rises in the majesty of her intelligence and benevolence, and enterprise, for the emancipation of the world.

It is equally clear, that the conflict which is to decide the destiny of the West, will be a conflict of institutions for the education of her sons, for purposes of superstition, or evangelical light; of despotism, or liberty.

· ·

The thing required for the civil and religious prosperity of the

West, is universal education, and moral culture, by institutions commensurate to that result—the all-pervading influence of schools, and colleges, and seminaries, and pastors, and churches. When the West is well supplied in this respect, though there may be great relative defects, there will be, as we believe, the stamina and the vitality of a perpetual civil and religious prosperity.

By whom shall the work of rearing the literary and religious institutions of the West be done?

Not by the West alone.

The West is able to do this great work for herself,—and would do it, provided the exigencies of her condition allowed to her the requisite time. The subject of education is no where more appreciated; and no people in the same time ever performed so great a work as has already been performed in the West. Such an extent of forest never fell before the arm of man in forty years, and gave place, as by enchantment, to such an empire of cities, and towns, and villages, and agriculture, and merchandise, and manufactures, and roads and rapid navigation, and schools, and colleges, and libraries, and literary enterprise, with such a number of pastors and churches, and such a relative amount of religious influence, as has been produced by the spontaneous effort of the religious denominations of the West. The later peopled states of New-England did by no means come as rapidly to the same state of relative, intellectual and moral culture as many portions of the West have already arrived at, in the short period of forty, thirty, and even twenty years.

But this work of self-supply is not complete, and by no human possibility could have been completed by the West, in her past condition.

No people ever did, in the first generation, fell the forest, and construct the roads, and rear the dwellings and public edifices, and provide the competent supply of schools and literary institutions. New-England did not. Her colleges were endowed extensively by foreign munificence, and her churches of the first generation were supplied chiefly from the mother country;—and yet the colonists of New-England were few in number, compact in territory, homogeneous in origin, language, manners, and doctrines; and were coerced to unity by common perils and necessities; and could be acted upon by immediate legislation; and could wait also for their institutions to grow with their growth and strengthen with their strength. But the population of the great West is not so, but is assembled from all the states of the Union, and from all the nations of Europe, and is rushing in like the waters of the flood, demanding for its moral preservation the immediate and universal action of those institutions which discipline the mind, and arm the conscience and the heart. And so various are the opinions and habits, and so recent and imperfect is the acquaintance, and so sparse are the settlements of the West, that no homogeneous public sentiment can be formed to legislate immediately into being the requisite institutions. And yet they are all needed immediately, in their utmost perfection and power. A nation is being "born in a day," and all the nurture of schools and literary institutions is needed, constantly and universally, to rear it up to a glorious and unperverted manhood.

It is no implication of the West, that in a single generation, she has not completed this work. In the circumstances of her condition she could not do it; and had it been done, we should believe that a miraculous, and not a human power had done it.

Who then, shall co-operate with our brethren of the West, for the consummation of this work so auspiciously begun? Shall the South be invoked? The South have difficulties of their own to encounter, and cannot do it; and the middle states have too much of the same work yet to do, to volunteer their aid abroad.

Whence, then, shall the aid come, but from those portions of the Union where the work of rearing these institutions has been most nearly accomplished, and their blessings most eminently enjoyed? And by whom, but by those who in their infancy were aided; and who, having freely received, are now called upon freely to give, and who, by a hard soil and habits of industry and economy, and by experience are qualified to endure hardness as good soldiers and pioneers in this great work? And be assured that those who go to the West with unostentatious benevolence, to identify themselves with the people and interests of that vast community, will be adopted with a warm heart and an unwavering right hand of fellowship.

But how shall this aid be extended to our brethren of the West in the manner most acceptable and efficacious?

Not by prayers and supplications only, nor by charities alone, nor by colonial emigrations; for these, though they might cultivate their own garden, would for obvious reasons be fenced in, and exert but a feeble general influence beyond their own inclosures. Those who go out to do good at the West should go out to mingle with the people of the West, and be absorbed in their multitude, as rain drops fall on the bosom of the ocean and mingle with that world of waters.

Nor is it by tracts, or Bibles, or itinerating missions, that the requisite intellectual and moral power can be applied. There must be permanent, powerful, literary and moral institutions, which, like the great orbs of attraction and light, shall send forth at once their power and their illumination, and without them all else will be inconstant and ephemeral. Let it not, however, for a moment be supposed, that the schools of the West are to be sustained by the emigration of an army of instructors from the East. For though for the present *necessity*, the aid of qualified instructors is not to be repelled, but invited; yet for any permanent reliance, it is but a drop of the bucket to the ocean.

Nothing is more certain, than that the great body of the teachers of the West must be educated at the West. It is by her own sons chiefly, that the great work is to be consummated which her civil, and literary, and religious prosperity demands.

But how shall the requisite supply of teachers for the sons and daughters of the West be raised up? It can be accomplished by the instrumentality of a learned and pious ministry, educated at the West.

Experience has evinced, that schools and popular education, in their best estate, go not far beyond the suburbs of the city of God. All attempts to legislate prosperous colleges and schools into being without the intervening influence of religious education and moral principle, and habits of intellectual culture which spring up in alliance with evangelical institutions, have failed. Schools wane, invariably, in those towns where the evangelical ministry is neglected, and the Sabbath is profaned, and the tavern supplants the worship of God. Thrift and knowledge in such places go out, while vice and irreligion come in.

But the ministry is a central luminary in each sphere, and soon sends out schools and seminaries as its satellites by the hands of sons and daughters of its own training. A land supplied with able and faithful ministers, will of course be filled with schools, academies, libraries, colleges, and all the apparatus for the perpetuity of republican institutions. It always has been so—it always will be.

But the ministry for the West must be educated at the West. The demands on the East, for herself and for pagan lands, forbid the East ever to supply our wants. Nor is it necessary. For the Spirit of God is with the churches of the West, and pious and talented young men are there in great numbers, willing, desiring, impatient to consecrate themselves to the glorious work. If we possessed the accommodations and the funds, we might easily send out a hundred ministers a year—a thousand ministers in ten years—around each of whom schools would arise, and instructors multiply, and churches spring up, and revivals extend, and all the elements of civil and religious prosperity abound.

But we have said that the ministry for the West must be a learned and talented ministry.

No opinion is more false and fatal than that mediocrity of talent and learning will suffice for the West. That if a minister is a good sort of a man, but somehow does not seem to be popular, and find employment, he had better go to the West. No; let him stay at home; and if among the urgent demands for ministerial labor here, he cannot find employment, let him conclude that he has mistaken his profession.

But let him not go to the West. The men who, *somehow*, do not succeed at the East, are the very men who will succeed still less at the West. If there be in the new settlements at the West a lack of schools and educated mind, there is no lack of shrewd and vigorous mind; and if they are not deep read in Latin and Greek, they are well read in men and things.

On their vast rivers, they go every where, and see every body, and know every thing, and judge with the tact of perspicacious common sense. They are disciplined to resolution and mental vigor by toils and perils, and enterprises; and often they are called to attend as umpires to the earnest discussions of their most able and eloquent men, which cannot fail to throw prosing dullness in the ministry to a hopeless distance. No where, if a minister is deficient, will he be more sure to be "weighed in the balance and found wanting." On the contrary, there is not a place on earth where piety, and talent, and learning, and argument, and popular eloquence are more highly appreciated, or rewarded with a more frank and enthusiastic admiration. There are chords in the heart of the West which vibrate to the touch of genius, and to the power of argumentative eloquence, with a sensibility and enthusiasm no where surpassed. A hundred ministers of cultivated mind and popular eloquence might find settlement in an hundred places, and without the aid of missions, and only to increase the demand for an hundred more.

Most unquestionably the West demands the instrumentality of the first order of minds in the ministry, and thoroughly furnished minds, to command attention, enlighten the understanding, form the conscience, and gain the heart, and bring into religious organization and order the uncommitted mind and families of the great world; and many a man who might guide respectfully a well-organized congregation here of homogeneous character, and moving onward under the impetus of long continued habits, might fail utterly to call around him the population of a new country.

Of course, the institutions which are to lead in this great work of rearing the future ministry of the West should be second to none in their endowments and adaptation to this end. For it is such a work in magnitude as human instrumentality was never before concentrated upon. All other nations have gone up slowly from semi-barbarism to a civilized manhood, while our nation was commenced with the best materials of a nation at that time the most favored nation in the world, and yet was delayed in its growth, through two centuries, by policy, and power, and war, and taxation, and want of capital. It is less than fifty years since our resources have begun to be developed in great power, and we have entered upon the career of internal improvement and national greatness; and at the East, until recently, these movements were slow, as capital gradually increased, and agriculture, and commerce, and art led the way. But the West is filling up as by ocean waves; and such is her prospective greatness, that the capital of the East and of Europe hold competition for her acceptance and use, so that in a day, she is rising up to the high eminence that all other nations have approached progressively through the revolution of centuries.

But what will become of the West, if her prosperity rushes up to such a majesty of power, while those great institutions linger which are necessary to form the mind, and the conscience, and the heart of that vast world. It must not be permitted. And yet what is done must be done quickly; for population will not wait, and commerce will not cast anchor, and manufactures will not shut off the steam nor shut down the gate, and agriculture, pushed by millions of freemen on their fertile soil, will not withhold her corrupting abundance.

We must educate! We must educate! or we must perish by our own prosperity. If we do not, short from the cradle to the grave will be our race. If in our haste to be rich and mighty, we outrun our literary and religious institutions, they will never overtake us; or only come up after the battle of liberty is fought and lost, as spoils to grace the victory, and as resources of inexorable despotism for the perpetuity of our bondage. And let no man at the East quiet himself, and dream of liberty, whatever may become of the West. Our alliance of blood, and political institutions, and common interests, is such, that we cannot stand aloof in the hour of her calamity, should it ever come. Her destiny is our destiny; and the day that her gallant ship goes down, our little boat sinks in the vortex!

It was to meet these exigences of our common country in the West, that the Lane Seminary was called into being by the munificence of the sons of the West; first by a donation from the two gentlemen whose name it bears, followed by the gift of sixty acres of land, on which the institution is located, by Mr. Elnathan Kemper, and the sale of fifty more at a reduced price and long credit by the same benefactor; to which have been added fifteen thousand dollars by the citizens of Cincinnati and the West, for the construction of two college buildings and two professors' houses. To this has been added by our friends on this side of the mountains, twenty thousand dollars from one individual, for the endowment of the professorship of Theology; and by others, thirty thousand, for the endowment of the two professorships of Biblical Literature and Ecclesiastical History.

What we now need is a chapel for the accommodation of students and a fast increasing community with a place of worship; the endowment of a professorship of Sacred Rhetoric, and a library. For the first, we have dared to rely on our friends in Boston and its vicinity. The library we hope to receive from our friends in New-York; and for the Professorship of Sacred Rhetoric we look up, hoping and believing that God will put into the heart of one or more individuals to endow it.

The motives which call on us to co-operate immediately in this glorious work of consummating the institutions of the West, essential to the perpetuity of her greatness and glory, are neither few, nor feeble, nor obscure.

The territory is eight thousand miles in circumference, extending from the Alleghany to the Rocky mountains, and from the Gulf of

Mexico to the Lakes of the North; and it is the largest territory, and most beneficent in climate, and soil, and mineral wealth, and commercial facilities, ever prepared for the habitation of man, and qualified to sustain in prosperity and happiness the densest population on the globe. By twenty-four thousand miles of steam navigation, and canals and rail roads, a market is brought near to every man, and the whole is brought into near neighborhood.

When I first entered the West, its vastness overpowered me with the impression of its uncontrollable greatness, in which all human effort must be lost. But when I perceived the active intercourse between the great cities, like the rapid circulation of a giant's blood; and heard merchants speak of just stepping up to Pittsburgh—only six hundred miles—and back in a few days; and others just from New-Orleans, or St. Louis, or the Far West; and others going thither; and when I heard my ministerial brethren negotiating exchanges in the near neighborhood—only one hundred miles up or down the river—and going and returning on Saturday and Monday, and without trespassing on the Sabbath;—then did I perceive how God, who seeth the end from the beginning, had prepared the West to be mighty, and still wieldable, that the moral energy of his word and spirit might take it up as a very little thing.

This vast territory is occupied now by ten states and will soon be by twelve. Forty years since it contained only about one hundred and fifty thousand souls; while it now contains little short of five millions. At the close of this century, if no calamity intervenes, it will contain, probably, one hundred millions—a day which some of our children may live to see; and when fully peopled, may accommodate three hundred millions. It is half as large as all Europe, four times as large as the Atlantic states, and twenty times as large as New-England. Was there ever such a spectacle—such a field in which to plant the seeds of an immortal harvest!—so vast a ship, so richly laden with the world's treasures and riches, whose helm is offered to the guiding influence of early forming institutions!

The certainty of success calls us to immediate effort. If we knew not what to do, if all was effort and expense in untried experiments, there might be some pretext for the paralysis of amazement and inaction. But we know what to do: the means are obvious, and well tried, and certain. The sun and the rain of heaven are not more sure to call forth a bounteous vegetation, than Bibles, and Sabbaths, and schools, and seminaries, are to diffuse intellectual light and warmth for the bounteous fruits of righteousness and peace. The corn and the acorn of the East are not more sure to vegetate at the West than the institutions which have blessed the East are to bless the West.

But these all-pervading orbs of illumination and centres of attraction must be established. Such is the gravitating tendency of society, that no spontaneous effort at arms-length will hold it up. It is by the constant energy and strong attraction of powerful institutions only that the needed intellectual and moral power can be applied: and the present is the age of founding them. If this work be done, and well done, our country is safe, and the world's hope is secure. The government of force will cease, and that of intelligence and virtue will take its place; and nation after nation cheered by our example, will follow in our footsteps, till the whole earth is free. There is no danger that our agriculture and arts will not prosper: the danger is, that our intelligence and virtue will falter and fall back into a dark minded, vicious populace—a poor, uneducated reckless mass of infuriated animalism, to rush on resistless as the tornado, or to burn as if set on fire of hell.

Until Europe, by universal education, is delivered from such masses of feudal ignorance and servitude, she sits upon a volcano, and despotism and revolution will arbitrate her destiny.

Consider, too, how quickly and how cheaply the guarantee of a perpetual and boundless prosperity can be secured. The West needs but a momentary aid, when almost as soon as received, should it be needed, she will repay and quadruple both principle and interest. Lend a hand to get up her institutions, to give ubiquity to her schools and Sabbaths and sanctuaries, while her forests are falling and her ocean floods of population rolling in, and afterwards we will not come here to ask for aid; for there is a wealth and chivalrous munificence there, which, when it has first performed the necessary work of self-preservation, will pour with you a noble tide of rival benevolence into that river which is "to make glad the city of our God."

. . . .

JOHN L. O'SULLIVAN

The True Title

Our legal title to Oregon, so far as law exists for such rights, is perfect. There is no doubt of this. Mr. Calhoun and Mr. Buchanan have settled that question, once for all. Flaw or break in the triple chain of that title, there is none. Not a foot of ground is left for England to stand upon, in any fair argument to maintain her pretensions. Poor Mr. Pakenham[1]—between the two Secretaries of State it has been his hard fate to have to deal with, he has been ground as between the upper and the nether millstones. He has been in the predicament of the third frog whom two others have got between them on a log, in a process we have sometimes witnessed on a warm summer morning by the side of a pond, when the unhappy victim in the *juste milieu* has been squeezed till fairly flattened out—Whether this is a sort of capital punishment among the frogs, or a mode of thinning off a superabundant population, we know not. Certain it is that it is often done, and equally certain that it has been most effectually done in the present case. Between Calhoun and Buchanan, poor Pakenham has certainly been made to look superlatively that. It is indeed a name of rather evil omen for England in America. Whether in arts or arms, in cabinet or camp, with sword or pen, it seems destined to achieve nothing but defeat and disgrace for the cause it represents. Alike in the annals of England's war and diplomacy, "Pakenham" will henceforth stand recorded forever as a *nomen infaustum*—the unluckiest of names.

And yet after all, unanswerable as is the demonstration of our legal title to Oregon—and the whole of Oregon, if a rood!—we have a still better title than any that can ever be constructed out of all these antiquated materials of old black-letter international law. Away, away with all these cobweb tissues of rights of discovery, exploration, settlement, continuity, &c. To state the truth at once in its naked simplicity, we are free to say that were the respective cases and arguments of the two parties, as to all

From *The New York Morning News,* December 27, 1845.
[1] [Sir Richard Pakenham (1797–1868), envoy extraordinary and minister plenipotentiary to the United States who represented the British interests on the Oregon question.—EDITOR]

128

these points of history and law, reversed—had England all ours, and we nothing but hers—our claim to Oregon would still be best and strongest. And that claim is by the right of our manifest destiny to overspread and to possess the whole of the continent which Providence has given for the development of the great experiment of liberty and federative self-government entrusted to us. It is a right such as that of the tree in the space of air and earth suitable for the full expansion of its principle and destiny of growth—such as that of the stream to the channel required for the still accumulating volume of its flow. It is in our future far more than in our past, or in the past history of Spanish exploration or French colonial rights, that our True Title is to be found. Consider only the wonderful law of growth which has been thus far exhibited in the increase of our population from the commencement of our present system of government —namely, that of *doubling every quarter of a century*. Carry this forward for only a hundred years from the present day—to a period which thousands of children already born among us will live to witness. Our present population being 20,000,000 will become under the continued operation of this law—and what should arrest its continued operation?—

In the first quarter of century . . . . 40 millions
  ,,   second   ,,   ,, ... 80   ,,
  ,,   third   ,,   ,, ... 160   ,,
  ,,   fourth   ,,   ,, ... 320   ,,

Three hundred millions, within little more than the ordinary term of hale and healthy old age! The duty and the right of providing the necessary accommodation for all this stupendous future of the American destiny—one existing position on this continent, led and established here as we have been by the finger of God himself—that pervading tendency westward, westward, which marks the slope of our national movement, and bears us ever on towards the Pacific, like the attraction felt by the head waters of its own rivers that hear and in their flow obey the call of the great ocean of their destiny—in these views of this high national question, we repeat, resides the title we prefer to dwell upon; the title constituting the true foundation of that deep and instinctive national sentiment which has been awakened throughout the length and breadth of the Union by the recent agitation of this subject; and which will never be satisfied with any settlement of it that will not sooner or later secure to us and our institutions and laws the peaceful possession of Oregon and the whole of Oregon.

Were England in ours or a similar position in regard to that portion of the North American continent, she would have, in her degree, rights of a similar nature. But such is not and can never become, her position. Oregon can never be to her or for her any thing but a mere hunting ground for furs and peltries. There is no population there to be worked and ground and sweated and drained of tribute to pay for their own subjugation, and to minister to the aggrandizement of their conquerors. Nor can she ever colonize it with any sort of transplanted population of her own. It is far too remote and too ungenial for any such purpose. In her hands it is and must always remain wholly useless and worthless for any purpose of human civilization or society. In our hands on the contrary, it must fast fill in with a population destined to establish, within the life of the existing generation, a noble young empire of the Pacific, vying in all the elements of greatness with that already overspreading the Atlantic and the great Mississippi valley. The God of nature and of nations has marked it for our own; and with His blessing we will firmly maintain the incontestable rights He has given, and fearlessly perform the high duties He has imposed.

WALT WHITMAN

Passage To India

1

Singing my days,
Singing the great achievements of the present,
Singing the strong light works of engineers,
Our modern wonders, (the antique ponderous Seven outvied,)
In the Old World the east the Suez canal,   5
The New by its mighty railroad spann'd,
The seas inlaid with eloquent gentle wires;
Yet first to sound, and ever sound, the cry with thee O soul,
The Past! the Past! the Past!

The Past—the dark unfathom'd retrospect!   10
The teeming gulf—the sleepers and the shadows!
The past—the infinite greatness of the past!
For what is the present after all but a growth out of the past?
(As a projectile form'd, impell'd, passing a certain line, still keeps
    on,
So the present, utterly form'd, impell'd by the past.)   15

2

Passage O soul to India!
Eclaircise the myths Asiatic, the primitive fables.

Not you alone proud truths of the world,
Nor you alone ye facts of modern science,
But myths and fables of eld, Asia's, Africa's fables,   20
The far-darting beams of the spirit, the unloos'd dreams,
The deep diving bibles and legends,

From *The Complete Writings of Walt Whitman,* IX (New York: G. P.
Putnam's Sons, 1902), 186–197.

The daring plots of the poets, the elder religions;
O you temples fairer than lilies pour'd over by the rising sun!
O you fables spurning the known, eluding the hold of the known,
   mounting to heaven!   25
You lofty and dazzling towers, pinnacled, red as roses, burnish'd
   with gold!
Towers of fables immortal fashion'd from mortal dreams!
You too I welcome and fully the same as the rest!
You too with joy I sing.

Passage to India!   30
Lo, soul, seest thou not God's purpose from the first?
The earth to be spann'd, connected by network,
The races, neighbors, to marry and be given in marriage,
The oceans to be cross'd, the distant brought near,
The lands to be welded together.   35

A worship new I sing,
You captains, voyagers, explorers, yours,
You engineers, you architects, machinists, yours,
You, not for trade or transportation only,
But in God's name, and for thy sake O soul.   40

3

Passage to India!
Lo soul for thee of tableaus twain,
I see in one the Suez canal initiated, open'd,
I see the procession of steamships, the Empress Eugenie's leading
   the van,
I mark from on deck the strange landscape, the pure sky, the level
   sand in the distance,   45
I pass swiftly the picturesque groups, the workmen gather'd,
The gigantic dredging machines.

In one again, different, (yea thine, all thine, O soul, the same,)
I see over my own continent the Pacific railroad surmounting every
   barrier,
I see continual trains of cars winding along the Platte carrying
   freight and passengers,   50
I hear the locomotives rushing and roaring, and the shrill steam-
   whistle,

I hear the echoes reverberate through the grandest scenery in the
    world,
I cross the Laramie plains, I note the rocks in grotesque shapes,
    the buttes,
I see the plentiful larkspur and wild onions, the barren, colorless
    sage-deserts,
I see in glimpses afar or towering immediately above me the great
    mountains, I see the Wind river and the Wahsatch mountains,   55
I see the Monument mountain and the Eagle's Nest, I pass the
    Promontory, I ascend the Nevadas,
I scan the noble Elk mountain and wind around its base,
I see the Humboldt range, I thread the valley and cross the river,
I see the clear waters of lake Tahoe, I see forests of majestic pines,
Or crossing the great desert, the alkaline plains, I behold enchanting
    mirages of waters and meadows,   60
Marking through these and after all, in duplicate slender lines,
Bridging the three or four thousand miles of land travel,
Tying the Eastern to the Western sea,
The road between Europe and Asia.

(Ah Genoese thy dream! thy dream!   65
Centuries after thou art laid in thy grave,
The shore thou foundest verifies thy dream.)

4

Passage to India!
Struggles of many a captain, tales of many a sailor dead,
Over my mood stealing and spreading they come,   70
Like clouds and cloudlets in the unreach'd sky.

Along all history, down the slopes,
As a rivulet running, sinking now, and now again to the surface
    rising,
A ceaseless thought, a varied train—lo, soul, to thee, thy sight they
    rise,
The plans, the voyages again, the expeditions,   75
Again Vasco de Gama sails forth,
Again the knowledge gain'd, the mariner's compass,
Lands found and nations born, thou born America,
For purpose vast, man's long probation fill'd,
Thou rondure of the world at last accomplish'd.   80

5

O vast Rondure, swimming in space,
Cover'd all over with visible power and beauty,
Alternate light and day and the teeming spiritual darkness,
Unspeakable high processions of sun and moon and countless stars
    above,
Below, the manifold grass and waters, animals, mountains, trees,   85
With inscrutable purpose, some hidden prophetic intention,
Now first it seems my thought begins to span thee.

Down from the gardens of Asia descending radiating,
Adam and Eve appear, then their myriad progeny after them,
Wandering, yearning, curious, with restless explorations,   90
With questionings, baffled, formless, feverish, with never-happy
    hearts,
With that sad incessant refrain, *Wherefore unsatisfied soul?* and
    Whither O mocking life?

Ah who shall soothe these feverish children?
Who justify these restless explorations?
Who speak the secret of impassive earth?   95
Who bind it to us? what is this separate Nature so unnatural?
What is this earth to our affections? (unloving earth, without a
    throb to answer ours,
Cold earth, the place of graves.)

Yet soul be sure the first intent remains, and shall be carried out,
Perhaps even now the time has arrived.   100

After the seas are all cross'd, (as they seem already cross'd,)
After the great captains and engineers have accomplish'd their
    work,
After the noble inventors, after the scientists, the chemist, the
    geologist, ethnologist,
Finally shall come the poet worthy that name,
The true son of God shall come singing his songs.   105

Then not your deeds only O voyagers, O scientists and inventors,
    shall be justified,
All these hearts as of fretted children shall be sooth'd,
All affection shall be fully responded to, the secret shall be told,
All these separations and gaps shall be taken up and hook'd and
    link'd together,
The whole earth, this cold, impassive, voiceless earth, shall be
    completely justified,   110

Trinitas divine shall be gloriously accomplish'd and compacted
    by the true son of God, the poet,
(He shall indeed pass the straits and conquer the mountains,
He shall double the cape of Good Hope to some purpose,)
Nature and Man shall be disjoin'd and diffused no more,
The true son of God shall absolutely fuse them.   115

6

Year at whose wide-flung door I sing!
Year of the purpose accomplish'd!
Year of the marriage of continents, climates and oceans!
(No mere doge of Venice now wedding the Adriatic,)
I see O year in you the vast terraqueous globe given and giving
    all,   120
Europe to Asia, Africa join'd, and they to the New World,
The lands, geographies, dancing before you, holding a festival
    garland,
As brides and bridegrooms hand in hand.

Passage to India!
Cooling airs from Caucasus far, soothing cradle of man,   125
The river Euphrates flowing, the past lit up again,

Lo soul, the retrospect brought forward,
The old, most populous, wealthiest of earth's lands,
The streams of the Indus and the Ganges and their many affluents,
(I my shores of America walking to-day behold, resuming all,)   130
The tale of Alexander on his warlike marches suddenly dying,
On one side China and on the other side Persia and Arabia,
To the south the great seas and the bay of Bengal,
The flowing literatures, tremendous epics, religions, castes,
Old occult Brahma interminably far back, the tender and junior
    Buddha,   135
Central and southern empires and all their belongings, possessors,
The wars of Tamerlane, the reign of Aurungzebe,
The traders, rulers, explorers, Moslems, Venetians, Byzantium, the
    Arabs, Portuguese,
The first travelers famous yet, Marco Polo, Batouta the Moor,
Doubts to be solv'd, the map incognita, blanks to be fill'd,   140
The foot of man unstay'd, the hands never at rest,
Thyself O soul that will not brook a challenge.

The mediaeval navigators rise before me,
The world of 1492, with its awaken'd enterprise,
Something swelling in humanity now like the sap of the earth in
    spring,   145
The sunset splendor of chivalry declining.

And who art thou sad shade?
Gigantic, visionary, thyself a visionary,
With majestic limbs and pious beaming eyes,
Spreading around with every look of thine a golden world,   150
Enhuing it with gorgeous hues.

As the chief histrion,
Down to the footlights walks in some great scena,
Dominating the rest I see the Admiral himself,
(History's type of courage, action, faith,)   155
Behold him sail from Palos leading his little fleet,
His voyage behold, his return, his great fame,
His misfortunes, calumniators, behold him a prisoner, chain'd,
Behold his dejection, poverty, death.

(Curious in time I stand, noting the efforts of heroes,   160
Is the deferment long? bitter the slander, poverty, death?
Lies the seed unreck'd for centuries in the ground? lo, to God's
    due occasion,
Uprising in the night, it sprouts, blooms,
And fills the earth with use and beauty.)

7

Passage indeed O soul to primal thought,   165
Not lands and seas alone, thy own clear freshness,
The young maturity of brood and bloom,
To realms of budding bibles.

O soul, repressless, I with thee and thou with me,
Thy circumnavigation of the world begin,   170
Of man, the voyage of his mind's return,
To reason's early paradise,
Back, back to wisdom's birth, to innocent intuitions,
Again with fair creation.

8

O we can wait no longer,   175
We too take ship O soul,
Joyous we too launch out on trackless seas,
Fearless for unknown shores on waves of ecstasy to sail,
Amid the wafting winds, (thou pressing me to thee, I thee to me,
    O soul,)
Caroling free, singing our song of God.   180
Chanting our chant of pleasant exploration.

With laugh and many a kiss,
(Let others deprecate, let others weep for sin, remorse, humilia-
    tion,)
O soul thou pleasest me, I thee.

Ah more than any priest O soul we too believe in God,   185
But with the mystery of God we dare not dally.

O soul thou pleasest me, I thee,
Sailing these seas or on the hills, or waking in the night,
Thoughts, silent thoughts, of Time and Space and Death, like
    waters flowing,
Bear me indeed as through the regions infinite,   190
Whose air I breathe, whose ripples hear, lave me all over,
Bathe me O God in thee, mounting to thee,
I and my soul to range in range of thee.

O Thou transcendent,
Nameless, the fibre and the breath,   195
Light of the light, shedding forth universes, thou centre of them,
Thou mightier centre of the true, the good, the loving,
Thou moral, spiritual fountain—affection's source—thou reservoir,
(O pensive soul of me—O thirst unsatisfied—waitest not there?
Waitest not haply for us somewhere there the Comrade perfect?)   200
Thou pulse—thou motive of the stars, suns, systems,
That, circling, move in order, safe, harmonious,
Athwart the shapeless vastnesses of space,
How should I think, how breathe a single breath, how speak, if
    out of myself,
I could not launch, to those, superior universes?   205

Swiftly I shrivel at the thought of God,
At Nature and its wonders, Time and Space and Death,
But that I, turning, call to thee O soul, thou actual Me,

And lo, thou gently masterest the orbs,
Thou matest Time, smilest content at Death,   210
And fillest, swellest full the vastnessess of Space.

Greater than stars or suns,
Bounding O soul thou journeyest forth;
What love than thine and ours could wider amplify?
What aspirations, wishes, outvie thine and ours O soul?   215
What dreams of the ideal? what plans of purity, perfection,
   strength,
What cheerful willingness for others' sake to give up all?
For others' sake to suffer all?

Reckoning ahead O soul, when thou, the time achiev'd,
The seas all cross'd, weather'd the capes, the voyage done,   220
Surrounded, copest, frontest God, yieldest, the aim attain'd,
As filled with friendship, love complete, the Elder Brother found,
The Younger melts in fondness in his arms.

9

Passage to more than India!
Are thy wings plumed indeed for such far flights?   225
O soul, voyagest thou indeed on voyages like those?
Disportest thou on waters such as those?
Soundest below the Sanscrit and the Vedas?
Then have thy bent unleash'd.

Passage to you, your shores, ye aged fierce enigmas!   230
Passage to you, to mastership of you, ye strangling problems!
You, strew'd with the wrecks of skeletons, that living, never
   reach'd you.

Passage to more than India!
O secret of the earth and sky!
Of you O waters of the sea! O winding creeks and rivers!   235
Of you O woods and fields! of you strong mountains of my land!
Of you O prairies! of you gray rocks!
O morning red! O clouds! O rains and snows!
O day and night, passage to you!

O sun and moon and all you stars! Sirius and Jupiter!   240
Passage to you!

Passage, immediate passage! the blood burns in my veins!

Away O soul! hoist instantly the anchor!
Cut the hawsers—haul out—shake out every sail!
Have we not stood here like trees in the ground long enough?   245
Have we not grovel'd here long enough, eating and drinking like
    mere brutes?
Have we not darken'd and dazed ourselves with books long enough?

Sail forth—steer for the deep waters only,
Reckless O soul, exploring, I with thee, and thou with me,
For we are bound where mariner has not yet dared to go,   250
And we will risk the ship, ourselves and all.

O my brave soul!
O farther farther sail!
O daring joy, but safe! are they not all the seas of God?
O farther, farther, farther sail!   255

ALBERT J. BEVERIDGE

The Star Of Empire

Speech opening the Republican Campaign for the
West in the Auditorium, at Chicago, September 25,
1900, in reply to Mr. Bryan's Indianapolis speech
accepting his second Democratic nomination for
President. This speech was used by the Republicans
as a National Campaign document.

"Westward the Star of Empire takes its Way." Not the star of kingly
power, for kingdoms are everywhere dissolving in the increasing rights of
men; not the star of autocratic oppression, for civilization is brightening
and the liberties of the people are broadening under every flag. But the
star of empire, as Washington used the word, when he called this Republic an "empire"; as Jefferson understood it, when he declared our form of
government ideal for extending "our empire"; as Marshall understood it,
when he closed a noble period of an immortal constitutional opinion by
naming the domain of the American people "our empire."

This is the "empire" of which the prophetic voice declared "Westward the Star of Empire takes its Way"—the star of the empire of liberty
and law, of commerce and communication, of social order and the Gospel
of our Lord—the star of the empire of the civilization of the world. Westward *that* star of empire takes its course. And to-day it illumines our path
of duty across the Pacific into the islands and lands where Providence has
called us.

In that path the American government is marching forward, opposed
at every step by those who deny the right of the Republic to plant the
institutions of the Flag where Events have planted that Flag itself. For
this is our purpose, to perform which the Opposition declares that the
Republic has no warrant in the Constitution, in morals or in the rights of
man. And I mean to examine to-night every argument they advance for
their policy of reaction and retreat.

It is not true, as the Opposition asserts, that every race without

From Albert J. Beveridge, *The Meaning of the Times and Other Speeches*
(Indianapolis: The Bobbs-Merrill Co., Inc., 1908), pp. 118–43.

instruction and guidance is naturally self-governing. If so, the Indians were capable of self-government. America belonged to them whether they were or were not capable of self-government. If they were capable of self-government it was not only wrong, but it was a crime to set up our independent government on their land without their consent. If this is true, the Puritans, instead of being noble, are despicable characters; and the patriots of 1776, to whom the Opposition compares the Filipinos, were only a swarm of land pirates. If the Opposition is right, the Zulus who owned the Transvaal were capable of self-government; and the Boers who expelled them, according to the Opposition, deserve the abhorrence of righteous men.

But while the Boers took the lands they occupy from the natives who peopled them; while we peopled this country in spite of the Indian who owned it; and while this may be justified by the welfare of the world which those events advanced, that is not what is to be done in the Philippines. The American government, as a government, will not appropriate the Filipinos' land or permit Americans as individuals to seize it. It will protect the Filipinos in their possessions. If any American secures real estate in the Philippines, it will be because he buys it from the owner. Under American administration the Filipino who owns his little plot of ground will experience a security in the possession of his property that he has never known before.

The English in Egypt and India have not taken the land from its owners; they have confirmed the occupants in their ownership. In Hawaii we have not taken the land from its owners; we have secured its owners in their peaceable possession. And our administration in the Philippines will also establish there that same security of property and life which is the very beginning of civilization itself.

If it be said that tropical countries can not be peopled by the Caucasian race, I answer that, even if true, it is no reason why they should not be governed by the Caucasian race. India is a tropical country. India is ruled by England to the advantage of India and England alike. Who denies that India's 300,000,000 are better off under English administration than under the bestial tyranny of native rulers, to whom the agony of their subjects was the highest form of amusement?

Dare Mr. Bryan say that he would have India back to its condition before England took it? If he dare not, he is answered. Dare he say that he would withdraw English rule now? If he dare not, he is answered. Dare he say that he would take the English "residents" from the Malay States and turn them back again to the rule of their brutal lords? If he dare not, he is answered. Dare he say that the Boers should restore the Transvaal to its original owners? If he dare not, he is answered. Dare he deny that the greatest progress shown upon the map of earth to-day is the progress of

Egypt during the last twenty years under English rule? If he dare not, he is answered. And he dare not. If he proclaims his faith in the Filipino people, who know not the meaning of self-government, I declare my faith in the American people, who have developed the realities of liberty.

Grant, for the purposes of argument, the Opposition's premise that the white man can not people the Philippines. Grant, also, that the Malays of those islands can not, unaided, establish civilization there; build roads, open mines, erect schools, maintain social order, repress piracy and administer safe government throughout the archipelago. And this must be granted; for they are the same race which inhabits the Malay Peninsula. What, then, is the conclusion demanded by the general welfare of the world?

Surely not that this land, rich in all that civilized man requires, and these people needing the very blessings they ignorantly repel, should be remanded to savagery and the wilderness! If you say this, you say that barbarism and undeveloped resources are better than civilization and the earth's resources developed. What is the conclusion, then, which the logic of civilization compels from these admitted premises? It is that the reign of law must be established throughout these islands, their resources developed and their people civilized by those in whose blood resides the genius of administration.

Such are all Teutonic and Celtic peoples. Such are the Dutch; behold their work in Java. Such are the English; behold their work all around the world. Such the German; behold his advance into the fields of world-regeneration and administration. Such were the French before Napoleon diverted their energies; behold their work in Canada, Louisiana and our great Northwest. And such, more than any people who ever lived, are the Americans, into whose hands God has given the antipodes to develop their resources, to regenerate their people and to establish there the civilization of law-born liberty and liberty-born law.

If the Opposition declares that we ought to set up a separate government over the Philippines because we are setting up a separate government over Cuba, I answer that such an error in Cuba does not justify the same error in the Philippines. I am speaking for myself alone, but speaking thus, I say, that for the good of Cuba more even than for the good of the United States, a separate government over Cuba, uncontrolled by the American Republic, *never should have been promised*.

Cuba is a mere extension of our Atlantic coast-line. It commands the ocean entrances to the Mississippi and the Isthmian Canal. Jefferson's dearest dream was that Cuba should belong to the United States. To possess this extension of American soil has been the wish of every far-seeing statesman from Jefferson to Blaine. Annexation to the greatest nation the world has ever seen is a prouder Cuban destiny than separate nationality.

As an American possession, Cuba might possibly have been fitted for statehood in a period not much longer than that in which Louisiana was prepared for statehood.

Even now the work of regeneration—of cleansing cities, building roads, establishing posts, erecting a system of universal education and the action of all the forces that make up our civilization—is speeding forward faster than at any time or place in human history—American administration! But yesterday there were less than ten thousand Cuban children in school; to-day there are nearly one hundred and fifty thousand Cuban children in school—American administration! But yesterday Havana was the source of our yellow-fever plagues; to-day it is nearly as healthy as New Orleans—American administration!

When we stop this work and withdraw our restraint, revolution will succeed revolution in Cuba, as in the Central and South American countries; Havana again fester with the yellow death; systematic education again degenerate into sporadic instances; and Cuba, which under our control should be a source of profit, power and glory to the Republic and herself, will be a source of irritation and of loss, of danger and disease to both. The United States needs Cuba for our protection; *but Cuba needs the United States for Cuba's salvation.*

The resolution for Cuban independence, hastily passed by all parties in Congress, at an excited hour, was an error which years of time, propinquity of location, common commerce, mutual interests and similar dangers surely will correct. The President, jealous of American honor, considers that resolution a promise. And American promise means performance. And so the unnatural experiment is to be tried. What war and nature—aye, what God hath joined together—is to be put asunder.

I speak for myself alone, but speaking thus, I say that it will be an evil day for Cuba when the Stars and Stripes come down from Morro Castle. I speak for myself alone, but I believe that in this my voice is the voice of the American millions, as it is the voice of the ultimate future, when I say that Porto Rico is ours and ours for ever; the Philippines are ours and ours for ever; and Cuba ought to have been ours, and by the free choice of her people some day will be ours, and ours for ever.

We have a foreign nation on our north; another on our southwest; and now to permit another foreign nation within cannon shot of our southeast coast, will indeed create conditions which will require that militarism which the Opposition to the Government pretends to fear. Think of Cuba in alliance with England or Germany or France! Think of Cuba a naval station and ally of one of the great foreign powers, every one of whom is a rival of America! And so my answer to Mr. Bryan's comparison is that, if we have made a mistake in Cuba, we ought not to make the same mistake in the Philippines.

. . . .

Consider, now, the Opposition's proposed method of procedure in the Philippines: It is to establish a stable government there, turn that government over to the Filipinos, and protect them and their government from molestation by any other nation.

Suppose the Opposition's plan in operation. Suppose a satisfactory government is established, turned over to the Filipinos and American troops withdrawn. The new government must experience feuds, factions and revolution. This is the history of every new government. It was so even with the American people. Witness Shays' Rebellion against the National Government, almost shaking its foundations; witness the Whiskey Rebellion in Pennsylvania, which required the first exercise of armed national power to maintain order with a state of the Union. And we were of a self-governing race—at that period we were almost wholly Anglo-Saxon.

How can we expect the Philippine Malays to escape this common fate of all new governments? Remember that as a race they have not that civil cohesion which binds a people into a nation. Remember that every island is envious of every other one; and that in each island every officer is a "general," jealous of his dignity, intriguing for advancement.

How long would this stable government, which the Opposition asks us to "establish," *remain* "stable," if we withdrew our forces? And if resistance broke out in the Visayas, if revolt sprang into flame among the murderous Moros, what would be our duty? It would be to reënter where we had withdraw and restore the stability of the government which the Opposition declares that we shall establish before we withdraw. And so the Opposition program constantly defeats itself and compels us to do over and over again the work which we must perform at the beginning. And all this without benefit to the Philippine people, without improvement to their lands and with immeasurable loss to ourselves recouped not from a single source of profit. But the American flag floating there for ever means not only established liberty, but permanent stability.

Again governments must have money. That is their first necessity; money for salaries, money for the army, money for public buildings, money for improvements. Before the revenues are established, the government must have money. If the revenues are inadequate, nevertheless the government must have money. Therefore, all governments are borrowers. Even the government of the American people—the richest people of history—is a borrower. Even the government of the British people, who for centuries have been accumulating wealth, must borrow; its bonds are in our own bank vaults. Much more, then, must little governments borrow money.

If, then, we "establish a stable government," as the Opposition demands, and turn that government over to the Filipinos, they also must borrow money. But suppose the Philippine government can not pay its debt when it falls due, as has been the case in many instances on our own continent within the last quarter of a century; as is the case to-day with one of the governments of Central America. If that loan is an English loan, England would seize the revenues of the Philippines for the payment of her debt, as she has done before and is doing now. So would France or Germany or whoever was the creditor nation. Should we have a right to interfere? Of course not, unless we were willing to guarantee the Philippine debt. If, then, the first purpose of the Opposition candidate is carried out, we must:

Keep "stable" the government which we first *"establish,"* or the very purpose of the establishment of that government is defeated.

If the second proposition of the Opposition is performed we must:

First: Control the finances of the Philippines perpetually; or,

Second: Guarantee the loans the Philippine government makes with other nations; or,

Third: Go to war with those nations to defeat their collection of their just debts.

Is this sound policy? Is it profitable? Is it moral? Is it just to the Filipinos, to the world, to ourselves? Is it humane to the masses of those children who need first of all, and more than all, order, law and peace? Is it prudent, wise, far-seeing statesmanship? *And does the adoption of a similar course in Cuba justify it in the Philippines?*

No. Here is the program of reason and righteousness, and Time and Events will make it the program of the Republic:

First: We have given Porto Rico such a civil government as her situation demands, under the Stars and Stripes.

Second: We will put down the rebellion and then give the Philippines such a civil government as the situation demands, under the Stars and Stripes.

Third: We are regenerating Cuba, and when our preparatory work is done, we should have given Cuba such a civil government as her situation may demand, under the Stars and Stripes.

The sovereignty of the Stars and Stripes can be nothing but a blessing to any people and to any land.

I do not advocate this course for commercial reasons, though these have their weight. All men who understand production and exchange, understand the commercial advantage resulting from our ownership of these rich possessions. But I waive this large consideration as insignificant, compared with the master argument of the progress of civilization, which under God, the American people are henceforth to lead until our day is done. For henceforward in the trooping of the colors of the nations they shall cluster around and follow the Republic's banner.

The mercantile argument is mighty with Americans in merely mercantile times, and it should be so; but the argument of destiny is the master argument in the hour of destiny, and it should be so. The American people never yet entered on a great movement for merely mercantile reasons. Sentiment and duty have started and controlled every noble current of American history. And at this historic hour, destiny is the controlling consideration in the prophetic statesmanship which conditions require of the American people.

It is destiny that the world shall be rescued from its natural wilderness and from savage men. Civilization is no less an evolution than the changing forms of animal and vegetable life. Surely and steadily the reign of law, which is the very spirit of liberty, takes the place of arbitrary caprice. Surely and steadily the methods of social order are bringing the whole earth under their subjection. And to deny that this is right, is to deny that civilization should increase. In this great work the American people must have their part. They are fitted for the work as no people have ever been fitted; and their work lies before them.

If the Opposition say that they grant this, but that the higher considerations of abstract human rights demand that the Philippines shall have such a government as they wish, regardless of the remainder of the world, I answer that the desire of the Filipinos is not the only factor in determining their government, just as the desire of no individual man is the only factor determining his conduct. It is written in the moral law of individuals that "No man liveth to himself alone"; and it is no less written in the moral law of peoples that "No people liveth to itself alone."

The world is interested in the Philippines, and it has a right to be. The world is interested in India, and it has a right to be. Civilization is interested in China and its government, and that is the duty of civilization. You can not take the Philippines out of the operation of those forces which are binding all mankind into one vast and united intelligence. When Circumstance has raised our flag above them, we dare not turn these misguided children over to destruction by themselves or spoliation by others, and then make answer when the God of nations requires them at our hands, "Am I my brother's keeper?"

If you admit that it is the purpose of that Intelligence that rules the universe to civilize and unify mankind, how is this to be accomplished? If you say that it is by leaving each people to themselves to work out their own salvation, I answer that history shows that civilization has been preserved only by the most superior nations extending it. And the method of extending civilization is by colonization where the superior nation can establish itself among the inferior races; or in place of them, if the inferior races can not exist under civilization, as in New Zealand, Australia and the like. The method is by administration where the superior nation can not, because of climatic conditions, establish itself among or supplant the inferior races, as in Java, India, and the like. And finally that method is by creating and developing commerce among all the peoples of the world.

It is thus that America itself was discovered; thus that this Republic was builded; thus that South Africa was reclaimed; thus that Australia was recovered from the Bushman and made the home of civilization; thus that Ceylon was taken from wild men and tangled jungle and brought beneath the rule of religion, law and industry. It is thus that Egypt is being redeemed, her deserts fertilized, her starving millions fed, her fellahs made men and the blessings of just government bestowed upon the land of the Pharaohs. It is thus that the regeneration of India has progressed, her cities been cleansed, the reign of hygiene and health gradually established in the very kingdom of pestilence and disease; and the arbitrary and infamous tyranny of petty princes, holding power of life and death over miserable subjects, reduced to the orderly administration of equal and unpurchased justice under equal and impartial laws.

History establishes these propositions:

First: Every people who have become great, have become colonizers or administrators;

Second: Coincident with this colonization and administration, their material and political greatness develops;

Third: Their decline is coincident with the abandonment of the policy of possession and administration, or departure from the true principles thereof.

And as a corollary to these propositions is this self-evident and contemporaneous truth:

Every progressive nation of Europe to-day is seeking lands to colonize and governments to administer.

And can this common instinct of the most progressive peoples of the world—this common conclusion of the ablest statesmen of other nations—be baseless?

If the Opposition asks why this is the mission of the American people now more than heretofore, I answer that before any people assumes these great tasks it goes through a process of consolidation and unification, just as a man achieves maturity before he assumes the tasks of a man. Great Britain never became a colonizing and administering power until the separate peoples of England, Scotland, Ireland and Wales, welded into a single indivisible people, were ready to go forth as a national unit and do the great work to which the world was calling it.

The German people did not embark upon this natural policy until separate duchies, principalities and kingdoms were finally welded by a common war, common blood, and common interests into a great single and indivisible people ready to go forth as a national unit to the great work to which the world was calling it.

The French became colonizers of lands and administrators of governments only when her great statesmen, from Richelieu to Colbert, had knit the separate and divided French people into a national unit and sent it forth to the work to which the world was calling it; and France declined only when she abandoned that natural law of national power and progress, and Napoleon diverted her energies to the internal strifes of Europe. Then her decline began. She lost Canada. The Corsican sold Louisiana to us. And to-day French statesmen at last realize the fatal operation of this law when once disobyed, and so again are seeking to become one of the colonizing and administering powers of earth.

The American Republic has been going through the process of fitting it for the execution of this natural law of civilization. Hitherto we have had local divisions. The proposition that we were a single people, a national unit, and not a sum of segregated factions, was denied. And it required war and commerce and time—the shedding of blood, the uniting of communities by railroads and telegraphs, the knitting together of the fabric of Nationality by that wonderful loom of human intelligence called the post; and finally, the common and united effort of a foreign war, to bring us to a consciousness of our power *as a people*. And there is never in nature a power without a corresponding purpose. Shall we now stop this process of nature?

We are this at last, a great national unit ready to carry out that universal law of civilization which requires of every people who have reached our high estate to become colonizers of new lands, administrators of orderly government over savage and senile peoples. And being thus prepared, the lands and peoples needing our administration are delivered to our keeping, not by our design, but by occurrence beyond our control. In the astronomy of Destiny, American Opportunity, American Duty and American Preparedness are in conjunction. Who shall oppose their progress?

These are the laws which history advises are the laws of civilization's growth. These, therefore, are the high ordinances of universal and racial morality which has for its ultimate object "that far-off divine event towards which civilization tends." And it is to this divine order of progress that I appeal in answer to the misapplied individual moralities that would give Australia back to its Bushmen, the United States to its Indians, Ceylon to its natives, and the whole world back to barbarism and night.

If the Opposition says that this program, written not in the statutes of man, but in the nature of things, will smother our institutions with a myriad of soldiers, I answer that the world to-day demonstrates that it will result in the reverse. If they point to Germany, and other nations with vast military establishments, to prove that colonization and administration over lands held as possessions and dependencies result in the supremacy of the soldiery over the common people, I answer that the examples do not sustain, but destroy the proposition.

Consider Germany. Her standing army in times of peace is 562,000 men. Does colonization cause or require them? No; because she maintained that mighty multitude before the present Emperor and his counsellors developed Germany's progressive colonial and administrative policy. No, again; because, of Germany's standing army of 562,000 men, less than 4,000 are in her possessions, the remainder of her mighty host being stationed within the Empire itself. No, again; because Austria, with no colonies at all, has a standing army in times of peace of over 361,000 men, none of whom is employed in the care of possessions. No, again; because France, a republic, has a standing army in times of peace of 616,000 men, of which less than 10,000 are employed in her colonies and possessions except in Algeria and Tunis, which are considered an immediate part of France. No, again; because Italy, with hardly a colonial possession, maintains a standing army in times of peace of nearly 325,000 men. No, again; because Spain, the world's second largest holder of possessions before we won them, maintained a standing army of less than 100,000 men, of whom less than 10,000 were kept in her misruled and oppressed possessions. No, again; because the greatest colonial power that the world has ever seen, the Empire of Great Britain, has a smaller standing army in times of peace than any power of Europe—less than half as many as Germany, almost two-thirds less than the soldiers of France, nearly one-third less than Italy, and one-third less than the soldiers maintained by Austria, an absolutely non-colonizing power.

. . . .

If we do our duty in the Philippines, it is admitted that we ought not to govern the Filipinos as fellow-citizens of the Republic. The Platform of the Opposition says that "to make the Filipinos citizens would endanger our civilization." To force upon Malays, who three hundred years ago were savages and who since that time have been schooled only in oppression, that form of self-government exercised by the citizens of the United States, would be to clothe an infant in the apparel of a giant and require of it a giant's strength and tasks. If we govern them, we must govern them with common sense. They must first be made familiar with the simplest principles of liberty—equal obedience to equal laws, impartial justice by unpurchasable courts, protection of property and of the right to labor—in short, with the *substance* of liberty which civilized government will establish among them.

The Filipinos must begin at the beginning and grow in the knowledge of free institutions, and, if possible, into the ultimate practice of free government by observing the operation of those institutions among them and by experiencing their benefits. They have experienced unjust, unequal and arbitrary taxation; this is the result of the institutions of tyranny. They must experience equal, just and scientific taxation; this is the result of free institutions. They have experienced arrest without cause, imprisonment without a hearing, and beheld justice bought and sold; these are the results of the institutions of tyranny. They must experience arrest only for cause publicly made known, conviction only after trial publicly conducted and justice impartial, unpurchasable and speedily administered; these are the results of free institutions.

They have experienced the violation of the home and robbery by public officers; these are the results of the institutions of tyranny. They must experience the sanctity of the fireside, the separation of Church and State, the punishment of soldier or public official practising outrage or extortion upon them; these are the results of free institutions. And these are the results which they will experience under the government of the American Institutions, and our *institutions* follow the flag.

The institutions of every nation follow its flag. German institutions follow the flag of the Fatherland. English institutions follow the banner of St. George. French institutions follow the tricolor of France. And just sò, American institutions follow the emblem of the Republic. Nay! Our institutions not only follow the flag, *they accompany it.* They troop beneath its fold. Wherever an American citizen goes, he carries the spirit of our institutions. On whatever soil his blood is shed to establish the sovereignty of our flag, there are planted the imperishable seeds of the institutions of our Nation; and there those institutions flourish in proportion as the soil where they are planted is prepared for them.

Free institutions are as definite, certain and concrete as our Constitution itself. Free speech is an institution of liberty. Free schools are an institution of liberty. Freedom of worship is an institution of liberty. Any American school-boy can catalogue free institutions. And as fast as the simplest of these institutions prepares these children Providence has given into our keeping for higher grades, just so fast more complex forms of our institutions will follow as naturally as childhood succeeds infancy, youth succeeds childhood and manhood crowns maturity. Our flag! Our institutions! Our Constitution! This is the immortal order in which American civilization marches.

And so the answer to the politician's battle-cry that "our Constitution follows the flag" is this great truth of popular liberty, OUR INSTITUTIONS FOLLOW THE FLAG.

We are a Nation. We can acquire territory. If we can acquire territory, we can govern it. If we can govern it, we can govern it as its situation may demand. If the Opposition says that power so broad is dangerous to the liberties of the American people, I answer that the American people's liberties can never be endangered at the hands of the American people; and, therefore, that their liberties can not be endangered by the exercise of this power, because this power is power exercised by the American people themselves.

"*Congress* shall have power to dispose of and make all needful rules and regulations respecting territory belonging to the United States," says the Constitution.

And what is Congress? The agent of the American people. The Constitution created Congress. But who created the Constitution? "We, the people," declares the Constitution itself.

The American people created the Constitution; it is their method. The American people established Congress; it is their instrument. The American people elect the members of Congress; they are the people's servants. Their laws are the people's laws. Their power is the people's power. And if you fear this power, you fear the people. If you want their power restricted, it is because you want the power of the people restricted; and a restriction of their power is a restriction of their liberty. So that the end of the logic of the Opposition is limitation upon the liberties of the American people, for fear that the liberties of the American people will suffer at the hands of the American people—which is absurd.

If the Opposition asserts that the powers which the Constitution gives to the legislative agents of the American people will not be exercised in righteousness, I answer that that can only be because the American people themselves are not righteous. It is the American people, through their agents, who exercise the power; and if those agents do not act as the people would have them, they will discharge those agents and annul their acts. The heart of the whole argument on the constitutional power of the government is faith in the wisdom and virtue of the people; and in that virtue and wisdom I believe, as every man must, who believes in a republic. In the end, the judgment of the masses is right. If this were not so, progress would be impossible, since only through the people is progress achieved.

The Opposition says that American liberties will be lost if we administer the substance of liberty to those children. Does any man believe that the American institution of free schools will be destroyed or impaired because we plant free schools throughout the Philippines? Does any man believe that equal rights will be impaired here, because we establish equal rights there?

The individual rights of Englishmen have not declined since England became an administrator of external governments; on the contrary, as England has extended her colonies, the individual rights of individual Englishmen have increased. The rights of the Crown have not enlarged as England's empire has extended; on the contrary, they have diminished. The period of England's great activity in external government has been precisely the period of the extension of the suffrage in England itself, of the enactment of laws for the protection of labor and the amelioration of all the conditions of life among the common people of England.

. . . .

This is no unprecedented struggle. It is the ever-old and yet the ever-new, because the ever-elemental contest between the forces of a growing nationality and those who resist it; between the forces of extending dominion and those who oppose it; between the forces that are making us the master people of the world and those who think that our activities should be confined to this continent for ever. It is the eternal duel between the forces of progress and reaction, of construction and disintegration, of growth and decay.

Both sides are and always have been sincere. Washington was sincere when he advocated the adoption of the Constitution; Patrick Henry was sincere when he resisted it as the death-blow to our liberties. Jefferson was sincere when he acquired the empire of Louisiana; Josiah Quincy was sincere when he declared in Congress that the Louisiana acquisition meant the dissolution of the Union.

Webster was sincere when he asserted the sovereignty of the Nation, the indestructibility of the Union, and declared that the Constitution could not follow the flag until the American people so decreed; and Calhoun was sincere when he pronounced the doctrine of state sovereignty, the right of nullification, and announced that the Constitution, carrying slavery, followed the flag in spite of the will of the American people. Lincoln was sincere when he proclaimed that the Union was older than the Constitution, that nationality was the indestructible destiny of the American people, and that he would maintain that nationality by arms; and those mistaken ones were sincere who sought to divide the American people and on the field of battle poured out their blood fighting for their faith.

But their sincerity did not make them *right*. Their earnestness, ability, courage could not give them victory. They were struggling against the Fates. They were resisting the onward forces which were making of the American people the master Nation of the world—the forces that established us first as a separate political body, then welded us into a national unit, indivisible; then extended our dominion from ocean to ocean over unexplored wilderness; and now in the ripeness of time fling our authority and unfurl our flag almost around the globe. It is the "divine event" of American principles among the governments of men for which these forces have been working since the Pilgrims landed on the red man's soil. Men—patriotic, brave and wise—have sought to stay that tremendous purpose of destiny, but their opposition was as the feeble finger of a babe against the resistless pour of the Gulf Stream's mighty current.

For God's hand was in it all. His plans were working out their glorious results. And just as futile is resistance to the continuance to-day of the eternal movement of the American people toward the mastery of the world. This is a destiny neither vague nor undesirable. It is definite, splendid and holy.

When nations shall war no more without the consent of the American Republic: what American heart thrills not with pride at that prospect? And yet our interests are weaving themselves so rapidly around the world that that time is almost here.

When governments stay the slaughter of human beings, because the American Republic demands it: what American heart thrills not with pride at that prospect? And yet to-night there sits in Constantinople a sovereign who knows that time is nearly here.

When the commerce of the world on which the world's peace hangs, traveling every ocean highway of earth, shall pass beneath the guns of the great Republic: what American heart thrills not at that prospect? Yet that time will be here before the first quarter of the twentieth century closes.

When any changing of the map of earth requires a conference of the Powers, and when, at any Congress of the Nations, the American Republic will preside as the most powerful of powers and most righteous of judges: what American heart thrills not at that prospect? And yet, that prospect is in sight, even as I speak.

It is the high and holy destiny of the American people, and from that destiny the American bugles will never sound retreat. "Westward the Star of Empire takes its way!" AMERICAN INSTITUTIONS FOLLOW THE AMERICAN FLAG.

part four

CIVIL WAR
AND
NATIONAL DESTINY

The mortar shell that burst over Fort Sumter in the early morning of April 12, 1861, signaled Confederate batteries ringing Charleston Harbor to open fire on Federal forces occupying the stronghold. That explosion announced the beginning of the bloody Civil War that would claim, through wounds and disease, the lives of 600,000 Americans. It also heralded the onset of history's direst threat to an undivided American destiny. To be sure, the nation was badly divided long before the act of secession and the ensuing war. Antipathy between an industrial North and an agricultural South, abetted by abolitionist and proslavery literature and by contention over western territories, had already spelled the loss of agreement on America's historic role. Yet whatever hopes for an undivided national destiny may have burned deep within American breasts before the war were in danger of being utterly extinguished by the gathering storm.

It comes as no surprise to find both Northern and Southern apologists during the conflict identifying their separate causes with the destiny of the nation. Both felt that they were defending an authentically *American* mission. Both invoked the help of the nation's God. Each viewed his own section as the citadel of the fundamental principles of American government. Each assumed that his military was the advance guard of the New Israel crossing the Red Sea of war.

Henry Ward Beecher stirred up considerable support for the Union side and confidently identified the Northern cause with the nation's destiny. Neither a profound nor an original religious thinker, Beecher was nevertheless one of the most influential and popular ministers of the nineteenth century. He had long used his platform at Plymouth (Congregational) Church of Brooklyn for the discussion of social and political issues. During the war years he directed his oratorical powers to a vigorous defense of the Union and a caustic indictment of the Confederacy.

When news of the firing on Fort Sumter reached New York, Beecher addressed his Plymouth congregation on the religious and national meaning of the impending war. The sermon, "The Battle Set in Array," set forth the themes that Beecher would reiterate during the next four years. Although Beecher professed an abhorrence for war, he insisted that God's chosen were usually called to suffer for their principles, war being the suffering facing God's American Israel. And although he warned against a vengeful spirit, his warning lost much of its force when he portrayed Southerners as "hot, narrow, boastful" and completely devoid of the sentiments of liberty and national patriotism. In a later sermon before the same congregation he would make the polarity between North and South absolute: "I thank them [the Confederacy] that they took another flag to do the Devil's work, and left our flag to do the work of God." Clearly Beecher believed Northern war efforts to be the instruments of God himself as the Union prepared to preserve America as the "chosen refuge of liberty for all the earth" and to stamp out slavery, the last major obstacle to American freedom. (Beecher was a Republican who campaigned for Lincoln in 1860, but he criticized Lincoln for the delay in issuing an emancipation proclamation. From the start Beecher viewed the war as a moral crusade against slavery.)

James Silver has demonstrated how religious leaders and associations were effective in arousing and sustaining the morale of the people in the South during the Civil War. "Because of the limited industrial resources of the South, the success of the Confederacy depended on the degree of intestinal fortitude developed by the man in the street and on the farm. He needed to identify himself as a member of God's chosen people and his country as a fulfillment of the destiny of history." Jewish and Catholic leaders performed significant roles in so boosting Confederate morale, but the strongest support came from Southern Protestantism.[1] Through sermons, tracts, and editorials composed for both civilians and soldiers, Protestant ministers and editors depicted the Southern struggle against Union forces as the attempt of a chosen people to preserve an American destiny abandoned by Yankee infidels.

There was no more active a sustainer of Confederate morale or more

[1] James W. Silver, *Confederate Morale and Church Propaganda* (New York: W. W. Norton & Company, Inc., 1967), pp. 15, 25, 48, 50, 57–59.

energetic a proponent of Southern destiny than Benjamin Morgan Palmer, minister of the First Presbyterian Church in New Orleans. In terms of intellectual capacity, Palmer stood in the shadow of his friend and teacher James Henley Thornwell, professor at Columbia (South Carolina) Theological Seminary and ardent defender of the institution of slavery. Yet Palmer possessed the talent for taking Thornwell's ideas and dramatically relating them to events of the moment. Shortly after Lincoln's election both Thornwell and Palmer preached on slavery as an institution ordained by God, an institution threatened by the victory of the Republican party. Palmer added that the Southern states should bind themselves into a sacred covenant to protect slavery and should "take all necessary steps looking to separate and independent existence." If war should follow on such actions, Palmer said, the South could be certain that "we defend the cause of God and religion" since "the abolition spirit is undeniably atheistic." Palmer's career of oratory on behalf of the Confederacy was launched; he would travel before the war's end throughout the Southern states championing Confederate destiny under God.[2]

On the first of nine Confederate fast days called by President Davis, Palmer delivered a sermon in New Orleans that described the South's divine mission in the war. As a fast-day address, "National Responsibility Before God" dwelt on public sins, but they were sins of the nation that preceded the rise of the Confederacy—that is, they were Yankee sins! As Palmer said, "the South has rather been 'sinned against than sinning.'" In the course of reciting national sins, Palmer elaborated the religious and political principles for which the South stood, but the climax was reached toward the end of the sermon where Palmer exulted in the destiny that the Confederacy encountered in the war. The South would fight to preserve the constitutional right of self-government. Palmer believed, therefore, that Southern destiny was in its deepest meaning *the American* destiny under God.

In "National Responsibility" Palmer alluded to certain convictions used in the justification of slavery: the curse of Ham that befell the black race and doomed it to perpetual servitude, the civilizing effects of the institution of slavery on a backward people, etc. In the antebellum South a defense of slavery had been worked out in great detail, often supported in large measure by proof texts from the Bible.[3] During the war Confederate spokesmen like Palmer incorporated slavery into their view of

---

[2] See Margaret Burr DesChamps, "Benjamin Morgan Palmer, Orator-Preacher of the Confederacy," *Southern Speech Journal*, Sept. 1953, pp. 14–22.

[3] See William Sumner Jenkins, *Pro-Slavery Thought in the Old South* (Chapel Hill: University of North Carolina Press, 1935).

American destiny: the slave's good fortune depended upon the future of the Confederacy since its institution of slavery shielded the Negro from a hostile world and provided him with Christianity and other fruits of Western civilization. Whereas an abolitionist like Beecher considered slavery to be the last great obstacle to the achievement of American freedom, a Southerner like Palmer argued that the abolition of the institution would be destructive of the Negro's future. The facile rationalization and oppressive paternalism involved in the proslavery position are detected easily enough, but it is equally evident that pressure for abolition on moral grounds did not receive widespread Northern support and that genuine concern for the welfare of the Negro was scarcely characteristic of Northern attitudes either before or after the war. For the most part the Negro slave became a pawn on the checkered board of American destiny, shifted about by both Northern and Southern advocates of the war.

Few persons were able to rise above sectional interpretations of national destiny and speak of the Civil War as a judgment of God falling upon the nation as a whole. Abraham Lincoln was one of those few. As the war dragged on and the lists of dead mounted, Lincoln agonized over the ultimate purpose of the tragedy. Late in 1862 he wrote in a personal note, "In the present civil war it is quite possible that God's purpose is something different from the purpose of either party—and yet the human instrumentalities, working just as they do, are of the best adaptation to effect His purpose." The war years deepened Lincoln's sense of the mystery of divine providence and heightened his awareness of the presumption involved in the easy identification of the designs of man with the will of God. His brooding over the ways of providence, however, by no means led to timidity in his pursuit of victory; on the contrary, it made even more apparent to him the need to bring the war to a close and restore a united nation dedicated to freedom, the "last, best hope of earth." As Lincoln prepared to issue the final Emancipation Proclamation, he included the freedom of the slave in that hope: "In *giving* freedom to the *slave*, we *assure* freedom to the *free*—honorable alike in what we give, and what we preserve. We shall nobly save, or meanly lose, the last, best hope of earth." (Annual Message to Congress, December 1, 1862.) The nation's destiny was for Lincoln that of beaming forth the rays of democratic freedom to the world. He saw that destiny being severely tested by a tragic and ultimately incomprehensible war. Yet, as Lincoln so vividly put it in the Gettysburg Address, the war might well provide the occasion for a renewed pledge to American destiny under God: "It is for us the living . . . to be here dedicated to the great task remaining before us—that from these honored dead we take increased devotion to that cause for which they gave the last full measure of devotion . . . that this nation, under God, shall have a new birth of freedom. . . ."[4]

Lincoln's Second Inaugural Address was the finest example of his mature religious interpretation of the Civil War and American destiny. Replete with biblical language and allusions to Old Testament prophecy, the address combined a belief that the war was a divine judgment upon the entire nation with a firm resolve to set the nation back on its course of justice, peace, and freedom.

The Civil War cost the American people a staggering amount of blood and property. But, as Robert Penn Warren has claimed, probably the most enduring cost was psychological. The war handed the Southerner "the Great Alibi," the feeling that his attitudes and actions are excusable because history conspired against him. "The race problem, according to the Great Alibi, is the doom defined by history—by New England slavers, New England and Middlewestern Abolitionists, cotton, climate, the Civil War, Reconstruction, Wall Street, the Jews. . . . Since the situation is given by history, the Southerner therefore is guiltless; is, in fact, an innocent victim of a cosmic conspiracy." Using his Great Alibi, the Southerner as loser of the war can convince himself that he is "trapped in history." The psychological heritage of the North is a different kind—what Warren calls "the Treasury of Virtue." If the Southerner believes himself trapped in history, "the Northerner, with his Treasury of Virtue, feels redeemed by history, automatically redeemed." Having won the war, preserved the Union, and eliminated slavery, the Northerner feels his history has given him virtue. "He has in his pocket . . . a plenary indulgence, for all sins past, present, and future, freely given by the hand of history."[5] Both the complacent fatalism of the Great Alibi and the smug self-righteousness of the Treasury of Virtue destroy the heavy sense of *responsibility* that Lincoln believed was bound up with American destiny under God. To feel conspired against by history, or to feel automatically redeemed by it— neither is to assume responsibility for one's historical destiny.

Much of the religious literature appearing immediately after the Civil War fell into one or the other of these psychological traps. Yet there were persons in all regions of the country who sought a maturer, more responsible understanding of the costly war through which they had passed. In the South, for example, Stephen Elliott, a native South Carolinian who became bishop of the Episcopal Church in Georgia, disavowed

[4] All Lincoln quotes are from William J. Wolf, *The Religion of Abraham Lincoln* (New York: The Seabury Press, Inc., 1963), pp. 147, 159, 172.
[5] Robert Penn Warren, *The Legacy of the Civil War* (New York: Random House, Inc., Vintage Books, 1964), pp. 53, 55–56, 59.

alibis. Although he had been an advocate of the Confederacy and found the *specific* purposes of God in allowing the Confederacy's defeat to be obscure, he repeatedly insisted that defeat served the *ultimate*, hidden purposes of God and urged his fellow Southerners to dedicate themselves to a sounder, less spurious nationhood in the future.[6] In Connecticut, Horace Bushnell, a Congregational minister and the most distinguished theologian to appear in America since Jonathan Edwards, also searched for a profounder meaning to the war than that represented by narrow sectional apologetics.

Bushnell's oration honoring the alumni of Yale who fell in the Civil War developed many of the themes found in Lincoln's Gettysburg Address. The speech, "Our Obligations to the Dead," clearly expressed Bushnell's resolute opposition to states' rights, slavery and secession, but without lapsing into the superficial confusion of Northern victory with absolute righteousness. Although we may wish it were otherwise, said Bushnell, history is tragic, and both individuals and nations reach maturity by the appropriation of the tragic features of their histories. The tragedy of the Civil War may nurture a common public sentiment, purchase for Americans a genuine historical consciousness, and yield an American government that is an organic covenant rather than simply a collection of states "kenneled under the Constitution." In short, the Civil War is a baptism of blood capable of redeeming America for her destiny under God—the destiny of exhibiting to the world the nature of democratic freedom. Bushnell's paradigm for interpreting the Civil War was, of course, a Christian doctrine of atonement. Just as reconciliation between God and man was achieved through vicarious sacrifice, so the drawing together of Americans into a common nation under a common destiny is accomplished through the tragic sacrifices of the war dead.

Thoughts like those of Bushnell and Lincoln focus on the Civil War as a possible resource for recognizing the tragic dimensions of our national existence and for critically assessing American goals. Yet, as Robert Penn Warren has seen, certain attitudes resulting from that war have frequently obscured our tragic experiences and weakened our critical powers. As Americans moved through the last three decades of the nineteenth century, their interpretations of national destiny would grow increasingly optimistic; it would seem to them that the blood of the Civil War was a small price to pay for progress and wealth.

6 See William A. Clebsch, "Baptism of Blood: A Study of Christian Contributions to the Interpretation of the Civil War in American History" (Th.D. dissertation, Union Theological Seminary, 1957), pp. 136–89. Cf. the selection by the Georgian Methodist Atticus G. Haygood in H. Shelton Smith, Robert T. Handy, Lefferts A. Loetscher, *American Christianity*, II (New York: Charles Scribner's Sons, 1963), 373–77.

SUGGESTED READING

Clebsch, William A. "Christian Interpretations of the Civil War," *Church History*, XXX, 2 (June, 1961), 212–22.

Filler, Louis. *The Crusade Against Slavery*. New York: Harper & Row, Publishers, Torchbooks, 1960.

Fredrickson, George M., *The Inner Civil War: Northern Intellectuals and the Crisis of the Union*. New York: Harper & Row, Publishers, Torchbooks, 1965.

Jenkins, William Sumner. *Pro-Slavery Thought in the Old South*. Chapel Hill: University of North Carolina Press, 1935.

Korn, Bertram W. *American Jewry and the Civil War*. New York: The World Publishing Company, Meridian Books, 1961.

Pressly, Thomas J. *Americans Interpret Their Civil War*. New York: The Free Press, 1962.

Silver, James W. *Confederate Morale and Church Propaganda*. New York: W. W. Norton & Company, Inc., 1967.

Wolf, William J. *The Religion of Abraham Lincoln*. New York: The Seabury Press, Inc., 1963.

HENRY WARD BEECHER

The Battle Set In Array

Exod. xiv. 15. *"And the Lord said unto Moses,*
Wherefore criest thou unto me?
speak unto the children of Israel,
that they go forward."

Moses was raised up to be the emancipator of three millions of people. At the age of forty, having, through a singular providence, been reared in the midst of luxury, in the proudest, most intelligent, and most civilized court on the globe, with a heart uncorrupt, with a genuine love of his own race and people, he began to act as their emancipator. He boldly slew one of their oppressors. And, seeing dissension among his brethren, he sought to bring them to peace. He was rejected, reproved, and reproached; and finding himself discovered, he fled, and, for the sake of liberty, became a fugitive and a martyr. For forty years, uncomplaining, he dwelt apart with his father-in-law, Jethro, in the wilderness, in the peaceful pursuits of a herdsman. At eighty—the time when most men lay down the burden of life, or have long laid it down—he began his life-work. He was called back by the voice of God; and now, accompanied by his brother, he returned, confronted the king, and, moved by Divine inspiration, demanded, repeatedly, the release of his people. The first demand was sanctioned by a terrific plague; a second, by a second terrible judgment; the third, by a third frightful devastation; the fourth, by a fourth dreadful blow; the fifth, by a fifth desolating, sweeping mischief. A sixth, a seventh, an eighth, and a ninth time, he demanded their release. And when was there ever, on the face of the earth, a man that, once having power, would let it go till life itself went with it? Pharaoh, who is the grand type of oppressors, held on in spite of the Divine command and of the Divine punishment. Then God let fly the last terrific judgment, and smote the first-born of Egypt; and there was wailing in every house of the midnight land. And then, in the midst of the first gush of grief and

From Henry Ward Beecher, *Patriotic Addresses,* ed. J. R. Howard (New York: Fords, Howard & Hulbert, 1889), pp. 269–88. Preached April 14, 1861, at Plymouth Church of Brooklyn.

anguish, the tyrant said, "Let them go! Let them go!" And he did let them go; he shoved them out; and they went pell-mell in great confusion on their way, taking up their line of march, and escaped from Egypt.

But as soon as the first anguish had passed away, Pharaoh came back to his old nature,—just as many men whose hearts are softened and whose lives are made better by affliction, come back to the old way of feeling and living, as soon as they have ceased to experience the first effects of the affliction,—and he followed on after the Israelites. As they lay encamped —these three millions of people, men, women, and children—just apart from the land of bondage, near the fork and head of the Red Sea, with great hills on either side of them, and the sea before them, some one brought panic into the camp, saying, "I see the signs of an advancing host! The air far on the horizon is filled with rising clouds!" Presently, through these clouds, began to be seen glancing spears, mounted horsemen, and a great swelling army. Such, to these lately enslaved, but just emancipated people, was the first token of the coming adversary. Surely, they were unable to cope with the disciplined cohorts of this Egyptian king. They, that were unused to war, that had never been allowed to hold weapons in their hands, that were a poor, despoiled people not only, but that had been subjected to the blighting touch of slavery, had lost courage. They did not dare to be free. And there is no wonder, therefore, that they reproached Moses, and said, "Because there were no graves in Egypt, hast thou taken us away to die in the wilderness?"

I have no doubt that, if Pharaoh's courtiers had heard that, they would have said, "Ah! they do not want to be free. They do not believe in freedom."

"Because there were no graves in Egypt, hast thou taken us away to die in the wilderness? Wherefore hast thou dealt thus with us, to carry us forth out of Egypt?"

Were these people miserable specimens of humanity? They were just what slavery makes everybody to be.

"Is not this the word that we did tell thee in Egypt, saying, Let us alone, that we may serve the Egyptians?"

They would rather have had peace with servitude, than liberty with the manly daring required to obtain it.

"For it had been better for us to serve the Egyptians, than that we should die in the wilderness."

That is just the difference between a man and a slave. They would rather have lived slaves, and eaten their pottage, than to suffer for the sake of liberty; a *man* would rather die in his tracks, than live in ease as a slave.

These, then, were the people that Moses undertook to emancipate, and this was the beginning of Moses's life-work.

"And Moses said unto the people, Fear ye not, stand still"—

That was wrong, but he did not know any better.

"Fear ye not, stand still, and see the salvation of the Lord, which he will show you to-day: for the Egyptians, whom ye have seen to-day, ye shall see them again no more forever. The Lord shall fight for you, and ye shall hold your peace."

He was a little too fast. He was right in respect to the result, but wrong in respect to the means.

"And the Lord said unto Moses, Wherefore criest thou unto me? Speak unto the children of Israel, that they go forward."

They were, after all, to do something and dare something for their liberty. No standing still, but going forward!

"Lift up the rod, and stretch out thine hand over the sea, and divide it; and the children of Israel shall go on dry ground through the midst of the sea."

You recollect the rest. They walked through the sea that lay as a protecting wall on either side of them. They reached the other side. They were divided from the camp of the Egyptians by a fiery cloud, and the Egyptians could not touch them. And what was the fate of the Egyptians? They attempted to follow the children of Israel through the sea, when the waters closed together, and their host was destroyed.

God has raised up many men, at different periods of the world, to bring his cause forth from its various exigencies. Wherever a man is called to defend a truth or a principle, a church or a people, a nation or an age, he may be said to be, like Moses, the leader of God's people. And in every period of the world God has shut up his people, at one time or another, to himself. He has brought their enemies behind them, as he brought the Egyptians behind the children of Israel. He has hedged them in on either hand. He has spread out the unfordable sea before them. He has so beset them with difficulties, when they were attempting to live for right, for duty, and for liberty, that they have been like Israel.

When men stand for a moral principle, their troubles are not a presumption that they are in the wrong. Since the world began, men that have stood for the right have had to stand for it, as Christ stood for the world, suffering for victory.

In the history which belongs peculiarly to us, over and over again the same thing has occurred. In that grand beginning struggle in which Luther figured so prominently, he stood in a doubtful conflict. He was in the minority; he was vehemently pressed with enemies on every side; nine times out of ten during his whole life the odds were against him. And yet he died victorious, and we reap the fruit of his victory.

In one of the consequences of that noble struggle, the assertion in the Netherlands of civil liberty and religious toleration, the same thing took place. Almost the entire globe was against this amphibious republic, until England cared for them; and England cared for them very doubtfully and very imperfectly. All the reigning influences, all the noblest of the commanding men of the Continent, were against them. The conflict was a long and dubious one, in which they suffered extremely, and conquered through their suffering.

In the resulting struggle in England, which was borrowed largely from the Continent,—the Puritan uprising, the Puritan struggle,—the same thing occurred. The Puritans were enveloped in darkness. Their enemies were more than their friends. The issue was exceedingly doubtful. Their very victory began in apparent defeat. For when at last, wearied and discouraged, they could no longer abide the restriction of their liberty in England, they fled away to plant colonies upon these shores. On the sea did they venture, but the ocean, black and wild, before they left it was covered with winter.

In every one of these instances darkness and the flood lay before the champions of truth and rectitude. God in his providence said to them, though they were without apparent instrumentalities, "Go forward! Venture everything! Endure everything! Yield the precious truths never! Live forever by them! Die with *them*, if you die at all."

The whole lesson of the past, then, is that safety and honor come by holding fast to one's principles; by pressing them with courage; by going into darkness and defeat cheerfully for them.

And now our turn has come. Right before us lies the Red Sea of war. It is red indeed. There is blood in it. We have come to the very edge of it, and the Word of God to us to-day is, "Speak unto this people that they go forward!" It is not of our procuring. It is not of our wishing. It is not our hand that has struck the first stroke, nor drawn the first blood. We have prayed against it. We have struggled against it. Ten thousand times we have cried, "Let this cup pass from us!" It has been overruled. We have yielded everything but manhood, and principle, and truth, and honor, and we have heard the voice of God saying, "Yield these never!" And these not being yielded, war has been let loose upon this land.

Now, let us look both ways into this matter, that we may decide what it is our duty to do.

1. There is no fact susceptible of proof in history, if it be not true that this Federal Government was created for the purposes of justice and liberty; and not liberty, either, with the construction that traitorous or befooled heads are attempting to give it,—liberty with a devil in it! We know very well what was the breadth and the clarity of the faith of those men who formed the early constitutions of this nation. If there was any peculiarity in their faith, it was that their notion of liberty was often extravagant. But there was no doubtfulness in their position. And the instruments which accompanied and preceded it, and the opinions of the men that framed it, put this fact beyond all controversy: that the Constitution of the United States was meant to be as we now hold it, as we now defend it, as we have held it, and as we have been defending it. And at length even this is conceded, as I shall have occasion to say further on, by the enemies of liberty in this country. The Vice-President of the so-called Southern Confederacy has stated recently that there was a blunder made in the construction of our Constitution on this very truth of universal liberty, thus admitting the grand fact that that immortal instrument, as held by the North, embodies the views of those who framed it; and that those views are unmistakably in favor of liberty to all.

2. There can be no disputing the fact that, from commercial and political causes, an element of slavery which had a temporary refuge in the beginning in this land swelled to an unforeseen and unexpected power, and for fifty years has held the administrative power of the country in its hands. No man acquainted with our politics hesitates to say, that while the spirit of liberty first suggested our national ideas and fashioned our national institutions, after that work was done the government passed into the hands of the slave-power; and that that power has administered these institutions during the last fifty years for its own purposes, or in a manner that has been antagonistic to the interests of this country.

3. Against this growing usurpation for the last twenty-five years there has been rising up and organizing a proper legal constitutional opposition, wishing not the circumscription or injury of any section in this land, but endeavoring to keep our institutions out of the hands of despotism and on the side of liberty. For twenty-five years there has been a struggle to see to it that those immortal instruments of liberty should not be wrested from their original intent,—that they should be maintained for the objects for which they were created.

4. What are the means that have been employed to maintain our

institutions? Free discussion. That, simply. We have gone before the people, in every proper form. For twenty years of defeat, though of growing influence, we have argued the questions of human rights and human liberty, and the doctrines of the Constitution and of our fathers; and we have maintained that the children should stand where the fathers did. At last the continent has consented. We began as a handful, in the midst of mobs and derision and obloquy. We have gone through the experience of Gethsemane and Calvary. The cause of Christ among his poor has suffered as the Master suffered, again and again and again; and at last the public sentiment of the North has been revolutionized. What! revolutionized away from the doctrines of the fathers? No; back to the doctrines of the fathers. Revolutionized against our institutions? No; in favor of our institutions. We have taken simply the old American principles. That is the history very simply stated. The children have gone back to the old landmarks. We stand for the doctrines and instruments that the fathers gave us.

5. The vast majority of this nation are now on the side of our American institutions, according to their original intent. We ask only this: that our government may be what it was made to be,—an instrument of justice and liberty. We ask no advantages, no new prerogatives, no privileges whatsoever. We merely say, "Let there be no intestine revolution in our institutions, but let them stand as they were made, and for the purposes for which they were created." Is there anything unreasonable, anything wrong in that? Is it wrong to reason? Is it wrong to discuss? Is it wrong to go before a free people with their own business, and, in the field, in the caucus, in the assembly, in all deliberative bodies, to argue fairly, and express the result by the American means,—the omnipotence of the vote? Is that wrong? It is what we have been doing for the last few years. By the prescribed methods of the Constitution, and in the spirit of liberty which it embodied and evoked, we have done our proper work. Before God we cleanse our hands of all imputation of designing injustice or of seeking wrong. We have not sought any one's damage. We have aimed at no invidious restrictions for any. We have simply said, "God, through our fathers, committed to us certain institutions, and we will maintain them to the end of our lives, and to the end of time."

6. Seven States, however, in a manner revolutionary not only of government, but in violation of the rights and customs of their own people, have disowned their country and made war upon it! There has been a spirit of patriotism in the North; but never, within my memory, in the South. I never heard a man from the South speak of himself as an American. Men from the South always speak of themselves as Southerners. When I was abroad, I never spoke of myself as a Northerner, but always as a citizen of the United States. I love our country; and it is a love of the

country, and not a love of the North alone, that pervades the people of the North. There has never been witnessed such patience, such self-denial, such magnanimity, such true patriotism, under such circumstances, as that which has been manifested in the North. And in the South the feeling has been sectional, local. The people there have been proud, not that they belong to the nation, but that they were born where the sun burns. They are hot, narrow, and boastful,—for out of China there is not so much conceit as exists among them. They have been devoid of that large spirit which takes in the race, and the nation, and its institutions, and its history, and that which its history prophesies,—the prerogative of carrying the banner of liberty to the Pacific from the Atlantic.

Now, these States, in a spirit entirely in agreement with their past developments, have revolutionized and disowned the United States of America, and set up a so-called government of their own. Shall we, now, go forward under these circumstances?

For the first time in the history of this nation there is a deliberate and extensive preparation for war, and this country has received the deadly thrust of bullet and bayonet from the hands of her own children. If we could have prevented it, this should not have taken place. But it is a fact! It hath happened! The question is no longer a question of choice. The war is brought to us. Shall we retreat, or shall we accept the hard conditions on which we are to maintain the grounds of our fathers? Hearing the voice of God in his providence saying, "Go forward!" shall we go?

I go with those that go furthest in describing the wretchedness and wickedness and monstrosity of war. The only point on which I should probably differ from any is this: that while war is an evil so presented to our senses that we measure and estimate it, there are other evils just as great, and much more terrible, whose deadly mischiefs have no power upon the senses. I hold that it is ten thousand times better to have war than to have slavery. I hold that to be corrupted silently by giving up manhood, by degenerating, by becoming craven, by yielding one right after another, is infinitely worse than war. Why, war is resurrection in comparison with the state to which we should be brought by such a course. And although war is a terrible evil, there are other evils that are more terrible. In our own peculiar case, though I would say nothing to garnish it, nothing to palliate it, nothing to alleviate it, nothing to make you more willing to have it, nothing to remove the just abhorrence which every man and patriot should have for it, yet I would say that, in the particular condition into which we have been brought, it will not be an unmixed evil. Eighty years of unexampled prosperity have gone far toward making us a people that judge of moral questions by their relation to our convenience and ease. We are in great danger of becoming a people that shall measure by earthly rules,—by the lowest standard of a commercial expediency. We have never suffered for our own principles. And now if it please God to do that which daily we pray that he may avert,—if it please God to wrap this nation in war,—one result will follow: we shall be called to suffer for our faith. We shall be called to the heroism of doing and daring, and bearing and suffering, for the things which we believe to be vital to the salvation of this people.

On what conditions, then, may we retreat from this war, and on what conditions may we have peace?

1. We may do it on condition that two-thirds of this nation shall implicitly yield up to the dictation of one-third. You can have peace on that ground. Italy could have had peace at the hands of Francis II. They had nothing to do but to say to that tyrant, "Here is my neck, put your foot on it," to obtain peace. The people of Hungary may have peace, if they will only say to him of Vienna, "Reign over us as you please; our lives are in your hands." There is never any trouble in having peace, if men will yield themselves to the control of those that have no business to control them. Two-thirds of this nation unquestionably stand on the side of the original articles of our Constitution and in the service of liberty, and one-third deny and reject them. Now if the two-thirds will give up to the one-third, we can have peace—for a little while.

2. We can have peace if we will legalize and establish the right of any discontented community to rebel, and to set up intestine governments within the government of the United States. Yield that principle, demoralize government, and you can have peace—for a little while. You cannot yield that principle and not demoralize government. And if it is right for seven States on the Gulf to secede, it is the right of seven States on the Lakes. If it is the right of seven States on the Lakes, it is the right of five or three States on the Ohio River. If it is the right of a number of States, it is the right of one State. And if it is the right of any State, there is not a State, a half of a State, a county, or a town, that has not the same right. It is the right of disintegration. It is a right that aims at the destruction of the attraction of governmental cohesion. It is a right that invalidates all power in government. And if you will grant this right; if you will consent to have this government broken up; if you are willing that our country should degenerate to the condition of wrangling and rival States,—you can have peace—for a little while.

3. We can have peace if we will agree fundamentally to change our Constitution, and, instead of maintaining a charter of universal freedom, to write it out as a deliberate charter of oppression.

Mr. Stephens, the Vice-President of the so-called Confederate States, declared, in a formal speech, that our Constitution was framed on a fundamental mistake, inasmuch as it took it for granted that men were born for freedom and equality. They have expunged the doctrine of universal liberty, and put in its place the doctrine of liberty for the strong and servitude for the weak. It is said that the African race, by reason of their nationality and savagism, are not fit for liberty, and that the white race, by reason of their nationality and civilization, are fit to govern them. It is merely a plea that weak persons are not fit to take care of themselves, and that strong persons are fit to take care of them; and it is a plea that is just as applicable to any other peoples as to the Anglo-Saxons and the Africans. It is simply a doctrine that might makes right. It may be stated in this form: "You are weak and I am strong, and I am therefore your lawful master." If it is good for the Africans and the Anglo-Saxons, it is good for all other races. And if it is good in reference to races, it is good in reference to individuals. Therefore there is not a workman, there is not a poor man, there is not a man that is low in station, at the North, who is not interested in this matter, who is not touched in his rights, and who is not insulted by the spirit that is latent in the new Constitution of the so-called Confederate States. It holds that there is appointed of God a governing class and a class to be governed,—a class that are born governors because they are strong and smart and well-to-do, and a class that are born servants because they are poor and weak and unable to take care of themselves. Now take that glorious, flaming sentence in the Declaration of Independence, which asserts the right of every man to life, liberty, and the pursuit of happiness, and which pronounces that right to be alike inalienable to all,—take that and strike it out, and put in its place this infernal article of the new Constitution of the Southern States, and you can have peace—for a little while. There is no trouble about having peace. What an unreasonable people we are! If we will only pay enough for peace we can have it.

This diabolical principle is also deliberately held and advocated by the churches of the South. The Southern churches are all sound on the question of the Bible, and infidel on the question of its contents! They believe that this is God's Book; they believe that this Book is the world's charter; and they believe that it teaches the religion of servitude. Every sermon that I have received within the last year from the South has been a various echo of this one atrocious idea, held in common with all the despotic preachers of Europe. Any man that has read Robert South's sermons, has read over and over again all the arguments contained in the raw, jejune productions of Southern clerical advocates for oppression. In all the discussions between Milton and Salmasius, and in all the writings of Roman priests that have sought to bolster up sacerdotal rule, these arguments have been put forth far more ably than our unscholarly Southerners have put them forth. But this is the ground which has been taken by the Christian Church of the South: that in Christ Jesus all men are not created equal,—that white masters are, but that black servants are not!

And that is not all. Not only is this new government framed on this ground, and not only have all the churches of the South taken this ground, so that it may be said of the Southern Confederacy as it was said of one of the old revolted tribes, "They have a priest to their house," but there has just now been raised up in the North a club of the same kind,—a society for the promotion of *national unity*, on the basis of a change of our national instruments of government. This society proposes to restore peace to this country. And how? Exactly as you restore uniformity of color in a room where some things are red, some blue, and some yellow,—by blowing the light out so that in darkness all things will be of the same color! We are very much divided in this land, one part believing in liberty, and the other believing in servitude; and it is proposed to bring these two parts together in unity, by destroying the distinction between them. What is this society's own statement, as contained in the letter which they have put forth with their articles? They make this formal assertion: that that portion of our original Declaration of Independence which makes all men free and equal has been misinterpreted, or is false. They endeavor to say it softly, but it is a thing that cannot be said softly. To breathe it, to whisper it, makes it louder than thunder!

Indeed, it is true that men are not physiologically equal. No man ever believed that they were. They do not weigh alike. They differ in respect to bone and tissue. They are not the same as regards mental caliber. Their dynamic forces are different. They are not capable of exerting the same amount of political influence. In the nations of Europe it was held that the royal head, *jure Divino*, had privileges which the nobles had not; that there belonged to the nobles prerogatives which did not belong to the commonalty; and that the political rights of the great common people were to be graduated according to their status in society. But our fathers said, God gives the same political rights to all alike. The people are king, and the people are nobles. They are equal in this: that they all stand before the same law of justice, and that justice is to be the same to one as to another. The richest and the poorest, the wisest and the most ignorant, the highest and the lowest, are on an equality before the law. The Declaration of Independence taught simply that every man born into life was born with such dignities, with such a nature conferred upon him, that, as a child of God, he has a right to confront government and legislature and laws, and say, "I demand, in common with every other man, equal justice, equal protection, to life, to liberty, and in the pursuit of happiness." And this is what our society in the North for the promotion of national unity undertake, in their first article, to say is a lie!

Now, you can have your American eagle as you want it. If, with the South, you will strike out his eyes, then you shall stand well with Mr. Davis and Mr. Stephens of the Confederate States; if, with the Christians of the South, you will pluck off his wings, you shall stand well with the

Southern churches; and if, with the new peace-makers that have risen up in the North, you will pull out his tailfeathers, you shall stand well with the society for the promotion of national unity! But when you have stricken out his eyes so that he can no longer see, when you have plucked off his wings so that he can no longer fly, and when you have pulled out his guiding tail-feathers so that he can no longer steer himself, but rolls in the dirt a mere buzzard, then will he be worth preserving? Such an eagle it is that they mean to depict upon the banner of America!

Now if any man is fierce for peace, and is willing to pay the price demanded for it, he can have it. On those conditions you can have peace as long as the Jews did. For three guilty days they were rid of the Saviour, and then he rose from the grave, with eternal power on his head, and beyond all touch of weakness or death, then ascended on high to the Source of eternal power, there to live, and to live forever!

4. We must accordingly, if we go on to purchase peace on these terms, become partners in slavery, and consent, for the sake of peace, to ratify this gigantic evil. We cannot wink at it. We are called to bear overt witness either for or against it. Every State in this Union, according to the new Constitution, must be open to slavery. It is the design of not a few men at the North to make this the issue at the next election: whether we shall not reconstruct this government according to the Constitution of the Confederate States, one feature of which is that slavery shall have liberty to go wherever it pleases,—that slavery shall have the right of incursion to any part of this country. If you consent to such a reconstruction as is proposed, you must open every one of your States to the incoming of slavery. Not only that, but every territory on this continent is to be opened to slavery. We are called to take the executive lancet, and the virus of slavery, and lift up the arm of this virgin continent and inoculate it with this terrific poison. If you will do these things, you are to be permitted to escape war.

5. Next in order must of course be silence. When we have gone so far, we shall no longer have any right of discussion, of debate, of criticism, —we shall no longer have any right of *agitation,* as it is called.

On these conditions we may have peace. If we reject these conditions we are to have separation, demoralization of government, and war.

Now are you prepared to take peace on these conditions? You will not get it on any other conditions. If you have peace, you are to stigmatize the whole history of the past; you are to yield your religious convictions; you are to give over the government into the hands of factious revolutionists; you are to suppress every manly sentiment, and every sympathy for the oppressed. Will you take peace on such a ground as that? So far as I myself am concerned, I utterly abhor peace on any such grounds. Give me war redder than blood, and fiercer than fire, if this terrific infliction is necessary that I may maintain my faith of God in human liberty, my faith of the fathers in the instruments of liberty, my faith in this land as the appointed abode and chosen refuge of liberty for all the earth! War is terrible, but that abyss of ignominy is yet more terrible!

What, then, if we will go forward in the providence of God, and maintain our integrity, are the steps that are before us?

1. Instead of yielding our convictions, it is time to cleanse them, to deepen them, to give them more power, to make them more earnest and more religious. There is no reason, now, why we should compromise. There is nothing to be gained by compromising. And it is time that parents should talk on the great doctrine of human rights in the family, and indoctrinate their children with an abhorrence for slavery, and a love for liberty. It is time for schools to have their scholars instructed in these matters. It is time for every church to make its pews flame and glow with enthusiasm for freedom, and with hatred for oppression. While the air of the South is full of pestilent doctrines of slavery, accursed be our communities if we will not be as zealous and enthusiastic for liberty as they are against it! If their air is filled with the storm and madness of oppression, let ours be full of the sweet peace and love of liberty!

2. We must draw the lines. A great many men have been on both sides. A great many men have been thrown backward and forward, like a shuttle, from one side to the other. It is now time for every man to choose one side or the other. We want no shufflers; we want no craven cowards; we want *men*; we want every man to stand forth, and say, "I am for liberty, and the Constitution, and the country, as our fathers gave them to us," or else, "I am against them."

Thousands, thank God, of great men have spoken to us; but I think that the war-voice of Sumter has done more to bring men together, and to produce unity of feeling among them on this subject, than the most eloquent-tongued orator.

We must say in this matter, my friends, as Christ said, "He that is not for us is against us." I will have no commerce, I will not cross palms with a man that disowns liberty in such a struggle as is before us! I will not give him shelter or house-room—except as a convicted sinner; then I will take him, as the prodigal was taken, in his rags and nakedness! But so long as he stands up with impudent face against the things that are dearest to God's heart, and dearest to the instincts of this people, I shall treat him as what he is,—a *traitor*! There ought to be but one feeling in the North, and that ought to be a feeling for liberty, which should sweep through the land like a mighty wind.

3. We must not stop to measure costs,—especially the costs of going

forward,—on any basis so mean and narrow as that of pecuniary prosperity. We must put our honor and religion into this struggle. God is
helping you; for, no matter how much you deplore the state of things, you
cannot help yourselves. You may take counsel with your Till and Safe
and Bank, you may look at your accounts on both sides, but your talking
and looking will make no difference with your affairs. The time is past in
which these things could be of any avail. This matter must now be settled.
You must have a part in settling it. The question is whether that shall be
a manly or an ignoble part!

There are many reasons which make a good and thorough battle
necessary. The Southern men are infatuated. They will not have peace.
They are in arms. They have fired upon the American flag! That glorious
banner has been borne through every climate, all over the globe, and for
fifty years not a land or people has been found to scorn it, or dishonor it.
At home, among the degenerate people of our own land, among Southern
citizens, for the first time, has this glorious national flag been abased, and
trampled to the ground! It is for our sons reverently to lift it, and to bear
it full high again, to victory and national supremacy! Our arms, in this
peculiar exigency, can lay the foundation of future union, in mutual
respect. The South firmly believes that *cowardice* is the universal attribute of Northern men! Until they are most thoroughly convinced to the
contrary, they will never cease arrogancy and aggression. But if now it
please God to crown our arms with victory, we shall have gone far toward
impressing Southern men with salutary respect. Good soldiers, brave men,
hard fighting, will do more toward quiet than all the compromises and
empty, wagging tongues in the world. Our reluctance to break peace, our
unwillingness to shed blood, our patience, have all been misinterpreted.
The more we have been generous and forbearing, the more thoroughly
were they sure that it was because we dared not fight!

With the North is the strength, the population, the courage. There
is not elsewhere on this continent that breadth of courage—the courage of
a man in distinction from the courage of a brute beast—which there is in
the free States of the North. It was General Scott who said that the New
Englanders were the hardest to get into a fight, and the most terrible to
meet in a conflict, of any men on the globe.

We have no braggart courage; we have no courage that rushes into
an affray for the love of fighting. We have that courage which comes from
calm intelligence. We have that courage which comes from broad moral
sentiment. We have no anger, but we have indignation. We have no irri-
table passion, but we have fixed will. We regard war and contest as terrible evils; but when, detesting them as we do, we are roused to enter into
them, our courage will be of the measure of our detestation. You may be
sure that the cause which can stir up the feelings of the North sufficiently

to bring them into such a conflict, will develop in them a courage that will be terrific to the men who have to meet it. I could wish no worse punishment to those that decry the courage of the North, than that they shall have to meet her when she is once brought out and fairly in the field.

4. We must aim at a peace built on foundations so solid, of God's immutable truth, that nothing can reach to unsettle it. Let this conflict beween liberty and slavery never come up again. Better have it thoroughly settled, though it take a score of years to settle it, than to have an intermittent fever for the next century, breaking out at every five or ten years. It is bad, you say. That has nothing to do with the point. Your house is on fire, and the question is, What will you do? You are in the struggle, and the question is, Will you go through it in the spirit of your ancestors, in the spirit of Christians and patriots, in the spirit that belongs to the age of the world in which you live, and settle it so that it shall not be in the power of mischief to unsettle it? Or will you dally? Will you delay? I know which you will do. *This question is now going forward* to a settlement.

5.   Let not our feelings be vengeful nor savage. We can go into this conflict with a spirit just as truly Christian as any that ever inspired us in the performance of a Christian duty. Indignation is very different from anger; conscience from revenge. Let the spirit of fury be far from us; but a spirit of earnestness, of willingness to do, to suffer, and to die, if need be, for our land and our principles,—that may be a religious spirit. We may consecrate it with prayer.

All through the struggle of the Revolution, men there were that preached on the Sabbath, and when not preaching went from tent to tent and performed kind offices to those that were sick or wounded, cheered those that were in despondency, encouraged those whose trials were severe, and led or accompanied their brethren to those conflicts which achieved liberty.

I believe that the old spirit will be found yet in the Church; and that in that patriotism which dares to do as well as teach, laymen and officers and pastors will be found no whit behind the Revolutionary day.

It is trying to live in suspense, to be in the tormenting whirl of rumor, now to see the banner up, and now to see it trailing in the dust. Early yesterday things seemed inauspicious. Toward evening all appeared calm and fair. To-day disastrous and depressing rumors were current. This evening I came hither sad from the tidings that that stronghold which seemed to guard the precious name and lasting fame of the noble and gallant Anderson had been given up; but since I came into this desk I have received a dispatch from one of our most illustrious citizens, saying that Sumter is reinforced, and that Moultrie is the fort that has been destroyed. But what if the rising sun to-morrow should reverse the message? What if the tidings that greet you in the morning should be but the echo of the old tidings of disaster? You live in hours in which you are to suffer suspense. Now lifted up, you will be prematurely cheering, and now cast down, you will be prematurely desponding. Look forward, then, past the individual steps, the various vicissitudes of experience, to the glorious end that is coming! Look beyond the present to that assured victory which awaits us in the future.

Young men, you will live to see more auspicious days. Later sent, delayed in your voyage into life, you will see the bright consummation, in part at least, of that victory of this land, by which, with mortal throes, it shall cast out from itself all morbific influences, and cleanse itself from slavery. And you that are in middle life shall see the ultimate triumph advancing beyond anything that you have yet known. The scepter shall not depart. The government shall not be shaken from its foundations.

Let no man, then, in this time of peril, fail to associate himself with that cause which is to be so entirely glorious. Let not your children, as they carry you to your burial, be ashamed to write upon your tombstone the truth of your history. Let every man that lives and owns himself an American, take the side of true American principles;—liberty for one, and liberty for all; liberty now, and liberty forever; liberty as the foundation of government, and liberty as the basis of union; liberty as against revolution, liberty, against anarchy, and liberty, against slavery; liberty here, and liberty everywhere, the world through!

When the trumpet of God has sounded, and that grand procession is forming; as Italy has risen, and is wheeling into the ranks; as Hungary, though mute, is beginning to beat time, and make ready for the march; as Poland, having long slept, has dreamt of liberty again, and is waking; as the thirty million serfs are hearing the roll of the drum, and are going forward toward citizenship,—let it not be your miserable fate, nor mine, to live in a nation that shall be seen reeling and staggering and wallowing in the orgies of despotism! We, too, have a right to march in this grand procession of liberty. By the memory of the fathers; by the sufferings of the Puritan ancestry; by the teaching of our national history; by our faith and hope of religion; by every line of the Declaration of Independence, and every article of our Constitution; by what we are and what our progenitors were,—we have a right to walk foremost in this procession of nations toward the bright future.

BENJAMIN M. PALMER

National Responsibility
Before God

2d. Chronicles, 6th Chapter, 34th, 35th verses:
> *"If thy people go out to war against*
> *their enemies by the way that thou*
> *shalt send them, and they pray unto*
> *thee toward this city which thou hast*
> *chosen, and the house which I have*
> *built for thy name; then hear thou*
> *from the heavens their prayer and*
> *their supplication, and maintain*
> *their cause."*

This day is one of surpassing solemnity. In the gravest period of our history, amidst the perils which attend the dismemberment of a great nation and the reconstruction of a new government, we are confronted with another more instant and appalling. Our late Confederates, denying us the right of self-government, have appealed to the sword and threaten to extinguish this right in our blood. Eleven tribes sought to go forth in peace from the house of political bondage: but the heart of our modern Pharaoh is hardened, that he will not let Israel go. In their distress, with the untried sea before and the chariots of Egypt behind, ten millions of people stretch forth their hands before Jehovah's throne, imploring him to "stir up his strength before Ephraim and Benjamin and Manasseh, and come and save them." It was a memorable day when the Hebrew tribes, having crossed the Jordan, stood, the one-half of them upon Mount Ebal and the other half upon Mount Gerizim, and pronounced the solemn Amen to the curses and blessings of the divine law as proclaimed by the Levites. Not less grand and awful is this scene to-day, when an infant nation strikes its covenant with the God of Heaven. This vast assembly is not simply a convention of individuals engaged in acts of personal wor-

From Benjamin M. Palmer, *National Responsibility Before God, A Discourse Delivered on the Day of Fasting, Humiliation and Prayer*, June 13, 1861 (New Orleans: Price-Current Steam Book & Job Printing Office, 1861).

ship. It is not even the Church holding communion through priestly rites. But, as an integral part of this young nation and in obedience to the call of our civil head, we are met to recognize the God of nations. Confessing the sins of our fathers with our own, and imploring the divine guidance through all our fortunes, the people of these Confederate States proclaim this day, "the Lord our God will we serve, and his voice will we obey." It is this sacramental feature of our worship which lends to it such dreadful solemnity. At the moment when we are crystalizing into a nation, at the very opening of our separate career, we bend the knee together before God—appealing to his justice in the adjudication of our cause, and submitting our destiny to his supreme arbitration. The bonds of this covenant, which we seal this day to the Lord, are entered upon the register in which the Recording Angel writes up the deeds of time, before the Eternal throne.

The question then arises at the threshold of our proceedings, what principles underlie and support this act of public and national homage? Our external actions are a mockery, except as they are concrete expressions of some secret and vital truth. As the body is but the organ of the soul, and each gesture but a symbol of the power which reigns within— so in all intelligent action some dominant idea resides, the soul by which it is quickened and informed. The worship now offered in this sanctuary will be found to turn upon the great truth, that the nation is in a clear sense a sort of *person* before God—girded with responsibilities which draw it within his comprehensive government. We must renounce the shallow nominalism which would make such a word as "nation" a dead abstraction, signifying only the aggregation of individuals. It is an incorporated society, and possesses a unity of life resembling the individuality of a single being. It can deliberate and concur in common conclusions which are carried out in a joint action, analogous to the powers of thought and will in a single mind. It stands in definite moral relations, out of which spring such duties and obligations that we can properly speak of the law of nations in which they are expounded, and by which the intercourse with every similar society is regulated. In these respects a nation becomes a *person* capable of executing a trust, and conscious both of rights and obligations. Each has its own precisely defined character, fulfils its appointed mission, is developed through a providential training, and is held to a strict providential reckoning. The importance of this principle is sufficiently apparent. It not only gives significance to these religious solemnities; but it suggests the duty of this new-born nation to consider the part assigned it in the great drama of History, and its dependence upon the blessing of Him who "ruleth in the kingdom of men and giveth it to whomsoever he will." I shall, therefore, be justified in pausing for a moment upon its illustration.

If we ascend the stream of history to its source, we find in Noah's prophetic utterances to his three sons, the fortunes of mankind presented in perfect outline. The benediction upon Shem marked his descendants out for a destiny predominantly religious; and through all time, in ancient days and in modern, both in a true direction and in a false, and as seen in the two representative nations of the Shemitic stock, history attests the fulfilment of this mission. Through the entire interval between Abraham and Christ, the Hebrews were appointed to testify for the unity of God against the idolatry of mankind; and all Hebrew history turns upon the execution of this trust as its pivot. Since the Christian era, the Arabians, belonging to the same group, moving in a false direction, but yielding a blind obedience to what may be termed their Shemitish instinct, gave birth to the Mohammedan imposture, a religion without a mystery and without a sacrifice, which, transforming a religious enthusiasm into martial fanaticism, has tinged the whole current of their history. Still further to mark the destiny of this group, the only members of it, which have left no permanent trace upon the history of mankind, were those upon the banks of the Euphrates, who were seduced by a fertile agriculture and a flourishing commerce from their religious trust, and lapsed into the idolatry and worldliness of the other races.

In like manner, enlargement was promised to Japhet; and through all the past, the hardy and aggressive families of this stock have spread over the larger portion of the earth's surface, fulfiling their mission as the organ of human civilization. In ancient and in modern times—through the Greeks and Romans once, through the English, French and Germans now—the world has been indebted to Japhet for its intellectual culture, for the discoveries of science, for the inventions of art, for the solution of all the great problems of State policy and public law. It would not be difficult to show how this general work of civilizing the world has been providentially subdivided between the families of this great stock—that as of old Greece was supremely devoted to intellectual culture, and Rome to political philosophy, so in later times the same partition of duties has practically been made between the great nations of Europe. Still further to show the controlling power of God over nations, wild and nomadic tribes have been held in reserve, bursting, at appointed times, the bounds of their enclosure and recruiting the wasted energies of a decaying civilization.

Upon Ham was pronounced the doom of perpetual servitude—proclaimed with double emphasis, as it is twice repeated that he shall be the servant of Japhet and the servant of Shem. Accordingly, history records not a single example of any member of this group lifting itself, by any process of self-development, above the savage condition. From first to last, their mental and moral characteristics, together with the guidance of Providence, have marked them for servitude; while their comparative advance in civilization and their participation in the blessings of salvation, have ever been suspended upon this decreed connexion with Japhet and with Shem.

These facts are beyond impeachment; and nothing can be more instructive than to see the outspreading landscape of all history embraced thus within the camera of Noah's brief prochecy. In the largest classification of the human race, we see the hand of God upon nations—not only "appointing the bounds of their habitations," but impressing upon each the type of character that fits it for its mission. If from this wide generalization we turn attention to particular States, we have the same evidence of their separateness and individuality. Thus, from the earliest moment that Egypt was cradled amidst the bulrushes of her own sacred Nile, she exhibits a character throughout and intensely Egyptian; a character as clearly distinct from the Hebrew and the Persian, as these in their turn differ from the Roman and the Greek. And the spaces which all these respectively fill upon the chart of universal history are as exclusively their own, as the places which they occupy upon the surface of the globe. It is noteworthy in this connection that as nations have their assigned missions, so they are preserved in being till their work is done; after which they sink into decrepitude, or are expunged from the roll of the living. Thus Greece was perpetuated until she had carried the arts of sculpture and painting, of poetry, eloquence and song, to a perfection which has never been surpassed; and when she could do no more in philosophy and science, she was trodden in the dust beneath the iron-heeled legions of Rome. When Rome, too, had built up an empire as wide as the world, and could do no more by her systems of jurisprudence and schemes of state-craft, she slid into a military despotism—and the world having no need of experiments in that direction, her mighty fabric gave way under the pressure of barbarian hordes, the present congress of European nations springing ultimately from the political chaos which was thereby induced. So it has been through all the past; so it will continue to be through all the future; and the grand conclusion is but the lesson which is impressed upon us to-day. This lesson is, that nations are in a weighty sense *persons* before God, with individual characters mysteriously impressed upon the parent stock, and fully developed through a providential training; that they work out their historic missions which are unequivocally assigned by a higher power; that girt about with grave responsibilities, they are held to account for their fidelity to their trusts: and that their solemn duty is to recognize in every stage of their career that Being by whose guidance and blessing they are conducted to their destinies. In the acknowledgment of this truth we to-day bow the knee before the God of Heaven, whom we have chosen to serve as the God of this nation forever.

Parallel with this truth of the nation's personal responsibility, is another which determines the form of our worship by humiliation and fasting as well as by prayer. I refer to the continuity of a nation's life through a long succession of individuals that die. While the elements which compose the nation are continually passing away, the nation remains entire without disintegration. As the body of a living man is continually wasting and as continually repaired, through the ceaseless flux of its particles; so in the state "one generation goeth and another generation cometh," but the nation preserves its identity through the whole succession. In consequence of this it is that, in God's government over them, the sins of a nation are often punished in generations long posterior to that which is immediately guilty. The measure of criminality being at last filled up by these, the accumulated chastisement descends. This principle our Lord declares to the Jews of his day: that they "filled up the measure of their fathers"; that "upon them would come all the righteous blood shed upon the earth, from the blood of righteous Abel unto the blood of Zacharias, the son of Barachias, whom they slew between the temple and the altar; verily I say unto you, all these things shall come upon this generation." It is in virtue of this principle that we undertake to confess the sins of our fathers as well as our own; which, upon any other ground, would be a mockery and a sham. As nations in their corporate form cannot be subject to the retributions of the final judgment, the divine government must be enforced alone by temporal sanctions; and the probation which nations enjoy passes along the current of national life through succeeding generations, bringing at last the avenging punishment upon one generation out of many which are equally implicated. If this should seem severe, it should be remembered that it is unavoidable under a state of discipline and probation; and it has the practical comfort, that repenting posterity may often, by humility and faith, turn aside the descending judgment, and secure still the favor and protection of Heaven, forfeited by their fathers.

Under this exposition of principles which underlie our worship, let us, my brethren, like Daniel of old, "confess our sins and the sins of our people, and present our supplication before the Lord our God, in this his holy mountain." There is obviously a distinction between the sins committed really by individuals, but which from their universality we may in a sense bewail as national, and those sins which are referrable to the nation itself in its organized and corporate form. For example, intemperance is painfully prevalent among all classes of our people; yet it is not properly chargeable upon the nation as an organic whole, except so far as the government by its unwise or insufficient legislation may be responsible for the same. So again, "because of swearing the land mourneth," that profane use of God's holy name which dishonors the lips of multitudes; and which one of England's classic writers describes as "the superfluity of naughtiness," "a sort of peppercorn rent" which men gratuitously pay to the Devil. Yet in a strict sense it is the sin of individuals who presumptuously say "our lips are our own, who is Lord over us!" In like manner, Sabbath-breaking is affirmed in Scripture to be one of those offences which peculiarly draw down upon a people the righteous resentment of God. Yet the nation is not held answerable for it, except as rulers in their official acts, or the law by its postal and other arrangements, may wantonly tread it in the dust. However proper it might be to comment upon these forms of transgression and to bewail them upon this day of public fasting, as the common sins of our people, I prefer for special reasons to restrict your attention to that class of sins which are properly national, as being committed by the people in their public association and in their corporate existence.

1. WE BEWAIL THEN, IN THE FIRST PLACE, THE FATAL ERROR OF OUR FATHERS IN NOT MAKING A CLEAR NATIONAL RECOGNITION OF GOD AT THE OUTSET OF THE NATION'S CAREER. The record of the divine dealings with America was, from the beginning, singularly a religious record. It was certainly remarkable that this Western Continent should have been locked up between two oceans from the knowledge of mankind, through fifteen centuries of the Christian era: and quite as remarkable that its discovery should be ordered at a time when an asylum was required for the victims of religious persecution in the old world. It is certainly true that religious zeal operated as a constraining motive with those who first took possession of these shores. In all the proclamations and grants of Spain and Portugal, the planting of the cross upon these heathen and savage coasts was urged as the leading motive for conquest and colonization—and the Continent was formally taken possession of by the first discoverers as distinctly in the name of Almighty God, as by the authority of their Christian Majesties, Ferdinand and Isabella. It is familiar even to our children that the hardships of the first settlement in these United States were cheerfully endured through the faith and patience of those who simply sought "amidst the depths of the desert gloom" "freedom to worship God." Yet will it be credited, when this most religious people, after the lapse of a century and a half, undertook to establish an independent government, there was a total ignoring of the divine claims and of all allegiance to the divine supremacy? It is true that in the eloquent paper which recited their grievances before the world, and proclaimed the Colonies independent of the British throne, the signers of the Declaration appealed to the Divine Omniscience "for the rectitude of their intentions," and pledged their faith to each other "with a firm reliance on the protection of divine Providence." It is therefore the more remarkable that, eleven

years after, in that great instrument by which the several States were linked together in a common nationality, and which was at once the public charter and the paramount law of the land, not a word is found from which one could possibly infer that such a being as God ever existed. The omission was a fearful one; and it is not surprising that He who proclaims his jealousy of his own glory, should let fall the blow which has shattered *that* nation. Probable reasons may be suggested for its explanation. It certainly was not due to the irreligiousness of the masses, for they were predominantly christian. But the public leaders of the time were largely tinctured with the free-thinking and infidel spirit which swept like a pestilence over Europe in the seventeenth and eighteenth centuries, and which brought forth at last its bitter fruit in the horrors of the French Revolution. It may have been due likewise to the jealousy entertained of any union between Church and State, at a time when the novel, grand and successful experiment was first tried of an entire separation between the two. But to whatever causes we refer it, the certain fact is that the American nation stood up before the world a helpless orphan, and entered upon its career without a God. Through almost a century of unparalleled prosperity, this error has been but partially retrieved; as the religious spirit of the people has silently compelled the appointment by executive authority, of days of public thanksgiving and prayer—yet to this day, in the great national act of incorporation there is no bond which connects the old American nation with the Providence and Government of Jehovah.

Thanks be unto God, my brethren, for the grace given our own Confederacy, in receding from this perilous atheism! When my eye first rested upon the Constitution adopted by the Confederate Congress, and I read in the first lines of our organic and fundamental law a clear, solemn, official recognition of Almighty God, my heart swelled with unutterable emotions of gratitude and joy. It was the return of the prodigal to the bosom of his father, of the poor exile who has long pined in some distant and bleak Siberia after the associations of his childhood's home. At length, the nation has a God: Alleluia! "the Lord reigneth let the earth rejoice." And now in the beautiful proclamation of our President our whole people through eleven States are called to ratify the covenant, and to set up the memorial stone thereof. It is indeed no ordinary State Paper, filled with cold and starched commonplaces, which by their icy formality so often freeze up the very piety they seem to invoke. But a religious unction pervades every clause and line; and the child of God can recognize the dialect which his ear loves to hear. It summons us to "recognize our dependence upon God," to "humble ourselves under the dispensations of divine providence," to "acknowledge his goodness" and "supplicate his merciful protection." Under the conviction that "none but a righteous cause can gain the divine favor," it "implores the Lord of

Hosts to guide and direct our policy in the paths of right, duty, justice and mercy; to unite our hearts and our efforts for the defence of our dearest rights; to strengthen our weakness, crown our arms with success, and enable us to secure a speedy, just and honorable peace," "to inspire us with a proper spirit and temper of heart and mind to bear our evils, to bless us with his favor and protection, and to bestow his gracious benediction upon our government and country." This is truly a Christian patriot's prayer. It breathes no malignant revenge; but it calls the nation to nestle beneath the wings of Almighty power and love. Upon this central truth—that "God is and that He is the rewarder of them that diligently seek him"—all of us can stand. Hebrew or Christian, Protestant or Catholic—all can subscribe this ultimate truth: and here we all meet to-day to say that He is our trust in whom nations as well as men "live and move and have their being." This day is therefore one of infinite solemnity; it is our nation's first Sabbath, when it meets to confess its God. If it shall hold fast to this testimony, it will have an immortal career: and had I a voice loud as seven thunders, I would proclaim from the Potomac to the Rio Grande, that a nation drives against the rocks which denies its responsibility before the God of Heaven. I speak this not as if it were my trade: but as a man, and in full view of all that constitutes true manhood, under the pressure and dictation of the highest philosophy, I affirm that to know and fear God is the perfection of wisdom. He is most a man, who brings up all parts of his nature with an equal culture; and to cleave sacrilegiously between these parts and to throw away those religious longings which can be satisfied only in God, is to forego our highest prerogative and to approximate the level of senseless apes chattering upon the trees of the forest. May God keep this nation under the power of those religious convictions, which to-day move the hearts of our people as they were never moved before!

2. WE HAVE SINNED AGAINST GOD IN THE IDOLATRY OF OUR HISTORY, AND IN THE BOASTFUL SPIRIT IT HAS NATURALLY BEGOTTEN. It is a melancholy proof of human frailty, that our noblest virtues so easily degenerate into the meanest vices. A generous heart cannot but rejoice in an honorable ancestry; and love of country is a filial virtue, which must feel complacency in a public history illustrated by magnanimity and truth. A just self-reliance too is only the off-shoot of true manliness; characteristic of all, whether nations or men, by whom any thing historic is ever achieved. Were these high virtues always sanctified by a religious sense of dependence upon God, they would never be corrupted into the weaknesses either of vanity or arrogance. But woe to the nation that with pride of heart lifts itself against God! The terrible infliction upon Nebuchadnezzar of old, is a lesson for all time. The poor monarch, driven among the

beasts of the field and drivelling in his insanity, proclaims through his affecting experience that all "those who walk in pride God is able to abase." Never was such a debt of gratitude for providential blessings contracted by any people, as that due to God from the American nation. He gave them a broad land and full of springs—He emptied out its former inhabitants who melted away as the Canaanites before Israel—and His gracious providence was a wall of fire around their armies through a long and painful war. Yet we have seen how speedily they forgot the God of their salvation, and made an idol of themselves. Looking out from their palaces and towers, they have cried, saying, "is not this great Babylon that we have built for the house of the kingdom, by the might of our power and for the honor of our majesty?" They have lifted up their golden image upon the plain of Dura, and "at the sound of the cornet, flute, harp, sackbut and psaltery, they have fallen down and worshipped it." With insufferable arrogance they have taunted other nations with their adherence to institutions and usages, which are the growth of time, and cannot perish in an hour. Assuming that Constitutional freedom can only be enjoyed under Republican forms, as propagandists of their own political faith, they have sometimes rudely challenged every other creed as heretical and monstrous. It is too often forgotten that forms of government are not the arbitrary products of legislation, but are an outgrowth from the nation's life—as it were, secreted from within and crystalizing around it as an external shell. Hence the burning resentment created by a crusade against usages which are endeared by habit and consecrated by time. Certainly from this charge of officious intermeddling, a portion of the American people have not been free, springing, even where it is most innocent, from the egotism and self-conceit which says, "we are the people, and wisdom will die with us." But it was reserved to our own day to carry this haughtiness to its climax, in denying the right even of political existence to those who will not pronounce the Shibboleth of Federalism. The empty menaces, too, which have been poured into our ears, and into the ears of all Europe, would be disgusting from their arrogance if they were not contemptible from their impotence. But in the public laughter which they have drawn down from all the world, we cannot fail to see the righteous retribution of God upon this national idolatry of self. Let us— so far as in the past we may have been implicated in this transgression— deeply repent of it. Let us, in the opening of our national career, lay deep the foundations of public virtue in a sense of dependence upon God. Let us, to the end of our history, aim to preserve that modesty of carriage which distinguishes the nobleman from the parvenu, and which always remembers that a nation is great only through the divine favor.

3. ANOTHER FORM OF NATIONAL SIN HAS BEEN A TOO GREAT DEVOTION

TO PARTY, COUPLED WITH THE FLAGRANT ABUSE OF THE ELECTIVE FRANCHISE. We may indulge no Utopian dreams of exemption from the collisions of party; nor would complete political repose, if long continued, be an advantage. Under a free government where men are permitted to think, they must be expected to differ. Discussion, too, gives light; for truth, like fire, comes out from the contact of flint and steel. Parties which spring from honest and different views of public policy, are seldom sectional. Embracing the whole country, they are perfectly consistent with genuine patriotism; and may even form bonds of union between those who might else be separated by local interests. The simple existence of parties, therefore, is not an evil; or if it be, like the antagonism between the forces of nature, it is conducive to a higher good. This presupposes, however, that the arena of conflict is the hall of legislation, and the weapons of warfare are those of honorable debate. But when it comes to this, that party usurps the place of country—when caucus becomes king, and by boot and thumbscrew all individuality of opinion is crushed out of men—when public platforms become the oracles of inspiration, higher than the constitution and the law—when tricksters and under-whippers, who drill the rank and file of party, take the place of statesmen who expound and defend great and lofty principles—when, above all, supple cunning carries out, by base and crooked measures, the decrees of secret cabals: then may be seen the handwriting upon the wall, and the glory has departed. Alas! my brethren, am I not reciting the sad and bitter tale of the past? What but this fell spirit of party has riven to its base a government which, a little while ago, we thought as enduring as the everlasting hills? The great statesmen passed away whose hearts could embrace a continent, and we came to men who, whatever their genius, fall under the cutting rebuke of Goldsmith—to men

> "Who, born for the universe, narrowed their mind,
> And to party gave up what was meant for mankind."

We have lived to see fulfilled in the reign of sectionalism the remarkable prophecy of Mr. Jefferson, uttered forty years ago with such startling emphasis: "I had ceased," writes he, "to pay any attention to public affairs, content to be a passenger in our bark to the shore from which I am not distant. But this momentous question (the Missouri controversy) *like a fire bell in the night*, awakened and filled me with terror. *I considered it at once as the knell of the Union.* It is hushed for a moment; but this is a reprieve only, not a final sentence. *A geographical line coinciding with a marked principle, moral and political, once conceived and held up to the angry passions of men, will never be obliterated.*" A turbulent and wicked faction, working through a generation and laying its obscene touch upon everything holy in Church and State, at length sprung like the old man of the sea astride of the nation's neck. The work of ruin was accomplished; and now the deep, awful chasm of eternal separation yawns between North and South. May God in his mercy forgive the authors of this mischief, for it never can be repaired!

But what shall be said of the *abuse of the ballot*, the very symbol and instrument of the people's power? What of the timidity, or indifference, or disgust of some who abstain from their privilege, and suffer every true interest of the country to pass by default into the hands of base and designing men? What, of the profaneness of others, like Esau, who for a mess of pottage sell their American birthright? What, of the political brokerage which trades in this dreadful immorality, and sets up the offices of government virtually at public outcry to the highest bidders? What, of the trained ruffianism which hustles with violence from the polls all honest men who can be browbeaten? "Oh! the offence is rank, and smells to Heaven!" Can my poor voice contribute aught this day towards arousing the public conscience to the enormity of measures, by which all national morality is secretly sapped, and the foundations of public liberty are surely undermined? Let us be deeply humbled before God for sins like these; and let us fervently pray they may belong only to the record of the past. For the love of God and Country, let us strive to bring back the purer days of the republic: when honest merit waited, like Cincinnatus at his plow, to be called forth for service, and before noisy candidates cried their wares at the hustings like fishwomen in the market—when a ribald press did not thrust its obtrusive gaze into the sanctities of private life, and the road to office did not lead through the pillory of public abuse and scandal—and when the votes of the people only expressed their virtuous and unbiased will. If not—then in the loss of our national virtue we shall become as incapable of serving God and history, as the poor nation which we have just seen stranded upon these abuses and wrecked forever. May these things be only of the past! May the brand of Cain be on the forehead of him who first attempts, in our new Government, to corrupt the ballot! May he go forth a fugitive from men, until his dishonor shall hide itself in a nameless grave!

4. As a nation, we have sinned in a grievous want of reverence for the authority and majesty of law. You remember that fine passage in Hooker which embalms, in words of amber, the whole philosophy of obedience: "of law there can be no less acknowledged than that her seat is in the bosom of God, her voice the harmony of the world; all things in heaven and earth do her homage; the very least as feeling her care, and the greatest as not exempted from her power; both angels and men and creatures of what condition soever, with uniform consent, admir-

ing her as the mother of their peace and joy." Like the attraction of gravitation in physics, law binds together all the spheres of human duty and holds them fast to the throne of God. In all the concentric circles of society, obedience is man's first obligation. Not one is so much a master, but he owes fealty to a power higher than his own. The spirit of insubordination is therefore the highest treason, for it breaks the tie which binds the universe of moral beings together: as though in nature apostate orbs should fly from their centres, and wildly clash in the regions of space.

But if disregard of law be in this general view a crime of such magnitude, it assumes a new malignity when committed by a people living under such a government as ours. Its distinctive folly and wickedness are seen in the fact that it involves the abdication of our supremacy. In a republic, the sovereign is the people; and the laws they obey are the expressions of their own will. To trample upon these is, therefore, to trail their own sovereignty in the mire, to abdicate their own power, to extinguish the national life by shameful felo-de-se. When a monarch like Charles V lays aside the insignia of his royal state and retires to a convent, we can understand the weariness of care and disgust of the world, which induced the step. But no censure mingles with our compassion, because the state survived. His abdication simply transferred the symbol and substance of power to the hands of another, and there was no break in the continuity of the nation's life. But where the people are the ruler no less than the ruled, abdication is a felony; for it can only take place through self-murder. Insubordination to authority is with us therefore the commencement of political destruction—at once the most flagrant and the most senseless of crimes. There is the greater necessity for grinding this truth into the minds of our people, inasmuch as through the simplicity of our republican institutions the ensigns of power are not flaunted before the eye. Under a monarchy, the king and his court become the symbol of authority, the living representative of the law in its majesty. It is an unquestionable advantage of that form of government, that law should be presented in this embodied and concrete form before the masses; who are insensibly taught reverence by the very pomp and ceremony, which many decry without considering this incidental benefit which accrues. But with us, the administration of law is necessarily stripped of this outward splendor: the people should, therefore, be taught the dignity of obedience, as springing from the self-respect which is due to their own sovereignty. Need I pause to show the disasters which, in a popular government, must flow from irreverence of the law? Alas! the present history of our own distracted land furnishes a commentary for the text. It is a sad tale—a tale, sad as that which renewed the grief of Aeneas before the Tyrian queen. It is this arrogant competition of individual opinion finding its climax in the pretensions of "a higher law," which has involved half the nation in the guilt of perjury, and broken the bond of the holiest covenant ever sworn between man and man. It is this same recklessness of obligation, which has lifted up the sword to butcher those who will not bend nor yield to a merciless proscription. It is the same spirit mounting to phrenzy, which has seized upon wise and venerable ministers of the church; who have turned away from the gospel of God, in order to hound on this war of exterminating and bitter revenge. And it is the same demon of misrule which, in three short months, has swept away every guard of private as well as public liberty; and erected, under the shadow of the tomb of Washington, a despotism as irresponsible and cruel as any which has ever crushed the hearts and hopes of mankind.

In this particular manifestation of lawlessness, the South has rather been "sinned against than sinning." But then we have the *lex talionis;* the spirit, whose unrelenting cry is "an eye for an eye—a tooth for a tooth." This right of retaliation finds recognition with us; not softened, as with the ancient Hebrews, by cities of refuge, whither the man-slayer may betake himself. By a too general consent individuals assume the prerogative of the magistrate, in redressing their own wrongs. It may be true, that certain outrages cannot be restrained by the inadequate defences of public law; and when the safety of society may require instant retribution at the hands of the sufferer, who is substantively transformed into the magistrate. But these cases are exceptional and extreme; and if not provided for by special enactment, they are at least sustained by a virtuous sentiment based upon the instinct of self-preservation, characterizing the State as well as the person. Yet, in a civilized and Christian land, when the broad shield of law is supposed to cover all the interests and rights of men, it is flagrant wickedness to live as though society was resolved into its primordial elements: amid all the paths of business or pleasure, to have the treacherous hand trembling upon the concealed weapon, which is ready, in the sudden brawl, to leap forth upon its unsuspecting victim. This spirit must be exorcised from the land, else it will work the destruction of government. Let us choose wise legislators, who shall frame a code sufficient for the public protection. Let us clothe our Judges with the purest ermine, that they may make the temple of justice awful and holy as the sanctuary of God. Let us create a robust and healthy public sentiment, which shall everywhere support the law by an influence as diffused and silent as the pressure of the atmosphere. Let us train our youth to habits of obedience, teaching boys to remain boys, else they will be beaten with rods. Thus may reverence for law pervade all classes; and the daily conduct of our citizens come up as the swelling chorus of that song, which Hooker beautifully describes as "the harmony of the world." We have sinned in this against our race and against God: let our repentance to-day be the deep bass, which shall give the keynote of that song.

5. As a people, we have been distinguished by a grovelling devotion to merely material interests. A nation loses its tone when it becomes intensely utilitarian. When noble deeds are weighed in the scales of merchandise; and expediency stands behind its counter to measure off virtue by the ell, and weigh honor by the pound avoirdupois. The American devotion to material interests is by no means inexplicable. A great and practical race like our own, thrown upon a new Continent, and turning its Saxon energy upon the development of hidden treasures, elsewhere unparalleled, finds its covetousness reacted upon by its own prosperity. The age too is an age of physical science, which, exploring the secrets of nature, and subordinating her powers to the uses of man, renders it utilitarian by system. Besides all this, the stimulus of our Republican institutions develops the activity of our people into almost superhuman energy, and sharpens their wit to the highest shrewdness. With the total obliteration of caste, we start together from the same level of democratic equality. Yet, with the avenues to power and distinction open to all aspirants, is it strange that a general competition should exist amongst our people in the accumulation of wealth, which is at once the most obvious and the most easily attained instrument of power? Thus, the greed of gain has rusted into the hearts of our people—the most sordid of all passions, and the most fruitful source of individual and national corruption. The prevalence of this spirit has exposed us to the bitter sarcasm that, as a nation, we have set up the Golden Calf in the midst of the camp as the God of our idolatry. Every interest of the land has suffered from the corroding influence of this sordid utilitarianism. It has infected our schools of learning, cutting down the standard of intellectual discipline until sound scholarship is fast becoming a thing obsolete as the mythology of Greece. It has contaminated our Courts of Justice, until jury trial has, in a measure, become a shield for crime, and immunity from punishment is regulated by a graduated tariff. It has seated itself in halls of legislation, and discounts at the tables of the money-changers the rights and claims which a just legislation should protect. The spirit of speculation sweeps over the land with its expansion of credit and its inflated prosperity, until, as periodically as the equinox, we look for financial disaster, which dashes to the ground colossal fortunes as easily as the hurricane lays prostrate the giants of the forest.

It is all wrong, my hearers: offensive to God, and ruinous to ourselves. And I do not wonder that, to save us from total demoralization, God has let loose upon us this political storm, in order to bring up from the depth of the nation's heart its dormant virtue. We are learning by the sacrifices of the times, in the same school with our heroic forefathers, that liberty is better than gold, and honor more precious than fortune. The accumulated treasures of past industry and thrift are now cheerfully laid upon the altar of your country's safety. Fathers are consecrating their sons to that Country's service, with an oath more solemn than that which bound Hannibal to eternal enmity with Rome: and tender mothers buckle the shield around them, as did the Spartan mothers of old, saying with equal heroism, "come back with it a conqueror, or be borne back upon it a martyr." I thank God for the storm. It has come in time to redeem us from ruin. Though the heavens be overcast, and lurid lightnings gleam from the bosom of each dark cloud, the moral atmosphere will be purged—and from our heroism shall spring sons and daughters capable of immortal destinies. Let me sound it out as with the trumpet of the Resurrection day: the men in all ages who have made history, have been men of faith—men who could hide a great principle deep in their heart, work it out as a potential and substantive fact, and abide the verdict of posterity. All the Poets, all the Statesmen, all the Warriors of the past, were men of faith. Believing in the grand and the true, they could put their heel upon the present; and lifting up the curtain which hides the far off future from other men, they drew up that future by a magnetic attraction to themselves, and lived abreast of it. Any man can do the things that can be done; but they who do the things that can't be done— they are the immortals. It is a heroic day in which to live! Let the pulse of a high and generous patriotism beat in our breasts: that the history we work out may be the school-book from which our children's children shall learn to be true, and brave, and pure, as it becomes the children of the great to be.

I had designed, in connexion with our national responsibilities, to speak of *the obligations we owe to our slave population.* But the subject is excluded by its own largeness from discussion now. It will bear postponement. When this unnatural war shall be concluded, and we shall be free from the impertinent interference with our domestic affairs by which we have been so long annoyed, there will be opportunity to say all that the moralist and christian should utter, and what it will be fitting the legislator and the master should hear. We can afford to bide the time.

In conclusion, permit me to say that the present is by far the most important and glorious struggle through which the nation has ever passed. The parallel which has been drawn between it and the contest of the Revolution has not been seen in its full significance by many even of those who have suggested it; certainly not by those who have derided it in terms of measureless contempt. The principles involved in this conflict are broader and deeper than those which underlay that of the Revolution, rendering it of far greater significance to us and to our posterity and to mankind at large. Our fathers fought for no abstract rights as men, but for chartered rights as Englishmen. They claimed that the fundamental principle of English liberty was invaded, when the Colonies were taxed without representation. They were abundantly able to pay the duty which was stamped upon the Royal paper, and the tax levied upon the tea which they threw into the harbor of Boston: but they were not able to submit to any infraction of their Constitutional rights. For this they resisted unto blood: and had the British Ministry been wise, the day had been long postponed before the Crown had lost its brightest jewel, and England found a rival in those very Colonies which once owed her fealty and love. But *our* Revolution rests upon the broader principle laid as the corner stone of the American Constitution: "that governments derive their just powers from the consent of the governed; and that whenever any form of government becomes destructive of the ends for which it was formed, it is the right of the People to alter, or to abolish it, and to institute a new government, organizing its powers in such form as to them shall seem most likely to effect their safety and happiness." The true issue of to-day is not precisely what it was in November last, nor in January last, nor yet in March, when was exhibited the spectacle of the inauguration at Washington. The issue which now unites our whole population as the heart of one man, is *whether ten millions of people have not the inherent right to institute such a government, "as to them shall seem most likely to secure their safety and happiness."* This right is denied to us; and its denial lays the foundation of a despotism under which we cannot consent to live, for it was distinctly repudiated in the Declaration of 1776. We should be unworthy of our Fathers, if we flinched from maintaining to the last extremity the one, great, cardinal principle of American constitutional freedom. I could perhaps manage to live, if Providence had so ordained, under the despotism of the Czar, for it is not wholly irresponsible: the order of the Nobles would be interposed between me and the absolute will of the Autocrat. I could perhaps submit even to the Turk; for he is held in check by fear of his own Janizaries. But I will not—so help me God!—I never will submit to the despotism of the mob. It is not the occupant of the White House who is the tyrant of to-day; but the starving millions behind the throne. Hence the wild outburst of revenge and hate, which now astonishes the world. It is the wail of concentrated agony and despair of the unpaid labor which asks for bread, and capital gives it a stone; and which hopes through our extermination and the deportation or massacre of our slaves, to find room for itself upon the broad Savannas of the South. May a merciful God help them of the North! They have sowed the wind, they must reap the whirlwind. They cannot retrieve the past, they must drive on and meet the future: perhaps to experience the fate of Acteon, and be eaten up by their own hounds.

The last hope of self-government upon this Continent lies in these eleven Confederated States. We have retained the one, primary truth upon which the whole fabric of public liberty was reared by our fathers, and

from which the North has openly apostatized. We have too in the institution of Slavery a great central fact, living and embodied, lifting itself
up from the bed of history as the mountain cliff from the bed of the deep,
blue sea; and in defending it against the assaults of a "rose-water philanthropy," we may place ourselves against all the past and feel the support
of God's immovable Providence. Dare we then—dare any of us, man,
woman or child—falter upon the path of such a destiny? Dare we quench
in eternal night the hope which for a hundred years has been shedding its
light upon the world, that man may be self-governed and free? I do not
doubt the bravery of our people—I do not distrust their willingness to
make all possible sacrifices to maintain their right. But I do fear the
absence of sufficient trust in the power and grace of Almighty God. Whatever may be the strength of our self-reliance, let it be built up through a
sacred confidence in God as our shield and buckler. Whatever hopes we
may cherish from the diplomatic influences which are destined to bear
upon this quarrel, let us remember the jealousy of Him who forbade
Israel to "go down into Egypt for horses." Let us trust in God, and with
an humble self-reliance take care of ourselves; prepared to recognize that
gracious Providence which will work our deliverance.

The division of the American people into two distinct nations has
not taken me by surprise. It was clearly enough foreshadowed by the parliamentary conflicts through which we have passed; and it has its root
deep down in the different nationalities, of which our eclectic population
is composed. The analogies of history should have led us to anticipate it.
Through all time, nations have been formed first by agglutination, and
then by separation. In their original weakness, the most heterogeneous
elements are combined and held together by the pressure of necessity: but
in their maturity, those concealed differences spring up, which have their
root often in the type of character impressed upon the parent stock; and
which no lapse of time can obliterate, and no political chemistry can
make permanently to coalesce. We have vainly read the history of our
fathers, if we failed to see that from the beginning two nations were in
the American womb; and through the whole period of gestation the sup-
planter has had his hand upon his brother's heel. The separation of
North and South was as surely decreed of God, and has as certainly been
accomplished by the outworking of great moral causes, as was the separation of the Colonies from their English mother; as the genesis of the
modern nations of Europe, out of the destruction of ancient Rome. In
effecting this separation, the most glorious opportunity has been missed
of demonstrating the power of our Republican principles, the progress of
American civilization, and the effective control of the Gospel over human
passions. In past ages, the sword has been the universal arbiter, and every
issue has been submitted to the ordeal of battle. How fondly many of us

hoped and pleaded for the rejection of this brutal argument; and for such an adjustment of our difficulties, as both the civilization and the religion of the age demanded! But our overtures of peace were first fraudulently entertained, and then insultingly rejected. I accept that rejection. I will go to my God, and will tell him how we have desired peace, I will tell him how we have sought to realize the scripture idea of "beating the sword into the plowshare": and then I will remit those who have rejected our treaties of amity and commerce, to his retributive judgment. But in this act, let us bow in low humility before His throne; confessing our sins with prayer and fasting, and trusting in His promise to reward them that diligently seek him. Oh! my country! "there is none like unto the God of Jeshurun, who rideth upon the heaven in thy help, and in his excellency on the sky. The eternal God is thy refuge, and underneath are the everlasting arms: and He shall thrust out the enemy from before thee, and shall say, destroy them. Israel then shall dwell in safety alone: the fountain of Jacob shall be upon a land of corn and wine; also his heavens shall drop dew. Happy art thou, O Israel: who is like unto thee, O People saved by the Lord, the shield of thy help, and who is the sword of thy excellency! and thine enemies shall be found liars unto thee, and thou shalt tread upon their high places."

ABRAHAM LINCOLN

Second Inaugural Address

March 4, 1865

Fellow-Countrymen:

At this second appearing to take the oath of the Presidential office there is less occasion for an extended address that there was at the first. Then a statement somewhat in detail of a course to be pursued seemed fitting and proper. Now, at the expiration of four years, during which public declarations have been constantly called forth on every point and phase of the great contest which still absorbs the attention and engrosses the energies of the nation, little that is new could be presented. The progress of our arms, upon which all else chiefly depends, is as well known to the public as to myself, and it is, I trust, reasonably satisfactory and encouraging to all. With high hope for the future, no prediction in regard to it is ventured.

On the occasion corresponding to this four years ago all thoughts were anxiously directed to an impending civil war. All dreaded it, all sought to avert it. While the inaugural address was being delivered from this place, devoted altogether to *saving* the Union without war, insurgent agents were in the city seeking to *destroy* it without war—seeking to dissolve the Union and divide effects by negotiation. Both parties deprecated war, but one of them would *make* war rather than let the nation survive, and the other would *accept* war rather than let it perish, and the war came.

One-eighth of the whole population were colored slaves, not distributed generally over the Union, but localized in the southern part of it. These slaves constituted a peculiar and powerful interest. All knew that this interest was somehow the cause of the war. To strengthen, perpetuate, and extend this interest was the object for which the insurgents would rend the Union even by war, while the Government claimed no right to do more than to restrict the territorial enlargement of it. Neither party

From *Inaugural Addresses of the Presidents of the United States* (Washington, D.C.: Government Printing Office, 1965), pp. 127–28.

expected for the war the magnitude or the duration which it has already attained. Neither anticipated that the *cause* of the conflict might cease with or even before the conflict itself should cease. Each looked for an easier triumph, and a result less fundamental and astounding. Both read the same Bible and pray to the same God, and each invokes His aid against the other. It may seem strange that any men should dare to ask a just God's assistance in wringing their bread from the sweat of other men's faces, but let us judge not, that we be not judged. The prayers of both could not be answered. That of neither has been answered fully. The Almighty has His own purposes. "Woe unto the world because of offenses; for it must needs be that offenses come, but woe to that man by whom the offense cometh." If we shall suppose that American slavery is one of those offenses which, in the providence of God, must needs come, but which, having continued through His appointed time, He now wills to remove, and that He gives to both North and South this terrible war as the woe due to those by whom the offense came, shall we discern therein any departure from those divine attributes which the believers in a living God always ascribe to Him? Fondly do we hope, fervently do we pray, that this mighty scourge of war may speedily pass away. Yet, if God wills that it continue until all the wealth piled by the bondsman's two hundred and fifty years of unrequited toil shall be sunk, and until every drop of blood drawn with the lash shall be paid by another drawn with the sword, as was said three thousand years ago, so still it must be said "the judgments of the Lord are true and righteous altogether."

With malice toward none, with charity for all, with firmness in the right as God gives us to see the right, let us strive on to finish the work we are in, to bind up the nation's wounds, to care for him who shall have borne the battle and for his widow and his orphan, to do all which may achieve and cherish a just and lasting peace among ourselves and with all nations.

HORACE BUSHNELL

Our Obligations To
The Dead

Brethren of the Alumni:—

To pay fit honors to our dead is one of the fraternal and custom-
ary offices of these anniversaries; never so nearly an office of high public
duty as now, when we find the roll of our membership starred with so
many names made sacred by the giving up of life for the Republic. We
knew them here in terms of cherished intimacy; some of them so lately
that we scarcely seem to have been parted from them; others of them we
have met here many times, returning to renew, with us, their tender and
pleasant recollections of the past; but we meet them here no more: they
are gone to make up the hecatomb offered for their and our great nation's
life. Hence it has been specially desired on this occasion, that we honor
their heroic sacrifice by some fit remembrance. Had the call of your committee been different, I should certainly not have responded.

And yet, over-willing as I have been to assume an office so entirely
grateful, it is a matter none the less difficult to settle on the best and most
proper way of doing the honors intended. I think you will agree with me,
that it cannot be satisfactorily done by preparing a string of obituary
notices of our dead; that would be more appropriate to some published
document, and no wise appropriate to a public discourse. Besides, to
withdraw them from the vaster roll of the dead, in which it was their
honor to die, and set them in a circle of mere literary clanship, bounding
our testimony of homage by the accident of their matriculation here with
us, would be rather to claim our honors in them, than to pay them honors
due to themselves. We should seem not even to appreciate the grand public motive to which they gave up their life. They honored us in dying for

An oration given at the Commemorative Celebration held in New Haven,
on Wednesday of Commencement Week, July 26, 1865, in honor of the
Alumni of Yale College, who fell in the War of the Rebellion. From
Horace Bushnell, *Building Eras in Religion* (New York: Charles Scribner's
Sons, 1881), pp. 319–55.

their country, and we fitly honor them, when we class them with the glorious brotherhood in which they fell. Reserving it therefore as my privilege, to make such reference specially to them as befits the occasion, I propose a more general subject in which due honors may be paid to all, viz., *The obligations we owe to the dead,*—all the dead who have fallen in this gigantic and fearfully bloody war.

. . . .

First of all then, we are to see that we give them their due share of the victory and the honors of victory. For it is one of our natural infirmities, against which we need to be carefully and even jealously guarded, that we fall so easily into the impression which puts them in the class of defeat and failure. Are they not dead? And who shall count the dead as being in the roll of victory? But the living return to greet us and be with us, and we listen eagerly to the story of the scenes in which they bore their part. We enjoy their exultations and exult with them. Their great leaders also return, to be crowded by our ovations, and deafened by our applauses. These, these, we too readily say, are the victors, considering no more the dead but with a certain feeling close akin to pity. If, sometime, the story of their fall is told us, the spot described, far in front or on the rampart's edge, where they left their bodies with the fatal gashes at which their souls went out, we listen with sympathy and sad respect, but we do not find how to count them in the lists of victory, and scarcely to include them in the general victory of the cause. All our associations run this way, and before we know it we have them down, most likely, on the losing side of the struggle. They belong, we fancy, to the waste of victory,—sad waste indeed! but not in any sense a part of victory itself. No, no, ye living! It is the ammunition spent that gains the battle, not the ammunition brought off from the field. These dead are the spent ammunition of the war, and theirs above all is the victory. Upon what indeed turned the question of the war itself, but on the dead that could be furnished; or what is no wise different, the life that could be contributed for that kind of expenditure? These grim heroes therefore, dead and dumb, that have strewed so many fields with their bodies,—these are the price and purchase-money of our triumph. A great many of us were ready to live, but these offered themselves, in a sense, to die, and by their cost the victory is won.

Nay, it is not quite enough, if we will know exactly who is entitled to a part in these honors, that we only remember these dead of the war. Buried generations back of them were also present in it, almost as truly as they. Thus, if we take the two most honored leaders, Grant and Sherman, who, besides the general victory they have gained for the cause, have won their sublime distinction as the greatest living commanders of the world, it will be impossible to think of them as having made or begotten their own lofty endowments. All great heroic men have seeds and roots, far back it may be, out of which they spring, and apart from which they could not spring at all; a sublime fatherhood and motherhood, in whose blood and life, however undistinguished, victory was long ago distilling for the great day to come of their people and nation.

. . . .

Still, it is not my intention to occupy you with the part fulfilled by these remoter generations of the past, but with the more general remembrance of such as have fallen in the war itself. I only refer you to these, to show you how very trivial and weak a thing it is, if we speak of our victories, to imagine that only such as come out of the war alive are entitled to credit and reverence on account of them.

But I pass to a point where the dead obtain a right of honor that is more distinctive, and belongs not to the living at all; or if in certain things partly to the living, yet only to them in some less sacred and prominent way. I speak here of the fact that, according to the true economy of the world, so many of its grandest and most noble benefits have and are to have a tragic origin, and to come as outgrowths only of blood. Whether it be that sin is in the world, and the whole creation groaneth in the necessary throes of its demonized life, we need not stay to inquire; for sin would be in the world and the demonizing spell would be upon it. Such was, and was to be, and is, the economy of it. Common life, the world's great life, is in the large way tragic. As the mild benignity and peaceful reign of Christ begins at the principle: "without shedding of blood, there is no remission," so, without shedding of blood, there is almost nothing great in the world, or to be expected for it. For the life is in the blood, —all life; and it is put flowing within, partly for the serving of a nobler use in flowing out on fit occasion, to quicken and consecrate whatever it touches. God could not plan a Peace-Society world, to live in the sweet amenities, and grow great and happy by simply thriving and feeding. There must be bleeding also. Sentiments must be born that are children of thunder; there must be heroes and heroic nationalities, and martyr testimonies, else there will be only mediocrities, insipidities, commonplace men, and common-place writings,—a sordid and mean peace, liberties without a pulse, and epics that are only eclogues.

And here it is that the dead of our war have done for us a work so precious, which is all their own,—they have bled for us; and by this simple sacrifice of blood they have opened for us a new great chapter of life. We were living before in trade and commerce, bragging of our new cities and our census reports, and our liberties that were also consciously mocked by our hypocrisies; having only the possibilities of great inspirations and not the fact, materialized more and more evidently in our habits and sentiments, strong principally in our discords and the impetuosity of our projects for money. But the blood of our dead has touched our souls with thoughts more serious and deeper, and begotten, as I trust, somewhat of that high-bred inspiration which is itself the possibility of genius, and of a true public greatness. Saying nothing then for the present of our victors and victories, let us see what we have gotten by the blood of our slain.

And first of all, in this blood our unity is cemented and forever sanctified. Something was gained for us here, at the beginning, by our sacrifices in the fields of our Revolution,—something, but not all. Had it not been for this common bleeding of the States in their common cause, it is doubtful whether our Constitution could ever have been carried. The discords of the Convention were imminent, as we know, and were only surmounted by compromises that left them still existing. They were simply kenneled under the Constitution and not reconciled, as began to be evident shortly in the doctrines of state sovereignty, and state nullification, here and there asserted. We had not bled enough, as yet, to merge our colonial distinctions and make us a proper nation. Our battles had not been upon a scale to thoroughly mass our feeling, or gulf us in a common cause and life. Against the state-rights doctrines, the logic of our Constitution was decisive, and they were refuted a thousand times over. But such things do not go by argument. No argument transmutes a discord, or composes a unity where there was none. The matter wanted here was blood, not logic, and this we now have on a scale large enough to meet our necessity. True it is blood on one side, and blood on the other, —all the better for that; for bad bleeding kills, and righteous bleeding sanctifies and quickens. The state-rights doctrine is now fairly bled away, and the unity died for, in a way of such prodigious devotion, is forever sealed and glorified.

Nor let any one be concerned for the sectional relations of defeat and victory. For there has all the while been a grand, suppressed sentiment of country in the general field of the rebellion, which is bursting up already into sovereignty out of the soil itself. There is even a chance that this sentiment may blaze into a passion hot enough to utterly burn up whatever fire itself can master. At all events it will put under the ban, from this time forth, all such instigators of treason as could turn their peaceful States into hells of desolation, and force even patriotic citizens to fight against the homage they bore their country. However this may be, the seeds of a true public life are in the soil, waiting to grow apace. It will be as when the flood of Noah receded. For the righteous man perchance began to bethink himself shortly, and to be troubled, that he took no seeds into the ark; but no sooner were the waters down, than the oaks and palms and all great trees sprung into life, under the dead old trunks of the forest, and the green world reappeared even greener than before; only the sections had all received new seeds, by a floating exchange, and put them forthwith into growth together with their own. So the unity now to be developed, after this war-deluge is over, is even like to be more cordial than it ever could have been. It will be no more thought of as a mere human compact, or composition, always to be debated by the letter, but it will be that bond of common life which God had touched with blood; a sacredly heroic, Providentially tragic unity, where God's cherubim stand guard over grudges and hates and remembered jealousies, and the sense of nationality becomes even a kind of religion. . . .

Passing to another point of view, we owe it to our dead in this terrible war, that they have given us the possibility of a great consciousness and great public sentiments. There must needs be something lofty in a people's action, and above all something heroic in their sacrifices for a cause, to sustain a great sentiment in them. They will try, in the smooth days of peace and golden thriftiness and wide-spreading growth, to have it, and perhaps will think they really have it, but they will only have semblances and counterfeits; patriotic professions that are showy and thin, swells and protestations that are only oratorical and have no true fire. All the worse if they have interests and institutions that are all the while mocking their principles; breeding factions that can be quieted only by connivances and compromises and political bargains, that sell out their muniments of right and nationality. Then you shall see all high devotion going down as by a law, till nothing is left but the dastard picture of a spent magistracy that, when every thing is falling into wreck, can only whimper that it sees not any thing it can do! Great sentiments go when they are not dismissed, and will not come when they are sent for. We cannot keep them by much talk, nor have them because we have heard of them and seen them in a classic halo. A lofty public consciousness arises only when things are loftily and nobly done. It is only when we are rallied by a cause, in that cause receive a great inspiration, in that inspiration give our bodies to the death, that at last, out of many such heroes dead, comes the possibility of great thoughts, fired by sacrifice, and a true public magnanimity.

In this view, we are not the same people that we were, and never can be again. Our young scholars, that before could only find the forms of great feeling in their classic studies, now catch the fire of it unsought. Emulous before of saying fine things for their country, they now choke for the impossibility of saying what they truly feel. The pitch of their life is raised. The tragic blood of the war is a kind of new capacity for them. They perceive what it is to have a country and a public devotion. Great aims are close at hand, and in such aims a finer type of manners. And what shall follow, but that, in their more invigorated, nobler life, they are seen hereafter to be manlier in thought and scholarship, and closer to genius in action.

I must also speak of the new great history sanctified by this war, and the blood of its fearfully bloody sacrifices. So much worth and character were never sacrificed in a human war before. And by this mournful offering, we have bought a really stupendous chapter of history. We had a little very beautiful history before, which we were beginning to cherish and fondly cultivate. But we had not enough of it to beget a full historic consciousness. As was just now intimated in a different way, no people ever become vigorously conscious, till they mightily do, and heroically suffer. The historic sense is close akin to tragedy. We say it accusingly often,—and foolishly,—that history cannot live on peace, but must feed itself on blood. The reason is that, without the blood, there is really nothing great enough in motive and action, taking the world as it is, to create a great people or story. If a gospel can be executed only in blood, if there is no power of salvation strong enough to carry the world's feeling which is not gained by dying for it, how shall a selfish race get far enough above itself, to be kindled by the story of its action in the dull routine of its common arts of peace? Doubtless it should be otherwise, even as goodness should be universal; but so it never has been, and upon the present footing of evil never can be. The great cause must be great as in the clashing of evil; and heroic inspirations, and the bleeding of heroic worth must be the zest of the story. Nations can sufficiently live only as they find how to energetically die. In this view, some of us have felt, for a long time, the want of a more historic life, to make us a truly great people. This want is now supplied; for now, at last, we may be said to have gotten a history. The story of this four years' war is the grandest chapter, I think, of heroic fact, and tragic devotion, and spontaneous public sacrifice, that has ever been made in our world. The great epic story of Troy is but a song in comparison. There was never a better, and never so great a cause; order against faction, law against conspiracy, liberty and right against the madness and defiant wrong of slavery, the unity and salvation of the greatest future nationality and freest government of the world, a perpetual state of war to be averted, and the preservation for mankind of an example of popular government and free society that is a token of promise for true manhood, and an omen of death to old abuse and prescriptive wrong the world over; this has been our cause, and it is something to say that we have borne ourselves worthily in it. Our noblest and best sons have given their life to it. We have dotted whole regions with battlefields. We have stained how many rivers, and bays, and how many hundred leagues of railroad, with our blood! We have suffered appalling defeats; twice at Bull Run, at Wilson's Creek, in the great campaign of the Peninsula, at Cedar Mountain, at Fredericksburg, at Chancellorsville, at Chickamauga, and upon the Red River, leaving our acres of dead on all these fields and many others less conspicuous; yet, abating no jot of courage and returning with resolve unbroken, we have

203 Our Obligations To The Dead

converted these defeats into only more impressive victories. In this manner too, with a better fortune nobly earned, we have hallowed, as names of glory and high victory, Pea Ridge, Donelson, Shiloh, Hilton Head, New Orleans, Vicksburg, Port Hudson, Stone River, Lookout Mountain, Resaca, Atlanta, Fort Fisher, Gettysburg, Nashville, Wilmington, Petersburg and Richmond, Bentonville, Mobile Bay, and, last of all, the forts of Mobile City. All these and a hundred others are now become, and in all future time are to be, names grandly historic. And to have them is to be how great a gift for the ages to come! By how many of the future children of the Republic will these spots be visited, and how many will return from their pilgrimages thither, blest in remembrances of the dead, to whom they owe their country!

Among the fallen too we have names that will glow with unfading lustre on whatever page they are written; our own brave Lyon, baptizing the cause in the blood of his early death; our Sedgwick, never found wanting at any point of command, equal in fact to the very highest command, and only too modest to receive it when offered; the grandly gifted young McPherson, who had already fought himself into the first rank of leadership, and was generally counted the peerless hope and prodigy of the armies; Reynolds also, and Kearney, and Reno, and Birney; and how many brilliant stars, or even constellations of stars, in the lower degrees of command, such as Rice, and Lowell, and Vincent, and Shaw, and Stedman, and a hundred others in like honor, for the heroic merit of their leadership and death! And yet, when I drop all particular names, dear as they may be, counting them only the smoke and not the fire, letting the unknown trains of dead heroes pack and mass and ascend, to shine, as by host, in the glorious Milky Way of their multitude,—men that left their business and all the dearest ties of home and family to fight their country's righteous war, and fought on till they fell,—then for the first time do I seem to feel the tide-swing of a great historic consciousness. God forbid that any prudishness of modesty should here detain us. Let us fear no more to say that we have won a history and the right to be a consciously historic people. Henceforth our new world even heads the old, having in this single chapter risen clean above it. The wars of Caesar, and Frederic, and Napoleon, were grand enough in their leadership, but there is no grand people or popular greatness in them, consequently no true dignity. In this war of ours it is the people, moving by their own decisive motion, in the sense of their own great cause. For this cause we have volunteered by the million, and in three thousand millions of money, and by the resolute bleeding of our men and the equally resolute bleeding of our self-taxation, we have bought and sanctified consentingly all these fields, all that is grand in this thoroughly principled history.

Again, it is not a new age of history only that we owe to the bloody sacrifices of this war, but in much the same manner the confidence of a new literary age; a benefit that we are specially called in such a place as this, and on such an occasion, to remember and fitly acknowledge. Great public throes are, mentally speaking, changes of base for some new thought-campaign in a people. Hence the brilliant new literature of the age of Queen Elizabeth; then of another golden era under Anne; and then still again, as in the arrival of another birth-time, after the Napoleonic wars of George the Fourth. The same thing has been noted, I believe, in respect to the wars of Greece and Germany. Only it is in such wars as raise the public sense and majesty of a people that the result is seen to follow. For it is the high-souled feeling raised that quickens high-souled thought, and puts the life of genius in the glow of new-born liberty. This we are now to expect, for the special reason also that we have here, for the first time, conquered a position. Thus it will be seen that no great writer becomes himself, in his full power, till he has gotten the sense of position. Much more true is this of a people. And here has been our weakness until now. We have held the place of cliency, we have taken our models and laws of criticism, and to a great extent our opinions, from the English motherhood of our language and mind. Under that kind of pupilage we live no longer; we are thoroughly weaned from it, and become a people in no secondary right. Henceforth we are not going to write English, but American. As we have gotten our position, we are now to have our own civilization, think our own thoughts, rhyme in our own measures, kindle our own fires, and make our own canons of criticism, even as we settle the proprieties of punishment for our own traitors. We are not henceforth to live as by cotton and corn and trade, keeping the downward slope of thrifty mediocrity. Our young men are not going out of college, staled, in the name of discipline, by their carefully conned lessons, to be launched on the voyage of life as ships without wind, but they are to have great sentiments, and mighty impulsions, and souls alive all through in fires of high devotion.

. . . .

I might also speak at large, if I had the time, of the immense benefit these dead have conferred upon our free institutions themselves, by the consecrating blood of their sacrifice. But I can only say that having taken the sword to be God's ministers, and to vindicate the law as his ordinance, they have done it even the more effectively in that they have died for it. It has been a wretched fault of our people that we have so nearly ignored the moral foundations of our government. Regarding it as a merely human creation, we have held it only by the tenure of convenience. Hence came the secession. For what we create by our will, may we not dissolve by the same? Bitter has been the cost of our pitifully weak philosophy. In these rivers of blood we have now bathed our institutions and they are henceforth to be hallowed in our sight. Government is now become Providential,—no more a mere creature of our human will, but a grandly moral affair. The awful stains of sacrifice are upon it, as upon the fields where our dead battled for it, and it is sacred for their sakes. The stamp of God's sovereignty is also upon it; for he has beheld their blood upon its gate-posts and made it the sign of his passover. Henceforth we are not to be manufacturing government, and defying in turn its sovereignty because we have made it ourselves; but we are to revere its sacred rights, rest in its sacred immunities, and have it even as the Caesar whom our Christ himself requires us to obey. Have we not also proved, written it down for all the ages to come, that the most horrible, God-defying crime of this world is unnecessary rebellion?

I might also speak of the immense contribution made for religion, by the sacrifices of these bleeding years. Religion, at the first, gave impulse, and, by a sublime recompense of reaction, it will also receive impulse. What then shall we look for but for a new era now to break forth, a day of new gifts and powers and holy endowments from on high, wherein great communities and friendly nations shall be girded in sacrifice, for the cause of Christ their Master?

But these illustrations must not be continued farther. Such are some of the benefits we are put in obligations for by the dead in this great war. And now it remains to ask, by what fitting tribute these obligations are to be paid? And it signifies little, first of all, to say: Let the widows of these dead be widows, and their children, children of the Republic. Let them also be the private care of us all. Let the childless families adopt these fatherless. Give the sons and daughters growing up the necessary education: open to them ways of industry; set them in opportunities of advancement. Let our whole people resolve themselves into a grand Sanitary Commission, for these after-blows of suffering and loss occasioned by the war.

Again, it is another of the sacred obligations we owe to the dead, that we sanctify their good name. Nothing can be more annoying to the sense of honor, than the mischievous facility of some, in letting down the merit and repute of the fallen by the flippant recollection of their faults, or, it may be, of their former vices. Who have earned immunity from this petty kind of criticism, if not they who have died for their country? . . .

A great work also is due from us to the dead, and quite as much for our own sakes as theirs, in the due memorizing of their names and acts. Let the nation's grand war monument be raised in massive granite, piercing the sky. Let every State, honored by such names as Sedgwick, and Lyon, and Mansfield, claim the right to their honors for the future ages, by raising, on some highest mountain top, or in some park of ornament, the conspicuous shaft or pillar, that will fitly represent the majesty of the men. The towns and villages will but honor themselves, when they set up their humbler monuments inscribed with the names of the fallen. Let the churches also, and the college halls and chapels, show their mural tablets, where both worship and learning may be quickened by the remembrance of heroic deeds and deaths. In this way, or some other, every name of our fallen Alumni should be conspicuously recorded in the College; that our sons coming hither may learn, first of all, that our mother gives her best to die for their country.

.   .   .   .

But there is one other and yet higher duty that we owe to these dead; viz., that we take their places and stand in their cause. It is even a great law of natural duty that the living shall come into the places and works of the dead. The same also is accepted and honored by Christianity, when it shows the Christian son, and brother, and friend, stepping into the places made vacant by the dead, to assume their blessed and great work unaccomplished, and die, if need be, in the testimony of a common martyrdom. They challenged, in this manner, if the commentators will suffer it, the vows of baptism, and "were baptized for the dead,"—consecrated upon the dead, for the work of the dead. God lays it upon us in the same way now, to own the bond of fealty that connects us with the fallen, in the conscious community and righteous kinship of their cause. And then, as brothers baptized for the dead,—Alumni, so to speak, of the Republic,—we are to execute their purpose and fulfill the idea that inspired them. Neither is it enough at this point to go off in a general heroic, promising, in high rhetoric, to give our life for the country in like manner. There is no present likelihood that we shall be called to do any such thing. No, but we have duties upon us that are closer at hand; viz., to wind up and settle this great tragedy in a way to exactly justify every drop of blood that has been shed in it. Like the blood of righteous Abel it cries both to us and to God, from every field, and river, and wood, and road, dotted by our pickets and swept by the march of our armies.

First of all we are sworn to see that no vestige of state sovereignty is left, and the perpetual, supreme sovereignty of the nation established. For what but this have our heroes died? Not one of them would have died for a government of mere optional continuance; not one for a government fit to be rebelled against. But they volunteered for a government in perfect right, and one to be perpetual as the stars, and they went to the death as against the crime of hell. Tell me also this,—if a government is good enough to die *for*, is it not good enough to die *by*, when it is violated? Not that every traitor is, of course, to be visited by the punishment of treason. It is not for me to say who, or how many or few, shall suffer that punishment. But I would willingly take the question to the dead victims of Belle Isle, and Salisbury, and Andersonville, and let them be the judges. There is no revenge in them now. The wild storms of their agony are laid, and the thoughts which bear sway in the world where they are gathered are those of the merciful Christ, and Christ is the judge before whose bar they know full well that their redress is sure. And yet I think it will be none the less their judgment that something is due to law and justice here. As, too, it was something for them to die for the law, I can imagine them to ask whether it is not something for the law to prove its vindicated honor in the fit punishment of such barbarities? May it not occur to them also to ask, whether proportion is not an everlasting attribute of justice? And if punctual retribution is to follow the sudden taking off of one, whether the deliberate and slow starvation of so many thousands is to be fitly ignored and raise no sword of judgment? Neither is it any thing to say, that the awful ruin of the rebellious country is itself a punishment upon the grandest scale, and ought to be sufficient; for the misery of it is, that it falls on the innocent and not on the leaders and projectors, who are the chief criminals. Our liberal friends abroad conjure us to follow the lead of their despotism, and cover up gently all these offenses, because they are only political. Ah! there is a difference which they need to learn. Doubtless governments may be bad enough to make political offenses innocent; nay, to make them even righteous. But we have not fought this dreadful war to a close, just to put our government upon a par with their oppressive dynasties! We scorn the parallel they give us; and we owe it even to them to say, that a government which is friendly, and free, and right, protecting all alike, and doing the most for all, is one of God's sacred finalities, which no hand may touch, or conspiracy assail, without committing the most damning crime, such as can be matched by no possible severities of justice. We are driven in thus on every side, upon the conclusion that examples ought to be and must be made. Only they must be few and such as can be taken apart from all sectional conditions; for we have sections to compose, and the ordinary uses of punishment in cases of private treason do not pertain where the crime is nearly geographic, and is scarcely different from public war.

One thing more we are also sworn upon the dead to do; viz., to see that every vestige of slavery is swept clean. We did not begin the war to extirpate slavery; but the war itself took hold of slavery on its way, and as this had been the gangrene of our wound from the first, we shortly put ourselves heartily to the cleansing, and shall not, as good surgeons, leave a part of the virus in it. We are not to extirpate the form and leave the fact. The whole black code must go; the law of passes, and the law of evidence, and the unequal laws of suit and impeachment for crime. We are bound, if possible, to make the emancipation work well; as it never can, till the old habit of domination, and the new grudges of exasperated pride and passion, are qualified by gentleness and consideration. Otherwise there will be no industry but only jangle; society in fact will be turned into a hell of poverty and confusion. And this kind of relationship never can be secured, till the dejected and despised race are put upon the footing of men, and allowed to assert themselves somehow in the laws. Putting aside all theoretic notions of equality, and regarding nothing but the practical want of the emancipation, negro suffrage appears to be indispensable. But the want is one thing, and the right of compelling it another. Our States have always made their own laws of suffrage, and if we want to resuscitate the state-rights doctrine, there is no so ready way as to rouse it by state wrongs. But there is always a way of doing what wants to be done,—pardon me if I name it even here; for our dead are not asking mere rhetoric of us, but duty. They call us to no whimpering over them, no sad weeping, or doling of soft sympathy, but to counsel and true action. I remember too, that we have taken more than a hundred thousand of these freedmen of the war to fight our common battle. I remember the massacre of Fort Pillow. I remember the fatal assault of Fort Wagner and the gallant Shaw sleeping there in the pile of his black followers. I remember the bloody fight and victory on the James, where the ground itself was black with dead. Ah, there is a debt of honor here! And honor is never so sacred as when it is due to the weak. Blasted and accursed be the soul that will forget these dead! If they had no offices or honors, if they fought and died in the plane of their humility,—Thou just God, forbid that we suffer them now to be robbed of the hope that inspired them!

Do then simply this, which we have a perfect constitutional right to do,—pass this very simple amendment, that the basis of representation in Congress shall hereafter be the number, in all the States alike, of the free male voters therein. Then the work is done; a general free suffrage follows by consent, and as soon as it probably ought. For these returning States will not be long content with half the offices they want, and half the power allowed them in the Republic. Negro suffrage is thus carried without even naming the word.

Need I add, that now, by these strange fortunes of the rebellion rushing on its Providential overthrow, immense responsibilities are put upon us, that are new. A new style of industry is to be inaugurated. The soil is to be distributed over again, villages are to be created, schools established, churches erected, preachers and teachers provided, and money for these purposes to be poured out in rivers of benefaction, even as it has been in the war. A whole hundred years of new creation will be needed to repair these wastes and regenerate these habits of wrong; and we are baptized for the dead, to go forth in God's name, ceasing not, and putting it upon our children never to cease, till the work is done.

My task is now finished; only, alas! too feebly. There are many things I might say, addressing you as Alumni, as professors and teachers, and as scholars training here for the new age to come. But you will anticipate my suggestions, and pass on by me, to conceive a better wisdom for yourselves. One thing only I will name, which is fitting, as we part, for us all, viz., that without any particle of vain assumption, we swear by our dead to be Americans. Our position is gained! Our die of history is struck! Thank God we have a country, and that country has the chance of a future! Ours be it henceforth to cherish that country, and assert that future; also, to invigorate both by our own civilization, adorn them by our literature, consolidate them in our religion. Ours be it also, in God's own time, to champion, by land and sea, the right of this whole continent to be an American world, and to have its own American laws, and liberties, and institutions.

part five

NATIONAL
PROGRESS
AND
WEALTH

During the last three decades of the nineteenth century American life passed through some transformations that substantially affected perspectives on the national destiny. The composition of the population was radically changed by millions of European immigrants settling in the United States. It has been estimated that by 1900 one-third of the population were either foreign born or the children of foreign-born parents. Of no less consequence were the alterations brought to American life by the twin phenomena of industrial expansion and the growth of cities. By 1860 the amount of capital invested in industry, railroads, commerce, and urban property had already outstripped the total economic value of American farms; after 1865 the nation's industry, greatly stimulated by manufacturing demands of the Civil War, surged ahead at an unprecedented pace. In those postwar years the urban population more than doubled as European immigrants and rural Americans made their way to burgeoning industrial centers.[1]

With these changes came all the social and economic problems associated with the industrial revolution: city blight and urban ghettos, rural depressions, exploited human and natural resources. Yet the prevalent

[1] For a discussion of these changes and their effects on American religion see Edwin Scott Gaustad, *A Religious History of America* (New York: Harper & Row, Publishers, 1966), pp. 227ff; and Winthrop S. Hudson, *Religion in America* (New York: Charles Scribner's Sons, 1965), pp. 207ff.

mood in post-Civil War America was one of forward-looking optimism. Beneath the surface of this optimistic exterior there seethed a potentially explosive discontent, but Americans in most walks of life assumed that both they as individuals and their nation as a whole were beckoned by a glorious future. Increased immigration produced a resurgence of nativist fears that all these foreigners would wreck the social, economic, and political structure of the nation; such apprehensions were more than counterbalanced, however, by the widely proclaimed belief that America was rapidly fulfilling her destiny as a refuge of freedom and opportunity for the oppressed and homeless of the world. Expanding national wealth was concentrated more and more into the holdings of a few corporations and families, but the ideology which long held sway was that the hand of providence was rewarding the American virtues of thrift and hard work by guiding both industrious individuals and the nation toward a splendid position of economic strength. God's New Israel began increasingly to turn in upon herself, behold her progress and wealth, and conclude that the Almighty could not have elected a more virtuous or more deserving people.

Rabbi Isaac Mayer Wise, an immigrant to this country from Bohemia in 1846, was not uncritical of nineteenth-century American society, but he did believe that the progress of Western civilization was culminating in America. Arriving in New York City with only two dollars in his pocket, Wise was to become the influential rabbi of Temple Bene Yeshurun in Cincinnati, a promoter of the Union of American Hebrew Congregations, a founder of Hebrew Union College, and the leading American spokesman for Reform Judaism. Wise's life in America was not the typical success story since he brought with him from Europe a solid formal education at the universities of Prague and Vienna. Yet, like so many other European Jews, he had been at best "tolerated" by a culture shaped by a State Church. "My father," he once said, "was not permitted to call even a handbreadth of land his own, therefore I never had a fatherland." Wise urged Jewish immigrants to become thoroughly Americanized, to discard as quickly as possible their European languages and habits. "The Jew must become an American, in order to gain the proud self-consciousness of the free-born man." Through Americanization and the retention of the essentials of his religion, the Jew could both attain full participation in American life and preserve his Jewish identity.[2]

Americanization did not mean for Wise the mindless approval of everything in American society. He fulminated against this country's ignorance of great literature, its worship of money, its ready acceptance of

2 See Israel Knox, *Rabbi in America: The Story of Isaac M. Wise* (Boston: Little, Brown and Company, 1957); and Jacob Rader Marcus, "The Americanization of Isaac Mayer Wise" (Cincinnati: privately printed, 1931).

Protestant influence on politics. Yet the note he sounded repeatedly was that America was the nation of the future. Her future was, in fact, the hope of humanity since she possessed liberty as "the soul of her existence." Wise gave classic expression to this idea in his 1869 lecture before the Theological and Religious Library Association of Cincinnati. There he portrayed America as the Promised Land of freedom progressively realizing her role in history through a combination of free choice and the law of providence.

Religious interpretations of American destiny after the Civil War seldom dwelt simply on America as the Promised Land of liberty. They usually extolled that destiny in terms of the nation's expanding wealth, employing the arguments of the then dominant laissez faire economic theory. If economic self-interest were allowed free play, it was held, every industrious man would serve the common good of society and contribute to the nation's increasing wealth. This theory was buttressed by the individualism of the so-called Protestant ethic that identified virtue with frugality and hard work; it was also supported by a providential view of history that saw the nation's progress proceeding according to laws of God incorporated within a system of unhindered economic competition.

Henry Ward Beecher, who had scarcely exhausted his persuasive powers during the Civil War, became one of America's most eloquent spokesmen for a national destiny pursued within a laissez faire system. Enjoying a liberal salary and large royalties from his publications, Beecher reasoned (like so many of his fellow clergy) that poverty more often springs from sin, than sin from poverty:

> There may be reasons of poverty which do not involve wrong; but looking comprehensively through city and town and village and country, the general truth will stand, that no man in this land suffers from poverty unless it be more than his fault—unless it be his sin.[3]

In 1877, when bloody railroad strikes broke out in American cities in protest of a ten percent wage cut, Beecher upbraided the railroad employees for not nobly bearing their poverty. He was not always so callous in his attitude toward the poor and occasionally even denounced the corporate swindles and frauds of his day. He consistently maintained, however, that wealth itself was a blessing to be actively sought and that the nation's wealth was a providentially bestowed means for achieving a significant place in history.

Beecher's Thanksgiving Day sermon of 1870, "The Tendencies of American Progress," clearly revealed his individualist ethic and his views

---

[3] Quoted in Henry F. May, *Protestant Churches and Industrial America* (New York: Harper & Row, Publishers, Torchbooks, 1967), p. 69.

of national wealth and progress. Running through the entire sermon was the conviction that American destiny under God was inextricably intertwined with American wealth. "May God give us magnanimity and power and riches," Beecher said, "that we may throw the shadow of our example upon the poor, the perishing, and the ready-to-be-destroyed, for their protection." John Winthrop's exemplary "city upon a hill" had become, in the rhetoric of people like Beecher, a tawdry megalopolis.

Laissez faire individualism attained its height as an ideology in this country at precisely the time when it was becoming inapplicable to social and economic reality. The appearance of large trusts and vast cities between Reconstruction and 1900 thwarted the dynamics of free competition and frustrated radical individualism. Nevertheless, laissez faire as an idea-system continued to spread; it became, in fact, a veritable American gospel reaching all levels of society. "This faith and philosophy became the most persuasive siren in American life," Ralph Henry Gabriel has written.

> It filled the highways with farm boys trekking to the city. It drained the towns and countryside of Europe. It persuaded the educated young man that the greatest rewards of life were to be found in the business world. It taught the ambitious that power lies in wealth rather than in political office. It penetrated the workshop and paralyzed the effort of the labor leader undertaking a crusade for justice to the working man.[4]

Captains of industry and builders of railroads became national heroes, saints in a cult of success. Horatio Alger's dime novels popularized the cult in a series of rags-to-riches stories which indoctrinated American lads in the belief that virtue is rewarded by wealth.

Andrew Carnegie, who rose from the position of bobbin boy to wealthy steelmaster, was one of the heroes of his age and an articulate defender of its ideology. His famous essay "Wealth," which first appeared in the *North American Review* in 1889, argued that the foundations of society and the progress of civilization rest upon certain "laws": the sacredness of property, free economic competition, and accumulation of wealth. Carnegie admitted that the development of civilization on the basis of these laws "may be sometimes hard for the individual," but he was convinced "it is best for the race, because it insures the survival of the fittest in every department." Carnegie, Beecher, and many other Americans of the time drew upon the social Darwinism of Herbert

---

[4] Ralph Henry Gabriel, *The Course of American Democratic Thought* (New York: The Ronald Press Company, 1956), pp. 163–64.

Spencer to give their laissez faire individualism theoretical respectability. The rough-and-tumble of economic competition was believed to effect the improvement of humanity by guaranteeing that only the fittest of the race would survive. Carnegie softened the harshness of his Darwinism by insisting that the wealthy man is obligated to abide by the law of stewardship, that is, he should distribute his wealth in such a way that it contributes to the common good and helps those who will help themselves. Carnegie was thoroughly persuaded, however, that obedience to the basic laws of economic competition would "some day . . . solve the problem of the Rich and the Poor, and . . . bring 'Peace on earth, among men Good-Will.' "

It fell principally to the influential clergy of the day to give the Gospel of Wealth religious sanction and, as custodians of the public conscience, to assure a nation scrambling for riches that it was in no danger of corrupting its character or abandoning its divine destiny. Russell Conwell, Baptist minister and founder of the Philadelphia Temple (out of which grew Temple University), assured Americans that the pursuit of wealth was an honorable task. In his lecture *Acres of Diamonds* which he delivered more than six thousand times across the eastern and middle western United States, Conwell admonished his hearers, "I say that you ought to get rich, and it is your duty to get rich." The reason is simple: "Money is power, and you ought to be reasonably ambitious to have it. You ought because you can do more good with it than you could without it." For those who doubted the good character of men of wealth and power Conwell had further words of comfort: "ninety-eight out of one hundred of the rich men of America are honest. That is why they are rich. That is why they are trusted with money."

The religious and moral justification of the Gospel of Wealth was rounded out in 1901 by William Lawrence, Episcopal bishop of Massachusetts. In his essay "The Relation of Wealth to Morals," Lawrence acknowledges that certain moral hazards attend wealth, but he insists that "in the long run, it is only to the man of morality that wealth comes," that on the whole "godliness is in league with riches." What is true for the individual is equally true for the nation. "Material prosperity is helping to make the national character sweeter, more joyous, more unselfish, more Christlike." "Clothed with her material forces, the great personality of this Nation may fulfill her divine destiny" of developing her education, industry, art—her culture as a whole. For Lawrence, American destiny has become thoroughly introverted. Acquisition of wealth through free economic competition "sweetens" the national character and encourages the growth of American culture—that is the extent of American destiny under God!

The Gospel of Wealth exercised a firm, prolonged control on the American mind; its control, however, was neither absolute nor endless.

Among farmers and industrial workers who were the victims of a monopolistic capitalism unchecked by government regulations, discontent smoldered and then burst forth in strikes and in protests from workingmen's associations and farmers' alliances. Critics of the ideology of acquisitiveness emerged among the intellectuals. American pragmatist philosopher Charles Peirce attacked his "century of greed," economist Thorstein Veblen condemned the Gospel of Wealth, journalist Finley Peter Dunne bitingly satirized the philanthropic activities of the captains of industry. During the early years of the twentieth century the muckrakers opened national sores created by the industrial revolution. The ground was being prepared for an emerging concept of a welfare state and the reforms of the progressive movement.

Religious resistance to uncontrolled capitalism was spearheaded by the movement known as "Social Christianity" or the "Social Gospel." The Social Gospel was never really a tightly organized movement; for the most part it was a religious outlook constituted by shared beliefs. Most of its representatives believed in the social principles of Jesus as reliable moral guides for the individual and for society, trusted in the basic goodness and worth of man, and expected "that, through the efforts of men of good will, the kingdom of God would soon become a reality, bringing with it social harmony and the elimination of the worst of social injustices."[5] Most proponents of the Social Gospel shared their age's wholehearted belief in progress. Critical though they were of the selfishness and atomistic individualism of the Gospel of Wealth, they were confident that honest efforts on the part of both government and individuals of good will would correct social injustices and that the nation could progressively achieve the Kingdom of God and the brotherhood of man.

Washington Gladden, commonly regarded as the "father of the Social Gospel," held to a progressive view of national destiny. Pastor of the First Congregational Church in Columbus, Ohio, Gladden was for two years an active member of the Columbus city council, but like most Social Gospelers he exerted his greatest influence through sermons, lectures, and books. On October 13, 1909, Gladden, then in his seventies, delivered a sermon at Minneapolis before the American Board of Commissioners for Foreign Missions. That sermon, "The Nation and the Kingdom," elucidated an understanding of American destiny long held by Gladden and his fellow Social Christians. Convinced that America was progressively Christianizing herself, Gladden advanced the claim that Christianity's mission to save the world was identical in all essential parts with the American mission. Gladden's sermon represented two tendencies

[5] Robert T. Handy, *The Social Gospel in America, 1870–1920* (New York: Oxford University Press, Inc., 1966), p. 10.

in late nineteenth- and early twentieth-century American religion: the tendency to link the coming Kingdom of God with American destiny, and the inclination to connect an intense Christian missionary impulse with a view of America's world role.

Events of the twentieth century would produce attitudes among the American people that would severely shake their optimism. Deep disappointment over the fact that the Great War was not a war to end all war, shock and despair over the Depression, anxiety over the threat of nuclear extinction—such feelings would render highly questionable, if not downright ludicrous, the assumption that America was moving steadily toward the Kingdom of God. Yet even the crises of the twentieth century would not totally invalidate Walt Whitman's description of America as the nation that "counts almost entirely upon the future." The American Israel could no longer depend upon an inevitable progress toward a spectacular place in history, but she could and would continue to count on the future to bring opportunities for renewal of her divine destiny.

SUGGESTED READING

Abell, Aaron I. *American Catholicism and Social Action: A Search for Social Justice, 1865–1950.* Garden City, N.Y.: Doubleday & Company, Inc., 1960.

Fine, Sidney. *Laissez-Faire and the General-Welfare State: A Study of Conflict in American Thought, 1865–1901.* Ann Arbor: The University of Michigan Press, 1956.

Hofstadter, Richard. *Social Darwinism in American Thought.* Boston: Beacon Press, 1955.

Hopkins, Charles Howard. *The Rise of the Social Gospel in American Protestantism, 1865–1915.* New Haven, Conn.: Yale University Press, 1940.

Kennedy, Gail, ed. *Democracy and the Gospel of Wealth.* Boston: D. C. Heath & Company, 1949.

Lerner, Max. "The Triumph of Laissez-Faire," in *Paths of American Thought*, edited by A. M. Schlesinger, Jr. and M. White, pp. 147–66. Boston: Houghton Mifflin Company, 1963.

May, Henry F., *Protestant Churches and Industrial America.* New York: Harper & Row, Publishers, Torchbooks, 1967.

ISAAC M. WISE

Our Country's
Place In History

The Committee of the Theological and Religious Library Association of our city having bestowed the privilege upon me to open a course of lectures, in which so many excellent and distinguished gentlemen participate, I must in the first place express my thanks to the Committee; and in the second place, make the humble confession, that looking upon the galaxy of orators to come after me (in time, of course,), and the intelligent audience before me, I do not consider myself equal to the task so kindly conferred upon me.

Weak men, in battle, seek shelter behind strong fortifications. I have been prudent enough to profit by the experience of others. Conscious of my deficiencies I seek shelter behind a strong subject—a subject dear and precious to all of us, our country, our promised land, the home and fortress of freedom, the blessed spot which flows with milk and honey, upon which we invoke God's gracious blessings. "Our Country's Place in History" is the subject of this lecture, to which I claim your kind attention; and I know you will bestow it, on account of this important theme.

HISTORY AND A PLACE IN IT

History is Providence realized. It is the experience of the human family, because it is the compendium of those events which effected the progress of our race. Individuals and nations, by an undefined impulse, are the actors who realize the plans of a higher power, to the detriment of all that is wicked, the development and preservation of all that is good, and tends to the elevation of man.

A lecture delivered before the Theological and Religious Library Association of Cincinnati, January 7, 1869. [I am grateful to my former student Marc J. Trister for his discovery of this and numerous other items by Wise that bear on the theme of this book.—EDITOR]

A cursory glance upon this physical universe proves the existence of such an impulse in the vast domain of creation as a force of nature, a universal law. Primary matter, imagine it as ether, gas, mist or chaos,— primary matter is potential, imbued with the desire of individuation (although no such term is known in physics), to form bodies of a separate existence. So this earth, those stars, and those suns were individualized from primary matter, other celestial bodies are, and will perpetually be formed by the same law, the same "Word of God." The great bodies of the universe, in the architecture of heaven, are active and co-operative individuals. The influence of each contributes directly or indirectly to the rotation and life of the whole; while the primary or non-individualized matter is apparently passive, without a role in the grand drama of the universe.

The same law precisely governs the destiny of man. The human family is a chaos of persons, each imbued with the desire, to rise above this chaos to individual immortality. Tribes and nations, composed of persons, are continually stimulated by the same innate desire, to rise above the level of the chaos to individual existence, to an active and co-operative attitude. Many rise above the chaos, and fulfill their destiny, to realize the designs of Providence; many more remain particles of the chaos, or meteors in the celestial plan.

Like the stars in the solar system, the nations who rose to individuality are clustered around the central and invisible omnipotence, and complete their rotation in obedience to immutable laws. Like the stars, every people must be a unit in the sum total of history—a unit without which the whole sum could not exist; an independent unit in its sphere, and an auxiliary one, attracting and being attracted, bearing and being borne, in the moral universe of Providence. So and not otherwise, we can imagine a government administered by the Supreme Wisdom. This theory rests upon the solid basis of analogy from nature's revelations, and explains the phenomenon of history. In this sense nations have their places in history.

NO FATALISM

This theory has nothing in common with fatalism, inasmuch as obedience to the dicta of reason is its direct opposite. It is not even inevitable necessity to the individual or the nation. Both are at liberty to choose their own course; although, if persisting in the deviation, it amounts to an entire failure of their existence to themselves, while others take their places in the realization of the Providential designs. Particles must, man wills, the object is God's. Let us explain. Every individual is appointed to fulfill that destiny in society, for which he is gifted with adequate capacities. This destiny must be fulfilled, although this or that particular individual may revolt, and neglect his appointment to the bitter end of self destruction. Others gifted with the same capacities will take that place in society and fulfill that same destiny. This is individual freedom and universal necessity. Nature offers many an analogy in this respect, one of which will suffice. There is the forest with its numerous trees. Every tree has the destiny to be a part of the forest. Trees die, therefore saplings must grow up to take their respective places. Every sapling has the natural destiny to grow and to take its place as a tree. But nature produces ten saplings, only one of which fulfills its destiny as a tree of the forest, the other nine die, to nourish the roots of that tree. The forest must; man wills. Precisely the same is the case with nations. Every nation has that destiny, to which time, geographical location and the capacities of the race enable it. It may not know, not understand, not attempt to fulfill its destiny, or do it but partially. But then other nations who do fulfill this particular destiny, will replace it, and the designs of Providence must be realized, exactly as the forest remains a forest, however many saplings perish before one becomes a tree. The Philistines might have fulfilled the destiny of the Hebrews, the Phoenicians that of the Greeks, the Macedonians that of Rome, and the Mexicans that of the United States. But they did not, and the succession was necessary to realize the design. There is no fatalism.

EXPLANATIONS

Without entering upon the principles of just and successful government, the logical sequence of our theory; we will only add this explanation: The destiny which a nation realizes in the designs of Providence, is its place in history. Furthermore, however different the destinies of the various nations, they are similar in one chief characteristic, whose name is PROGRESS. Nations which contribute nothing to the progress of humanity, fulfill no destiny. Nations contributing no longer to the progress of humanity, have ceased to fulfill their destiny, and are in a state of dissolution. Nations, which contribute most to the progress of humanity, fulfill the highest national destiny. For history, as we have said already, "is the compendium of those events which effected the progress of the human race." We are ready now, to discuss our country's place in history.

THE CLOSE OF THE FIFTEENTH CENTURY

Let us open our text book and cast a glance on the state of affairs towards the close of the fifteenth century. In the political arena, personal liberty was submerged in huge centralized empires with a fair beginning of standing armies as the right hand of despotism. From and after the crusades, the small sovereignties vanished, and with them the last trace of personal freedom and patriarchal government, without any beneficent change in the feudal system. The serf, the peasant, and the burgher, with the exception of a few cities, was the beast of burden, the commodity, the chattel of the lawless nobleman whose life and fortune were property of the crown. The law was barbarous, and barbarism was the law, modified in exceptional cases by conscientious or prudent rulers. . . .

The Church was no better than the State. Europe was one huge despotism. John Wikliff [*sic*] was dead (1384). His followers were few and harmless. Huss and Hieronimus of Prague had ended on the Pyre (1415–16). The Taborites and Orphanites were massacred and the Calixtines subjected again to the sovereign church (1433). A century of quarrels in the church was successfully closed, the reforms proposed by the councils of Basel and Kostnitz were set aside and overcome, the head of the church was so well established in his rights and privileges, the lower clergy and the people so well trained into submission and silence, that Alexander VI occupied undisturbed the highest dignity in Christendom. The inquisition extended its paternal arms from the North sea into the Pyrenean peninsula; the Jews were driven out of Spain, and everything was nicely fixed for the perpetuation of despotism in State and Church. There was no escape from the terrible arm of absolutism. It reached to the very ends of the then known earth, and extended its horrible dominion into the very realms of heaven. The nations failing to fulfill their destiny, the old world having arrived at a dead lock, a new nation, a new world had to be born, and born they were.

THE TRAVAIL

Mark the wonderful travail at the birth of a new world and a new chapter of history. In the chaos of that despotism, two peculiar germs of a new creation were discernible. We can only call them two unconscious passions. The love of knowledge and of discovery, were those two germs. Philosophy pressed in the straight jacket of orthodox scholasticism, in the dogmatic prison could not be entirely expunged after all. The long dispute of Nominalists and Realists, as well as the dissensions among church authorities, and especially the philosophical and scientific labors of the Arabs, carried into Christendom by Spanish Jews and their books—began to undermine the authority of scholasticism and to secularize philosophy. Men, although few and far apart, especially in Italy and Germany, began to thirst passionately after better knowledge. Although they were unconscious of the object of their desire and its influence upon the new state of affairs which was to come; nevertheless they felt the desire after better knowledge, and were compelled by an impulse from a higher power, to seek it. This gradually gave birth to the humanists, a class of doctors whose knowledge was quite limited, and whose freedom of research was still more so, because the despotism of Church and State extended over all departments of the mind, as well as over the youngest daughter of that age, the child of Guttenberg [sic] and Faust. Nevertheless they worked, although they knew not to what purpose. Popes, potentates and other mighty men, with the iron rod of oppression in one hand, assisted with the other in rearing a new fortress to humanity, without knowing what they did. The same was the case with that peculiar desire, to discover unknown islands, unknown roads on the high sea. Nobody knew exactly why, wherefore or whereto. It was a passion, an impulse from a higher power, for which none could account, had they even attempted it. The Italians and especially the Portuguese, were almost frantic with this passion. These were the travails of that age. These were the silent and seemingly insignificant causes which inspired Columbus with the irresistible passion to discover, he knew not what.

THE DISCOVERY OF AMERICA

Contrary to the wisdom of all the wise men of his age, contrary to the resolves of the maritime experts and the maritime nations of his days, Columbus, compelled by the irresistible power of that nameless Spirit of the universe, steered out upon the unknown multitudiness of water, with the daring scheme to discover a direct route to India. Again, contrary to the hopes of those who sent him, of those who accompanied him, and contrary to his own expectation—to the most lofty flight of his imagination—he discovered a new world. A new world, in virgin purity, emerged from the deep, burst upon the enlarged horizon of human knowledge. A new world, so much larger than old princess Europe, and seated so much more secure between her wide oceans than Europe was on the back of the disguised, arbitrary and despotic Jupiter. A new world whose plains are wider, whose rivers broader, whose mountains higher and whose destiny so much loftier than those of her older sisters. A new world, the youngest daughter of Rhea, the proud heiress of their fortunes and their charms. A new world was discovered. Mankind had travailed and given birth to a new world.

Who schemed this masterly design of progress? Who understood its importance at the time? Who comprehended the passionate yearning of that age after knowledge and discovery? None on earth. God alone did. There is no fatalism.

MEXICO AND SOUTH AMERICA

Mankind is very slow in comprehending the designs of Providence. A century passed over the discovery of America without deriving any durable benefit from that great event. The love of discovery degenerated into an adventurous and avaricious spirit. Monarchs and violent men were allied for the sole purpose of plundering the new country, enslaving and exterminating its aborigines, and subjecting the new world to the despotic scepter of the old. Mexico, Peru, and other regions of South America and the West Indies, were thinly colonized to find gold, to acquire new domains for tyrannical crowns, new territory for defunct inhabitants. They failed in the choice of a destiny and could not succeed.

THE REFORMATION

Meanwhile the love for better knowledge progressed rapidly in central Europe, especially in Italy, Germany, France, Holland and England. Commerce, and with it the free cities and municipal rights gained considerable importance. The Jews driven from Spain, Portugal and Naples, carried their commercial spirit, their rich literature, and Free Masonry with its cosmopolitan spirit into other parts of Christendom, especially to Holland and Italy. The love of learning, the growing power of the press, and the increase of commerce, liberalized and humanized nations, and roused in them that spirit of liberty which, in the first instance, resulted in the Protestant Reformation, which severed the sinews of ecclesiastical despotism, and paralyzed the right arm of worldly tyranny. From the day when Martin Luther nailed his theses to the church door, to the outbreak of the Thirty Years' War was a century of fierce contest between growing freedom and tenacious despotism, rising philosophy and declining dogmatics, which roused a feeling of independence, a spirit of liberty, and conscious sentiment of self-respect in the hearts of tens of thousands, who could no longer find a home in Europe, and they were driven to America.

THE PURITAN FATHERS

During and after the Thirty Years' War in Germany and the concomitant convulsions in other countries, the liberal element lost considerable ground in Europe. The persecuted of all classes and denominations sought refuge in North America. True, not all like the Puritan Fathers, came to these shores with the pure desire to be free, and unmolested in their form of worship: nevertheless the vast majority of immigrants came to avoid persecution. Also most of the mere adventurers, to say nothing of English Catholics, French Huguenots, German, Dutch and Slavonic sects, Jews, Quakers and Deists; also most of the mere adventurers came to these shores with a certain spirit of liberty and independence, which was strengthened here by the influence of society and by the circumstances, that every pioneer in the forests of the Atlantic shore, or on the broad plains of the West, was sovereign on his domain, out of every foreign government's reach, and compelled to be his own governor, cabinet, legislature, general and army of defence. This made of the original settlers not only matter-of-fact men, capable of self-government, but also independent sons of freedom who abhorred the very idea of subjection and persecution. This spirit increased in intensity with the growth of the population in number and intelligence. The martial spirit also was developed by the course of events. The combat against ferocious beasts; the wars of "the Israelites against the Philistines," of "God's chosen people against the Indian Gentiles," and the struggles of France and England on this continent, made the American soldier. To all these growing elements in the early stage of American history one more must be counted, and that is the preservation of one language for all the colonies. This was the cornerstone to national greatness.

THE REVOLUTION

It is, therefore, quite natural, that the slightest irritation by the British Government, reaching outside of the commercial centers to the sovereigns of the forests and the broad plains, should arm them to resolute resistance. Being all sovereigns and soldiers themselves, and having learned an excellent lesson of Oliver Cromwell and his ironsiders, the only true cousins of Americans—the tea pennies and stamp shillings which among any other people would have passed unnoticed, sufficed to set the colonies ablaze, and to enact one of the brightest chapters in history. Glory to the memory of the heroes of the revolution, to the generous godfathers of liberty. Glory to the memory of George Washington and his heroic compatriots. They were the chosen instruments in the hands of Providence, to turn the wheel of events in favor of liberty forever; and they proved worthy of their great mission, of their immortal work. The hearts of a grateful people, canonized with honor and glory, are the indestructible materials of the monument of George Washington and his compatriots. The millions of oppressed men and women in all countries, whose chains have been broken and whose prisons have been razed, are the grand chorus, who sing the praise of the American revolution; and we, the lords and ladies of this broad land of freedom, re-echo the Hallelujah from ocean to ocean, from Maine's rocky coast to the silvery mirror of the Pacific and the sunny gulf of Mexico.

THE CHOICE OF DESTINY

The revolution was the first grasp after the destiny of the nation, to which it was fully prepared by the spirit of the age, geographical location and special capacities, growing out naturally of former events in the regular routine of cause and effect. But now the question rose what to make of the thirteen independent republics. A new kingdom was the natural suggestion. But who besides God was to be the king of kings and the lord of lords? Washington, like Gideon, was too good a man to be a king. Still had he accepted that dignity, he could not have maintained it for any length of time. Those who understood the spirit of the people which came forth victoriously from the revolution could think of a republic only, on the broadest principles of personal freedom and municipal rights, civil and religious liberty in the most extensive sense of these terms. The framers of the Constitution were wise enough to understand the spirit of their people, courageous enough to confront the destiny of the nation, and honest enough to express their full conviction in the paragraphs of the Constitution and its immortal preamble. The people of the United States, on accepting this Constitution, had formally and solemnly chosen its destiny, to be now and forever the palladium of liberty and its divinely appointed banner-bearer, for the progress and redemption of mankind. It is a glorious destiny, a lofty ideal, which the fathers of our country have chosen for her; an ideal which must inspire every citizen with the holy desire, to take his proper place in the ranks of the people which follows this ideal, this guiding star, this glowing sun of human prosperity; an ideal which in the midst of selfishness, passion, avarice and debasing materialism, must be and was powerful enough, to rally the myriads of free men around the banners of our country and, with death-defying bravery, wield the sword in her protection to the undisturbed fulfillment of her destiny.

ILLUSTRATION

With the adoption of the Constitution, our country assumed her place in history. It was done by the free choice of the people. Although it must be admitted that a chain of natural causes and effects, from the fifteenth century to the end of the eighteenth, together with geographical causes, educated the colonists to this destiny; nevertheless it can not be denied that every important step in the progress of our early history resulted from free choice, from personal freedom, demonstrating clearly the theory of individual freedom and universal necessity in the government of mankind. This theory, in the government of a nation, is reduced to the practical problem of finding the just equilibrium of personal freedom and the necessary power of the government, the solution of which is the great object of constitutional statesmanship. Our Constitution of the United States is the original American attempt in solution of that problem. This being of itself a contribution to the progress of mankind, it entitled our country to a place in history. But she occupies a larger chapter in the records of humanity than a written document confers; a place which might be best illustrated by historical parallels.

Being the heiress of the preceding phases of civilization, numerous parallels suggest themselves. Let us select one.

The United States occupy the same place in modern history as Greece did in antiquity. Greece, surrounded by water and blessed with numerous harbors, was favored with an extensive commerce and continual intercourse with the world. The same precisely is the case with our country. The oceans are broad enough to protect us against foreign interference in our domestic affairs, which no council of European powers will ever arrange. At the same time our harbors are numerous enough to shelter the navies of the whole world, and to keep us in constant intercourse with all nations. Distances were the great obstacles in our way. But the American mind removed them. The application of steam to navigation and the electro-magnetic force to the telegraph brought us in connection with the world, as closely as Greece ever was, to Egypt, Phoenicia or Italy, and reduced our wide-stretched territories, for all practical purposes, to a compass no larger than that of ancient Greece. Greece was the heiress of an ancient civilization, which was poured into her lap by immigrants from Egypt, Phoenicia, Assyria, Syria and Asia Minor, and the constant intercourse with all those and other nations. Our country is the heiress of the European civilization. All her shipwrecked men and shipwrecked ideas continually pour into our lap with a wealth of thoughts, designs, energies, learning, skill and enterprise which steadily fill our mental coffers, and enlarge our horizon of conceptions. Greece remoulded all those foreign elements into one preeminently Grecial form; so do we continually assimilate and Americanize, absorb and recast all the foreign elements which we receive. So powerful is the affinity of freedom among men that it unites and amalgamates them quicker than any other agency. While the German in Poland, after centuries of domicil, is still a German, the first American-born generation of Germans is American. While the Poles in France remain foreigners, among us they are fastly incorporated. While Czechs in the heart of Germany, after centuries of mutual intercourse, are still Bohemian in feeling, language, customs and ideals; it is extremely easy for us to sustain one language for the whole country. This is one of the most wonderful influences which we know liberty to exercise on man.

Greece did not stop short at her heritage from abroad, but enlarged it, by native genius, to Grecian art, philosophy, science, government and religion; so do we. Our form of government is new. The patent-office at Washington, that great museum of mind, speaks volumes in praise of native genius. The practical sphere, to which necessity has confined and schooled us, testifies sufficiently, that whenever our turn shall come in the idealistic sphere, we will not be found missing in the production of an originally American art, science, philosophy and religion. Greece educated ten thousands of emissaries, to carry her wealth into Asia, Africa and Europe; so do we. We educate millions of free men, to carry our national wealth all over the earth. The very example of our successful revolution set France and all Europe ablaze with hopes of liberty. The millions of letters and journals which we send annually across the ocean, are so many rays of light to oppressed nations, and rouse the millions to think, reflect, wish and hope for freedom, and to appreciate its blessings. Every Negro in our midst is an emissary for the future humanization and civilization of Africa. Those very Chinamen who do now the work of washerwomen in the far West, are our boarding scholars, to become the future teachers of Eastern Asia, which is already near our doors. The very result of our late rebellion encouraged and inspired millions of European hearts with hopes of redemption, and proved that the republic is stronger than any monarchy. This is as important to humanity as our declaration of independence was. Greece, by the conflux of the various families of man, was inhabited by a peculiar people; so is our country. We are originally English, Irish, French, Dutch, German, Polish, Spanish, or Scandinavian; but we are neither. We are Americans. Every child born on this soil is Americanized. Our country has a peculiar people to work out a new and peculiar destiny.

The heiress of the civilized world's blood, experience and wisdom, as Greece was in days of yore; the mistress of the vast domain fortified by heaving oceans, really wealthy as none was before her; the favored high priestess of the goddess of liberty, with the diadem of honor and the breast-plate of justice—though young, gay, fast, blundering and wild— occupies already a prominent place in history. Her commerce influences the commerce of the world, as only a few old countries do. But commerce, the source of wealth and the missionary of civilization, is one of the handmaids of progress. Her inventions in the mechanical arts, her strikes and associations of mechanics and laborers, revolutionize the system of labor all over the world, and redeem the laboring man from the oppression of hard labor, the despotism of capital and cunningness. These are powerful contributions to the progress of humanity. Still, industry herself is but another handmaid of progress. Liberty is the cause, progenitor, preserver and protector of all the blessings which we enjoy and impart to others. Liberty is progress itself. The chapter of liberty in the modern record of nations is our country's place in history. All other blessings of the human family grow from the soil of liberty, warmed by the genial rays of this glorious sun, and fructified by the stream of justice. Liberty is our place in history, our national destiny, our ideal, the very soul of our existence. As long as we cling tenaciously to our destiny and long steadily after our ideal, we will maintain our country's place in history. Greece, Rome and all the other empires afford no precedences to our future, for ours is a new world and a new destiny, which is entirely in our hands. Political parties may struggle and strive for the ascendancy. The conservative and the progressive elements of society are its centripetal and centrifugal forces which cause regular rotation, as long as they are governed by the center of gravity, the ideal of liberty. Money may govern the actions of tens of thousands; it is after all the mere foam on the surface which invariably disappears, as often as the ocean exerts its freedom of heaving up its billows. Sects may quarrel over particular dogmas, doctors disagree on the precise nature of the center of the earth. Liberty neutralizes their disputes, and begets new forms of religion and science. Nothing can arrest our progress, nothing drag down our country from her high place in history, except our own wickedness working a wilful desertion of our destiny, the desertion from the ideal of liberty. As long as we cling to this ideal, we will be in honor, glory, wealth and prosperity.

In the family, in school, in the academy, in church, on the public forum, in the press and everywhere else educate champions for the host of freedom; they are our country's guard. Warm, rouse, inspire every heart for liberty; this is our strength, our prosperity, our future, our destiny. Freedom to all nations; freedom to every man, this is our country's place in history; liberty in the name of my God and my country.

HENRY WARD BEECHER

The Tendencies Of
American Progress

It is well for us to pause, in our career, to consider whither our
national life is tending. For we are too apt to become so engrossed in our
private affairs as to have but a dim and feeble sense of our relations to the
life of the whole community. Or, if we cast a glance upon the tendencies
of our times, it is apt to be superficial—a judgment which follows rather
our disposition than our reason. To the hopeful, things are always bright;
and they are always dark to the cautious. Prosperous men think the country is doing well; and the unfortunate see the signs of impending mischief
and of quick-coming ruin on every hand. Men are apt to judge of the drift
of things by the impressions made upon them by the things which are
nearest, or by the welfare of the special cause to which they are giving
their time and zeal. If that zone of life and force which is in contact with
them is stormy, they feel that it is stormy away to the horizon, though but
just a step beyond it may be tranquil; and if the affairs in which men
have embarked their chief zeal and their affections are withstood, and are
declining, they are apt to think that the whole work of God in the world
is weary and slow-paced.

While, then, it is proper that we should recognize superficial prosperity, and personal prosperity, and all forms of experience from the personal stand-point, we are far more earnest to inquire whether under the
surface the tendency of things is onward and upward, or level, or working
downward. But in order to this we must have some determinate rule or
measure. We must not judge by the eye, nor by our senses, nor by a
transient criterion.

The most obvious, and historically the first, condition of prosperity
in any community is physical thrift, material wealth; and surely there can
be no national life of any great worth without that. For there must be
prosperity in material things if there is to be prosperity in moral things

From Henry Ward Beecher, *The Original Plymouth Pulpit,* vol. V.
(Boston: Pilgrim Press, 1871), pp. 203–19.

in the last estate. Still, a nation may be prospered in the field, and at the loom, and on the ship, and on the shore, and yet be degraded and declining. For material welfare, although it be an indispensable element of national prosperity, is the lowest, and is to be subordinated to all others. Above it is the social and civil development of a nation. Far superior in importance to mere physical wealth is the wealth which comes from institutions, from laws, from the conduct of the people, and from the whole course of civilized society. But yet higher than this is moral and spiritual good. For without faith civilization itself soon becomes tame and powerless.

The highest prosperity, then, is associated with spiritual good. Next to that is social; and lowest of all is material. And in this order we are to judge of prosperity. That material good is prosperous which is working toward the social and toward the spiritual. That social and civil condition of society is wholesome which recognizes the higher law of religious development.

Now, in looking upon our national condition it is not enough that we see unbounded prosperity on the farm, at the forge, in the shop: we must ask whether this prosperity lies in the line of intelligence, of real virtue; whether it guides itself by moral principle.

On the other hand, in looking upon the imperfections and positive evils which attend the various elements of national life, men are not to be discouraged because there is much in them that is still evil; nor because in some places things are going backward, like eddies upon mighty rivers. For this is the law of all progress. But are things, *on the whole*, tending toward, or away from, moral elements? That will determine the question of prosperity.

Look, then, at our own condition territorially. What other nation has such a field for extension, such a field for development, such a field for material prosperity? Russia alone, perhaps, of all nations, has a territory as extensive as America. In all except bulk though, how different! Our climate, from the north line to the very gulf, is congenial to industry. There is no league in which climatic influences forbid prosperity; but the Russian climate is too rigorous. Through perhaps one third, or one-half —through vast spaces at any rate, it is unfavorable even to life itself, and life can never be developed into any great degree of society-force. Our soil, except a central tract (and that less barren than men suppose) is cultivatable throughout. Theirs is largely sterile. Our population is English-speaking, and homogeneous in ideas, though heterogeneous in origin. But all this, a prodigious condition of power if other things favor, is useless,—and, worse than useless, will be corrupting—if there are not other elements of prosperity than merely that which is given us, of territory.

Then, our people carry with them everywhere self-government, and *a genius for it*. Partly, this is the quality of race. We spring mainly from a stock in which inheres the tendency to government, and self-government. And partly it is a thing learned. Our people have learned it; and government, therefore, and laws, go with every colony just as surely as yokes and harnesses go with their teams and herds. Men never emigrate without carrying their household wealth and the material for employing the soil in husbandry. But tools and implements are no more necessary in their judgment than are the institutions and the customs which make men societies. Wherever you throw a hundred Americans, you may be sure that almost their first thought will be to constitute themselves into a body politic. They do it as naturally as water comes together in crystals when cold congeals it. They come by a kind of elective affinity under laws and under constitutions.

Contrast that great and unfortunate nation, France, with our own in this respect. Their self-governing instinct seems never to have been developed. The tendency is feeble, and cultivation has never been applied to it. How to be governed they but just know; and how to govern themselves, not at all. But with us this is one of the most marked national features, the indispensable necessity of being governed, and the indispensable determination to let nobody do it for us, but to do it ourselves.

Our people, also, carry institutions which are to moral force what machinery is to physical force. Institutions are but the condensations of power. They are artificial persons, as it were, to whom is given an unweariable existence—a life longer than the life of those that made them. They are the devices of civilization for storing up and preserving and fitting out moral things, and are indispensable to the strength and constancy and perpetuity of communal life.

But all these are but conditions. What now are the general tendencies of the material prosperity of America which are being developed, with such a territory, with such a people on it, with such civic advantages? On the whole, are they toward intelligence, and morality, and a higher spiritual growth?

1. The mass of our working population, I think, were never so well clothed, so bountifully fed and so well housed, as they are now; and the tendency is not backward, but forward. Our working population, to the very lowest stage and class, tend to more refinement in their food, more taste in their apparel, and more culture in their dwellings, year by year. In other words, the lowest material conditions are working upward, and not downward. Plainness of apparel, and of circumstances surrounding, are not signs and tokens either of civil growth or of Christianity. The general impression is, that, as nations are better, they will be economical. I think, on the contrary, they will be profuse, and have the means of being so. The impression is that they will be unadorned. I think they will

be more glorious than Solomon was, in all his apparel. The impression is that the law of simplicity in the sense of littleness of having and using characterizes virtue and religion. Far from it. As you go toward the savage state, you go away from complexity, from multitudinous power, down toward simplicity, and when you come to the lowest state—to the simplicity of men that wear skins and leather apparel, and live in huts and caves —you come to the fool's ideal of prosperity. But from that low animal condition starts development, and nations go on opening their faculties; and every faculty becomes a market, and demands supply. And the more culture a man has, the more parts of his nature there are which ask for material, for institutions, for raiment, for comforts of every kind, the more there is in the single man demanding these things, the more must his circumstances open up, and become rich and potential. And in looking upon the condition of the community, if you find that they are increasing in the variety of their food, in the quality of their food, and in the excellence of cooking their food; if you find that their dwellings are growing better and better from period to period; if you find that their furniture is more beautiful, answering other ends than merely the mechanical and physical ends—ministering to taste, ministering, if you will, to luxury—if you find these things, they are signs of upward development and of growth. These are the signs which we find all the way through our people, clear down to the bottom. And we are beginning to find them, as I knew we should, among the Freedmen themselves. For no sooner was their bondage broken than they began to feel that they were no longer animals, but men, and began, partly from imitation, and partly from that instinct which is common to all men, to gather around about themselves these evidences of growth, development, power.

We do not think that anywhere on the globe men, on the whole, live so well as in America—or grumble so much! But that is an indispensable thing. For as men live better, their criterion of life grows with the betterment. Taste increases in a greater ratio, oftentimes, than possession; and men are dissatisfied, not so much by what they have, as by the proportion which what they have bears to their ideal. It is our ideals that make us grumblers. And so there is some comfort in that.

The tendency, also, is to augment the conveniences, the beauty and the resources of homes. There is universal social ambition among the laborers of America. They feel the dignity of citizenship. Power, with its responsibility, has produced upon them the effect that we knew it would. It has educated, it has inspired, it has developed them. And the consequence is, that they feel, not that they are a class of work men, but that they are members of society. They call themselves *citizens*. They belong to the common people. They are a part of the one great loaf; and though each one is but a crumb, unbroken, every crumb is loaf. And this, too, is a sign of growth in the right direction. Show me a man who is content with things just as they have been, when he has it in his power to make them better, and I will show you a man whose tendency is the wrong way. He is by just so much less than a man who is contented with inferior conditions of manhood.

There are other signs of thrift. The great fermentation and combinations everywhere pervading working men are full of promise—and vexation! They vex the present, but they will bless the future. This has nothing to do with the wisdom or the folly of any of the particular measures which the laboring men may take. All causes which come up from the bottom of society find their way up by the hardest; and mistakes are the rude nurses of ignorant men—rude, but faithful. No class and no nation ever was raised from the bottom by very much help from the top. Thus far men have scarcely discerned, and certainly have not learned, that superiority is an ordination of God, and makes the superior class the nurses and helpers of the inferior. But aristocracy has grown out of superiority, for the most part. As soon as any class has had the power to rise, it has separated itself from the lower class, and called itself cream, and desired to be skimmed off!

And so it has been that class after class, as we go down in society, have been obliged to fight their own battle, and largely to fight it against those who should have been their helpers; and instead of succor from those who were wiser and stronger than themselves, they have had resistance.

Now, it is not strange that when men are fighting their way up from the bottom of society, they are at first ignorant of the best modes; that they make mistakes in the instruments selected, and in the measures devised. It is not presumption against the validity and excellence of any cause that its advocates are making many mistakes. Nothing could be worse than contentment in degradation. And there is nothing, with all its mistakes, that is more auspicious than aspiration and enterprise among laboring men. Therefore when I behold them counseling, and gathering themselves into innumerable forms of association, and learning among themselves brotherhood, and forming habits of common thought, common purposes, and common government, whatever may be the inconvenience of the present, I regard such things as pre-eminently auspicious. They show that the laboring classes are not dead; that they are not inert; that they are a living mass; and that they mean to live to some purpose, and are finding out the way to do it. My heart goes with these my fellow-citizens under such circumstances, even when my head does not.

Very significant, too, is the assimilative power of American institutions, as shown in the condition and the conduct of foreign labor in our midst. For it is not our native-born citizens alone that are laborious, that are enterprising, that are accumulating property, that are good citizens, and obedient to the law. There have been thrown upon our shores vast masses, now almost uncountable, of men born under other skies, other institutions, and other customs, with other ideas. They are poured upon us by millions. Many have feared that they would change the color of the nation; that they would gradually undermine its laws; that, like the flowing of the stream which will chafe even rocks, so at last, by continual attrition, this vast mass of men pouring in upon our institutions would take the temper out of them. But they have not. Our institutions are stronger to-day, with all their population from abroad in them and under them, than they were fifty years ago, or even twenty-five years ago. And in those periods of critical peril when everything seemed put in jeopardy, there was no part of our whole population from the north to the south, or from the east to the west, that was more patriotic than our foreign population. And when, afterward, still other moral perils ensued, and the credit of the nation was at stake, there were no parts of our population, taking the country through, that were honester and truer to the national integrity than our foreign population.

And why should they desire to destroy those institutions for which they voyaged the deep and left their own land? It is the peculiar advantage of popular laws and institutions, that they are just such laws and institutions as common men want, and therefore are just such as common men do not want to destroy. Except in a few cities, and, to be plain, except from one nationality, we have scarcely heard a word of lawlessness from the great throng of our foreign population. The Irish are an ingenuous people. They are very frank and open, and they usually speak out what they think, and frequently act too openly and impulsively; and I must admit that there has been some trouble springing from them. Yet I say, without hesitation, that in fifty years all the trouble will have been a cheap price to have paid for the good qualities which that stock will infuse into the Anglo-Saxon stock. It is *good* stock, though it is very hard to work up. But with this single exception good-naturedly named, where have we found trouble from our foreign population?

With occasional and sporadic exceptions, where have we found better citizenship than among them? Where have we found men that, on the whole, not only were conducting themselves better, but were contributing more directly to the welfare of the state, or of the regions where they had settled down, than our emigrant population? They mingle among us; and in one generation they are as indistinguishable from us as if they and their parents had been born in our midst. They do not clog our courts; they do not mob our streets; they do not make aggression upon law nor upon civil liberty. Their virtues, their wisdom, and their industry we ought to recognize, both with surprise and with gratitude.

Nor do I believe that it will be in the power of China to do what all Scandinavia cannot do. I am just as little afraid of the East, or the West —no, I do not know which way China is—I am as little afraid of the *Oriental* as I am of the European. Coming with another tongue, not easily to be changed, and coming with a very different race-temperament, and with very different culture, it may take longer to digest them; but I think that even a Chinaman, when he has been thoroughly swallowed by American institutions, will, though he lies long by them, be at last digested, and that he will make good blood withal. So that I am not afraid of the importation of Chinamen. And though they do not understand it, others will, when I say, *All hail!* and *Welcome!*

There may be many who object to the Chinese on account of their compulsory carriage hither. They are ashamed to admit that this country is shut against the poor and the laboring classes of any land under heaven; but they find fault with the carriage of them by enforced emigration. "Let them come freely," say they. Oh yes, let them come freely, say I, only let them *come!* As for letting them come freely, here are both hands for that. But the difficulty is not that it is an enforced emigration, but that it is a competitious labor. And on that ground I say, shame, *shame* be to any class of men who have themselves made their fortunes by bringing in cheap labor against our own native labor, and have established themselves with our full welcome, and then turn to repel others who come just as they came, bearing what they bore—willingness to work, and ability to work cheaper than our own laborers!

For the law of God is that men, as they come up, cannot afford to work cheap. Nothing can work cheap except that which *is* cheap. If you have only a hand to sell, with no thought in it, and no skill in it, you can afford to sell that hand cheap; but if that hand has forty years of experience and thought; if that hand represents the whole machinery of your mind and soul, you cannot afford to sell it cheap—and I do not want to have you. And in every community there must be these classes. The lowest and most ignorant, who have never gone to school, nor had the means of culture of any sort, will of course work cheap; and they will work cheap because they bring so little in their work. But as working is instruction, they come up; and every step they come up they give more, and ask more, and get more because they give more. It is the *quid pro quo* that makes the price all the time. It is the great law of equivalents.

And so, while one class of foreign population, taking advantage of the opportunity offered, have been laying the foundations of a moderate competence, and have been going up, the prices of their labor have been rising. And I do not object to that. I want the prices of their labor to rise, because I believe that they give more in the same number of hours than they did when they were unskilled laborers.

But we want another class below them. And when *they* come up, we shall want another class below *them*. "The workman is worthy of his hire"; but it is one of the misfortunes of ignorance that it does not know how to be wise.

The very thing that we need more now than almost anything of the lower interests of our land, is labor. With our vast intermediary territories—that land which for a hundred years will hardly see seed-corn for lack of the hands to open the furrows and plant it—are we in a condition to turn away any man who will come here honestly to labor and to thrive? I say, God bless the Swede; and God bless the Dane; and God bless the German, a hundred times over; and God bless the Frenchman and the Italian, if they come here to be good citizens; and God bless the canny Scotchman, and the sturdy Englishman, and the mercurial Irishman; and God bless a little more the Chinaman,—because he needs a little more!

On the whole, then, there is occasion for courage and for thanks in regard to labor, and in regard to the laborer. Labor is remunerative. The field for it is almost illimitable. Its product is wonderful. The laborers are no longer brute beasts. A change is going on perpetually. There is fermentation, there is circulation, there is emulation; and little by little our laboring classes are coming up in intelligence; in organizing power; in forecast; in refinement; in the amplitude of their domestic conditions; in all the things that go to make men happy here, and that make virtue easy and aspiration natural.

And it is a theme for thanksgiving to-day that, while other nations are receiving the terrible scourge; while upon almost a whole continent labor is suspended, or works only at the forge and the foundry, for purposes of destruction, throughout the length and breadth of this great land labor whistles, and sings, and is happy.

2. Again, the general aspect of wealth in America is such as to give occasion for thanksgiving to-day. The prodigious facilities for developing wealth are only just beginning to be perceived by the mass. The future fortunes of America will be fabulous. I suppose that there are to be fortunes on this continent, compared with which what were called fortunes once will seem like penury. The power of organizing seems to be almost the only limit. The wealth is here. It is easy to be developed. It is easy to be concentrated. It is growing easier every decade of years to be administered. And to be the owner of a million dollars will not make a man eligible to the class of rich men much longer. I look forward into that "golden" future, literally, which is opening before us, and marvel whether the most poetic dreams of growing wealth may not fall short of the reality. By and by there is to be a genius shown—there are yet to be reputations, and very noble reputations—for organizing and amassing wealth, compared with which we have had almost nothing in the past history of nations.

There are some who think that riches are always and only danger-ous. Riches are dangerous simply because they are power; and all power is dangerous. Power is dangerous whether it be legislative or moral power. Even variety of influence is dangerous. And wealth is more dan-gerous than other forms simply because it is a more various power, and has certain facilities for adaptation and use which belong to almost no other power. But it is impossible to civilize a community without riches. I boldly affirm that no nation ever yet rose from a barbarous state except through the mediation of wealth earned. I affirm that the preaching of the Gospel to the heathen will be invalid and void if it does not make them active workmen, and teach them how to make money. And although the evidences of the conversion of the individual are not that he knows how to make money; yet in a nation no religion is a good religion that does not teach industry, and the thrift which comes from industry. For the law of communities is not analogous to the law of the individual. It is possible, in a great, rich, civilized community, for an individual man to be powerful, and preëminently so, and yet be poor; but no poor man can be of very great validity in a poor community. The community must be rich if he is to have power. It is the contrast, it is the self-denial, it is the moral efficiency without those other and external instrumentalities, that make him so marked, if he labors with voluntary poverty. But no *com-munity* can develop into permanent civilization unless it has power min-istered to it very largely through the civilizing influences of wealth. This alone will give the activity required; this alone will give the leisure in which men soften, and meliorate, and grow beautiful.

Now, the dangers of wealth in America are very great. They are even greater than we fear. Organized wealth is one great danger which lies ahead, looming up gigantically. And yet, wealth must be organized. The community will have to find ways in which to protect itself, however. If wealth be organized to do as it pleases, it becomes very dangerous. Nevertheless, organized wealth is yet to be a benefactor of the community to an extent that we have never suspected. It tends now to despotism; but it is because it is in the nascent stages.

Great corporations are dangerous. They do not need to be. Scores of millionaires organized together in concert to accomplish great ends need not be any more dangerous than the State is. There may be an empyrean of wealth; and it may be mischievous; but it does not need to be. At pres-ent it is so, and is to be watched against. Wealth tends to control all other power in society. Especially is it so in democratic societies, where we have no kings, no nobles, no fixed estate of honor, no titles, no positions which are permanent, and where wealth and character make the distinction, very largely, between man and man. Under such circumstances wealth tends to absorb into its own hands all the power in society. But it is not necessarily so. It is not necessary that riches should control courts and legislatures, and the franchise itself. It is not necessary that wealth, which owns the market, should also own the civil power, though it is a danger that is to be met and overcome. It tends to feed the lower nature; it tends to change refinement to luxury, and luxury to corruption; but it does not need to do this.

These are valid, imminent, pressing dangers, that never have been exaggerated; and yet they are not dangers which necessarily attend the accumulation and organization of great wealth in any community. It will require the vigilance of statesmen, and of philanthropists, and of good citizens, to guard against the dangers of wealth. But it is not philosophical to look only on the diseases of a community. It is wise to look at its hygienic qualities as well.

Is harm and danger, then, all that wealth is accomplishing in our midst? No. It is the almoner of employment, as it is the almoner of bread. It is the almoner of the family. It is the almoner of unnumbered households. It is the almoner of independence. And are we to forget that capital—that is, wealth in activity—with all its friction, is far safer than invested wealth, lying dead? It is money that is working that keeps bright, and it is money that is working that keeps men bright. Although working money is by various exigencies brought into circumstances where it must be limited, overruled, and curtailed, yet we are not to forget on this account that at the same time it is that which is vivifying industry to the bottom of society, and that is carrying out on its broad hands and arms innumerable blessings to every part of the community. The very circulation of the community would cease, almost, the moment that wealth should cease to exist. It is the blood that carries nutrition into every part of the whole system.

Riches, therefore, may be said to be the poor man's providence, provided it is riches in use, and not invested. When men have retired from business, and their wealth is laid up, there is less danger from it; but there is less benefit from it at the same time. The dangers which we see threatening us are not less than real; but looking comprehensively at the general tendency of wealth in America, it is working in subordination to intelligence and to domestic virtue. There is a vast deal of ignorant using of wealth. A great many men use their property for ostentation; and a great many employ it for useless pride; and a great many use it for selfishness, and even for vice. But how to use money is an art just as much to be learned as how to make it. There are a great many men that know how to make money, who do not know how to use it; and there are a great many men that know how to spend money, who do not know how to make it. Both sides are to be learned. Neither comes by nature. There is art in it as much as there is in learning to paint, or to carve, or to fabricate at the blacksmith's forge, or at the joiner's bench. And men must not be expected to learn it in a generation. There are hundreds and thousands of men who began with literally nothing, and have ended with two or three hundred thousand dollars which they have to organize and commute into forms of civilization; and is it strange that a great many men do not know how to do it; that they sometimes build and furnish extravagantly and out of taste? My wonder is that there is so much taste and discretion exercised. For if you go through town after town, and village after village,. and city after city, you will find that extravagant building and furnishing are the exception—not the rule. The rule is that wealth which has been earned wisely is being expended discreetly. I think that wealth to-day is being used more for building up American homes than for almost all other purposes. I think that the people live in better houses here than they do in any other country, the world over. I am sure they do. Men of the same rank in life, of the same professions, and of the same conditions of wealth, live in better houses, more amply stored, and with more conveniences, here than anywhere else. There is more ingenuity in the construction of houses here—and it requires more ingenuity to keep them constructed!—than in any other land on the globe.

.   .   .   .

It is not strange to find a man who works at the forge all day, grim and grizzly, going home at night to pursue historical reading. I know farmers that I should dislike to meet in an argument (unless I was on the same side with them!). And they are not cases here and there, selected. It is characteristic of our working people, and of men that are well to do, that they are growing up to make the town in which they live beautiful and intelligent. Their houses themselves are often models of taste and convenience, and are setting examples which one by one the neighbors follow. And so, in the train of industry comes wealth, and of wealth, taste, and of taste, beneficence; and refinement flashes throughout the land. And when I hear men speaking bitterly against wealth, I notice that almost invariably they are men who have not got it. When I hear them deride moneyed men, moneyed kings, moneyed princes, it seems to me that they have not well considered the facts. They only think of here and there, it may be, a Croesus. But if you follow the more moderate fortunes; if you look into the whole career of money in this land, not the Nile, when it comes down with its annual freshet and distributes the slime which is the riches of Egypt over the circumjacent territory, is so great a blessing to Egypt, as is the great diffusion of wealth in this country to America. And nowhere else does wealth so directly point towards virtue in morality, and spirituality in religion, as in America.

So then,I am not afraid to rejoice. Get rich, if you can. Pay anything for riches. Anything? Yes, pay yourself; pay weariness; pay head-cracking thought; pay anything but this—do not pay your honor, nor your affection, nor your simplicity, nor your faith in man, nor your love to God. But whatever you can take out of the body, pay. And when you shall have amassed wealth, it will be God's power, if you are wise to use it, by which you can make your home happier, the community more refined, and the whole land more civilized.

Wealth in America, also, is public-spirited (I thought I had got through; but I find two or three more heads). The classes that are amassing money furnish a large proportion of all the funds by which the active charities of society are carried on. The buildings which decorate our community are from the hands, mostly, of wealthy men. Architecture is the adopted child of wealth. The fine arts could scarcely exist but for the interposition of wealth. The universities, and academies, and colleges, and public libraries, and reading rooms, and halls for lectures, are the fruit of liberal wealth in America. Cornell, Vassar, Cooper, Williston, Lawrence, and a hundred others, are significant American names. And there are more coming forward, who yet will not simply be known by their money among those that love them, but whose names will become symbolic of some great public charity, or some great public spirit.

Wealth is searching out the neglected classes; is distributing from our cities vagabond children; is opening schools for the laboring classes, to teach them all mechanic arts. I may safely say that no public need can be wisely presented to the wealth of America, and not be liberally, and at times munificently, taken care of. In other lands, governments give much for public institutions; but in America the great bulk of the means required to build up the institutions of civilization, and to support them, is contributed by the people, and by the business men of the people.

Wealth, then, like its owners, has its devil and its temptation; it has its mistakes and perversions; it has its great dangers to society; but its blessings are a hundred-fold. And, on the whole, the general tendency of wealth is such as to lead me to-day to thank God for the increasing wealth of America. May it ever be sanctified. May it ever learn nobler uses, and aspire higher and higher, until the symbolism of the heavenly state, where the very streets are paved with gold, shall be reproduced in the realities and actualities of our life here on earth.

3. I meant to speak of the cause of education, and the reasons for thanksgiving in that direction; and also of the progress of civilization, and all forms of refinement. I can, however, not even mention them, in detail. I only, in closing, shall speak of the religious condition of the land, as a grand reason for thanksgiving.

4. There are many signs, which, if taken alone, will distress the mind, and so distress many timid souls. Such is the prevalence of scientific scepticism, such is the subversion of old landmarks, and the setting aside of cherished beliefs, and the letting go of old systems, and the coming in

of violent actions and reactions of men that have drunk new wine (for truth is intoxicating to men whose heads are not strong), that there is an impression that religion is losing ground; that it is becoming an old story —a superstition. But this scene is enacted every three or four hundred years; and religion comes up every time stronger and stronger. I think religion is like the grass of the meadow, which, when burnt over, lies black and charred, but the ashes of which are a stimulating manure, which afterwards fosters a growth that is stronger than that to which the violence was done. And my faith in religion is not in the church, and not in doctrines, and not in books, and not in ministers, nor in anything external to man, but in that nature which God created, and which makes religion indispensable to man. Until man himself dies, there will be a faith, and that faith will fashion to itself both beliefs and services of devotion.

On the other hand, there was never, probably, so intelligent a faith as there is to-day, in so many men. Never were there so many men who thought so much on the subject of religion, and read so much, and argued so much, and looked so far into the themes of their belief as to-day. Not among the educated classes alone, but among plain people of the country, I think there is more reading, and more thinking, and more real heart-interest in religion than ever before.

Then there is a drawing together, a more kindred feeling, which is taking the place of the rancor and sectarian bitterness which prevailed not a great while ago, in many directions.

And it is very noticeable that the different sects of religion are softening, and that men are coming together in conference who only a few years ago thought it their duty to hate and club one another. This growing spirit of love and fellowship in differing churches is one of the signs of the growth of religion.

Religious ethics, also, are more widely diffused. Though there may not be in the general mind as much belief in doctrinal religion as there once was, there is more belief in the ethics of religion than there was ever before. The standards of belief that are set up by the word of God are more universally accepted and applied to-day than formerly they were. Governments conform to the Christian spirit more than ever they did before. Jurisprudence seeks to measure itself more than ever according to the equity that was in Christ Jesus. The heart is regulating itself more by those great laws of simplicity and truth and righteousness, or justice, if I may so say, than ever before. And even business is seeking, among all its contortions, to cast the devil of dishonesty out of itself. I think business never before acknowledged so high a standard as it does to-day. And while the belief in creeds and formularies may have changed, the belief in ethical standards of religion was never so universally employed as to-day.

And humanity—which is sympathy for man in his sorrow and in his need—when was there ever so much of it? When, in any age of the world since Christ was lifted up on Calvary, has such a scene been presented as to-day is witnessed, when France is humbled? My heart is sore for her. And though I know that the wheat before it is bread must be ground; and though I believe in the loaf, yet, when the wheat is living men, I cannot bear to see the grinding. To-day, one vast nation is treading another vast nation under foot; and all the outlying world around— England, with all her dependencies, Germany itself, America, Italy, and all the other nations—by bazars, by fairs, by collections in churches, and by contributions of public-spirited men, is pouring out a tide of wealth to relieve the sufferers. And if war must be, humanity stands by to bind up the wounds that war makes. When before was there such a looking-on, such a spectatorship? In regard to the inhuman wars of the world, human- ity was never so wide-spread. Never was there such sensibility among the nations of the earth as there is to-day. A benevolent or cordial and coop- erative kindness in the upbuilding of society never was wiser than to-day. And faith in God—not perhaps according to your definition nor according to mine, but faith in an overruling power; faith in an unerring wisdom; faith in a goodness which is paternal; faith in One who looks upon the whole human race as his family, and not as a despot looks upon his sub- jects; faith that leads men to see roseate colors in the heaven, and not crushing bolts; faith in God, as the almighty good, was never stronger, and never was growing so fast, nor so deep.

Here, then, is our survey. Our territorial condition is prosperous. Our material prosperity is eminent, and it is tending upward rather than downward. Our labor and our laborers are prospering; and they are work- ing upward. Wealth, with all its tendencies, on the whole, is on the line of development toward moral and not toward physical things. Education is widely prevalent, and is taking in more perfectly every class. Refine- ment is becoming the indispensable element of all prosperity. Religion itself, though losing many of its antique forms and services, as a spirit and as a controlling influence, was never so strong. I thank God for all the signs of the times. I thank God for the health and for the prosperity of the nation.

And now, I have but one word to say more: as we have been put in the van among nations to develop principles in their practical forms that were only known as seed-corn in other lands, my heart's ambition is, first, for the welfare of this whole land, for the sake of the burden of the popu- lation which it carries. God bless America. Not because I was born in it; not because it is my America, and because I receive the reflection of its glory, and a dividend of its power. I am not insensible to these things; yet not on those accounts that are personal to me do I implore God's blessing upon America; but because this continent carries such a burden of humanity that its weal or woe will be like an eternal weal or woe, infinite, endless. May God, for the sake of neighboring peoples, bless this land. And as God is making us wise, and rich, and strong, and expert, and fearless, may He take the lion and the bear out of our nature, and give us the spirit of the dove, that we may stand frowning on our shores against no foreign people; that we may be no band of robbers to filch and to steal from the feeble and the poor. May God give us magnanimity and power and riches, that we may throw the shadow of our example upon the poor, the perishing, and the ready-to-be-destroyed, for their protection. And cursed—cursed of God, and of men cursed—be that man who counsels the red right hand of war except when it is needful to fight for our own existence! We have no war that we want to wage except the war of righteousness in ourselves. It is not for us to bombard and destroy other nations, and to follow the vices of tyrannies. What is the use of the reign of the common people, where is the glory of democracy, if it can but ape, and with greater cruelty, the mischiefs of despotism? Let kings war; let aristocrats war; but the common people of a great republic should own the brotherhood of man. And, instead of raising aloft the red hand, let them throw the nursing arm of protection around about their neighbors, and call all men their brethren, and dwell together in fealty, in unity, in sympathy, and in happiness.

THE RIGHT REVEREND WILLIAM LAWRENCE

The Relation Of Wealth
To Morals

There is a certain distrust on the part of our people as to the effect of material prosperity on their morality. We shrink with some foreboding at the great increase of riches, and question whether in the long run material prosperity does not tend toward the disintegration of character.

History seems to support us in our distrust. Visions arise of their fall from splendor of Tyre and Sidon, Babylon, Rome, and Venice, and of great nations too. The question is started whether England is not today, in the pride of her wealth and power, sowing the wind from which in time she will reap the whirlwind.

Experience seems to add its support. Is it not from the ranks of the poor that the leaders of the people have always risen? Recall Abraham Lincoln and patriots of every generation.

The Bible has sustained the same note. Were ever stronger words of warning uttered against the deceitfulness of riches than those spoken by the peasant Jesus, who Himself had no place to lay His head? And the Church has through the centuries upheld poverty as one of the surest paths to Heaven; it has been a mark of the saint.

To be sure, in spite of history, experience, and the Bible, men have gone on their way making money and hailing with joy each age of material prosperity. The answer is: "This only proves the case; men are of the world, riches are deceitful, and the Bible is true; the world is given over to Mammon. In the increase of material wealth and the accumulation of riches the man who seeks the higher life has no part."

In the face of this comes the statement of the chief statistician of our census—from one, therefore, who speaks with authority: "The present census, when completed, will unquestionably show that the visible material wealth in this country now has a value of ninety billion dollars. This is an addition since 1890 of twenty-five billion dollars. This is a saving greater than all the people of the Western Continent had been able to

From *The World's Work*, I. (January 1901), 286–92.

make from the discovery of Columbus to the breaking out of the Civil War."

If our reasoning from history, experience, and the Bible is correct, we, a Christian people, have rubbed a sponge over the pages of the Bible, and are in for orgies and a downfall to which the fall of Rome is a very tame incident.

May it not be well, however, to revise our inferences from history, experience, and the Bible? History tells us that, while riches have been an item and an indirect cause of national decay, innumerable other conditions entered in. Therefore, while wealth has been a source of danger, it has not necessarily led to demoralization.

That leaders have sprung from the ranks of the poor is true and always will be true, so long as force of character exists in every class. But there are other conditions than a lack of wealth at the source of their uprising.

And as to the Bible:—while every word that can be quoted against the rich is as true as any other word, other words and deeds are as true; and the parables of our Lord on the stewardship of wealth, His association with the wealthy, strike another and complementary note. Both notes are essential to the harmony of His life and teachings. His thought was not of the conditions, rich or poor, but of a higher life, the character rising out of the conditions—fortunately, for we are released from that subtle hypocrisy which has beset the Christian through the ages, bemoaning the deceitfulness of riches, and at the same time, working with all his might to earn a competence, and a fortune if he can.

MAN "BORN TO BE RICH"

Now we are in a position to affirm that neither history, experience, nor the Bible necessarily sustains the common distrust of the effect of material wealth on morality. Our path of study is made more clear. Two positive principles lead us out on our path.

The first is that man, when he is strong, will conquer Nature, open up her resources, and harness them to his service. This is his play, his exercise, his divine mission.

"Man," says Emerson, "is born to be rich. He is thoroughly related, and is tempted out by his appetites and fancies to the conquest of this and that piece of Nature, until he finds his well-being in the use of the planet, and of more planets than his own. Wealth requires, besides the crust of bread and the roof, the freedom of city, the freedom of the earth." "The strong race is strong on these terms."

Man draws to himself material wealth as surely, as naturally, and as necessarily as the oak draws the elements into itself from the earth.

The other principle is that, in the long run, it is only to the man of morality that wealth comes. We believe in the harmony of God's Universe. We know that it is only by working along His laws natural and spiritual that we can work with efficiency. Only by working along the lines of right thinking and right living can the secrets and wealth of Nature be revealed. We, like the Psalmist, occasionally see the wicked prosper, but only occasionally.

Put two men in adjoining fields, one man strong and normal, the other weak and listless. One picks up his spade, turns over the earth, and works till sunset. The other turns over a few clods, gets a drink from the spring, takes a nap, and loafs back to his work. In a few years one will be rich for his needs, and the other a pauper dependent on the first, and growling at his prosperity.

Put ten thousand immoral men to live and work in one fertile valley and ten thousand moral men to live and work in the next valley, and the question is soon answered as to who wins the material wealth. Godliness is in league with riches.

Now we return with an easier mind and clearer conscience to the problem of our twenty-five billion dollars in a decade.

My question is: Is the material prosperity of this Nation favorable or unfavorable to the morality of the people?

The first thought is, Who has prospered? Who has got the money?

I take it that the loudest answer would be, "The millionaires, the capitalists, and the incompetent but luxurious rich"; and, as we think of that twenty-five billion, our thoughts run over the yachts, the palaces, and the luxuries that flaunt themselves before the public.

WHO THE RICH ARE

As I was beginning to write this paper an Irishman with his horse and wagon drew up at my back door. Note that I say *his* horse and wagon. Twenty years ago that Irishman, then hardly twenty years old, landed in Boston, illiterate, uncouth, scarcely able to make himself understood in English. There was no symptom of brains, alertness, or ambition. He got a job to tend a few cows. Soon the American atmosphere began to take hold. He discovered that here every man has his chance. With his first earnings he bought a suit of clothes; he gained self-respect. Then he sent money home; then he got a job to drive a horse; he opened an account at the savings bank; then evening school; more money in the bank. He changed to a better job, married a thrifty wife, and today he owns his house, stable, horse, wagon, and bicycle; has a good sum at the bank, supports five children, and has half a dozen men working under him. He is a capitalist, and his yearly earnings represent the income on $30,000. He had no "pull"; he has made his own way by grit, physical strength, and increasing intelligence. He has had material prosperity. His older brother, who paid his passage over, has had material prosperity, and his younger brother, whose passage my friend paid, has had material prosperity.

Now we are beginning to get an idea as to where the savings are. They are in the hands of hundreds of thousands of just such men, and of scores of thousands of men whose incomes ten years ago were two and five thousand, and are now five and ten thousand; and of thousands of others whose incomes have risen from ten to thirty thousand. So that, when you get to the multi-millionaires, you have only a fraction to distribute among them. And of them the fact is that only a small fraction of their income can be spent upon their own pleasure and luxury; the bulk of what they get has to be reinvested, and becomes the means whereby thousands earn their wages. They are simply trustees of a fraction of the national property.

When, then, the question is asked, "Is the material prosperity of this nation favorable or unfavorable to the morality of the people?" I say with all emphasis, "In the long run, and by all means, favorable!"

In other words, to seek for and earn wealth is a sign of a natural, vigorous, and strong character. Wherever strong men are, there they will turn into the activities of life. In the ages of chivalry you will find them on the crusades or seeking the Golden Fleece; in college life you will find them high in rank, in the boat, or on the athletic field; in an industrial age you will find them eager, straining every nerve in the development of the great industries. The race is to the strong. The search for material wealth is therefore as natural and necessary to the man as is the pushing out of its roots for more moisture and food to the oak. This is man's play, his exercise, the expression of his powers, his personality. You can no more suppress it than you can suppress the tide of the ocean. For one man who seeks money for its own sake there are ten who seek it for the satisfaction of the seeking, the power there is in it, and the use they can make of it. There is the exhilaration of feeling one's self grow in one's surroundings; the man reaches out, lays hold of this, that, and the other interest, scheme, and problem. He is building up a fortune? Yes, but his joy is also that he is building up a stronger, abler, and more powerful man. There are two men that have none of this ambition: the gilded, listless youth and the ragged, listless pauper to whom he tosses a dime; they are in the same class.

We are now ready to take up the subject in a little more detail. How is it favorable? The parable of my Irish friend gives the answer.

In the first place, and as I have already suggested, the effort to make his living and add to his comforts and power gives free play to a man's activities and leads to a development of his faculties. In an age and country where the greater openings are in commercial lines, there the stronger men and the mass of them will move. It is not a question of worldliness or of love of money, but of the natural use and legitimate play of men's faculties. An effort to suppress this action is not a religious duty, but a disastrous error, sure to fail.

SELF-RESPECT AND SELF-MASTERY

Besides this natural play of the faculties comes the development of self-respect and ambition. In the uprise from a lower to a higher civilization, these are the basal elements. Watch the cart-loads of Polish or Italian immigrants as they are hauled away from the dock. Study their lifeless expression, their hang-dog look, and their almost cowering posture. Follow them and study them five years later: note the gradual straightening of the body, the kindling of the eye, and the alertness of the whole person as the men, women, and children begin to realize their opportunities, bring in their wages, and move to better quarters. Petty temptations and deep degradations that might have overwhelmed them on their arrival cannot now touch them.

With this comes also the power of self-mastery. The savage eats what he kills and spends what he has. In the movement towards civilization through material wealth, questions come up for decision every hour. Shall I spend? Shall I save? How shall I spend? How can I earn more? Shall I go into partnership with a capital of ten dollars, or shall I wait until I have fifty dollars?

Wage earners are not today, as they were in earlier days, hungering for the bare physical necessities of life. They are hungering now, and it marks an upward movement in civilization, for higher things, education, social life, relaxation, and the development of the higher faculties.

To be sure, a certain fraction wilt under the strain, take to drink, to lust, to laziness. There is always the thin line of stragglers behind every army, but the great body of the American people are marching upwards in prosperity through the mastery of their lower tastes and passions to the development of the higher. From rags to clothes, from filth to cleanliness, from disease to health; from bare walls to pictures; from ignorance to education; from narrow and petty talk to books and music and art; from superstition to a more rational religion; from crudity to refinement; from self-centralization to the conception of a social unity.

Here in this last phrase we strike the next step in development. In this increase of wealth, this rapid communication which goes with it, this shrinking of the earth's surface and unifying of peoples through commerce, men and women are realizing their relations to society.

That there are those who in the deepest poverty sustain the spirit of unselfishness and exhibit a self-sacrifice for others which puts their richer neighbors to the blush we know by experience. At the same time, the fact is that for the mass and in the long run grinding poverty does grind down the character; in the struggle for bare existence and for the very life of one's children there is developed an intense self-centralization and a hardness which is destructive of the social instinct and of the finer graces. When, however, through the increase of wealth man has extended his interests, his vision, and his opportunities, "he is thoroughly related." His lines run out in every direction; he lays his finger upon all the broader interests of life, the school, the church, and the college. He reaches through commerce to the ends of the earth. He discovers one bond which is essential to the social unity in this commercial age—the bond of faith in other men; for in credit, on belief in others, our whole social and commercial fabric is built. And when a man has reached this point, he has indeed reached one of the high plateaus of character: from this rise the higher mountain peaks of Christian graces, but here he is on the standing-ground of the higher civilization.

As I write I can almost feel the silent protest of some critics. Are not these qualities, self-respect, self-mastery, a sense of social unity, and mutual confidence, the commonplaces of life? Is this the only response of material wealth in its relation to morality?

These are to us now the commonplaces of life: they are at the same time the fundamentals of character and of morality. If material prosperity has been one of the great instruments (and I believe it has) in bringing the great body of our people even to approach this plateau of character, it has more than justified itself.

One might, however, mention other and finer qualities that follow in these days the train of prosperity. I instance only one. We will strike up one mountain peak: it is that of joyful and grateful service.

THE PRIVILEGE OF GRATEFUL SERVICE

In other days we have heard much of "the sweet uses of adversity": the note still lingers in sermons and will linger as long as Christianity stands. There is, however, the other note that sounds strong in these days, —the privilege of grateful service.

I have in mind now a man of wealth (you can conjure up many like him) who lives handsomely and entertains; he has everything that purveys to his health and comfort. All these things are tributary to what? To the man's efficiency in his complete devotion to the social, educational, and charitable interests to which he gives his life. He is Christ's as much as was St. Paul, he is consecrated as was St. Francis of Assisi; and in recognition of the bounty with which God has blessed him he does not sell all that he has, but he uses all that he has, and, as he believes, in the wisest way, for the relief of the poor, the upbuilding of social standards, and the upholding of righteousness among the people. The Christian centuries, with all their asceticism and monasticism, with their great and noble saints, have, I believe, never witnessed a sweeter, more gracious, and more complete consecration than that which exists in the lives of hundreds of men and women in the cities and towns of this country, who, out of a sense of grateful service to God for His bounty, are giving themselves with all joy to the welfare of the people. And if ever Christ's words have been obeyed to the letter, they are obeyed today by those who are living out His precepts of the stewardship of wealth.

As we think of the voluntary and glad service given to society, to the State, the Church, to education, art, and charity, of the army of able men and women who, without thought of pay, are serving upon directories of savings banks and national banks, life insurance companies, railroads, mills, trusts and corporations, public commissions, and offices of all sorts, schools and colleges, churches and charities; as we run our thoughts over the free services of the doctors, of the lawyers, for their poorer clients, we are amazed at the magnitude of unpaid service, which is now taken for granted, and at the cheerful and glad spirit in which it is carried through. Material prosperity is helping to make the national character sweeter, more joyous, more unselfish, more Christlike. That is my answer to the question as to the relation of material prosperity to morality.

Again I feel a silent protest. Is not the writer going rather far? We did not believe that our twenty-five billions would lead to orgies; but is he not getting rather close to the millennium? Are there no shadows and dark spaces in the radiance which he seems to think that wealth is shedding around us?

Yes, my friendly critic, there are, and to a mention of a few of them I give the pages that are left.

THE SPIRIT OF COMMERCIALISM

First and most pervasive, I name the spirit of commercialism. It crops up in many forms and places, hydra-headed.

Is it any wonder? When one realizes that in the last ten years seventy millions of people have earned their living, paid their bills, and have at the same time increased the property of the Nation by twenty-five billions of dollars, we reach a slight conception of the intensity, the industry, the enterprise, and the ability with which those people have thought, worked, and reaped. One wonders that religion, charity, or culture have survived the strain at all. When the eye and ambition of a strong man are set upon a purpose, he sometimes neglects other considerations; he is not over nice about the rights of others; he occasionally overrides the weak, crushes out the helpless, and forgets to stop and pick up those that have fallen by the way.

We know how that was in England: we remember the report of the Commission by Lord Shaftesbury as to the horrible condition of the miners, men, women, and children. That was simply one phase in the development of the great movement of modern industrialism. It was a neglect and forgetfulness under a new pressure, rather than deliberate cruelty. The facts once known, attention called,—and reforms began; and they have been going on in behalf of the working people ever since. Much, very much, has been done.

As conditions change, much remains to do. The better adjustment of rights, wages, and taxes will call for the highest intelligence and strongest character. Again, the small tradesman has driven away the little counter where a widow earned her living, the larger tradesman has wiped out the small tradesman, and the department store is now finishing off some of the large tradesmen. It is hard, but it is a part of the great economic movement. It endangers some of the fundamentals of morality, and destroys for the time some of the finer graces.

Ephemeral success sometimes follows deceit, and that breeds a body of commercial frauds; but they cannot endure. A fortune is won by an unscrupulous adventurer; and a hundred fortunes are lost and characters spoiled in trying to follow suit. An ignorant man happens upon wealth or by some mysterious commercial ability wins wealth, and he then thinks himself omniscient. He, not God, is his own creator. He goes to church, but he is Godless. When a nation of people have been seeking for clothes, houses, and comforts in the upbuilding of civilization, is it any wonder that they do not realize that a man's life consisteth not in the abundance of things that he possesseth? There are deceit, hardness, materialism, and vulgarity in the commercial world; and to me the vulgarest of all is not the diamond-studded operator, but the horde of mothers crushing each other around the bargain counter in the endeavor to get something, and that so small, for nothing. The worst of commercialism is that it does not stop at the office, but enters the home, taints the marriage vow, and poisons social life at its springs.

Beyond these rudimentary forms of commercialism, there is another, even more dangerous, because it threatens the liberties and rights of the people. The eye of the public is on it now. I refer to the relation of concentrated masses of wealth to the public service.

I have no time to more than suggest a few of the conditions that have led up to this. Industrial enterprise has drawn many of the strongest and ablest men from political to commercial interests; society and legislation now do for the people what in other days the landlord did; they are concerned more and more with industrial, commercial, and financial questions, from the national tariff to the size of a house-drain. Just at this time, and because of our great industrial development and prosperity, a horde of ignorant voters waiting to be moulded by any strong leader have come to this shore. The wide distribution of wealth has driven merchants and mechanics, widows and trustees of orphans, doctors and ministers, to invest their savings in great enterprises, corporations, and trusts, which, to succeed, must be directed by a few men. We have therefore this situation: a few men responsible for the safekeeping and development of enormous properties, dependent upon legislation, and a great mass of voters, many of them ignorant, represented by their own kind in city or state government, strongly organized by a leader who is in it for what he can get out of it, and who is ever alert with his legislative cohorts to "strike" the great corporations. The people believe that the officers of great corporations so manage that they can get what they want, call it by assessment, bribery, ransom, or what you will, and they brand those otherwise respectable men as cowards and traitors to public liberty.

THE RICH MAN AND THE BURGLAR

A burglar breaks into your house, awakes you, and "strikes" you for $500 which is in your safe downstairs. You expostulate: he answers that he will burn your house. But your children, you cry, will they be safe? He does not know: he wants the money. But if you give it to him, he will try the same on other people. It is against all public duty for you to yield. Again, the threat that he will burn your house; and you, miserable, conscience-stricken that you are doing a cowardly thing, and one against the safety of the public, crawl downstairs, open the safe, and hand over the cash. You have saved your house and children, but how about your duty to the public and your neighbors, as well as to yourself?

This is very much the position of the great trustees of capital, the heads of our great corporations, at the hands of the modern bandit. Shall they jeopardize the income of women and children, merchants and mechanics, and perhaps drive them into poverty? Or shall they accept the situation, yield to the threat, and trust to the authorities to seize the robber, or through an aroused public opinion so to vote, act, and legislate as to change the law and stop this modern brigandage? That some of the promoters and managers of great corporations are unscrupulous is undoubtedly true. The jail is none too good for them, if only the law would touch them. Nor have we a word of apology or justification for any man who yields to or encourages blackmail. The difficulty, however, is not a simple one. It concerns more than the directors and the politicians; it relates to the rights and liberties of the people. I do not have so much fear of the rich man in office, as I do of the poor but weak man in office and the rich man outside. Through the interplay of aroused public opinion, better legislation, and intelligent action, the relief will come. A younger generation, with its eye keen upon that danger-point is coming to the front.

In some cities of China the houses have no windows on the street, only bare walls and the little door. The families are isolated, narrow, and selfish: there is no public spirit. When the Chinese boy returns home from his Christian Mission School, touched with the spirit of Christian civilization, his first work in bringing civilization to his home is to take a crowbar, knock a hole in the front wall, and make a window, that he may see out and the people see in. He unifies society and creates a public opinion. What is needed as our next step in civilization is to break a hole and make a window that the public may see into the great corporations and trusts and, what is just as important, that the managers may see out and recognize the sentiment of the public.

Light and action—heroic action! There are men today waiting and wanting to act, to throw off the shackles of the modern bandit; but they dare not alone; their trusts are too great. What is wanted is a group of men, high in position, great in power, who at great cost, if need be, will stand and say, "Thus far, up to the lines of the nicest honor, shalt thou go, and no farther."

The people have their eye upon the public service. An administration may pay political debts by pushing ignorant and unworthy men into the lower offices, but when it comes to filling positions of great responsibility the President could not, and would not if he could, appoint men less worthy than Wood in Cuba, Allen in Porto Rico, and Taft in the Philippines, men of force, intelligence, and character. Collegiate education does not insure character, but it does sift men and insure intelligence; and, as President Pritchett of the Massachusetts Institute of Technology pointed out in his inaugural address, though less than one per cent of our population are college men, yet from this very small fraction a majority of the legislative, executive, and judicial places of the General Government which have to do in any large way with shaping the policy and determining the character of the government, are chosen.

THE DANGER FROM LUXURY

One other dark shadow, and I am done. The persistent companion of riches,—luxury and an ability to have what you want. That vice and license are rampant in certain quarters is clear; that vulgar wealth flaunts itself in the face of the people is beyond question; and that the people are rather amused at the spectacle must be confessed. The theatre syndicate will turn on to the boards whatever the people want; and the general tone of the plays speaks not well for the taste and morality of the people. The strain of temptation overwhelms a fraction of our youth. But one has no more right to test the result of prosperity by the small class of the lazy and luxurious than he has to test the result of poverty by the lazy tramp.

With all this said, the great mass of the people are self-restrained and simple. Material prosperity has come apace, and on the whole it uplifts. Responsibility sobers men and nations. We have learned how to win wealth: we are learning how to use and spend it. Every year marks a long step in advance in material prosperity, and character must march in step. Without wealth, character is liable to narrow and harden. Without character, wealth will destroy. Wealth is upon us, increasing wealth. The call of today is, then, for the uplift of character,—the support of industry, education, art, and every means of culture; the encouragement of the higher life; and, above all, the deepening of the religious faith of the people; the rekindling of the spirit, that, clothed with her material forces, the great personality of this Nation may fulfill her divine destiny.

I have been clear, I trust, in my opinion that material prosperity is in the long run favorable to morality. Let me be as clear in the statement of that eternal truth, that neither a man's nor a nation's life consists in the abundance of things that he possesseth.

In the investment of wealth in honest enterprise and business, lies our path of character. In the investment of wealth in all that goes towards the uplift of the people in education, art, and religion is another path of character. Above all, and first of all, stands the personal life. The immoral rich man is a traitor to himself, to his material as well as spiritual interests. Material prosperity is upon us; it is marching with us. Character must keep step, ay, character must lead. We want great riches; we want also great men.

WASHINGTON GLADDEN

The Nation And
The Kingdom

Is. LX, 4, 5. *Lift up thine eyes round about, and
see; they all gather themselves
together, they come unto thee; thy
sons shall come from far and thy
daughters shall be carried in the arms.
Then thou shalt see and be radiant,
and thy heart shall thrill and be
enlarged; because the abundance of
the sea shall be turned unto thee,
the wealth of the nations shall come
unto thee.*

This is part of a fervent apostrophe to the nation as the servant of
Jehovah, that ideal in which was concentrated the hopes of the great
unknown prophet of the exile. What kindles his expectation is his vision
of a regenerated society, a society from which injustice and oppression
and misery and want and all iniquity and wrong shall be put away; in
which peace and good will shall abide and order and security shall reign.
The prophet represents Jehovah as pledging his protection and care to
this holy nation, this peculiar people; they are indeed to represent him;
it is through them that he is to be made known in the earth, and therefore all his resources are at their disposal to enrich them and defend them,
and crown them with his benediction. "Violence shall no more be heard
in thy land, desolation nor destruction within thy borders, but thou shalt
call thy walls Salvation and thy gates praise."

What the prophet beholds in his vision is the kingdom of God, the
reign of righteousness and truth and love in the earth. Was it not the
same kingdom that John the Baptist announced, and that Jesus described
in the Sermon on the Mount, and that the Revelator pictured in his glow-

From Washington Gladden, *The Nation and the Kingdom: Annual Sermon Before the American Board of Commissioners for Foreign Missions*
(Boston, 1909).

ing representation of the new Jerusalem coming down out of heaven from God to fill the earth? In this prophecy, spoken five or six hundred years before Christ, the prophet depicts that glorious society; in his vision he sees it established, and in the words that I have read to you, he is describing the mighty attraction that it is exerting upon the population of the world. They are flocking into it, nations and tribes and peoples. "Who are these that fly as a cloud, and as the doves to their windows? . . . Strangers shall build up thy walls, and their kings shall minister unto thee. . . . Thy gates shall be open continually, they shall not be shut day nor night, that men may bring unto thee the wealth of the nations and their kings led captive." As the prophet conceives it, this transfigured society, when the world once gets a fair look at it, will have irresistible attraction for the children of men. They will come into it in crowds, they will throng its gates, they will bring the strength and the glory and the honor of the nation into it.

Let us get it clearly before our minds what it is that exerts such a powerful influence over the minds of men. Let us listen to what this prophet has to say about it. "For behold," saith Jehovah, "I create a new heaven and a new earth, and the former things shall not be remembered, not come into mind. But be ye glad and rejoice forever in that which I create. For, behold, I create Jerusalem a rejoicing, and her people a joy. . . . And they shall build houses, and inhabit them, and they shall plant vineyards, and eat the fruit of them. They shall not build, and another inhabit; they shall not plant, and another eat; for as the days of a tree shall be the days of my people, and my chosen shall long enjoy the work of their hands. . . . The wolf and the lamb shall feed together, and the lion shall eat straw like the ox; and dust shall be the serpent's meat. They shall not hurt nor destroy in all my holy mountain, saith the Lord. . . . They shall build the old wastes, they shall raise up the former desolations. . . . For your shame ye shall have double. . . . therefore in their land they shall possess double; everlasting joy shall be unto them. For I the Lord hate robbery with iniquity, and I will give them their recompense in truth, and I will make an everlasting covenant with them."

The establishment and maintenance of sound and fair social conditions, so that there should be no oppression nor injustice, but a square deal for everybody; so that the strong should not be permitted to prey upon the weak; so that the law of helpfulness should prevail, instead of the law of ravin; this was the primary cause of the phenomena which we are considering. Such sound and fair social conditions would bring to the community in which they were established and maintained, unexampled and marvelous prosperity; and this prosperity and peace and happiness would promptly advertise themselves, and set up an irresistible attraction. Such a society as this would be a magnet that would draw to itself, all the children of men. They would all want to be in it.

It is not necessary to conceive that the peoples from all parts of the world would abandon their homes and flock to the particular territory in which these social conditions were established; that is simply the outward costume of the spiritual fact. Even if the prophet himself conceived of it in this limited way, there is no reason why we should not discern the larger truth, that such conditions established in one community tend to repeat themselves in other communities, and these spread themselves over the world. The movement described is not geographical; it is social, it is moral; the kingdom of heaven is not advanced by gathering all the peoples into one place, but by inspiring them all with a common purpose. If New Zealand, on the opposite side of the globe, sets up a better method of social organization, the nations come to her light, and the kings to the brightness of her rising, by adopting the same methods; by putting in operation on their own soil the principles which have brought to her order and welfare. And such imitation as this is sure to take place. If any people in the world can establish and maintain conditions similar to those which the prophet here describes, the day is not distant when all the other peoples will follow its example. The result will not be immediate; the world may wait for a good while to see how the scheme works before accepting it, but eventually it will win. Righteousness and truth, justice and fair play, kindness and friendship are what the world needs, and when the world sees them organized into society and bringing forth their natural fruits in society, the world will lay hold on them, and cleave unto them. That is the way the kingdom of God is coming, by the mighty contagion of social justice.

It is touching to see the eagerness with which "poor sad humanity" has always turned toward any clear promise of the establishment on earth of this kingdom. When John the Baptist came proclaiming it, the people crowded to listen to him; they thought the real thing which the prophet had foretold was surely coming, and they were in haste to join themselves to it. And when Jesus took up the same theme in his Sermon on the Mount, the multitude thronged to hear him. What would have happened if the social aim of Jesus could have been realized then and there, if the society which is outlined in that great discourse could have been established in that little country of Palestine, we may faintly imagine. But there was simply no room in that quarter, nor anywhere else on the earth at that time, for the establishment of such a social order.

It is correctly asserted (says Dr. Rauschenbusch)[1] that the apos-

---

[1] (Walter Rauschenbusch—Baptist clergyman, professor at Rochester Theological Seminary, Social Gospel leader. His *A Theology for the Social Gospel* briefly systematized the beliefs of Social Christianity. The quotation above is from his *Christianity and the Social Crisis* [1907].—EDITOR)

tles undertook no special propaganda. Paul held no anti-slavery meetings, and Peter made no public protest against the organized grafting in the Roman system of tax farming. Of course they did not. Even the most ardent Christian socialist of our day would have stepped softly if he had been in their place. The right of public agitation was very limited in the Roman empire. Any attempt to arouse the people against the oppression of the government or the special privileges of the possessing classes, would have been choked off with relentless promptness. If, for instance, any one had been known to sow discontent among the vast and ever threatening slave population, which was not Negro but white, he would have had short shrift. Society was tensely alert against any possible slave-rising. If a slave killed his master, the law provided that every slave of the household should be killed, even if there was no trace of complicity. Upper-class philosophers might permit themselves very noble and beautiful sentiments, only because there was no connection between them and the masses, and their sentiments ended in perfumed smoke. Under such circumstances, any prudent man will husband his chance of life and usefulness, and drop the seeds of truth warily. If the conviction of William Lloyd Garrison had burned in Paul, we should probably not know that Paul had ever existed. There is no parallel between such a situation and our own in a country where we are ourselves the citizen-kings and where the right of moral agitation is almost unlimited.

This is the reason why the social aims of Jesus were not realized in his day. Doubtless he knew that they would not be. The seed had to grow secretly for many a generation before the blade of the Christian social organism could appear above the earth. The full corn in the ear was millenniums away. It would only be by centuries of indirect influence that liberty would be gradually enlarged, and room made in the earth for the establishment of a Christian social order.

So we have never yet had upon the earth a society representing, on any large scale, the principles of the teaching of Jesus. We have had many societies whose main reliance was on military force; many societies resting upon slavery or serfdom; many societies founded on feudal distinctions of ruling and serving classes; many societies whose regulative principle was competition, or a struggle for advantage and mastery; but we have never yet seen a society which rested upon the law of brotherhood and the principle of service.

Yet it is toward this that we have been steadily traveling ever since the day when the old prophet held up before the eyes of men his social ideal. One obstacle after another has been taken out of the way of its coming. The Roman empire crumbled, under the disintegrating influences which it set in motion; feudalism has disappeared; slavery has been abolished; political democracy with freedom of speech and of the press is the rule of the foremost people of the world; and large elements in our social life have been, to a very great degree, Christianized. Philanthropy, the principle of compassion and kindness, has been largely organized into the social life of this nation; the defective and dependent classes are the wards of the state. A considerable part of the life of civilized society is controlled by Christian principle. We have come to a day in which it does not seem quixotic to believe that the principles of Christianity are soon to prevail; that all social relations are to be Christianized. Listen to these words spoken a year and a half ago, not at a missionary meeting, not by a minister, but by a journalist who is not a church man, spoken at a political banquet in a western city:

> The whole world is coming into a new era. It is an era as distinct from the nineteenth century as the reformation is distinct from the middle ages. This new era is manifest in Russia as well as in Kansas; in England as well as in Nebraska. It is manifest in religion as well as in politics, in business as well as in art. It is *the era of humanization, the era of brotherhood....* Whether commerce will admit it or not, the chief concern of business today is not so entirely the accumulation of wealth as it was in the latter part of the nineteenth century, but instead, one of the chief concerns of business is the distribution of wealth.... The spirit of mutual kindness has been moving slowly for centuries through the world. The seed was sown two thousand years ago and *the plant is now preparing to burst into bloom,* and the next thousand years may see some real fruit of the spirit of brotherhood.

It is a great testimony, and it is a true testimony. This keen watcher from the mountaintops of the movements of humanity brings in a report which is surely entitled to credit. What is it that he sees and declares? It is the fulfillment of the prophet's vision, the realization of the Master's teaching in the Sermon on the Mount. It is all coming true. It is no longer a dream, it is proving to be a reality. The city of God, the New Jerusalem, which the Revelator saw coming down from heaven, is beginning to materialize before our eyes. It is still very fragmentary, very inchoate; it is like a new building rising on ground that has been occupied, and is but partially cleared; much debris and unsightliness is still visible; but we can begin to discern something of the plan and to rejoice in the beauty yet to be revealed.

While the witness whom I just quoted discerned signs of this dawning in other lands than ours, while, indeed, there are in some other Christian countries omens no less auspicious than those which are visible around us, yet we may thankfully confess that the promise which meets our eyes in our own country is for us the clearest and the most convincing.

That the prophecy is beginning to come true of America is not to many of us incredible. These words of the text, as we read them, sometimes sound like a current history of the United States.

> Lift up thine eyes round about, and see; they all gather them-
> selves together, they come to thee; thy sons shall come from far, and
> thy daughters shall be carried in the arms. Then shalt thou see and
> be radiant, and thy heart shall thrill and be enlarged because the
> abundance of the sea shall be turned unto thee; the wealth of the
> nations shall come unto thee.

Have we not thus brought clearly before our minds the fact that the nation is to be an important agency in bringing in the kingdom? Has not the time come when we must learn to look for the employment of the nations by the divine Power, in the evangelization of the world? Is there not work to do in the salvation of the world which can only be done on the scale of the nation, and by the enlistment of national resources; and is it not needful that we, who have this missionary work on our hands, should be well aware of this fact and should make large room for it in all our estimates and endeavors?

This is certainly the prophetic conception. It was through the nation that the kingdom of God was to be set up in the world. The contact of that holy nation, the socialized nation, with other nations was to result in the transformation of the other nations into the same type of national life, with righteousness reigning and plenty and peace prevailing. All these glowing promises made by the old prophets, of the triumphs yet to be won for the kingdom of God in the world, are made to the nation and not to the church. We have given to them so long a purely spiritual significance that it is difficult for us to realize that it was to a political rather than an ecclesiastical organization that all these promises are addressed. You may say that the nation was conceived as a theocracy, and that is true, but that is God's plan for every nation; he desires no other relation to any nation than that which he maintained toward Israel. It was the people Israel, and not the priesthood, which was to be equipped for moral and spiritual leadership; it was of Israel that Jehovah testified. "Behold, I have given him for a witness to the peoples, a leader and commander to the peoples." Any one who will read through these prophecies of the later Isaiah, with his eye upon these references to the part which the nation is to play in the conversion of the world, will get some new idea of the magnitude of the missionary movement.

In truth, the evangel which the divine love is seeking to proclaim to all the peoples, is a truth so large that it can only be adequately uttered by a nation's voice. There is, indeed, a message for the individual, and this the individual can utter, not indeed in its completeness, but in such manner that it may meet the needs of him who hears it. To the individual, in his darkness and his loneliness, bending under a nameless burden, groping in paths that lead he knows not whither, without hope and without God in the world, our gospel has a message of light and comfort and salvation, and blessed is he who hears it, and blessed is he to whom is given the joy of speaking it. This is the message to which the emphasis of our missionary preaching and teaching has hitherto been given, and great and beautiful have been the gains that have been gathered from this sowing, in transformed characters and regenerated homes. God forbid that this emphasis should ever be weakened, or that the brightness of this hope of salvation for the individual should ever be dimmed. How much need there is of filling the world with new life and power, we shall see very soon.

Nevertheless, the gospel has been very imperfectly heard by any one to whom it has brought no other tidings than that of personal salvation. For in truth the individual is saved only when he is put into right relations to the community in which he lives, and the establishment of these right relations among men is the very work that Christ came to do. The individual gospel and the social gospel are therefore vitally related, inseparably bound together, and salvation can no more come to the man apart from the community, than life can come to the branch when it is separated from the vine. And the social gospel can be adequately presented only in the terms of the common life. No man can know what it is except as he sees it exemplified in the life of the community. The family can show it to us in part, but only in part; the church can illustrate only certain of the gentler and humbler phases of the common life; to know what Christianity is, we must see it at work on the scale of the nation. If we want the nations of the earth to understand Christianity, we have got to have a Christianized nation to show them. Small samples will not serve. The real question is, after all, what Christianity is able to do for the civilization of a people. The keen-witted Orientals to whom we are making our appeal, the Japanese, the Chinamen, the Hindus, the Turks, understand this perfectly, and we must be ready for a rigid application of this test. It is perfectly fair. We are judging them in the same way. The religions of the world are forced by the contacts and collisions of world polities into a struggle for existence; the evolutionary processes are sifting them; and we shall see the survival of the fittest—that religion which best meets the deepest needs of human nature. Doubtless each will make some contribution to that synthesis of faith which the ages are working out, but none of us doubts which one of them will stamp its character most strongly upon the final result. But the elements are yet in the crucible, and Christianity is listening to the challenge of the millions to whom it offers the way and the truth and the life. And that challenge, as I have

said, is addressed to the larger incarnation of its spirit in the life of the
nation. The keen critics, to whom we are proffering our solution of the
problem of life, are practically replying to us: "We must be shown. By its
fruits we are judging your religion. That is the word of your own
Founder. And we must find its fruits in the national life. The individual
types that you send us in the missionaries may be satisfactory, but what
we need to know is that these are not exceptions, that the society out of
which they come is fairly represented by them. Yours is a Christian nation,
so we are told. We want to know what a Christian nation is like. We
want to see what Christianity is doing for all classes of your people, for
all departments of your national life."

This is the challenge by which our missionaries are halted on the
frontiers of all the old civilizations. It is a challenge that must be met.
If we cannot answer these questions satisfactorily, our missionary enterprise will have no large results.

It is needless to say that we sometimes find such questions embar-
rassing. For, in truth, as I have already said, our society is yet very imperfectly Christianized. That suppositious Chinese official whose "letters"
made some stir a few years ago was within the truth when he said: "You
profess Christianity but your civilization has never been Christian,
whereas ours is Confucian through and through." It is true that our
industrial society has been economic rather than Christian, and that our
political society has been too closely assimilated in its ruling ideas, to our
industrial society. The Christian conception of human relations has never
been consistently applied to these great departments of our national life,
and it is the sad truth that the Christian church has only recently begun
to see that it is its business to make this application. That critic whose
words I was just quoting says again, "Whether your religion be better
than ours, I do not at present dispute, but it is certain that it has less
influence on your society." This must be confessed to be a grave defect in
the type of Christianity with which we are familiar. It has been quite too
much employed, not in saving the world, but in saving people out of the
world. Of course we have always had some interest in promoting righteousness and justice here on earth, but this has been a subordinate interest; if we could get people ready to die, the question how they lived
together here did not so much concern us. Thus it has come about that
the influence of our religion on our industrial society and on political
society has been a superficial—oblique and not direct, incidental rather
than central—and not a controlling influence, and the national life therefore gives very imperfect expression to the Christian idea. Nevertheless,
in spite of our failure to apply our Christianity as thoroughly as we
ought to have applied it to these great departments of our national life,
its indirect and partial influence has been felt in every part of the life of

the nation; and just as it is, we need not shrink from the challenge of the rival faiths. We admit that America is not as consistently Christian, as China is Confucian; if it were, it would be a far better country than it is. We admit that grave and deadly evils yet mingle with our civilization; that poverty and vice and crime still infest the social order; that our industry in many of its phases is brutalized by greed; that we have harbored the growth of a plutocracy, whose presence on our soil is a shame and a curse to us, and have bred, at the other end of the scale, a proletariat whose helpless misery is the dismay of our philanthropy; we confess our public service is grievously disfigured and debased by inefficiency and corruption, and that multitudes of men seek public office as the opportunity of unscrupulous greed and ambition. With that tariff wrangle still sounding in our ears, in which there were so few public servants who were not ready to sacrifice the good of all to the gain of a few, it is quite impossible for any American to claim that the law of Christ rules our legislation. And yet, while we confess all these things with sorrow and shame, we must not shut our eyes to the saving virtues which do yet appear in the life of our own people. The nation is not yet sanctified, but we may say of it what they said of the people who were added to the church in the Pentecostal revival, that it is being saved.

Most of that which is bad in our present condition was worse two hundred years ago, or one hundred years ago; in spite of all that has been brought to light by pessimists and muckrakers, the health of the nation is sounder, its moral forces are stronger today than they ever were before. Much of that which startles and confounds us is due to the deepened and clarified ethical feeling of the people. The interests were just as selfish and insistent when the Dingley bill and the McKinley bill[2] were framed, as they were last summer, but nobody paid much attention to them; today the people are mad all through at the exhibition of egotism. This does not indicate a falling but a rapidly rising standard of political morality. Most of the other disturbing violations of social and political distemper fall under the same judgment. While, therefore, we acknowledge with humiliation that our nation still falls far below our ideal of a Christian nation, and while we are resolved by the grace of God to bring it a great deal nearer to that standard before this century is very old, yet even now, just as it is, we are not ashamed to put its civilization side by side with any civilization that is not Christian and let the world judge between them. With other Christian lands we make no comparison, that

---

[2] (The McKinley Tariff Act [1890] placed prohibitory duties on imports in an effort to protect established, and foster new, industries. The Dingley Tariff Act [1897] enacted the highest protective tariff imposed by Congress up to that time.—EDITOR)

is beside the point; but where in the world today is there a non-Christian country whose people enjoy so large a measure of well-being as ours possess? Where is the path to life as free as on this Christian soil? Where is property as secure, where is enterprise as unconfined, where is life as precious? Where, in any non-Christian land, is there any such provision as that to which we are accustomed, for the alleviation of human suffering and the care and comfort of the disabled and the unfortunate? Where else are the gates of knowledge thrown wide open to the children of the poor? Tell us of any country outside Christendom where woman enjoys the honor and the freedom that here are her inheritance.

It is not necessary to pause for answer to these questions. The answer is coming in the tides of immigration always pouring into our harbors. Wherever communications are opened between our own country and non-Christian countries, the multitudes that throng to seek the protection and the opportunity which our flag symbolizes are convincing witnesses to the value of our civilization. Defective as our national performance is when measured by the high standards of Christian morality, it yet embodies principles and forces and produces results which appeal, with irresistible power to the heart of universal humanity.

In the great chapter of his on "The Advent of Humanity" in his book on *The New Epoch for Faith*, Dr. Gordon[3] puts high among the agencies which are leading in that advent, the United States of America. It is not, I am sure, the fond conceit of a patriot, it is the reasoned judgment of a philosophical historian. Grievous as her shortcomings have been, I think it is true that "throughout the civilized world, government at the end of the nineteenth century is a very different thing from what it was at the beginning; and in bringing about this vast change, the influence of the United States has been predominant." And I hope that it is not in any petty national pride, but with profound and humble thankfulness for our great inheritance, that we are able to join with Dr. Gordon in saying: "In the ideas upon which it was founded, in the nature and scope of its political institutions, in the striking intellectual hospitality of its people, in the object and issues of its great war, and in the human foundation which it asserts for religion, the United States has been, in this century, the foremost servant of the idea of humanity."

I believe that the people of all the nations are beginning to discern something of the loftiness of our national ideals, and to turn with wistful hope to America for leadership. And what has caught the world's attention is the illustration in the life of the nation of the Christian virtues.

---

3 [George A. Gordon—Congregational minister of Old South Church in Boston and a liberal theologian with a strong philosophical bent.—EDITOR]

Dr. Gordon's estimate was made up at the end of the nineteenth century; but the first decade of the twentieth has lifted it into clearer light.

Ask China who it was that sturdily and successfully resisted the attempts of the powers to partition her territory among themselves, and established the policy of the open door; and who it was that sent back a good part of the indemnity money, and who it is that has just been seeking within the last few months to rouse the conscience of the nations of the world against the accursed opium traffic. China knows that in all these matters the United States has been her friend, and she knows that what this nation has done in these great matters has been done because she is, in some imperfect sense, a Christian nation.

Ask Japan what evidence she has had within the last year that this nation means to deal with other nations on Christian principles, and whether Christian principles, thus incarnated in the life of a nation, do not commend themselves to her as sound principles of national life.

Ask the European nations who it was that urged the reassembling of the Hague tribunal, and led the way toward the arbitration of national disputes and the establishment of peace and good will among men.

Ask the whole world who it was that laid a strong but gentle hand upon Russia and Japan when they were devouring each other, and brought them into an honorable peace. It was our President, you say, and he was acting on his own responsibility. Yes, but he never more perfectly represented the spirit of the nation than in that unofficial act, and all the world knows it. And all the world knows that the spirit of the nation as revealed in that act was the Christian spirit, and all the world stood still, reverently beholding a great nation going forth to claim the blessing of the peacemakers.

May we not say that the world has seen in the years just past such a manifestation of the glory of Christianity as it never before has witnessed, in these acts by which, on a national scale, the spirit of Christianity has been exemplified? There have been great preachers of the gospel, great missionaries of the cross, but few, I believe, who have presented the principles of our religion to the non-Christian world more convincingly than William McKinley and John Hay and John W. Foster and Theodore Roosevelt and Elihu Root and William H. Taft. Through the testimony of these witnesses the peoples of the non-Christian lands have gained a conception of the real genius of Christianity which they never had before. This exhibition must have its effect upon all our evangelical enterprises. I cannot doubt that because of these benign interventions of our national government the people of many of the Eastern lands must be more ready than they have ever been to listen to the message of the gospel of Christ.

. . . .

The gospel begins with the statement that Jesus went about in all

Galilee, teaching in the synagogues, and preaching the gospel of the king-dom and healing all manner of disease and all manner of sickness among the people. The gospel begins in every mission field with this benign ministry to human suffering. There are few cities in the Orient where the multitude has not learned that the men and women who bear the name of Christ have wonderful power to heal the sick and give strength to the lame and sight to the blind. Everywhere the medical work of our missions is reaching down to the humblest and the neediest and easing their pains and soothing their wounds, and wiping away their tears. Their experience of a skill which to them is marvelous excites their admiration; but they cannot help seeing that their skill is born of compassion, and that wins their hearts. And when they sit down in the hospitals and the dispen-saries to hear the surgeon read to them the gospel story, they find out who it was that awakened in human hearts this impulse to care for the sick and the suffering.

The advent among them of the American family is also a revelation. I am aware that among some of these ancient peoples the family relation is greatly cherished, and there are features of that family life which we might well seek to imitate; but after all that can be said of Confucianism, the Christian home is not to be classed with any other institution on the earth as a training school of human character. How deadly are the evil tendencies which assail the foundations of the family in America, I do not need to try to tell; and the wreckage of households here produces conditions quite as deplorable as any that the Orient can exhibit. When we compare the lowest levels of our own social condition with the lowest coolie of India or Turkey or China, there is not much to choose. It may be that we can show the world a deeper degradation than that into which any Eastern nation has sunk, for the higher and fairer are the social ideals, the fouler is the deformity when they are trampled under foot. The worst is always the perversion of the best. The purest thing in the world is the heart of a good woman, and the vilest is the heart of a bad one. The infidel who scoffs at the God of Horace Bushnell or Phillips Brooks is a more revolting character than was the one who shut his heart against the God of John Calvin.

But civilizations are not rightly estimated on their lowest level; it is by their growth and not by their abortions that we must judge them. And when the best types of the Christian family are set over against the best types of the family in any non-Christian nation, there is no call for argu-ment or demonstration. Certain it is that nothing can be done for China or for India or for Turkey, comparable with that which is done when the Christian family is transplanted to their soil, and they are permitted to look upon it with their own eyes, to witness its blossoming and its fruit-age; to see for themselves what Christianity makes of womanhood and childhood; to feel the force of the mighty contrast between the Christian home and the best form of family life elsewhere existing. We sometimes hear arguments, on the score of economy, for celibate missionaries; and we all share the loneliness and pain of missionary parents in being parted so many years from their children; but, after all, nothing can take the place in our missionary work of that object lesson which the Christian family presents to the non-Christian people. We could not make them understand what our religion means if we could not show them this. It is by just such fruits as these that we wish to have them know it. Doubtless, the Hindus and Confucians are apt to regard their domestic institution as superior to those of other peoples, and there is much superficial comment by Europeans and Americans in which certain features of those systems are eulogized to the disparagement of our own; but all that is needed is that the differing types of family life be placed side by side. The home in which the wife is apt to be a menial; in which it is a very rare thing for her to be able "to read for profit or recreation," from which she can never depart without seeking permission; in which a social meal is a thing unknown, since men and women never eat together; in which the appearance of a girl baby is generally regarded as a calamity, and from which multitudes of them are cast forth to die and many more are sold into degrading slavery; such homes as these need only to stand side by side with the homes in which the missionaries live, in order that those who dwell in them may understand the meaning of the Christian religion. . . .

We may say that the missionary work is in truth a method of revelation. It is, to these non-Christian peoples, God's continuing revelation. God has always been revealing himself to men; he has manifested much of his goodness and truth to these non-Christian peoples. It is part of our great happiness that we, in these latter days, are able to discern this so clearly and to rejoice in it. Our missionaries, above all others, are teaching us to recognize the elements of value in all the other religions. We go forth not to destroy but to fulfill their form of faith. We expect to find in them much that is in harmony with our own belief, and some elements by which our own faith may be strengthened. Nevertheless, we know that we have something to give, something very vital and precious, and we believe that the larger truth with which we have been entrusted is ours that we may share it. This, I say, is God's method of revelation. His word to us is "Freely have ye received, freely give." But the substance of this revelation, now as always, is conveyed by personal contact. "In him was life, and the life was the light of men." There is no way of teaching men what Christianity is except by living it among them. What the missionary says is of secondary importance; what the missionary is and does—the missionary and his wife and children, in the relations of everyday life, in buying and selling, in work and in play, in the home and in the school and in the hospital and in the street, in the presence of sickness and misfortune and danger and death—all this is of primary importance. The missionary may be able to interpret to them, to some good purpose, the law and the prophets and the psalms and the gospels, but the missionary and his family are the living epistles out of which they have the greater part of what they know about Christ and his religion.

. . . .

I once heard a brilliant Japanese scholar, who had been lecturing on the Oriental faiths, plumply asked in the presence of his audience, by one who undoubtedly expected a different answer, whether, after all, Christianity was in any respect superior to other faiths. He hesitated a little, but his answer came at length, clear and frank: "Yes, I think that the Christian faith in the Fatherhood of God is something better than any other religion has to offer." If that is true, there is nothing more to say. The case is concluded. If that is true, our one great business is to reveal this truth to those who do not know it. And it can only be revealed from life to life. Men can never know what friendship with God means except as they see that friendship incarnating itself in the terms and relations of human life; they must see it upholding and inspiring us, giving us comfort and courage, and peace and power. Such lives as these, hid with Christ in God, are the continuing revelation, and it is quite impossible for us, by any other method, to present to the people of other faiths, the real meaning of the Christian religion. This intimate and vital knowledge of what is seminal and essential in Christianity must be communicated to those who need it as we have been communicating it through the consecrated lives of the men and women who become their neighbors and companions, and show them by a testimony which no logic can confute and no prejudice withstand, what it means to have for a friend the God and Father of our Lord Jesus Christ.

It is the patent subsoiling that has been going on for a hundred years, on all the fields of Christian missions, which has opened the minds of the peoples to that great testimony which the nation is now prepared to utter, and which as I have tried to show is destined to appeal, with increasing power, to the great populations of the East.

Thus I have sought to bring before your minds the fact that the work which is so dear to us is going forward along other lines than those we are pursuing, and by the aid of mightier forces than we can muster. When we pray "Thy kingdom come," we are not always awake to the breadth of the grace by which our prayers are answered, "For God fulfills himself in many ways."

I am sure that we can all see how vitally related these two movements are; the spiritual movement, for which we stand; the national movement, which is part of God's providence. He is doing great things through the powers that be whom he has ordained, but he cannot do them without us. It would be strange if such a vision as this should lead us to disparage our work and relax our diligence; rather, is it a rousing call to us to fling ourselves into it with a courage and a confidence that we have never known. God has commissioned this nation, within the last few years, in some unwonted and impressive ways, to show the non-Christian nations what Christianity means; and in that call is a mighty summons to the Christians of this country to illuminate and enforce the message of the nation, to clothe it with crowning light and constraining love.

It is not a futile or a hopeless enterprise. See what mighty forces God is summoning to carry it forward. For these great nations, the nations that are bearing the standards of modern civilization, are under compulsion to behave like Christians. Their policy must needs be, increasingly, a Christian policy. There is no other way out, for any of them, in God's providence. Look at England! Reeling, alas! and somewhat incoherent, under the obsession of naval supremacy, but that is the bad side of England; we all have our bad sides. Look at what she has had to do for Egypt. Look at that South African nation which she has just welded together out of those peoples with which only yesterday she was in a deadly struggle. Was there ever anything finer than the magnanimity with which England has clothed the conquered Boers at once with full citizenship, trusting them utterly and putting the responsibility of self-government upon them? Could any nation have done this whose mind was not saturated with the Sermon on the Mount? It was Jesus Christ who taught her how to do it. For India, too, she has got to do a great deal of the same sort of thing, and she will do it, yes, she will do it under John Morley's head. John Morley may not be posing before the theological professors as a typical Christian, but for John Morley, as the Secretary of State for India, no path is open but that which is worked out by the ethics of the Christ. Whatever he believes, he has got to behave like a Christian. And this is the way the world is going. Doubt it not, beloved, doubt it not.

The earth is circling onward out of shadow into light,
The stars keep watch above our head however dark the night.
For every martyr-stripe there glows a bar of morning bright,
And love is marching on!

Lead on, O cross of martyr-faith, with thee is victory!
Shine forth, O stars and reddening dawn, the full day yet shall be,
On earth his kingdom cometh, and with joy our eyes shall see
Our God is marching on.

There are just two things for us to do. We must pour the love of our hearts and the strength of our lives into this work of preparing the way for him among the peoples. And we must make this nation fit to be a witness for him, so that when the banner of our country and the banner of the cross are seen floating together, it shall be evident to all men that the day has come when mercy and truth are met together, and righteousness and peace have kissed each other.

part six

AMERICAN DESTINY
AND
WORLD WAR

The United States hesitated before entering the two world wars. Each time most U.S. citizens initially preferred that their nation hold herself aloof from what they took to be strictly European conflicts. But after U.S. entrance, American spokesmen for the Allied cause envisioned war as an instrument for the achievement of a higher destiny.

Long before this country committed its men and arms to the First World War, a number of Americans were agitating for military preparedness and direct support of the Allied forces. Most wanted to avoid involvement in the struggle, however, and chose to believe that their nation should operate on the European scene through the power of moral example rather than by force of arms. Woodrow Wilson won the 1916 presidential election as the man who "kept us out of war," and many citizens hoped with Wilson that German belligerency could be negotiated away. "There is such a thing as a man being too proud to fight," Wilson said. "There is such a thing as a nation being so right that it does not need to convince others by force that it is right."[1]

Early in 1917 the Germans proved to be unmoved by moral suasion and announced the reopening of unrestricted submarine warfare. The subsequent loss of eight U.S. ships and the discovery of a German plot to involve the United States in a war with Mexico and Japan led to President

---

[1] Quoted in John Morton Blum, *Woodrow Wilson and the Politics of Morality* (Boston: Little, Brown and Company, 1956), p. 101.

Wilson's appearance before a special session of Congress on April 2 to ask for a declaration of war. Wilson's was one of history's least bellicose war speeches. "It is a fearful thing," he said, "to lead this great peaceful people into war, into the most terrible and disastrous of all wars, civilization itself seeming to be in the balance." Now that the nation has been forced into this course of action, however, the fight must be for those principles of freedom which it has ever been the destiny of America to safeguard: "We shall fight for the things which we have always carried nearest our hearts—for democracy, for the right of those who submit to authority to have a voice in their own Governments, for the rights and liberties of small nations, for a universal dominion of right by such a concert of free peoples as shall bring peace and safety to all nations, and make the world itself at last free." American engagement in war could be for no paltry purpose of merely defending American interests. For Wilson and millions of other Americans it had to be a war to end war, a war to make the whole world safe for democracy.

American public opinion was mobilized for the war effort by the government's Committee on Public Information. Operating under the direction of journalist George Creel, the C.P.I. employed the talents of hundreds of writers and artists to launch one of the most effective propaganda campaigns in modern history. The chief aim of the propaganda was to convince the American people that their nation was at war to preserve freedom and democracy in the world and that the "Huns" were the very creatures of Satan, completely devoid of human compassion and totally committed to wrecking the free world. As a result, the Great War came to be seen as an Armageddon, a battle waged by the saints against unmitigated evil.

American clergymen became leading advocates of the righteousness of the nation's cause. It is inaccurate to conclude, however, as one study has done,[2] that the clergy were dupes of a well-planned British and American government propaganda movement. The clergy did not have to be duped. They drew upon their own religious traditions of Israelite war, holy crusade, and "just war" theory in order both to ground their pro-war arguments and to give shape to their militant rhetoric. It is clear, however, that the clergy's and the government's cause were one. The clergy were ardent and effective defenders of Wilson's claim that this expeditionary war was being waged on behalf of free men everywhere, and they were prime contributors to the opinion that a holy American army was moving against an altogether evil force. It followed that pacifism was deemed a cowardly, unscriptural position. Randolph H. McKim,

---

[2] Ray H. Abrams, *Preachers Present Arms* (Philadelphia: Round Table Press, 1933), pp. xvi, 79ff. et passim.

Episcopal rector at Epiphany Church in Washington, D.C., summed up an argument frequently heard during the war: "If any man demands how we can make war in the name of Christ, the Prince of Peace, let him remember those words of His, 'I came not to send peace but a sword.' Yes, if He bids us love truth and righteousness, He also bids us hate false-hood and wrong and injustice and cruelty. And he calls us to fight against these things, not only by argument but by the sword, when occasion arises."[3] Words of damnation for the Germans—especially for their leaders —also came easily to the clergy. Revivalist Billy Sunday expressed the imprecation in his own inimitably uncouth fashion: "If you turn hell upside down, you will find 'Made in Germany' stamped on the bottom."

Numerous sermons sought to represent American action abroad as a serious attempt to realize the national destiny. A sermon on patriotism by the Right Reverend Monsignor C. F. Thomas of St. Patrick's Church in Washington, D.C., was typical of religious interpretations of American destiny during World War I. Delivered on Washington's Birthday at a memorial mass held for the Knights of Columbus, the sermon was one of a host preached by Catholics, Protestants, and Jews on that sacred day in 1918. All over the District of Columbia patriotic and religious groups gathered for ceremonies eulogizing George Washington and celebrating the principles of freedom for which he stood and for which, it was believed, Americans were currently called to fight. In his Washington tabernacle, Billy Sunday closed a prayer with the remark that it did not really matter if Germany had fifty guns to our one since "the Lord on our side is worth more guns than old Krupp can make." At the Eighth Street Temple, Rabbi Abram Simon said, "We are fighting the old fight of freedom and advancement against intolerance and oppression. This is the fight that George Washington made."[4] Mgr. Thomas's sermon paralleled the hard-ships of the children of Israel in the wilderness with the hardships of the New Israel at war, pleaded for unity and sacrifice in support of America's mission of preserving the liberties of democratic government, and closed with the claim that the American war task was "just and righteous." Thomas's address pulled together under the rubric of American destiny the war claims declared by Wilson and the government propaganda. Typical of speeches during American sacred ceremonies, it interpreted war deaths as sacrifices made for the fulfillment of American destiny under God.

A majority of Americans either heartily supported or did not seri-ously object to the Treaty of Versailles and the plan for a League of

3 Randolph H. McKim, *For God and Country, or the Christian Pupit in War-Time* (New York: E. P. Dutton & Co., Inc., 1918), pp. 117–18.
4 *Washington Post*, Feb. 23, 1918, p. 2.

Nations that Wilson brought back from the Paris Peace Conference in 1919. Nevertheless, in a final vote in March, 1920, the Senate rejected the treaty and the league. Reasons for this rejection were numerous and complex, but a fierce Republican opposition to Wilson, plus the president's own blunder in refusing to marshall bipartisan support for the treaty, were crucial factors. Even though the league and the treaty were defeated, Wilson's speeches on their behalf clearly articulated what the American people had come to believe the U.S. mission in the war had been.

In his speech for ratification before the Senate in 1919, Wilson admitted that he had to make undesirable compromises in the treaty, but he lodged the hope for future world peace, and for rectification of the errors of the treaty, in the League of Nations. Wilson painted a highly idealized picture of American destiny during the war and after. Clemenceau of France and Lloyd George of Great Britain scarcely accepted the picture Wilson had drawn, although it accurately reflected the self-understanding of the American people at the time.

As Wilson continued his defense of the treaty and the league in a speaking tour across the nation, his words revealed less and less concern for the facts. He talked of the "high-minded, statesmanlike cooperation" at the peace conference and described the United States as interested in nothing less than the "liberation and salvation of the world."[5] But all the rhetoric was of no avail, for America was beginning to turn from the kind of international leadership to which Wilson believed God had called her. The 1920s were years of isolationism and narrowing nationalism. Although the United States made some token gestures toward international peace efforts, the nation kept her distance from the real work of the league and raised around herself an economic wall of protective tariffs. The ugliest forms of chauvinism appeared in open hostility toward foreigners and in suspicion of foreign ideas. During the years between the two world wars numerous Americans, particularly clergymen, repented of their wholehearted endorsement of war, and religious pacifism became a widely accepted and respectable position. The coming of the Great Depression, the renewal of political and military upheavals in Europe, and a general war-weariness in the country led to a feeling of disillusionment and to a sense of frustration over the failure of the Great War to yield a secure peace and an enduring prosperity. Not only did the New Israel refuse to heed Wilson's plea that she assume a role of world leadership; embarrassed and disappointed by the fruits of war, she hesitated to call any role her own.

[5] For Wilson's speeches during his tour see *War and Peace*, II, ed. R. S. Baker and W. E. Dodd (New York: Harper & Row, Publishers, 1927), 1–416.

When the totalitarian powers revealed their strategies of aggression in the 1930s, most Americans indicated their disapproval—but with a sense of thankfulness that they were isolated from such disturbing affairs. The attacks on Poland, France, and Britain finally convinced the United States that she might eventually stand alone before the Axis forces. Step by step she abandoned her neutrality. With the attack on Pearl Harbor and the subsequent declaration of war, the nation was forced once again to interpret her reason-for-being within the greater context of world affairs. Propaganda released through films, radio, public speeches, newspapers, and popular magazines again mobilized public support for the national war effort, but on the whole there was less war hysteria this time and much less talk of a holy crusade aimed at the final destruction of evil. Because of the disappointments of World War I, Americans were more inclined to view their participation in World War II as a tragic necessity rather than as a glorious blow for righteousness. It was surely seen as a fight for freedom and justice against aggressive tyranny, but not as a struggle for the redemption of the world.

The Federal Council of Churches may serve as a barometer of the change in attitude that occurred between the two wars. At the conclusion of the First World War the Council had wired Wilson that the proposed League of Nations was the "political expression of the Kingdom of God on earth." In a statement released in 1942, the council spoke much more cautiously, characterizing the current war as a struggle between nations representing the institutions of free men against those representing tyranny and adding, "We do not hold that a victory of the United Nations would in itself guarantee the achievement of any Christian goals." Allied victory would simply create much more favorable circumstances for the Christian religion. "A victory of the United Nations would at least afford in many lands a degree of freedom in Christian service of which so far as the human eye can see an Axis victory would rob us."[6] There was evidence of yet another change: Although during the Second World War there was a noticeable decline in religious pacifism, most religious groups came to acknowledge the integrity of that position and supported the right of conscientious objection.

Though American leaders were reluctant to depict America's role in the war as a holy crusade for the redemption of the world, they did not hesitate to appeal to the nation's deep-seated sense of election in their description of war aims. Franklin D. Roosevelt, whose official statements and radio addresses were second only to those of Winston Churchill in their capacity to arouse and sustain the spirit of a people, frequently defined America's role in the war in terms of the national destiny. The

[6] *Christian Century*, Dec. 23, 1942, p. 1602.

president's annual message to Congress on January 6, 1942, suggested a far-reaching national mission at stake in the war: America had joined the free world in the noble task of preserving the divine heritage of human dignity against a cynical contempt for the human race. Roosevelt did see the war as a clear conflict between good and evil, but missing from his address was both the narrow jingoism and the naive utopianism so evident during the First War.

Almost as soon as World War II started, interpretations of American destiny began to center on the problem of how to establish a just and durable peace once an Allied victory had been attained. Thoughtful men turned their attention to the possibility of a United Nations organization which would provide a workable alternative to the settlement of disputes by war. The interlocking nature of American destiny, Allied war aims, and national responsibility for world peace was ably delineated by the Christian ethicist Reinhold Niebuhr in 1943. Written at the time of the formation of the British-American Alliance (which was to be a step toward the United Nations), Niebuhr's brief but trenchant essay, "Anglo-Saxon Destiny and Responsibility," differentiated between a self-righteous and a responsible sense of Anglo-American destiny. Niebuhr claimed that a proper religious understanding of a high national calling can stimulate the pursuit of justice and peace without giving rein to proud messianism and destructive vindictiveness. The essay was one of the finest expressions of Niebuhr's political realism, and it possessed a religious insight reminiscent of Lincoln's during the Civil War.

The nuclear obliteration of Hiroshima and Nagasaki toward the war's end was a terrifying warning that civilization could not survive another total war. It was also awesome proof that the American isolationism of the twenties and thirties had been a deceptive means of achieving national security. The destiny of America was inextricably bound up with the destiny of the globe. Interpretations of America's mission in the world would continue to vary, however. The cold war with Russia, the limited wars in Korea and Vietnam, the various revolutions throughout the world all would raise maddening questions about the nature and extent of America's international responsibility. Serious problems at home would pose even more startling questions: Did a New American Israel any longer exist? Could America really claim a unified destiny under God?

SUGGESTED READING

Abrams, Ray H. "The Churches and the Clergy in World War II," *Annals of the American Academy of Political and Social Science*, Mar. 1948, pp. 110–19.

————, *Preachers Present Arms*. Philadelphia: Round Table Press, 1933.

Aron, Raymond. *The Century of Total War*. Garden City, N.Y.: Doubleday & Company, Inc., 1954.

Bainton, Roland H. *Christian Attitudes Toward War and Peace*. Nashville: Abingdon Press, 1960.

Blum, John Morton. *Woodrow Wilson and the Politics of Morality*. Boston: Little, Brown and Company, 1956.

Johnson, F. Ernest. "The Impact of the War on Religion in America," *American Journal of Sociology*, Nov. 1942, pp. 353–60.

May, Henry F. *The End of American Innocence*. New York: Alfred A. Knopf, Inc., 1959.

Niebuhr, Reinhold. *Love and Justice*, edited by D. B. Robertson. New York: World Publishing Company, Meridian Books, 1967.

THE RIGHT REVEREND MONSIGNOR C. F. THOMAS

Patriotism

I am glad to welcome you here on this occasion and to aid in your celebration of this memorial day. I applaud your sentiments of love and devotion which prompt you to come. Your presence at this solemn Mass renews your consecration to the highest duties of religion and patriotism.

This day is sacred to the memory of Washington, who still remains first in the hearts of his countrymen for his successful work and heroic sacrifices in winning liberty and freedom for this favored land of ours. The day is honored, and through its memories we are kept in mind of the solemn pledges we inherit to perpetuate what he achieved to remotest generations. And your noble and admirable fraternity links itself closely to all the deepest sentiments or loftiest ideals which the honoring of the day calls forth.

The greatness of Washington shines out in his generosity of soul and largeness of nature, as well as in his genuine courage and heroism. And through them was he able to render grateful recognition for the valuable patriotic services of our forefathers in the faith in bringing about the glorious results of the American Revolution.

Far be it from us to glory in fidelity to truth and duty; but we have inviolably kept the trust handed down to us, and every generation of us has striven to uphold, increase, defend and enrich the precious inheritance of our republican institutions in liberty and freedom.

Your organization has from the beginning served to emphasize the loyalty of energy towards the upbuilding of tendencies and movements, and of succor and support in times of emergency, peril and disaster. And recent sacrifices and services have demonstrated the ever living element or instinct of patriotism which pervades and permeates our being. In every corner of this vast land, loud has been the response to our country's call in the hour of need and danger, and in this response the clearest tones have been sounded by the enthusiastic and brave and unselfish action of the Knights of Columbus.

Delivered at a Memorial Mass on Washington's Birthday at St. Patrick's Church, Washington, D.C. From *War Addresses from Catholic Pulpit and Platform* (New York: Joseph F. Wagner, Inc., n.d.), pp. 171–77.

This action to which I refer, which has been and is an important factor in the means of defense adopted against the impending peril, and which has received just and merited approbation from private sources and Government authorities, has certainly been duplicated by others; but it evidences a spirit which the whole American people must thoroughly learn. The preservation of what our fathers won on many hard fought fields of battle and completely achieved by patient struggle and heroic sacrifices, the fulfillment of the mission attained by this nation, or entrusted to it, by their victory, is to be the result of many trials and much hardship.

It was a glorious day when this young nation was declared and acknowledged to be free and independent; and when it set out—emerging from the bondage of Old World ideas—to confer on the human race new and incalculable truths founded in the aspirations of democracy. Our fathers indulged in the vision of untold splendor, of radiant happiness, of true civilization, when the States would eventually unfold their capacities to the fullest extent and the people would develop the inherent powers of the human soul and reach almost Utopian heights of success and peace. True to the inspiration imparted, and faithful to the traditions handed down, the citizens of these United States have furnished valuable contributions to the best and purest civilization, and have built up a vast nation, solid in its integrity, strong in its assurance of permanence, vast in its power of achievement, rich in its resources and opulent in its advantages. The providence of God seems to have smiled on their efforts and to have exceedingly blessed their endeavors; and the nation has advanced far beyond the most sanguine expectations of its founders and fathers.

But I think that many have been prone to rest satisfied with the progress so far obtained, or to imagine that the greatness of the nation is so strong that one need not fear the peril of defeat or the disaster of subjugation. They fold themselves, as it were, within their self-conceit or self-consciousness and consider it impossible for all this glory and grandeur, all this power and prestige to be swept away and our institutions demolished. They resent the forcing of the present emergency upon us as unwarranted, as if there was no danger to us from the cataclysm which has befallen the Old World systems and life. It has been hard to convince a great number of our fellow citizens that our participation in this was justifiable, or that our rights and liberties were in any way jeopardized. Failure to rouse universal enthusiasm and support, bitter and severe denunciation of governmental action, attempts to thwart measures of defence or means of aggressive prosecution of the war prove, not perhaps any lack of genuine loyalty or appreciation of the need of adequate defence, but the conviction of an overweening confidence in the unassailable character of our institutions or of a want of the conviction of the necessity of intense personal sacrifice and patriotism.

The ancient Hebrews were led out of Egypt to found a theocratic state in the land of Canaan. Under the guidance of Moses they were fitting themselves for a high divine purpose. They were drilling to influence the world by their preservation of the knowledge of the true God and by the principles and ideas flowing therefrom. But they did not realize what the cost of progress towards that end involved and were not disposed to endure without protest the hardships, pain, hunger and fatigue, the disgust and perils of their pilgrimage towards the shining goal of their liberty from oppression. Disappointment and anger oft moved them to bitter sarcasm and deep murmuring of their lot. Rebuke and resentment against their great captain were frequent because of their sorry plights and severe sufferings into which he led them. They were willing enough to rejoice in liberty acquired and in glory attained, but were too selfish to undergo the trials through which alone they could lay hold onto the end of their desires and efforts. They were glad enough to be free from Pharaoh's yoke and Egyptian bondage, but even the sufferings of that time and ignominy of that lot seemed to them in the desert more tolerable than the hardships they were encountering on their journey to the promised land.

There is in this country a spirit—evident and pronounced—which acknowledges the high state of our progress and the glories of our material prosperity, the incomparable advantages here secured and enjoyed, the magnificent opportunity for the realization of the highest results of democracy; but does not appreciate the need or necessity of sustaining the trials and hardships through which all these can and must be enlarged, strengthened and perpetuated. This nation is grand in the prospects of happiness it holds out to the human race, almost divine in the prophecy it enfolds of future perfection of human life. The principles upon which it is erected are truer than it was ever the fortune of man to invent for the benefit of mankind; the elements which tell for progress and development, for enlightenment and happiness, are here more rooted than ever before in the history of the world. But it must not be forgotten that the enjoyment of our possession, and the perpetuation of our inheritance, even the solidification of our work or achievements, require and demand on our part, now more than ever, the greatest amount of personal sacrifice, endurance, devotion and heroism. We cannot expect to retain or to preserve the present results of past endeavors, the fruit of our fathers' labors and struggles, unless we are determined at all costs, and all hazards, to maintain the precious ideas, spirit, principles, as well as the material accomplishments which they bequeathed to us.

Even after the Hebrews had rooted themselves in Canaan, and attained a kingdom and established themselves as a dominant people in all that Eastern country they found themselves attacked on every side—

exposed to incursions from hostile tribes, to subjugation by neighboring nations—always in conflict with dangers and perils, with envy and fear from abroad, and always obliged to intense exertion for defence and for the perpetuation of the glorious principality they had set up. No nation, no people, have endured who were not endowed with the deepest instincts of patriotism and the most unselfish spirit of devotion and sacrifice. And the ancient Hebrews had ingrained into them by severe measures and bitter experience the lesson of suffering and hardship.

We have now to learn the same lesson. We have never been compelled to learn it before. We must learn it now in face of the danger that confronts us. We are to continue. The Providence of God destines this nation to last—indefinitely, we confidently trust. The whole world looks to us to carry to the future what will save the future from disorder, confusion, anarchy, perhaps dissolution. But our trust cannot be fulfilled without the loyalty, love, personal aid and patriotic efforts of each and every individual.

If I read aright the meaning of this day, if I understand at all the significance of this celebration, if I have caught in the least degree the spirit of the immortal Washington, I must emphasize the need of the individual devotion of every citizen of this Republic to the fortunes, whatever they be, in store for it. We may be eager to avail ourselves of the advantages and privileges; we must be just as eager to sustain the trials and help to ward off the dangers that may assail it. We are all anxious that our liberties be preserved; we must be just as anxious to stand behind it when these liberties are threatened with extinction. We rejoice to share in the happiness here conferred upon us; we must be just as willing to sorrow with the country in its misfortunes. And when the country sorrows, when its freedom hangs in the balance, when all that for which it stands finds itself a target for outside attack, when its fondest hopes and yearnings are in danger of being frustrated, there is demanded a universal unity among the citizens—unity of thought, unity of effort, unity of aim, unity in personal devotion and self-sacrifice.

There has been a union here among us ever since Washington's day. There never was seen in the whole history of the world such a union as has existed among us. But that union has now to be perfected by privations we endure and the cost we pay in this time of our nation's greatest crisis.

Perhaps the emergency has arisen precisely to teach us this union. We have not yet really become a nation. There have been so many divergent interests among us. There have been conflicting aims. There are so many different nationalities here beginning to establish themselves. We have been a melting pot; and we have not yet solved the problem—never before presented except to the Roman Empire of old—of amalgamating into one nation members of various other nationalities. We thought we had succeeded. Professor Charles William Elliott, twenty-two years ago, wrote that we had succeeded. But the present crisis proves we had not. And, in my judgment, there was need of some such circumstances as the present to give us the opportunity to appreciate the benefits of the life and the blessings we enjoy, and by appreciation be urged and impelled and driven to give of the best and dearest in us for the defence of the home of our hearts and the land of our abode. Man never values what comes to him easily. A nation never realizes its happiness or its greatness until the hour when its life is threatened. The soul never takes in the grandeur of life eternal until the mortal life is about to end. So here in these United States I believe there would not and will not be a united people unless we now realize that our future as a people, and as individuals, depends on the personal hardships we suffer, and the sacrifices we offer, in order that safety be secured and our institutions be solidified.

I speak for an undivided nation. I speak for unity of action in the crisis we face. I speak for union of endeavor to secure victory for the American arms now engaged in deadly conflict for the perpetuation of American liberties. I speak for universal sacrifice, and for the devotion of each and every individual, in the giving up of even earthly life itself for the cause which is now the cause of America.

In the work of preparation for the task the Government has undertaken, in the gathering together the elements which shall form a powerful army and equip it to the highest point of efficiency much has been accomplished. Criticism has been severe. Lethargy was deep. Objections were numerous. Supineness was inconceivably great. Opposition was intense in some quarters. But the success has been phenomenal. And there is no reason to fear but that our forces will be equal to the burden placed upon them and fit to give a good and glorious account of themselves on the day of battle and in the hour of actual conflict.

Yet much more remains to be done, and the whole nation must be aroused. Every section must be brought to take part. No man, no woman must be found who does not do all possible, suffer all that is required, positively and willingly sustain hardship and trial, privation and pain, in the endeavor to contribute effectively to the success of the cause everyone has or should have at heart. And the spectacle must be offered to the entire world, of all the millions of which we are made up, rising en masse, struggling, rushing, rolling onward with force irresistible, with ardor the greatest and love the deepest, with unselfishness, to crush the foe of American life and liberty and to render safe for all time to come what we and the nation stand for.

A more inspiring example is not possible, a greater incentive could not be found towards unifying the people of this country in the spirit of heroic patriotism, of enthusiastic support and self-sacrificing devotion to the fortunes and needs of the country than has been given by the Knights of Columbus in what they have done and are still doing to help prepare the nation for its gigantic struggle and to aid in securing victory for its arms.

The day is a fitting occasion to renew and spread over the land a feeling of pride in American institutions, American greatness, American prosperity and a sense of assurance that it will all survive; to reawaken in all the liveliest sentiments of patriotism which cannot exist without the determination to suffer what may be necessary to insure safety and victory, and to send out through the entire land the call for union in hardship and trial as indispensable for union in joy and peace.

And this gathering affords opportunity of imparting to the whole country the stimulus, and of communicating to it the spirit which has animated the Knights of Columbus in every part of the Republic and prompted them to undertake, and enabled them to accomplish the great work which is so prolific of magnificent results in the perfecting of the morale and strength of our forces.

The cause is just and righteous. Our sanctuary has been violated. Our rights despised. Our honor assailed in its tenderest spot. Our champions have gone forth to avenge the insult, to regain the confidence of the world in our greatness and power. And it is incumbent upon every man and woman who glories in the name of American, and who lives under the protection of American freedom and enjoys the benefits of American liberty, to strengthen the arms of those champions by the offering of his energies and possessions. Unless they succeed—and they cannot succeed without the undivided action of our millions—this will no longer be the home of the brave and the land of the free.

WOODROW WILSON

Presenting The Treaty
For Ratification

Address to the Senate of the United States,
July 10, 1919.

Gentlemen of the Senate:

The treaty of peace with Germany was signed at Versailles on the twenty-eighth of June. I avail myself of the earliest opportunity to lay the treaty before you for ratification and to inform you with regard to the work of the Conference by which that treaty was formulated.

The treaty constitutes nothing less than a world settlement. It would not be possible for me either to summarize or to construe its manifold provisions in an address which must of necessity be something less than a treatise. My services and all the information I possess will be at your disposal and at the disposal of your Committee on Foreign Relations at any time, either informally or in session, as you may prefer; and I hope that you will not hesitate to make use of them. I shall at this time, prior to your own study of the document, attempt only a general characterization of its scope and purpose.

In one sense, no doubt, there is no need that I should report to you what was attempted and done at Paris. You have been daily cognizant of what was going on there,—of the problems with which the Peace Conference had to deal and of the difficulty of laying down straight lines of settlement anywhere on a field on which the old lines of international relationship, and the new alike, followed so intricate a pattern and were for the most part cut so deep by historical circumstances which dominated action even where it would have been best to ignore or reverse them. The cross currents of politics and of interest must have been evident to you. It would be presuming in me to attempt to explain the questions which arose or the many diverse elements that entered into them. I shall attempt something less ambitious than that and more clearly suggested by my duty

From *War and Peace,* I, *The Public Papers of Woodrow Wilson,* ed. S. T. Baker and W. E. Dodd (New York: Harper & Row, Publishers, 1927), 537–52.

to report to the Congress the part it seemed necessary for my colleagues and me to play as the representatives of the Government of the United States.

That part was dictated by the role America had played in the war and by the expectations that had been created in the minds of the peoples with whom we had associated ourselves in that great struggle.

The United States entered the war upon a different footing from every other nation except our associates on this side of the sea. We entered it, not because our material interests were directly threatened or because any special treaty obligations to which we were parties had been violated, but only because we saw the supremacy, and even the validity, of right everywhere put in jeopardy and free government likely to be everywhere imperiled by the intolerable aggression of a power which respected neither right nor obligation and whose every system of government flouted the rights of the citizen as against the autocratic authority of his governors. And in the settlements of the peace we have sought no special reparation for ourselves, but only the restoration of right and the assurance of liberty everywhere that the effects of the settlement were to be felt. We entered the war as the disinterested champions of right and we interested ourselves in the terms of the peace in no other capacity.

The hopes of the nations allied against the Central Powers were at a very low ebb when our soldiers began to pour across the sea. There was everywhere amongst them, except in their stoutest spirits, a somber foreboding of disaster. The war ended in November, eight months ago, but you have only to recall what was feared in midsummer last, four short months before the armistice, to realize what it was that our timely aid accomplished alike for their morale and their physical safety. That first, never-to-be-forgotten action at Chateau-Thierry had already taken place. Our redoubtable soldiers and marines had already closed the gap the enemy had succeeded in opening for their advance upon Paris,—had already turned the tide of battle back towards the frontiers of France and begun the rout that was to save Europe and the world. Thereafter the Germans were to be always forced back, back, were never to thrust successfully forward again. And yet there was no confident hope. Anxious men and women, leading spirits of France, attended the celebration of the Fourth of July last year in Paris out of generous courtesy,—with no heart for festivity, little zest for hope. But they came away with something new at their hearts; they have themselves told us so. The mere sight of our men,—of their vigor, of the confidence that showed itself in every movement of their stalwart figures and every turn of their swinging march, in their steady comprehending eyes and easy discipline, in the indomitable air that added spirit to everything they did,—made everyone who saw them that memorable day realize that something had happened that was much more than a mere incident in the fighting, something very different from the mere arrival of fresh troops. A great moral force had flung itself into the struggle. The fine physical force of those spirited men spoke of something more than bodily vigor. They carried the great ideals of a free people at their hearts and with that vision were unconquerable. Their very presence brought reassurance; their fighting made victory certain.

They were recognized as crusaders, and as their thousands swelled to millions their strength was seen to mean salvation. And they were fit men to carry such a hope and make good the assurance it forecast. Finer men never went into battle; and their officers were worthy of them. This is not the occasion upon which to utter a eulogy of the armies America sent to France, but perhaps, since I am speaking of their mission, I may speak also of the pride I shared with every American who saw or dealt with them there. They were the sort of men America would wish to be represented by, the sort of men every American would wish to claim as fellow countrymen and comrades in a great cause. They were terrible in battle, and gentle and helpful out of it, remembering the mothers and the sisters, the wives and the little children at home. They were free men under arms, not forgetting their ideals of duty in the midst of tasks of violence. I am proud to have had the privilege of being associated with them and of calling myself their leader.

But I speak now of what they meant to the men by whose sides they fought and to the people with whom they mingled with such utter simplicity, as friends who asked only to be of service. They were for all the visible embodiment of America. What they did made America and all that she stood for a living reality in the thoughts not only of the people of France but also of tens of millions of men and women throughout all the toiling nations of a world standing everywhere in peril of its freedom and of the loss of everything it held dear, in deadly fear that its bonds were never to be loosed, its hopes forever to be mocked and disappointed.

And the compulsion of what they stood for was upon us who represented America at the peace table. It was our duty to see to it that every decision we took part in contributed, so far as we were able to influence it, to quiet the fears and realize the hopes of the peoples who had been living in that shadow, the nations that had come by our assistance to their freedom. It was our duty to do everything that it was within our power to do to make the triumph of freedom and of right a lasting triumph in the assurance of which men might everywhere live without fear.

Old entanglements of every kind stood in the way,—promises which Governments had made to one another in the days when might and right were confused and the power of the victor was without restraint. Engagements which contemplated any dispositions of territory, any extensions of sovereignty that might seem to be to the interest of those who had the

power to insist upon them, had been entered into without thought of
what the peoples concerned might wish or profit by; and these could not
always be honorably brushed aside. It was not easy to graft the new order
of ideas on the old, and some of the fruits of the grafting may, I fear, for
a time be bitter. But, with very few exceptions, the men who sat with us
at the peace table desired as sincerely as we did to get away from the bad
influences, the illegitimate purposes, the demoralizing ambitions, the
international counsels and expedients out of which the sinister designs of
Germany had sprung as a natural growth.

It had been our privilege to formulate the principles which were
accepted as the basis of the peace, but they had been accepted, not because
we had come in to hasten and assure the victory and insisted upon them,
but because they were readily acceded to as the principles to which
honorable and enlightened minds everywhere had been bred. They spoke
the conscience of the world as well as the conscience of America, and I
am happy to pay my tribute of respect and gratitude to the able, forward-
looking men with whom it was my privilege to cooperate for their unfail-
ing spirit of cooperation, their constant effort to accommodate the interests they represented to the principles we were all agreed upon. The
difficulties, which were many, lay in the circumstances, not often in the
men. Almost without exception the men who led had caught the truce
and full vision of the problem of peace as an indivisible whole, a problem, not of mere adjustments of interest, but of justice and right action.

The atmosphere in which the Conference worked seemed created,
not by the ambitions of strong governments, but by the hopes and aspirations of small nations and of peoples hitherto under bondage to the
power that victory had shattered and destroyed. Two great empires had
been forced into political bankruptcy, and we were the receivers. Our task
was not only to make peace with the Central Empires and remedy the
wrongs their armies had done. The Central Empires had lived in open
violation of many of the very rights for which the war had been fought,
dominating alien peoples over whom they had no natural right to rule,
enforcing, not obedience, but veritable bondage, exploiting those who
were weak for the benefit of those who were masters and overlords only
by force of arms. There could be no peace until the whole order of Central
Europe was set right.

That meant that new nations were to be created,—Poland, Czecho-
Slovakia, Hungary itself. No part of ancient Poland had ever in any true
sense become a part of Germany, or of Austria, or of Russia. Bohemia was
alien in every thought and hope to the monarchy of which she had so
long been an artificial part; and the uneasy partnership between Austria
and Hungary had been one rather of interest than of kinship or sympathy. The Slavs whom Austria had chosen to force into her empire on

the south were kept to their obedience by nothing but fear. Their hearts were with their kinsmen in the Balkans. These were all arrangements of power, not arrangements of natural union or association. It was the imperative task of those who would make peace and make it intelligently to establish a new order which would rest upon the free choice of peoples rather than upon the arbitrary authority of Hapsburgs or Hohenzollerns.

More than that, great populations bound by sympathy and actual kin to Rumania were also linked against their will to the conglomerate Austro-Hungarian monarchy or to other alien sovereignties, and it was part of the task of peace to make a new Rumania as well as a new slavic state clustering about Serbia.

And no natural frontiers could be found to these new fields of adjustment and redemption. It was necessary to look constantly forward to other related tasks. The German colonies were to be disposed of. They had not been governed; they had been exploited merely, without thought of the interest or even the ordinary human rights of their inhabitants.

The Turkish Empire, moreover, had fallen apart, as the Austro-Hungarian had. It had never had any real unity. It had been held together only by pitiless, inhuman force. Its peoples cried aloud for release, for succor from unspeakable distress, for all that the new day of hope seemed at last to bring within its dawn. Peoples hitherto in utter darkness were to be led out into the same light and given at last a helping hand. Undeveloped peoples and peoples ready for recognition but not yet ready to assume the full responsibilities of statehood were to be given adequate guarantees of friendly protection, guidance and assistance.

And out of the execution of these great enterprises of liberty sprang opportunities to attempt what statesmen had never found the way before to do; an opportunity to throw safeguards about the rights of racial, national and religious minorities by solemn international covenant; an opportunity to limit and regulate military establishments where they were most likely to be mischievous; an opportunity to effect a complete and systematic internationalization of waterways and railways which were necessary to the free economic life of more than one nation and to clear many of the normal channels of commerce of unfair obstructions of law or of privilege; and the very welcome opportunity to secure for labor the concerted protection of definite international pledges of principle and practice.

These were not tasks which the Conference looked about it to find and went out of its way to perform. They were inseparable from the settlements of peace. They were thrust upon it by circumstances which could not be overlooked. The war had created them. In all quarters of the world old-established relationships had been disturbed or broken and affairs were at loose ends, needing to be mended or united again, but could not be made what they were before. They had to be set right by applying some uniform principle of justice or enlightened expediency. And they could not be adjusted by merely prescribing in a treaty what should be done. New states were to be set up which could not hope to live through their first period of weakness without assured support by the great nations that had consented to their creation and won for them their independence. Ill-governed colonies could not be put in the hands of governments which were to act as trustees for their people and not as their masters if there was to be no common authority among the nations to which they were to be responsible in the execution of their trust. Future international conventions with regard to the control of waterways, with regard to illicit traffic of many kinds, in arms or in deadly drugs, or with regard to the adjustment of many varying international administrative arrangements could not be assured if the treaty were to provide no permanent common international agency, if its execution in such matters was to be left to the slow and uncertain processes of cooperation by ordinary methods of negotiation. If the Peace Conference itself was to be the end of cooperative authority and common counsel among the governments to which the world was looking to enforce justice and give pledges of an enduring settlement, regions like the Saar basin could not be put under a temporary administrative regime which did not involve a transfer of political sovereignty and which contemplated a final determination of its political connections by popular vote to be taken at a distant date; no free city like Danzig could be created which was, under elaborate international guarantees, to accept exceptional obligations with regard to the use of its port and exceptional relations with a State of which it was not to form a part; properly safe-guarded plebiscites could not be provided for where populations were at some future date to make choice what sovereignty they would live under; no certain and uniform method of arbitration could be secured for the settlement of anticipated difficulties of final decision with regard to many matters dealt with in the treaty itself; the long-continued supervision of the task of reparation which Germany was to undertake to complete within the next generation might entirely break down; the reconsideration and revision of administrative arrangements and restrictions which the treaty prescribed but which it was recognized might not prove of lasting advantage or entirely fair if too long enforced would be impracticable. The promises governments were making to one another about the way in which labor was to be dealt with, by law not only but in fact as well, would remain a mere humane thesis if there was to be no common tribunal of opinion and judgment to which liberal statesmen could resort for the influences which alone might secure their redemption. A league of free nations had become a practical necessity. Examine the treaty of peace and you will find that everywhere throughout its manifold provisions its framers have felt obliged to turn to the League of Nations as an indispensable instrumentality for the maintenance of the new order it has been their purpose to set up in the world,—the world of civilized men.

That there should be a League of Nations to steady the counsels and maintain the peaceful understandings of the world, to make, not treaties alone, but the accepted principles of international law as well, the actual rule of conduct among the governments of the world, had been one of the agreements accepted from the first as the basis of peace with the Central Powers. The statesmen of all the belligerent countries were agreed that such a league must be created to sustain the settlements that were to be effected. But at first I think there was a feeling among some of them that, while it must be attempted, the formation of such a league was perhaps a counsel of perfection which practical men, long experienced in the world of affairs, must agree to very cautiously and with many misgivings. It was only as the difficult work of arranging an all but universal adjustment of the world's affairs advanced from day to day from one stage of conference to another that it became evident to them that what they were seeking would be little more than something written upon paper, to be interpreted and applied by such methods as the chances of politics might make available if they did not provide a means of common counsel which all were obliged to accept, a common authority whose decisions would be recognized as decisions which all must respect.

And so the most practical, the most skeptical among them turned more and more to the League as the authority through which international action was to be secured, the authority without which, as they had come to see it, it would be difficult to give assured effect either to this treaty or to any other international understanding upon which they were to depend for the maintenance of peace. The fact that the Covenant of the League was the first substantive part of the treaty to be worked out and agreed upon, while all else was in solution, helped to make the formulation of the rest easier. The Conference was, after all, not to be ephemeral. The concert of nations was to continue, under a definite Covenant which had been agreed upon and which all were convinced was workable. They could go forward with confidence to make arrangements intended to be permanent. The most practical of the conferees were at last the most ready to refer to the League of Nations the superintendence of all interests which did not admit of immediate determination, of all administrative problems which were to require a continuing oversight. What had seemed a counsel of perfection had come to seem a plain counsel of necessity. The League of Nations was the practical statesman's hope of success in many of the most difficult things he was attempting.

And it had validated itself in the thought of every member of the Conference as something much bigger, much greater every way, than a mere instrument for carrying out the provisions of a particular treaty. It was universally recognized that all the peoples of the world demanded of the Conference that it should create such a continuing concert of free nations as would make wars of aggression and spoliation such as this that has just ended forever impossible. A cry had gone out from every home in every stricken land from which sons and brothers and fathers had gone forth to the great sacrifice that such a sacrifice should never again be exacted. It was manifest why it had been exacted. It had been exacted because one nation desired dominion and other nations had known no means of defense except armaments and alliances. War had lain at the heart of every arrangement of the Europe,—of every arrangement of the world,—that preceded the war. Restive peoples had been told that fleets and armies, which they toiled to sustain, meant peace; and they now knew that they had been lied to: that fleets and armies had been maintained to promote national ambitions and meant war. They knew that no old policy meant anything else but force, force,—always force. And they knew that it was intolerable. Every true heart in the world, and every enlightened judgment demanded that, at whatever cost of independent action, every government that took thought for its people or for justice or for ordered freedom should lend itself to a new purpose and utterly destroy the old order of international politics. Statesmen might see difficulties, but the people could see none and could brook no denial. A war in which they had been bled white to beat the terror that lay concealed in every Balance of Power must not end in a mere victory of arms and a new balance. The monster that had resorted to arms must be put in chains that could not be broken. The united power of free nations must put a stop to aggression, and the world must be given peace. If there was not the will or the intelligence to accomplish that now, there must be another and a final war and the world must be swept clean of every power that could renew the terror. The League of Nations was not merely an instrument to adjust and remedy old wrongs under a new treaty of peace; it was the only hope for mankind. Again and again had the demon of war been cast out of the house of the peoples and the house swept clean by a treaty of peace; only to prepare a time when he would enter in again with spirits worse than himself. The house must now be given a tenant who could hold it against all such. Convenient, indeed indispensable, as statesmen found the newly planned League of Nations to be for the execution of present plans of peace and reparation, they saw it in a new aspect before their work was finished. They saw it as the main object of the peace, as the only thing that could complete it or make it worth while. They saw it as the hope of the world, and that hope they did not dare to disappoint. Shall we or any other free people hesitate to accept this great duty? Dare we reject it and break the heart of the world?

And so the result of the Conference of Peace, so far as Germany is concerned, stands complete. The difficulties encountered were very many. Sometimes they seemed insuperable. It was impossible to accommodate the interests of so great a body of nations,—interests which directly or indirectly affected almost every nation in the world,—without many minor compromises. The treaty, as a result, is not exactly what we would have written. It is probably not what any one of the national delegations would have written. But results were worked out which on the whole bear test. I think that it will be found that the compromises which were accepted as inevitable nowhere cut to the heart of any principle. The work of the Conference squares, as a whole, with the principles agreed upon as the basis of the peace as well as with the practical possibilities of the international situations which had to be faced and dealt with as facts.

I shall presently have occasion to lay before you a special treaty with France, whose object is the temporary protection of France from unprovoked aggression by the power with whom this treaty of peace has been negotiated. Its terms link it with this treaty. I take the liberty, however, of reserving it for special explication on another occasion.

The rôle which America was to play in the Conference seemed determined, as I have said, before my colleagues and I got to Paris,— determined by the universal expectations of the nations whose representatives, drawn from all quarters of the globe, we were to deal with. It was universally recognized that America had entered the war to promote no private or peculiar interest of her own but only as the champion of rights which she was glad to share with free men and lovers of justice everywhere. We had formulated the principles upon which the armistice had been agreed to and the parleys of peace undertaken,—and no one doubted that our desire was to see the treaty of peace formulated along the actual lines of those principles,—and desired nothing else. We were welcomed as disinterested friends. We were resorted to as arbiters in many a difficult matter. It was recognized that our material aid would be indispensable in the days to come, when industry and credit would have to be brought back to their normal operation again and communities beaten to the ground assisted to their feet once more, and it was taken for granted, I am proud to say, that we would play the helpful friend in these things as in all others without prejudice or favor. We were generously accepted as the unaffected champions of what was right. It was a very responsible role to play; but I am happy to report that the fine group of Americans who helped with their expert advice in each part of the varied settlements sought in every transaction to justify the high confidence reposed in them.

And that confidence, it seems to me, is the measure of our opportunity and of our duty in the days to come, in which the new hope of the peoples of the world is to be fulfilled or disappointed. The fact that America is the friend of the nations, whether they be rivals or associates, is no new fact; it is only the discovery of it by the rest of the world that is new.

America may be said to have just reached her majority as a world power. It was almost exactly twenty-one years ago that the results of the war with Spain put us unexpectedly in possession of rich islands on the other side of the world and brought us into association with other governments in the control of the West Indies. It was regarded as a sinister and ominous thing by the statesmen of more than one European chancellery that we should have extended our power beyond the confines of our continental dominions. They were accustomed to think of new neighbors as a new menace, of rivals as watchful enemies. There were persons amongst us at home who looked with deep disapproval and avowed anxiety on such extensions of our national authority over distant islands and over peoples whom they feared we might exploit, not serve and assist. But we have not exploited them. We have been their friends and have sought to serve them. And our dominion has been a menace to no other nation. We redeemed our honor to the utmost in our dealings with Cuba. She is weak but absolutely free; and it is her trust in us that makes her free. Weak peoples everywhere stand ready to give us any authority among them that will assure them a like friendly oversight and direction. They know that there is no ground for fear in receiving us as their mentors and guides. Our isolation was ended twenty years ago; and now fear of us is ended also, our counsel and association sought after and desired. There can be no question of our ceasing to be a world power. The only question is whether we can refuse the moral leadership that is offered us, whether we shall accept or reject the confidence of the world.

The war and the Conference of Peace now sitting in Paris seem to me to have answered that question. Our participation in the war established our position among the nations and nothing but our own mistaken action can alter it. It was not an accident or a matter of sudden choice that we are no longer isolated and devoted to a policy which has only our own interest and advantage for its object. It was our duty to go in, if we were indeed the champions of liberty and of right. We answered to the call of duty in a way so spirited, so utterly without thought of what we spent of blood or treasure, so effective, so worthy of the admiration of true men everywhere, so wrought out of the stuff of all that was heroic, that the whole world saw at last, in the flesh, in noble action, a great ideal asserted and vindicated, by a Nation they had deemed material and now found to be compact of the spiritual forces that must free men of every nation from every unworthy bondage. It is thus that a new role and a new responsibility have come to this great Nation that we honor and which we would all wish to lift to yet higher levels of service and achievement.

The stage is set, the destiny disclosed. It has come about by no plan of our conceiving, but by the hand of God who led us into this way. We cannot turn back. We can only go forward, with lifted eyes and freshened spirit, to follow the vision. It was of this that we dreamed at our birth. America shall in truth show the way. The light streams upon the path ahead, and nowhere else.

FRANKLIN D. ROOSEVELT

Annual Message
To Congress

January 6, 1942

Mr. Vice President, Mr. Speaker,
Members of the Senate and of the
House of Representatives:

In fulfilling my duty to report upon the state of the Union, I am proud to say to you that the spirit of the American people was never higher than it is today—the Union was never more closely knit together— this country was never more deeply determined to face the solemn tasks before it.

The response of the American people has been instantaneous. It will be sustained until our security is assured.

Exactly one year ago today I said to this Congress: "When the dictators are ready to make war upon us, they will not wait for an act of war on our part.... They—not we—will choose the time and the place and the method of their attack."

We know now their choice of the time: a peaceful Sunday morning —December 7, 1941.

We know their choice of the place: an American outpost in the Pacific.

We know their choice of the method: the method of Hitler himself.

Japan's scheme of conquest goes back half a century. It was not merely a policy of seeking living room: it was a plan which included the subjugation of all the peoples in the Far East and in the islands of the Pacific, and the domination of that ocean by Japanese military and naval control of the western coasts of North, Central, and South America.

The development of this ambitious conspiracy was marked by the war against China in 1894; the subsequent occupation of Korea; the war

From *The War Messages of Franklin D. Roosevelt,* December 8, 1941, to April 13, 1945 (Washington, D.C., 1945), pp. 26–30.

against Russia in 1904; the illegal fortification of the mandated Pacific islands following 1920; the seizure of Manchuria in 1931; and the invasion of China in 1937.

A similar policy of criminal conquest was adopted by Italy. The Fascists first revealed their imperial designs in Libya and Tripoli. In 1935 they seized Abyssinia. Their goal was the domination of all North Africa, Egypt, parts of France, and the entire Mediterranean world.

But the dreams of empire of the Japanese and Fascist leaders were modest in comparison with the gargantuan aspirations of Hitler and his Nazis. Even before they came to power in 1933, their plans for conquest had been drawn. Those plans provided for ultimate domination, not of any one section of the world, but of the whole earth and all the oceans on it.

With Hitler's formation of the Berlin-Rome-Tokyo alliance, all these plans of conquest became a single plan. Under this, in addition to her own schemes of conquest, Japan's role was to cut off our supply of weapons of war to Britain, Russia, and China—weapons which increasingly were speeding the day of Hitler's doom. The act of Japan at Pearl Harbor was intended to stun us—to terrify us to such an extent that we would divert our industrial and military strength to the Pacific area, or even to our own continental defense.

The plan failed in its purpose. We have not been stunned. We have not been terrified or confused. This reassembling of the Seventy-seventh Congress is proof of that; for the mood of quiet, grim resolution which here prevails bodes ill for those who conspired and collaborated to murder world peace.

That mood is stronger than any mere desire for revenge. It expresses the will of the American people to make very certain that the world will never suffer again.

Admittedly, we have been faced with hard choices. It was bitter, for example, not to be able to relieve the heroic and historic defenders of Wake Island. It was bitter for us not to be able to land a million men and a thousand ships in the Philippine Islands.

But this adds only to our determination to see to it that the Stars and Stripes will fly again over Wake and Guam; and that the brave people of the Philippines will be rid of Japanese imperialism; and will live in freedom, security, and independence.

Powerful and offensive actions must and will be taken in proper time. The consolidation of the United Nations total war effort against our common enemies is being achieved.

That is the purpose of conferences which have been held during the past two weeks in Washington, in Moscow, and in Chungking. That is the primary objective of the declaration of solidarity signed in Washington on January 1, 1942, by twenty-six nations united against the Axis powers.

Difficult choices may have to be made in the months to come. We will not shrink from such decisions. We and those united with us will make those decisions with courage and determination.

Plans have been laid here and in the other capitals for coordinated and cooperative action by all the United Nations—military action and economic action. Already we have established unified command of land, sea, and air forces in the Southwestern Pacific theater of war. There will be a continuation of conferences and consultations among military staffs, so that the plans and operations of each will fit into a general strategy designed to crush the enemy. We shall not fight isolated wars—each nation going its own way. These twenty-six nations are united—not in spirit and determination alone, but in the broad conduct of the war in all its phases.

For the first time since the Japanese and the Fascists and the Nazis started along their blood-stained course of conquest they now face the fact that superior forces are assembling against them. Gone forever are the days when the aggressors could attack and destroy their victims one by one without unity of resistance. We of the United Nations will so disperse our forces that we can strike at the common enemy wherever the greatest damage can be done.

The militarists in Berlin and Tokyo started this war. But the massed, angered forces of common humanity will finish it.

Destruction of the material and spiritual centers of civilization—this has been and still is the purpose of Hitler and his Italian and Japanese chessmen. They would wreck the power of the British Commonwealth and Russia and China and the Netherlands—and then combine all their forces to achieve their ultimate goal, the conquest of the United States.

They know that victory for us means victory for freedom.

They know that victory for us means victory for the institution of democracy—the ideal of the family, the simple principles of common decency and humanity.

They know that victory for us means victory for religion.

And they could not tolerate that. The world is too small to provide adequate "living room" for both Hitler and God. In proof of that Nazis have now announced their plan for enforcing their new German, pagan religion throughout the world—the plan by which the Holy Bible and the Cross of Mercy would be displaced by "Mein Kampf" and the swastika and the naked sword.

Our own objectives are clear: the objective of smashing the militarism imposed by war lords upon their enslaved peoples—the objective of liberating the subjugated nations—the objective of establishing and securing freedom of speech, freedom of religion, freedom from want, and freedom from fear everywhere in the world.

We shall not stop short of these objectives—nor shall we be satisfied merely to gain them and then call it a day. I know that I speak for the American people—and I have good reason to believe I speak also for all the other peoples who fight with us—when I say that this time we are determined not only to win the war, but also to maintain the security of the peace which will follow.

But modern methods of warfare make it a task not only of shooting and fighting but an even more urgent one of working and producing.

Victory requires the actual weapons of war and the means of transporting them to a dozen points of combat.

It will not be sufficient for us and the other United Nations to produce a slightly superior supply of munitions to that of Germany, Japan, Italy, and the stolen industries in the countries which they have overrun.

The superiority of the United Nations in munitions and ships must be overwhelming—so overwhelming that the Axis nations can never hope to catch up with it. In order to attain this overwhelming superiority the United States must build planes and tanks and guns and ships to the utmost limit of our national capacity. We have the ability and capacity to produce arms not only for our own forces but also for the armies, navies, and air forces fighting on our side.

And our overwhelming superiority of armament must be adequate to put weapons of war at the proper time into the hands of those men in the conquered nations who stand ready to seize the first opportunity to revolt against their German and Japanese oppressors and against the traitors in their own ranks, known by the already infamous name of "Quislings." As we get guns to the patriots in those lands, they too will fire shots heard "round the world."

This production of ours in the United States must be raised far above its present levels, even though it will mean the dislocation of the lives and occupations of millions of our own people. We must raise our sights all along the production line. Let no man say it cannot be done. It must be done and we have undertaken to do it.

I have just sent a letter of directive to the appropriate departments and agencies of our government, ordering that immediate steps be taken:

1. To increase our production rate of airplanes so rapidly that in this year, 1942, we shall produce 60,000 planes, 10,000 more than the goal set a year and a half ago. This includes 45,000 combat planes —bombers, dive bombers, pursuit planes. The rate of increase will be continued, so that next year, 1943, we shall produce 125,000 airplanes, including 100,000 combat planes.

2. To increase our production rate of tanks so rapidly that in this year, 1942, we shall produce 45,000 tanks; and to continue that increase so that next year, 1943, we shall produce 75,000 tanks.

3. To increase our production rate of antiaircraft guns so rapidly that in this year, 1942, we shall produce 20,000 of them; and to continue that increase so that next year, 1943, we shall produce 35,000 antiaircraft guns.

4. To increase our production rate of merchant ships so rapidly that in this year, 1942, we shall build 8,000,000 dead-weight tons as compared with a 1941 production of 1,100,000. We shall continue that increase so that next year, 1943, we shall build 10,000,000 tons.

These figures and similar figures for a multitude of other implements of war will give the Japanese and Nazis a little idea of just what they accomplished in the attack on Pearl Harbor.

Our task is hard—our task is unprecedented—and the time is short. We must strain every existing armament-producing facility to the utmost. We must convert every available plant and tool to war production. That goes all the way from the greatest plants to the smallest—from the huge automobile industry to the village machine shop.

Production for war is based on men and women—the human hands and brains which collectively we call Labor. Our workers stand ready to work long hours; to turn out more in a day's work; to keep the wheels turning and the fires burning twenty-four hours a day and seven days a week. They realize well that on the speed and efficiency of their work depend the lives of their sons and their brothers on the fighting fronts.

Production for war is based on metals and raw materials—steel, copper, rubber, aluminum, zinc, tin. Greater and greater quantities of them will have to be diverted to war purposes. Civilian use of them will have to be cut further and still further, and, in many cases, completely eliminated.

War costs money. So far, we have hardly even begun to pay for it. We have devoted only 15 percent of our national income to national defense. As will appear in my Budget Message tomorrow, our war program for the coming fiscal year will cost 56 billion dollars or, in other words, more than one half of the estimated annual national income. This means cutting luxuries and other non-essentials. In a word, it means an "all-out" war by individual effort and family effort in a united country.

Only this all-out scale of production will hasten the ultimate all-out victory. Speed will count. Lost ground can always be regained—lost time never. Speed will save lives; speed will save this nation which is in peril; speed will save our freedom and civilization—and slowness has never been an American characteristic.

As the United States goes into its full stride, we must always be on guard against misconceptions which will arise naturally or which will be planted among us by our enemies.

We must guard against complacency. We must not underrate the enemy. He is powerful and cunning—and cruel and ruthless. He will stop at nothing which gives him a chance to kill and to destroy. . . .

We must, on the other hand, guard against defeatism. . . .

We must guard against divisions among ourselves and among all the other United Nations. We must be particularly vigilant against racial discrimination in any of its ugly forms. Hitler will try again to breed mistrust and suspicion between one individual and another, one group and another, one race and another, one government and another. . . .

We canot wage this war in a defensive spirit. As our power and our resources are fully mobilized, we shall carry the attack against the enemy —we shall hit him and hit him again wherever and whenever we can reach him.

We must keep him far from our shores, for we intend to bring this battle to him on his own home grounds.

American armed forces must be used at any place in all the world where it seems advisable to engage the forces of the enemy. In some cases these operations will be defensive, in order to protect key positions. In other cases, these operations will be offensive, in order to strike at the common enemy, with a view to his complete encirclement and eventual total defeat.

. . . .

If any of our enemies, from Europe or from Asia, attempt long-range raids by "suicide" squadrons of bombing planes, they will do so only in the hope of terrorizing our people and disrupting our morale. Our people are not afraid of that. We know that we may have to pay a heavy price for freedom. We will pay this price with a will. Whatever the price, it is a thousand times worth it. No matter what our enemies in their desperation may attempt to do to us, we will say as the people of London have said, "We can take it." And what's more, we can give it back—and we will give it back—with compound interest.

When our enemies challenged our country to stand up and fight, they challenged each and every one of us. And each and every one of us has accepted the challenge—for himself and for the nation.

There were only some four hundred United States marines who in the heroic and historic defense of Wake Island inflicted such great losses on the enemy. Some of those men were killed in action; and others are now prisoners of war. When the survivors of that great fight are liberated and restored to their homes, they will learn that a hundred and thirty million of their fellow citizens have been inspired to render their own full share of service and sacrifice.

Our men on the fighting fronts have already proved that Americans today are just as rugged and just as tough as any of the heroes whose exploits we celebrate on the Fourth of July.

Many people ask, "When will this war end?" There is only one answer to that. It will end just as soon as we make it end, by our combined efforts, our combined strength, our combined determination to fight through and work through until the end—the end of militarism in Germany and Italy and Japan. Most certainly we shall not settle for less.

That is the spirit in which discussions have been conducted during the visit of the British Prime Minister to Washington. Mr. Churchill and I understand each other, our motives and our purposes. Together, during the past two weeks, we have faced squarely the major military and economic problems of this greatest world war.

All in our nation have been cheered by Mr. Churchill's visit. We have been deeply stirred by his great message to us. We wish him a safe return to his home. He is welcome in our midst, now and in days to come.

We are fighting on the same side with the British people, who fought alone for long, terrible months, and withstood the enemy with fortitude and tenacity and skill.

We are fighting on the same side with the Russian people who have seen the Nazi hordes swarm up to the very gates of Moscow, and who with almost superhuman will and courage have forced the invaders back into retreat.

We are fighting on the same side as the brave people of China who for four and a half long years have withstood bombs and starvation and have whipped the invaders time and again in spite of superior Japanese equipment and arms.

We are fighting on the same side as the indomitable Dutch.

We are fighting on the same side as all the other governments in exile, whom Hitler and all his armies and all his Gestapo have not been able to conquer.

But we of the United Nations are not making all this sacrifice of human effort and human lives to return to the kind of world we had after the last world war.

We are fighting today for security, for progress, and for peace, not only for ourselves, but for all men, not only for one generation, but for all generations. We are fighting to cleanse the world of ancient evils, ancient ills.

Our enemies are guided by brutal cynicism, by unholy contempt for the human race. We are inspired by a faith which goes back through all the years to the first chapter of the Book of Genesis: "God created man in His own image."

We on our side are striving to be true to that divine heritage. We are fighting, as our fathers have fought, to uphold the doctrine that all men are equal in the sight of God. Those on the other side are striving to destroy this deep belief and to create a world in their own image—a world of tyranny and cruelty and serfdom.

This is the conflict that day and night now pervades our lives. No compromise can end that conflict. There never has been—there never can be—successful compromise between good and evil. Only total victory can reward the champions of tolerance, and decency, and freedom, and faith.

REINHOLD NIEBUHR

Anglo-Saxon Destiny
And Responsibility

It is becoming increasingly apparent that, whether any other conditions of a stable peace will be fulfilled or not, an Anglo-American alliance, which must be the cornerstone of any durable world order, is in the process of formation. Mr. Churchill's unequivocal words at Harvard, Governor Dewey's statement in favor of lasting co-operation with Britain, and the Republican postwar statement in which isolationism is renounced, all point to at least one step forward in our foreign policy.

This partnership between the English-speaking peoples can of course become a new menace to international justice and peace if it stands alone. The world cannot be organized by an Anglo-Saxon hegemony. Such a leadership could be ten times more just than the Nazis were and yet not be just enough to avoid arousing the resentment of Europe and Asia, in fact, of the entire world. Whatever Britain and America do together must be immediately related to a wider co-operation with the other two great powers, Russia and China, and must finally be made a part of a total constitutional or quasi-constitutional system of the world order in which all the nations, large and small, will have their due responsibilities and rights.

Nevertheless the further steps that must be taken to insure a stable peace all depend upon this first step of Anglo-American solidarity; for if Britain and America cannot agree together, all other necessary agreements become improbable.

The position of the Anglo-Saxon peoples at the crucial and strategic point in the building of a world community is a fact of such tremendous significance that it can only be adequately comprehended in religious terms. It is a position of destiny and carries with it tremendous responsibilities. Without a religious sense of the meaning of destiny, such a position as Britain and America now hold is inevitably corrupted by pride

From *Christianity and Crisis,* October 4, 1943. Reprinted by permission of Reinhold Niebuhr.

and the lust of power. We may in fact be certain that this corruption will not be absent from our political life. But if the churches in Britain and America are able to speak to the several nations as the prophets spoke to Israel, it may be possible to mitigate the pride sufficiently to allow these two nations to serve the world community creatively.

THE PROPHETIC IDEA OF DESTINY

The prophet Amos was certain of two things. One was that Israel had been particularly chosen of God; and the other was that this special mission gave the nation not a special security but a special peril. "You only have I chosen," he declared in God's name, "therefore will I visit you with your iniquities." It would serve no good purpose to try to compare the special destiny of the Anglo-Saxon peoples with that of Israel in olden times. Certainly no one would be so rash today as to claim the kind of destiny for our nations that the prophet's word "only" implies. Nevertheless only those who have no sense of the profundities of history would deny that various nations and classes, various social groups and races are at various times placed in such a position that a special measure of the divine mission in history falls upon them. In that sense God has chosen us in this fateful period of world history.

The world requires a wider degree of community. It must escape international anarchy or perish. If the world community is to be genuine, it cannot, of course, be superimposed by Anglo-Saxon or any other power. All peoples and nations must find their rightful place in the fellowship. Nevertheless, neither the world community nor any other form of human society ever moves as logically or abstractly as some of the "planners" and blueprinters imagine. Some nation or group always has a higher degree of power and responsibility in the formation of community than others.

It so happens that the combined power of the British Empire and the United States is at present greater than any other power. It is also true that the political ideals that are woven into the texture of their history are less incompatible with international justice than any other previous power of history.

THE COMPONENTS OF DESTINY

Yet as soon as one has said this, one is forced to make qualifications. All historical destiny is compounded of virtue and grace. If the position that any nation or group of nations holds is attributed to the virtue of those nations alone, one has the beginning of that pharisaism which destroys virtue, whether in individual or in national life. The fact is that no nation or individual is ever good enough to deserve the position of leadership that some nations and individuals achieve. If the history that leads to a special mission is carefully analyzed, it always becomes apparent that factors other than the virtues of the leader are partly responsible for the position the individual or collective leader holds. Those who do not believe in God's providence in history will call these factors "accidents" or "fortune." The religious man perceives them as gifts of grace. The grace that determines the lives of men and nations is manifest in all special circumstances, favors, and fortunes of geography and climate, of history and fate that lead to eminence despite the weakness and sinfulness of the beneficiary of such eminence.

These elements in history are either purely accidental or they stand under divine providence. If they are purely accidental, then history itself has no meaning; for in that case it would be the fruit of caprice. That is why secularists usually obscure these factors of history; for it is not possible for man to live in a completely capricious world. But if they are obscured, the sense of destiny becomes purely a vehicle of pride. Those who achieve a special position in history claim a right to it either by virtue of their power or by virtue of their goodness. The Nazi sense of destiny is completely amoral because it regards power as the sole source of eminence. This amoral sense of destiny has been developed more explicitly by the Nazis than by any other modern nation; but no powerful nation is completely free of the pretension that its power is the sole source of its right to rule. Ideas of "manifest destiny" in our own history have this same source.

THE RULE OF THE VIRTUOUS

The idea that we have a right to rule because of our superior virtue is of a higher order than the amoral idea that we have a right to rule because of our power. It recognizes the moral element in history. It is nevertheless a dangerous idea because it obscures the immoral elements in all historical success. If Germany has been the particular bearer of the idea of destiny through power, the Anglo-Saxon world has been constantly tempted to express its sense of destiny pharisaically and to claim eminence by the right of its virtue. It is this element in Anglo-Saxon politics that has subjected it to the charge of "cant" from Continental nations. We have not heard the end of this charge from either Germany or France, from either the Continent or Russia, because there is an element of truth in the charge.

There is no cure for the pride of a virtuous nation but pure religion.

The pride of a powerful nation may be humbled by the impotence that defeat brings. The pride of a virtuous nation cannot be humbled by moral and political criticisms because in comparative terms it may actually be virtuous. The democratic traditions of the Anglo-Saxon world are actually the potential basis of a just world order. But the historical achievements of this world are full of violations and contradictions of these principles. "In God's sight" they are not just; and they know it if they place themselves under the divine scrutiny, that is, if they regard their own history prayerfully rather than comparatively and measure themselves by what is demanded of them rather than by comparing their success with the failure of others.

Thus a contrite recognition of our own sins destroys the illusion of eminence through virtue and lays the foundation for the apprehension of "grace" in our national life. We know that we have the position that we hold in the world today partly by reason of factors and forces in the complex pattern of history that we did not create and from which we do not deserve to benefit. If we apprehend this religiously, the sense of destiny ceases to be a vehicle of pride and becomes the occasion for a new sense of responsibility.

THE PERILS OF EMINENCE

If we know that we have been chosen beyond our deserts, we must also begin to realize that we have not been chosen for our particular task in order that our own life may be aggrandized. We ought not derive either special security or special advantages from our high historical mission. The real fact is that we are placed in a precarious moral and historical position by our special mission. It can be justified only if it results in good for the whole community of mankind. Woe unto us if we fail. For our failure will bring judgment upon both us and the world. That is the meaning of the prophetic word, "Therefore will I visit you with your iniquities." This word must be translated by the church today into meanings relevant to our own history. If this is not done, we are bound to fail. For the natural pride of great nations is such that any special historical success quickly aggravates it until it becomes the source of moral and political confusion.

Without a religious sense of humility and responsibility the Anglo-Saxon world will fail to come to terms with the two great non-Christian nations, Russia and China. It will fail to understand to what degree what is good in the new Russian order represents values of equal justice that we should have, but did not, achieve, and to what extent the evils of tyranny in Russia are simply a false answer to our own unsolved problem of social justice. It will fail to understand to what degree the white man's pride is the chief obstacle in building a world community that brings Asia fully into the world community. It is worth remembering in this connection that long before the Nazi elaborated the idea of Nordic superiority the Anglo-Saxon world betrayed an arrogance toward the darker peoples of which the Latin world, for instance, was comparatively free. Our racial pride is incompatible with our responsibilities in the world community. If we do not succeed in chastening it, we shall fail in our task.

If we should imagine that our victory in this great World War were a justification of our virtue and if our moral pride thus becomes accentuated, we shall fail in our task of finally bringing the fallen foes into the world community on terms that will bring health both to them and the total community. If we should give ourselves to the illusion that this war was a simple contest between right and wrong, and that the victory was a simple triumph of right over wrong; if we fail to understand to what degree Nazi tyranny grew on the soil of our general international anarchy; if we lack the spiritual humility to see these facts of history, we shall be bound to corrupt the peace by vindictiveness.

SELF-RIGHTEOUSNESS LEADS TO
VINDICTIVENESS

There are already many ominous signs of this vindictiveness, and a careful analysis of various manifestations of the spirit of vengeance reveals very clearly how self-righteousness is the presupposition of vengeance. It is also quite easy to foresee the consequences of any peace that is built upon the assumption that the elimination of Nazi evil will eliminate evil from the world. All these perils are the insecurities to which we are exposed in our historical eminence. They represent the always overhanging divine judgment. They are the modern counterparts of what Amos foresaw in his words, "Therefore will I visit you with your iniquities."

We may be fairly sure that the Anglo-Saxon world will not be good enough or sufficiently contrite to fulfill its historical mission with complete success. It nevertheless has a great opportunity to fulfill it with relative success. But if this is to be accomplished, the Christian church must understand its prophetic mission. It must cease to vacillate between ascetic withdrawal from the world "power politics" and a too simple identification of the nation's purposes with the divine Will. It must contend against both irresponsibility and complacency in our national life.

The world community cannot be realized if the Anglo-Saxon world fails in its historic mission. If it is afraid of the perils of that mission and is affrighted by the moral ambiguities of "power politics," it will fail just as seriously as if it accepts its mission without a religious sense of contrition. It may be that the former temptation is still the primary temptation for America, and the second one that to which Britain is particularly prone. But the differences between the two great parts of the Anglo-Saxon world are less than the similarities. In both cases the Christian faith is still in sufficiently close relation to the national life to encourage the hope that it will help to purify the nations for their mission; in both cases, however, the Christian forces are to some degree the salt that has lost its savor. If the nations should fail therefore, the failure would be the consequence of the prior failure of the Christian church.

part seven

THE
NATIONAL DESTINY
IN
CRISIS

Since the middle of the twentieth century America has been undergoing a crisis of self-understanding. Disturbing events both within and beyond her boundaries have been forcing her to an agonizing reassessment of her identity and mission. Race problems at home have set Americans to pondering whether their nation can justly be termed a Promised Land of liberty. Is it too late to include in the national destiny all those citizens who have been driven or excluded from the mainstream of society by the repeated blows of poverty and prejudice? Events on the international scene have stirred equally disquieting doubts. What is the role of America in a world caught in what seems to be a terminal balance of power? What are the limits—are there *any* limits—of American power in the nation's mission of safeguarding "the right of democratic freedom" around the globe? Indeed, can such a mission be honestly claimed in the light of America's actions abroad?

Doubts and questions such as these have arisen at other points in the American story. That this is so, however, does little to relieve for contemporary Americans the gravity of the situation reflected by such doubts and questions. The remaining readings in this book cluster around two problems which have become the foci of recent interpretations of American destiny. The interpretations vary widely, but all share the belief that the problems with which they deal have placed the nation at the crossroads of her existence.

AMERICA'S WORLD ROLE

American attitudes toward the nation's mission in the world were influenced considerably by the general "turn to religion" in the 1950s. Surveys conducted during that decade indicated a marked increase in church attendance and in the construction of new churches; they also reported that the large majority of Americans professed a belief in God, held that the Bible was the inspired word of God and thought that religion was "of very great importance."[1] The evangelistic crusades of Billy Graham and his imitators reached the peak of their popularity in the 1950s; Norman Vincent Peale's *The Power of Positive Thinking* and other books of religious self-help made the best seller lists. This surge of piety was by no means confined to ecclesiastical institutions. It was a revival of religiosity within the national religion, and its influence spread to the highest councils of the land. President Dwight D. Eisenhower became both a leading spokesman and the stellar symbol of the revival. Eisenhower broke precedent by opening his first inaugural address with a prayer. He instituted the practice of regular Prayer Breakfasts at the White House and appointed a Congregational minister as the "president's pastor." Under his direction the nation added "under God" to the pledge of allegiance and the postmaster general held a ceremony commemorating a new postage stamp bearing the motto "In God We Trust." Americans looked upon Eisenhower the man as a desirable blend of religion, patriotism, and moral principle (moral principle supposedly unsullied by partisan politics). His statement made during his years as president of Columbia University became the watchword of Americanism in the 1950s: "Democracy is the political expression of a deeply felt religion."[2]

The climate was right for the turn to piety that occurred during the Eisenhower years. The anxiety produced by the destructive use of nuclear power at the close of World War II and the tensions of the ensuing cold war ultimately drove many Americans to seek security in the warm folds of religiosity. Just as clearly, much of the religion of the day was in close league with anticommunism. The usual contrast drawn by public rhetoric was one between the "religious principles of democracy" and "godless communism." Even if all the religious fervor did not align itself with the

---

[1] See Will Herberg, *Protestant-Catholic-Jew* (Garden City, N.Y.: Doubleday & Company, Inc., 1960), pp. 1ff., 72ff.

[2] For a summary of Eisenhower's religion (public and private) and its relation to his political views see Merlin Gustafson, "The Religion of a President," *Christian Century*, Apr. 30, 1969, pp. 610–13. Cf. William Lee Miller, *Piety Along the Potomac* (Boston: Houghton Mifflin Company, 1964).

extremism of Senator Joseph McCarthy's Communist-hunt (some of it did), much of it was thoroughly bound up with a national urge to launch a "moral crusade" against atheistic communism. Religious interpretations of American destiny, therefore, tended to support a foreign policy which operated on the assumption that the nation's mission abroad was to stem the tide of a demonic Communist force which threatened to engulf the world. That assumption, though occasionally checked and often challenged, continued into the 1960s.

President Eisenhower indicated the pattern for America's response to communism in his first inaugural address, a pattern that had already been set by the Truman administration. Eisenhower portrayed the world as dividing itself into two opposing forces: "Freedom is pitted against slavery; lightness against the dark," and he called upon free people to unite against their common foe. "To produce this unity, to meet the challenge of our time, destiny has laid upon our country the responsibility of the free world's leadership." Eisenhower's secretary of state, John Foster Dulles, shared the president's vision of America's leadership in a divided world and acted to shape a foreign policy that sought to live up to that vision.

A dedicated and intelligent Presbyterian layman, Dulles had directed a church commission in the 1940s that studied the "Bases of a Just and Durable Peace." As secretary of state he argued that the possibility of a stable world peace resided in the firm leadership of the American nation, a nation called to its noble mission by God and specially equipped for that mission by the religious and moral principles which she possessed at the core of her political being.[3] Holding that conviction, Dulles worked for the strengthening of the North Atlantic Treaty Organization, piloted the formation of the Southeast Asia Treaty Organization, and generally sought to unify the Western alliance against the Communist menace. Although the United States under Dulles's secretaryship did not attain either the secure world peace or the firm Western unity that he had envisaged (the Suez crisis and the weakness of SEATO were strong proofs to the contrary), he never ceased defending an American foreign policy dedicated to the energetic deterrence of an aggressive communism.

Secretary Dulles delineated the major features of his theory of foreign relations and grounded them in his view of American destiny in a speech of February 26, 1956. In that address, "Freedom's New Task," he described a recent shift in the Soviet "plan of conquest" from the tactics of "intolerance and violence" to the tactics of economic assistance. He designated the response that the United States must make and felt that

---

[3] See Henry P. Van Dusen, ed., *The Spiritual Legacy of John Foster Dulles* (Philadelphia: The Westminster Press, 1960), pp. 5–85.

the response would be readily forthcoming since our nation "was conceived with a sense of mission" and had been assigned by providence the task of extending freedom throughout the world.

Dulles's philosophy of foreign relations was called "brinkmanship" by his critics. Dulles himself invited the criticism when he said in 1956, "The ability to get to the verge without getting into the war is the necessary art. If you cannot master it, you inevitably get into war. If you try to run away from it, if you are scared to go to the brink, you are lost."[4] Brinkmanship as a method of dealing with crises in international affairs did not die with Secretary Dulles, and his conviction that America was providentially chosen to lead the free world in stopping the spread of communism certainly lived on after the man. Yet the arrival of the 1960s marked a transition to a somewhat less belligerent American attitude toward Russian communism and to an emphasis on negotiation. The change was reflected in the inaugural address of President John F. Kennedy. "Let us never negotiate out of fear," Kennedy said, "But let us never fear to negotiate." President Kennedy spurned catchwords like "godless communism" and "America's moral crusade" that had riddled the rhetoric of the 1950s and had pictured the world as divided into realms of light and darkness. He continued to speak of the need to check the spread of communism, particularly through economic aid to underdeveloped countries, but he insisted that the primary purpose of foreign aid programs should not be the winning of allies but the raising of living standards and the consolidation of democracies.

Although Kennedy avoided pious clichés and kept his own Catholic faith a private matter, his public statements frequently drew upon religious themes. Mention has already been made of the way in which his inaugural address built on the motifs of the American civil religion. His remarks on America's world role often appealed to the sentiment lying at the heart of the civil religion: the sense of a special American destiny under God. President Kennedy's 1962 Fourth of July speech to the governors of the states made explicit reference to that sentiment. This nation's attempt to live up to the destiny disclosed in the Declaration of Independence, Kennedy said, must be grounded in two correlative courses of action: the encouragement and recognition of national independence everywhere, and a contribution to the cooperative interdependence of nations.

America found herself on the verge of nuclear war during the Cuban missile crisis. After Khrushchev agreed, at Kennedy's firm insistence, to dismantle the rocket sites in Cuba, the cold war between the Soviet Union and the United States thawed somewhat. Relations were

4 *Life,* Jan. 16, 1956, p. 78.

further improved with the signing of the Nuclear Test-Ban Treaty by the United States, Great Britain, and the Soviet Union in August, 1963. American fears of communism were now directed increasingly toward Red China, and talk of the American mission abroad focused more and more on Asia.

During the closing years of the 1960s the hottest item in the debate over the nature and extent of America's mission abroad became this country's costly involvement in the Vietnamese war. In the SEATO agreements made during the 1950s, America pledged herself to the protection of Southeast Asia against outside aggression. She immediately found herself dealing with an area plagued by bitter religious controversies, corrupt dictatorships insensitive to the needs of the people, and a style of political and social life unresponsive to the principles of Western democracy. Pleading obligation to aid South Vietnam in her struggle against the Viet Cong, the United States during the Kennedy years steadily increased her manpower and war material. As North Vietnam openly supported the Viet Cong with troops and supplies, the Johnson administration escalated the war with frequent bombings of the North and eventually stationed over 500,000 American servicemen in Vietnam. By the close of President Johnson's term of office, some 30,000 Americans had died in Vietnam. America was involved in one of the most expansive "limited wars" of history.

Spokesmen for the Johnson administration defended the American presence in Vietnam with the claim that the United States should meet its "long-standing commitments" to protect the right of independent nations to self-determination and "freedom from aggression." America's participation in the war was interpreted as an unfortunate but necessary means of preventing Asia from falling, area by area, under the control of communism.

The theme of American destiny, together with its religious underpinnings and its influence on American foreign policy in Southeast Asia, was forcefully brought to the attention of the American people by Senator J. William Fulbright, chairman of the Senate Foreign Relations Committee and foremost critic of U.S. policy in Vietnam. In the introduction to his *The Arrogance of Power* he summarized his criticisms of America's sense of omnipotence. Fulbright was convinced that the American presumption which confuses power with virtue and identifies fortunate national circumstances with the special blessings of God has led this nation into tragedies like the Vietnamese war. Although Senator Fulbright attacked one traditional view of American destiny—the one that holds that America is obligated actively to convert the entire world to an American way of doing things—he did not deny that the nation has a service to perform in the world, namely the "service of her own example."

It is impossible to say whether the crisis in foreign relations will eventually be the occasion for America's dismissal of the motivational myth that she is a messiah destined to redeem the world for democracy. The myth is deeply rooted in the American mind, has survived other crises and, like all inspirations that drive a people to action, manifests considerable resiliency in the face of hard facts which threaten its undoing. Abandonment of the messianic myth is not completely outside the realm of possibility, however, inasmuch as it has always competed in the American experience with another religious perspective on the national mission: the view of America as an example to the nations. This other perspective has a deep mythic and historic wellspring and is capable of directing more American energy toward solving the nation's manifold domestic problems. If the belief in America as an example avoids isolationism and is joined to a measured calculation of what the nation can and cannot do abroad, it may provide a viable alternative to American messianism.

THE BLACK AMERICAN

If the war in Vietnam has become a serious challenge to America's understanding of her destiny abroad, the black American's struggle for justice has become a critical test of the nation's view of destiny at home. The Negro's vivid demonstration of his plight through both the civil rights and the black power movements has cut deeply into the American conscience. The black demands that have been made on the society have called attention to diseases of prejudice, poverty, and inequity afflicting all regions and institutions in the land. Have these diseases seriously disabled, or have they destroyed, America as the Promised Land of freedom and equal opportunity? Should the downtrodden of our society seek to become a redeeming remnant within the American Israel, or are they called to separate themselves as a people from a thoroughly degenerate and hypocritical New Israel? Is their task one of rectifying America's destiny under God, or one of discovering their own myths and their own independent destiny? These questions lie at the center of the race crisis.

All of the motifs surrounding the belief in the election of a people by God are vital parts of the American Negro past. Themes like Deliverance from Bondage, Wilderness Wandering, Promised Land, and the Coming Kingdom of God were firmly embedded in the Negro experience by slave songs and spirituals and by the biblical preaching of the Negro church. It does appear that Negro Christianity, even after it ceased to be a slave religion, was predominantly otherworldly in outlook. The spirituals promised eternal rest after a lifetime of demeaning labor and the preaching minimized the sufferings and inequities of this life.[5] Under the influence of this kind of religion, the black American was led to hope for redemption only on the other side of the grave; he was encouraged to seek his true destiny totally outside the constricting boundaries of a white society. Yet Negro religion did not always lead its devotees to such other-worldliness. Despite white Protestantism's persistent efforts to keep the Negro in a subservient, compliant status by providing an opiate religion, black religious zeal often joined forces with a black passion for justice. The Old Testament, which furnished so much of the power of Negro preaching, was too explicitly this-worldly in its hope for the future, too prophetically critical of social injustice, too militantly aggressive in its words to the chosen people to be totally glossed over as a pie-in-the-sky treatise. The slave preacher Nat Turner seems to have been at least partially motivated toward his famous rebellion by an Old Testament instinct for warfare against the enemies of the Lord, and his followers looked to him as a prophet chosen to lead them to the Promised Land of freedom.[6] As early as 1829 David Walker and Robert A. Young, both free Negro abolitionists, prophesied that there would arise among their people a Messiah who would lead in the liberation of the slaves.[7] The historian Vincent Harding has observed that Afro-American intellectual history is replete with hopes for a Black Messiah (conceived either individually or collectively) who will rise up to deliver black Americans from their bondage.[8]

Otherworldly accretions that adhered to the black view of destiny in the past have recently been scrubbed off. Negro spokesmen have been lifting themes like Chosen People, Messiah and Promised Land into an activistic point of view aimed directly at America's social maladies. As the following readings make clear, however, a debate has raged within the black community itself over the tactics and ideology proper to the realization of the black American's task and over the connection of that task with America as a whole.

Dr. Martin Luther King, Jr., was catapulted into national attention by the Montgomery, Alabama, bus boycott in 1955/56. As president of the Southern Christian Leadership Conference, he quickly became a moving force behind the Negro's bid for justice and an articulate interpreter of

[5] E. Franklin Frazier, *The Negro Church in America* (New York: Schocken Books, Inc., 1966), pp. 12–16, 44–46.
[6] See Leslie H. Fishel and Benjamin Quarles, eds., *The Negro American* (Glenview, Ill.: Scott, Foresman & Company, 1967), p. 120.
[7] John Hope Franklin, *From Slavery to Freedom*, 3rd ed. (New York: Alfred A. Knopf, Inc., 1967), pp. 243, 250.
[8] Vincent Harding, "The Religion of Black Power," in *The Religious Situation: 1968*, ed. Donald R. Cutler (Boston: Beacon Press, 1968), p. 13.

the Negro's mission in American society. Before his death in the spring of 1968, Dr. King had come under severe criticism from black power militants as well as white segregationists, but he remained for large groups of Negroes a Moses calling his people out of the bondage of segregation and discrimination. The vision that energized King's nonviolent campaign was much broader than the attainment of immediate goals like the integration of public transportation, restaurants, and schools or the winning of voting rights for black Americans. It was a vision often expressed in the rolling cadence of his speeches: a vision of America united by the bonds of justice and brotherhood. "I have a dream," King said in his speech during the March on Washington in August, 1963. "It is a dream deeply rooted in the American dream. I have a dream that one day this nation will rise up and live out the true meaning of its creed: 'We hold these truths to be self-evident, that all men are created equal.'"

King's view of the pressing urgency of the civil rights movement and its part in the realization of the American dream was the subject of his "Letter from Birmingham Jail." Written in response to the charge by several white Southern clergymen that civil rights agitation in Birmingham was "unwise and untimely," the letter was a stinging indictment of the disgruntled white moderate and gave an able description of the aims and techniques of "nonviolent direct action." The letter portrayed the Negro people as a remnant of the New Israel called to redeem America for her destiny of freedom and equality.

In the 1960s a new mood spread through the black revolutionary movement, a mood that tended to withdraw from the tactics, aims, and vision of Martin Luther King. Convinced that the techniques of nonviolent resistance were both humiliating and ineffectual, a vocal group of American blacks called for direct confrontation with an adamant white power structure—a confrontation that need not rule out returning violence for violence. Persuaded that integration was simply another means of submerging a distinct and healthy black identity in the sea of white middle-class mediocrity, they urged their people to turn to forms of separation and independence—separation in education, in politics, in dress and speech, in music, in living arrangements, in business. Believing that they had been asked by King to achieve the impossible task of loving the white man while still harboring self-hatred, they issued a plea for self-love and the celebration of blackness. Feeling more affinity with the poor and oppressed people of the world than with the affluent white mainstream of American society, they began to seek connections with other nonwhite people and to search out the African roots of their heritage. Keenly aware that America's pursuit of her destiny had been undertaken at their expense but not on their behalf, they insisted that their own separate identity as a black people must be comprehended and actualized before they could—if ever—embrace the larger American destiny.

Elijah Muhammad, leader of the Nation of Islam, has for many years presented a separatist argument from the Black Muslim point of view. Founded in Detroit in 1931 by Wali Fard, the Black Muslim religion came under the leadership of Elijah Muhammad in 1934, at first made slow progress, then spread rapidly after World War II as it struck a responsive chord in an emerging black consciousness in the United States. Estimates of the membership of the Nation of Islam range all the way from 10,000 to a quarter of a million.[9] The influence of the religion has reached well beyond its official membership, however. Particularly in the teeming Negro ghettos of the cities and among blacks in prison, the militant expressions of Muslim belief have found attentive ears. The Muslim doctrines that black men are a morally and culturally superior race, that they are the chosen people of Allah, that white men are a race of devils who have corrupted "the so-called Negro" with their Christian religion and civilization—all these doctrines have found suitable soil for growth in the black frustrations created by an oppressive white society. As the following selection from the work of Elijah Muhammad makes clear, the Black Muslim religion promises the American Negro a separate, independent destiny. Black people are to unify and purify themselves and prepare for the final conflict between good and evil, the conflict between the black community and the white community. White America's certain future is total ruin; out of the ashes Allah will erect a separate nation for his own Chosen Black People.

The call for Black Power, given its first widely resounding utterance by Stokely Carmichael in the summer of 1966, provided the American Negro with a more pragmatic rallying point than the apocalypticism of Elijah Muhammad. The term "Black Power" did not denote an altogether homogeneous position; it was a motto that evoked diverse images for both blacks and whites. The term has come to possess this much unity, however: it has been a call for an effective Negro economic and political force launched against a well-entrenched, defensive white power structure. And in most cases it has been a call for black independence, which is believed to be the precondition of black development and of any black contribution to the larger American society.

Religious intimations have often been expressed in the pleas for Black Power. Even the remarks of those who have claimed a secular position have abounded with religious symbols and myths.[10] An explicitly religious interpretation of Black Power was offered by Dr. Nathan Wright, Jr., Plans Committee chairman of the 1967 National Conference on Black

[9] E. U. Essien-Udom, *Black Nationalism* (New York: Dell Publishing Co., Inc., 1964), pp. 18; 378–79, n.8.

[10] Harding, "Religion of Black Power," pp. 13–15. Cf. the symposium on Black Power in *Negro Digest*, Nov. 1966.

Power and executive director of the Department of Urban Work of the Episcopal Diocese of Newark, New Jersey. In a 1966 speech in Harlem Dr. Wright submitted that the demand for Black Power involves a just claim by black people to self-development and self-respect. He also saw in the demand the possibility of the American Negro contributing to an as yet far too limited national destiny. The black people of America are, he said, "like the Jews of old, a people peculiarly elected to transmit and to perform no less than a sacred trust," namely the trust of calling the whole of America to a social maturity through the responsible use of power.

The race crisis has raised to prominence key issues inherent in America's claim to the title "New Israel." All of these issues culminate in the question whether, during the remaining decades of the twentieth century, Americans of all races will ultimately be able to repair a national fabric badly weakened by long years of prejudice and injustice, or whether they will completely rend that cloth by pursuing independent, radically contradictory destinies. It would appear that only the former course of action could prevent the sense of American election from becoming a pious cover for a national destiny that is morally and religiously bankrupt.

SUGGESTED READING

America's World Role

Barnett, Frank R., William C. Mott, and John C. Neff, eds. *Peace and War in the Modern Age*. Garden City, N.Y.: Doubleday & Company, Inc., 1965.

Gettleman, Marvin E., ed. *Viet Nam: History, Documents, and Opinions on a Major World Crisis*. Greenwich, Conn.: Fawcett Publications, Inc., 1965.

Jack, Homer A., ed. *Religion and Peace*. New York: The Bobbs-Merrill Co., Inc., 1966.

Jessup, John K. et al. *The National Purpose*. New York: Holt, Rinehart & Winston, Inc., 1960.

Raskin, Marcus G. and Bernard B. Fall, eds. *The Viet-Nam Reader*. New York: Random House, Inc., 1965.

Thompson, Kenneth W. *Christian Ethics and the Dilemmas of Foreign Policy*. Durham, N.C.: Duke University Press, 1959.

The Black American

Carmichael, Stokely and Charles V. Hamilton. *Black Power; the Politics of Liberation in America*. New York: Random House, Inc., 1967.

Cleage, Albert B., Jr. *The Black Messiah*. New York: Sheed & Ward, 1968.

Frazier, E. Franklin. *The Negro Church in America*. New York: Schocken Books, Inc., 1966.

Harding, Vincent. "The Uses of the Afro-American Past," in *The Religious Situation: 1969*, edited by Donald R. Cutler, pp. 829–40. Boston: Beacon Press, 1969.

Lincoln, C. Eric. *The Black Muslims in America*. Boston: Beacon Press, 1961.

Malcolm X. *The Autobiography of Malcolm X*. New York: Grove Press, 1966.

America's World Role

JOHN FOSTER DULLES

Freedom's New Task

As we meet here at Independence Square, our thoughts inevitably turn to the world scene where freedom is at stake.

It is a moment of unusual significance. The Soviet rulers are reforming their lines. The Soviet 20th Congress, which adjourned last night, was busy revising the Soviet Communist creed. We cannot yet fully appraise what has happened. And, in any event, it takes time for doctrinal changes to get fully reflected in the mind and conduct of the party members.

But two things at least we know. One is that there is already a notable shift in Soviet foreign policy. And the other is that those Soviet policies which they change are being changed not because they succeeded, but because they have been thwarted by the free world.

Until recently, the foreign policy of Soviet communism was based on fanatical intolerance of all other systems and upon the organization of violence to overthrow all other systems. Marx, Lenin, and Stalin all taught that it was necessary to hate all who differed from the Soviet Communist creed; and they also taught that only by violence could international communism achieve its destined goals.

But the free nations, when confronted by this policy, grew more strong, more resolute and more united. Consequently the Soviet pattern of hatred and violence produced ever diminishing returns.

In Europe, the defensive strength of NATO, was rounded out by the addition of the Federal Republic of Germany.

In the western Pacific, freedom was consolidated by adding to our ANZUS, Philippine and Japanese treaties, the new mutual defense treaties with Korea and with the Republic of China. And the Congress, you will recall, authorized the President to use the Armed Forces of the United States in the Formosa area, if necessary, for its defense.

An address delivered to the Philadelphia Bulletin Forum, Philadelphia, Pennsylvania, February 26, 1956. From *Vital Speeches of the Day*, March 15, 1956, pp. 329–31.

In southeast Asia, the western powers joined with Asian powers in a treaty for collective security, and they transformed the Indochina struggle against colonialism to a struggle by truly independent nations—Vietnam, Laos, and Cambodia—to maintain their freedom.

In the Middle East, the northern tier concept, without challenging the concept of Arab unity, has drawn together for collective defense four nations which, for 2,500 miles, lie just south of Russia's frontiers.

Back of these formulations of free world resolve lay the vast mobile power of the United States which constituted a formidable deterrent to open armed aggression.

So the Soviets had either to give up their expansionist aims or turn to other means to advance them.

Lenin and Stalin had taught that, under these circumstances, there should be no giving up, but rather a shift to new methods.

So, last year, the Soviet rulers concluded that the time had come to change basically their approach to the non-Communist world.

II

In May of 1955, the Soviet rulers signed the Austrian State Treaty; they made their pilgrimage of repentance to Tito; they offered to establish diplomatic relations with Germany and to make a belated peace with Japan. In Asia, the Chinese Communists, at the Bandung Conference, gave at least lip service to methods other than outright violence.

The Soviet rulers trumpeted all this throughout the world as proof that Soviet Communist policy was no longer predatory.

We hoped that this was so. But we were highly skeptical. We well knew that under Leninism any tactic is admissible and that the change had come about, not through change of heart, but because old methods had failed.

On the other hand, we knew that the new Soviet tactics of increased tolerance and less dependence upon violence required a basic change in Soviet Communist doctrine. This can, in the long run, have major internal consequences and set up within Russia powerful liberalizing trends.

But the fanatical teaching of a generation cannot be erased all at once. Also the change had not gone so far that there could not almost overnight be a sudden reversal to the old practice of intolerance and violence. Also we could only safely assume that the new tactics were designed as a new means of conquest. So we did not relax our vigilance or allow our military posture to slump.

But, on the other hand, we do not assume fatalistically that there can be no evolution within Russia or that Russia's rulers will always be predatory. Some day—I would not attempt to guess when—Russia will be governed by men who put the welfare of the Russian people above world conquest. It is our basic policy to seek to advance the coming of that day.

So last spring, when Soviet conduct began to change, we determined to do all that we safely could to make that change a first installment toward an eventual Russian state that would be a normal, not abnormal, member of the society of nations.

One major step we took was to join with Britain and France to invite the Russian rulers to a conference of heads of government. At that summit Conference at Geneva President Eisenhower did more than any other man could have done to open up to the Soviet rulers the vista of a new era of friendly relations between our countries.

We cannot yet measure what has been the full effect of that Conference. The gains will be measurable only in the future. For the time being the Soviet rulers, finding that the road of intolerance and violence was blocked, have subordinated those elements of their old creed in the hope that, in a new garb, they could still pursue conquest. Now they pursue their foreign-policy goals with less manifestation of intolerance and less emphasis on violence. Their foreign policy now puts large emphasis upon seeking political cooperation with left-wing Socialists, whom formerly they detested. Finally there is heavy emphasis on trade and economic assistance. It is this economic aspect of the Soviet "new look" that I would consider today.

III

This Soviet economic campaign is a varied one. It includes the barter of surplus arms into areas where tensions were already high. There are highly publicized purchases of agricultural commodities from a few countries where mounting surpluses have exposed the vulnerabilities of economies lacking in diversity. Incidentally the Soviet bloc, with typical cynicism, has re-exported some of these commodities to markets that the original sellers normally would supply. And the Soviet bloc has made loans to a selected number of countries.

This policy has been directed especially toward certain peoples in the Near East and South Asia. There the Soviet rulers believe that they can also exploit historic grievances for their own ends.

But the new Soviet policy roams far and wide. Even African and South American countries are receiving Soviet economic propositions.

What is the import of this new economic campaign of the Soviet bloc countries?

The first thing to note is that Soviet capital exports divert resources from the Soviet people who still lack many of the ordinary decencies of life. On this we have the testimony of Mr. Khrushchev in his recent speech to the Twentieth Communist Party Congress. There he stated:

"It must be said that we do not yet have an adequate quantity of consumer goods, that there is a shortage of housing, and that many of the important problems connected with raising the people's living standards have not yet been solved." Still quoting Mr. Khrushchev:

"Production of many important foodstuffs and manufactured goods still lags behind growing demands. Some towns and communities are still insufficiently supplied with such items as milk, butter, and fruit. There are even cases where supplies of potatoes and other vegetables are irregular. There are also difficulties in supplying the population with certain high-grade manufactured goods."

The Soviet Union, of course, has the capacity to do much to lift up the living standards of the Russian people, which Mr. Khrushchev described, and to give them opportunities for greater happiness. There was indeed a moment when it seemed that this might become the Soviet policy. Mr. Malenkov, as the Prime Minister who first succeeded Stalin, advocated more consumer goods and better quality goods for the Soviet people. But Mr. Malenkov was quickly removed from leadership, and his successors resumed the policy of forcing the Russian people to work primarily to build up the power machine of the state. The output of consumer goods—food, clothing, and housing—was firmly relegated to a secondary place.

Under these conditions, can we accept at face value the Soviet professions that its foreign economic activities are primarily designed to help others?

Actually in this campaign the Soviet Union is seeking to advance its interests.

It is important, therefore, to examine how the Soviet Union sees its interests.

IV

Throughout its 38 years of existence, the Soviet pattern has been unvarying. Whenever the opportunity has arisen the Soviet Union has swallowed up its neighbors, or made satellites of them, or subordinated them in other ways.

The future may well produce a different Russia. But today changes in creed and conduct are looked upon as ways to make it easier to achieve old goals of conquest. If there is less apparent intolerance and less reliance

on violence, there is perhaps more reliance than ever on division, entice-
ment, and duplicity.

On December 29, 1955, speaking to the Supreme Soviet, Mr. Khrushchev stated the fundamental precept: "If certain people think that our
confidence in the victory of socialism, the teaching of Marxist-Leninism,
is a violation of the Geneva spirit, they obviously have an incorrect notion
of the Geneva spirit. They ought to remember once and for all that we
never renounced and we will never renounce our ideas, our struggle for
the victory of communism."

In his lengthy speech to the Twentieth Party Congress, Mr. Khrushchev promised "fundamental social transformations"—this means a Communist Party dictatorship—to any nation unwary enough to allow its
political life to be undermined by the Communist apparatus.

We must assume that the intent behind the Soviet economic campaign is to subvert and communize the nations that are its targets.

V

The United States is engaged in programs of economic assistance to
the less developed countries. Our programs have been in progress for a
number of years and have totaled billions of dollars.

By these programs, we too hope to advance our legitimate national
interests. We have never pretended otherwise.

But again the crucial question is: What are those interests and how
are they intended to be served?

Our interests will be fully served if other nations maintain their
independence and strengthen their free institutions. We have no further
aims than these. We want a world environment of freedom. We have
shown this time after time by electing to give freedom where we could
have had conquest. Our historic policy, reflecting the will and the views
of our own free people, is wholly compatible with the interests of the less-
developed countries as their leaders themselves have defined them.

VI

The political leaders in the economically less-developed countries
are entirely capable of judging the purposes and principles of other
nations. They are, for the most part, men of political experience. In many
cases they have had an active part in winning for their countries political
independence. They have no desire to preside over the loss of that
independence.

The wisdom and patriotism of the political leaders of the newly independent nations are among freedom's greatest assets. These men are not blind to Soviet purposes and past actions.

But we must also recognize that the Soviet Communist experiment has won for itself a considerable popular prestige in the less-developed countries. In these countries "industrialization" is a word of magic. It is a slogan that the people have come to believe will solve all domestic economic and political problems. The peoples of these countries do not like to be dependent upon the industrialized West for manufactured goods. For the most part, they now have political independence, but they do not yet have what they consider to be adequate economic independence.

The neighboring Asian peoples have seen the Soviet Union within a generation develop itself into a major industrial power. These observers are but dimly aware of the fact that the Soviet rate of progress was possible only because natural conditions favored, and that even so its cost in human servitude has been tragically high. They are like those of us who admire the pyramids, the palaces, the temples, and the coliseums which despotic rulers once produced out of slave labor. We are only dimly conscious of the cost in terms of human misery.

So it is with the peoples of less-developed lands who are informed in extravagant terms of the industrial monuments which have been built by the Soviet masters of 220 million subject peoples.

And when Soviet propaganda says to less-developed peoples, "See what we have done for ourselves; with our help, you can do the same," there is a strong temptation to accept that so-called help.

The political leaders of these countries, however wise they may be and however patriotic they may be, will find it difficult to resist the public pressures which Soviet propaganda arouses, unless there is some alternative.

The industrial nations of the West, with matured and vigorous economies and much well-being, can and must provide such an alternative.

VII

Western efforts to advance the economic well-being of the less-developed countries are nothing new. We need not be panicked by the new Soviet economic policy.

With or without the so-called competition of the Soviet Union, we propose to go forward with sound policies to aid the economic progress of less developed countries.

Normally, under our system, private capital could and should do the job. And, indeed, much private capital today flows into many less-developed countries. But it flows only where the political and economic risks are deemed tolerable. In much of the world, these risks are such that private capital is not ready to take them. If capital is to be found, a substantial part must be provided on a public basis which spreads the risk so that it is not appreciable in terms of any single individual.

This is one of the purposes of our mutual security program which now, in one form or another, is in its eighth year. The economic part of that program amounts this year (ending June 30) to about $1,700,000,000. Much of this is used to help our allies, particularly in the Far East and in Asia, to support adequate military establishments of their own. Of the total, approximately $600 million will assist, by loan or grant in capital developments in other lands.

This year we are asking Congress to appropriate for next year's economic program $100 million more than is available for this year. The capacity to spend wisely depends on many factors, and we should not appropriate, in a panic, merely because of Soviet economic activities. There is, however, need for somewhat greater flexibility, and for greater continuity, as regards support for long-range projects.

Some of the development projects which are most significant will take several years to complete. It is difficult for the countries concerned to arrange for financing these projects unless United States support can be relied upon not just for one year at a time, but for several years. Also, with United States support, it is easier for them to procure funds from other sources, such as the World Bank.

We believe, therefore, that the United States Government should have authority to commit some such amount as $100 million a year for several years for long-range projects which will develop to an important degree the economic strength of less-developed countries. Without that limited, long-range authority we take a risk which is quite unjustified having regard to the relatively small cost of avoiding it.

VIII

If our Nation and the other free nations play their proper part, we can face the future not with complacency—that would be disastrous—but with confidence.

I do not wish to minimize the threat of the Soviet "new look," of which the economic campaign is a part. Economic assistance knows no territorial limits. And we must count on the Soviets and their local Communist parties to press their policies with vigor.

But we should reflect that Communist successes in the world so far have come when Red armies were at hand. No people has willingly accepted the Soviet type of Communist dictatorship.

Communist open aggression has now been checked by the cohesion, resolution, vigilance, and strength of the free nations. Let us never forget that this is what deflected the Soviet rulers from primary reliance upon violence to which they were dedicated by creed and which they are skilled to practice.

They came up against the granite of a declared and strong resolve. If that granite should turn to putty, then violence and threat of war could again become the order of the day.

Meanwhile, we have new problems. These will require new efforts; without relaxation of the old cohesion, resolution, vigilance, and strength. But the new efforts will be of a kind that is in accord with our tradition. This Nation was conceived with a sense of mission and dedicated to the extension of freedom throughout the world. President Lincoln, speaking at this very Independence Hall, said of our Declaration of Independence, that there was "something in that Declaration giving liberty, not alone to the people of this country, but hope for the world for all future time. It was that which gave promise that in due time the weights should be lifted from the shoulders of all men and that all men should have an equal chance."

That has been the spirit which has animated our people since they came together as a nation. We have, it is true, acquired much for ourselves. But also we have had in large measure the greatest of all satisfactions—that is the satisfaction which comes from creating and from sharing.

We have created at home and we have also created abroad. We have shared here at home and we have shared abroad. Today the greatest opportunity for creation and for sharing lies in those areas which, possessed of great economic and human potentials, have not yet realized the opportunities which are theirs.

We have unprecedented resources with which to create and with which to share. Our 160 million people, working in freedom and with ample leisure, produce over three times as much as do the 220 million of the Soviet Union working in servitude. Our industrial techniques are beyond compare. Our desire to create and to share with others is not a political plot; it is an expression of the spirit which has long animated our Nation. It is not a product of Government; it is a product of the faith of our people.

Let me conclude with words which Benjamin Franklin wrote from Paris on May 1, 1777:

> "It is a common observation here that our cause is the cause of all mankind, and that we are fighting for their liberty in defending our own. It is a glorious task assigned us by Providence; which has, I trust, given us spirit and virtue equal to it, and will at last crown it with success."

JOHN F. KENNEDY

The Doctrine Of
National Independence

It is a high honor for any citizen of the great Republic to speak at this Hall of Independence on this day of Independence. To speak as President of the United States, to the chief executives of our fifty states, is both an opportunity and an obligation. The necessity for comity between the national government and the several states is an indelible lesson of our history.

Because our system is designed to encourage both differences and dissent, because its checks and balances are designed to preserve the rights of the individual and the locality against pre-eminent central authority, you and I both recognize how dependent we are, one upon the other, for the successful operation of our unique and happy form of government. Our system and our freedom permit the legislative to be pitted upon occasions against the executive, the state against the federal government, the city against the countryside, party against party, interest against interest, all in competition or in contention one with another. Our task in the White House—is to weave from all these tangled threads a fabric of law and progress. Others may confine themselves to debate, discussion and that ultimate luxury, free advice. Our responsibility is one of decision, for to govern is to choose.

Thus in a very real sense you and I are the executors of the testament handed down by those who gathered in this historic hall 186 years ago today. For they gathered to affix their names to a document which was above all else a document not of rhetoric, but of bold decision. It was, it is true, a document of protest, but protests had been made before. It set forth their grievances with eloquence, but such eloquence had been heard before. But what distinguished this paper from all the others was the final, irrevocable decision that it took to assert the independence of

An address delivered at Independence Hall, Philadelphia, Pennsylvania, July 4, 1962. From John F. Kennedy, *The Burden and the Glory*, ed. Allan Nevins (New York: Harper and Row, Publishers, 1964), pp. 108–12.

free states in place of colonies and to commit to that goal their lives, their fortunes and their sacred honor.

Today, 186 years later, that Declaration, whose yellowing parchment and fading, almost illegible lines I saw in the past week in the National Archives in Washington, is still a revolutionary document. To read it today is to hear a trumpet call. For that Declaration unleashed not merely a revolution against the British, but a revolution in human affairs. Its authors were highly conscious of its world-wide implications, and George Washington declared that liberty and self-government were, in his words, "finally staked on the experiment entrusted to the hands of the American people."

This prophecy has been borne out for 186 years. This doctrine of national independence has shaken the globe, and it remains the most powerful force anywhere in the world today. There are those struggling to eke out a bare existence in a barren land who have never heard of free enterprise, but who cherish the idea of independence. There are those who are grappling with overpowering problems of illiteracy and ill health, and who are ill-equipped to hold free elections, but they are determined to hold fast to their national independence. Even those unwilling or unable to take part in any struggle between East and West are strongly on the side of their own national independence—the independence of Berlin or Laos or Vietnam, the longing for independence behind the Iron Curtain, the peaceful transition to independence in those newly emerging areas whose troubles some hope to exploit.

The theory of independence, as old as man himself, was not invented in this hall, but it was in this hall that the theory became a practice, that the word went out to all the world that "the God who gave us life gave us liberty at the same time."

And today this nation, conceived in revolution, nurtured in liberty, matured in independence, has no intention of abdicating its leadership in that world-wide movement for independence to any nation or society committed to systematic human suppression.

As apt and applicable as this historic Declaration of Independence is today, we would do well to honor that other historic document drafted in this hall, the Constitution of the United States, for it stressed not independence but interdependence, not the individual liberty of one but the indivisible liberty of all.

In most of the old colonial world the struggle for independence is coming to an end. Even in areas behind the Curtain, that which Jefferson called "the disease of liberty" still appears to be infectious. With the passing of ancient empires, today less than 2 percent of the world's population lives in territories officially termed "dependent." As this effort for independence, inspired by the spirit of the American Declaration of

Independence, now approaches a successful close, a great new effort for interdependence is transforming the world about us. And the spirit of that new effort is the same spirit which gave birth to the American Constitution.

That spirit is today most clearly seen across the Atlantic Ocean. The nations of Western Europe, long divided by feuds more bitter than any which existed among the thirteen colonies, are joining together, seeking, as our forefathers sought, to find freedom in diversity and unity in strength.

The United States looks on this vast new enterprise with hope and admiration. We do not regard a strong and united Europe as a rival but as a partner. To aid its progress has been the basic objective of our foreign policy for seventeen years. We believe that a united Europe will be capable of playing a greater role in the common defense, of responding more generously to the needs of poorer nations, of joining with the United States and others in lowering trade barriers, resolving problems of currency and commodities, and developing coordinated policies in all other economic, diplomatic and political areas. We see in such a Europe a partner with whom we could deal on a basis of full equality in all the great and burdensome tasks of building and defending a community of free nations.

It would be premature at this time to do more than to indicate the high regard with which we view the formation of this partnership. The first order of business is for our European friends to go forward in forming the more perfect union which will someday make this partnership possible.

A great new edifice is not built overnight. It was eleven years from the Declaration of Independence to the writing of the Constitution. The construction of workable federal institutions required still another generation. The greatest works of our nation's founders lay not in documents and declarations, but in creative, determined action. The building of the new house of Europe has followed this same practical and purposeful course. Building the Atlantic Partnership will not be cheaply or easily finished.

But I will say here and now on this day of Independence that the United States will be ready for a Declaration of Interdependence, that we will be prepared to discuss with a United Europe the ways and means of forming a concrete Atlantic Partnership, a mutually beneficial partnership between the new union now emerging in Europe and the old American union founded here 175 years ago.

All this will not be completed in a year, but let the world know it is our goal.

In urging the adoption of the United States Constitution, Alexander

Hamilton told his fellow New Yorkers to "think continentally." Today Americans must learn to think intercontinentally.

Acting on our own by ourselves, we cannot establish justice throughout the world. We cannot insure its domestic tranquillity, or provide for its common defense, or promote its general welfare, or secure the blessings of liberty to ourselves and our posterity. But joined with other free nations, we can do all this and more. We can assist the developing nations to throw off the yoke of poverty. We can balance our world-wide trade and payments at the highest possible level of growth. We can mount a deterrent powerful enough to deter any aggression, and ultimately we can help achieve a world of law and free choice, banishing the world of war and coercion.

For the Atlantic Partnership of which I speak would not look inward only, preoccupied with its own welfare and advancement. It must look outward to cooperate with all nations in meeting their common concern. It would serve as a nucleus for the eventual union of all free men, those who are now free and those who are avowing that someday they will be free.

On Washington's birthday in 1861, standing right there, President Elect Abraham Lincoln spoke at this hall on his way to the nation's capital. And he paid a brief and eloquent tribute to the men who wrote, and fought for, and who died for, the Declaration of Independence. Its essence, he said, was its promise not only of liberty "to the people of this country, but hope to the world . . . [hope] that in due time the weights should be lifted from the shoulders of all men, and that *all* should have an equal chance."

On this fourth day of July, 1962, we who are gathered at this same hall, entrusted with the fate and future of our states and nation, declare now our vow to do our part to lift the weights from the shoulders of all, to join other men and nations in preserving both peace and freedom, and to regard any threat to the peace or freedom of one as a threat to the peace and freedom of all. "And for the support of this Declaration, with a firm reliance on the Protection of Divine Providence, we mutually pledge to each other our lives, our Fortunes, and our sacred Honor."

J. WILLIAM FULBRIGHT

The Arrogance Of Power

America is the most fortunate of nations—fortunate in her rich territory, fortunate in having had a century of relative peace in which to develop that territory, fortunate in her diverse and talented population, fortunate in the institutions devised by the founding fathers and in the wisdom of those who have adapted those institutions to a changing world.

For the most part America has made good use of her blessings, especially in her internal life but also in her foreign relations. Having done so much and succeeded so well, America is now at that historical point at which a great nation is in danger of losing its perspective on what exactly is within the realm of its power and what is beyond it. Other great nations, reaching this critical juncture, have aspired to too much, and by overextension of effort have declined and then fallen.

The causes of the malady are not entirely clear but its recurrence is one of the uniformities of history: power tends to confuse itself with virtue and a great nation is peculiarly susceptible to the idea that its power is a sign of God's favor, conferring upon it a special responsibility for other nations—to make them richer and happier and wiser, to remake them, that is, in its own shining image. Power confuses itself with virtue and tends also to take itself for omnipotence. Once imbued with the idea of a mission, a great nation easily assumes that it has the means as well as the duty to do God's work. The Lord, after all, surely would not choose you as His agent and then deny you the sword with which to work His will. German soldiers in the First World War wore belt buckles imprinted with the words "*Gott mit uns.*" It was approximately under this kind of infatuation—an exaggerated sense of power and an imaginary sense of mission—that the Athenians attacked Syracuse, and Napoleon and then Hitler invaded Russia. In plain words, they overextended their commitments and they came to grief.

I do not think for a moment that America, with her deeply rooted democratic traditions, is likely to embark upon a campaign to dominate the world in the manner of a Hitler or Napoleon. What I do fear is that she may be drifting into commitments which, though generous and benevolent in intent, are so far-reaching as to exceed even America's great capacities. At the same time, it is my hope—and I emphasize it because it underlies all of the criticisms and proposals to be made in these pages— that America will escape those fatal temptations of power which have ruined other great nations and will instead confine herself to doing only that good in the world which she *can* do, both by direct effort and by the force of her own example.

The stakes are high indeed: they include not only America's continued greatness but nothing less than the survival of the human race in an era when, for the first time in human history, a living generation has the power of veto over the survival of the next.

THE POWER DRIVE OF NATIONS

When the abstractions and subtleties of political science have been exhausted, there remain the most basic unanswered questions about war and peace and why nations contest the issues they contest and why they even care about then. As Aldous Huxley has written:

> There may be arguments about the best way of raising wheat in a cold climate or of re-afforesting a denuded mountain. But such arguments never lead to organized slaughter. Organized slaughter is the result of arguments about such questions as the following: Which is the best nation? The best religion? The best political theory? The best form of government? Why are other people so stupid and wicked? Why can't they see how good and intelligent *we* are? Why do they resist our beneficent efforts to bring them under our control and make them like ourselves?[1]

Many of the wars fought by man—I am tempted to say most—have been fought over such abstractions. The more I puzzle over the great wars of history, the more I am inclined to the view that the causes attributed to them—territory, markets, resources, the defense or perpetuation of great principles—were not the root causes at all but rather explanations or excuses for certain unfathomable drives of human nature. For lack of a clear and precise understanding of exactly what these motives are, I

---

[1] Aldous Huxley, "The Politics of Ecology" (Santa Barbara: Center for the Study of Democratic Institutions, 1963), p. 6.

refer to them as the "arrogance of power"—as a psychological need that nations seem to have in order to prove that they are bigger, better, or stronger than other nations. Implicit in this drive is the assumption, even on the part of normally peaceful nations, that force is the ultimate proof of superiority—that when a nation shows that it has the stronger army, it is also proving that it has better people, better institutions, better principles, and, in general, a better civilization.

Evidence for my proposition is found in the remarkable discrepancy between the apparent and hidden causes of some modern wars and the discrepancy between their causes and ultimate consequences.

The precipitating cause of the Franco-Prussian War of 1870, for example, was a dispute over the succession to the Spanish throne, and the ostensible "underlying" cause was French resistance to the unification of Germany. The war was followed by the completion of German unification—which probably could have been achieved without war—but it was also followed by the loss of Alsace-Lorraine, the humiliation of France, and the emergence of Germany as the greatest power in Europe, which could not have been achieved without war. The peace treaty, incidentally, said nothing about the Spanish throne, which everyone apparently had forgotten. One wonders to what extent the Germans were motivated simply by the desire to cut those haughty Frenchmen down to size and have a good excuse to build another monument in Berlin.

The United States went to war in 1898 for the stated purpose of liberating Cuba from Spanish tyranny, but after winning the war—a war which Spain had been willing to pay a high price to avoid—the United States brought the liberated Cubans under an American protectorate and incidentally annexed the Philippines, because, according to President McKinley, the Lord told him it was America's duty "to educate the Filipinos, and uplift and civilize and Christianize them, and by God's grace do the very best we could by them, as our fellowmen for whom Christ also died."[2]

Isn't it interesting that the voice was the voice of the Lord but the words were those of Theodore Roosevelt, Henry Cabot Lodge, and Admiral Mahan, those "imperialists of 1898" who wanted America to have an empire just because a big, powerful country like the United States *ought* to have an empire? The spirit of the times was expressed by Albert Beveridge, soon thereafter to be elected to the United States Senate, who proclaimed Americans to be "a conquering race": "We must obey our blood and occupy new markets and if necessary new lands," he said, because "In the Almighty's infinite plan ... debased civilizations and

---

[2] Quoted in Samuel Flagg Bemis, *A Diplomatic History of the United States* (New York: Holt, Rinehart & Winston, Inc., 1955), p. 472.

decaying races" must disappear "before the higher civilization of the nobler and more virile types of man."[3]

In 1914 all Europe went to war, ostensibly because the heir to the Austrian throne had been assassinated at Sarajevo, but really because that murder became the symbolic focus of the incredibly delicate sensibilities of the great nations of Europe. The events of the summer of 1914 were a melodrama of abnormal psychology: Austria had to humiliate Serbia in order not to be humiliated herself, but Austria's effort at recovering self-esteem was profoundly humiliating to Russia; Russia was allied to France, who had been feeling generally humiliated since 1871, and Austria in turn was allied to Germany, whose pride required that she support Austria no matter how insanely Austria behaved and who may in any case have felt that it would be fun to give the German Army another swing down the Champs-Élysées. For these ennobling reasons the world was plunged into a war which took tens of millions of lives, precipitated the Russian Revolution, and set in motion the events that led to another world war, a war which took tens of millions more lives and precipitated the worldwide revolutions of our time, revolutions whose consequences are beyond the foresight of any of us now alive.

The causes and consequences of war may have more to do with pathology than with politics, more to do with irrational pressures of pride and pain than with rational calculations of advantage and profit. There is a Washington story, perhaps apocryphal, that the military intellectuals in the Pentagon conducted an experiment in which they fed data derived from the events of the summer of 1914 into a computer and that, after weighing and digesting the evidence, the machine assured its users that there was no danger of war. What this "proves," if anything, is that computers are more rational than men; it also suggests that if there is a root cause of human conflict and of the power drive of nations, it lies not in economic aspirations, historical forces, or the workings of the balance of power, but in the ordinary hopes and fears of the human mind.

It has been said that buried in every woman's secret soul is a drum majorette; it might also be said that in all of our souls there is a bit of the missionary. We all like telling people what to do, which is perfectly all right except that most people do not like being told what to do. I have given my wife some splendid suggestions on household management but she has been so consistently ungrateful for my advice that I have stopped offering it. The phenomenon is explained by the Canadian psychiatrist and former Director-General of the World Health Organization, Brock Chisholm, who writes:

[3] Quoted in Barbara Tuchman, *The Proud Tower* (New York: The Macmillan Company, 1966), p. 153.

...Man's method of dealing with difficulties in the past has always been to tell everyone else how they should behave. We've all been doing that for centuries.

It should be clear by now that this no longer does any good. Everybody has by now been told by everybody else how he should behave.... The criticism is not effective; it never has been, and it never is going to be....[4]

Ineffective though it has been, the giving—and enforcement—of all this unsolicited advice has at least until recently been compatible with the survival of the human race. Man is now, however, for the first time, in a situation in which the survival of his species is in jeopardy. Other forms of life have been endangered and many destroyed by changes in their natural environment; man is menaced by a change of environmet which he himself has wrought by the invention of nuclear weapons and ballistic missiles. Our power to kill has become universal, creating a radically new situation which, if we are to survive, requires us to adopt some radically new attitudes about the giving and enforcement of advice and in general about human and international relations.

The enormity of the danger of extinction of our species is dulled by the frequency with which it is stated, as if a familiar threat of catastrophe were no threat at all. We seem to feel somehow that because the hydrogen bomb has not killed us yet, it is never going to kill us. This is a dangerous assumption because it encourages the retention of traditional attitudes about world politics when our responsibility, in Dr. Chisholm's words, is nothing less than "to re-examine all of the attitudes of our ancestors and to select from those attitudes things which we, on our own authority in these present circumstances, with our knowledge, recognize as still valid in this new kind of world...."[5]

The attitude above all others which I feel sure is no longer valid is the arrogance of power, the tendency of great nations to equate power with virtue and major responsibilities with a universal mission. The dilemmas involved are pre-eminently American dilemmas, not because America has weaknesses that others do not have but because America is powerful as no nation has ever been before, and the discrepancy between her power and the power of others appears to be increasing. One may hope that America, with her vast resources and democratic traditions, with her diverse and creative populations, will find the wisdom to match her power; but one can hardly be confident because the wisdom required is greater wisdom than any great nation has ever shown before. It must

---

[4] Brock Chisholm, *Prescription for Survival* (New York: Columbia University Press, 1957), p. 54.
[5] Ibid., p. 9.

be rooted, as Dr. Chisholm says, in the re-examination of "all of the attitudes of our ancestors."

It is a tall order. Perhaps one can begin to fill it by an attempt to assess the attitudes of Americans toward other peoples and some of the effects of America's power on small countries whom she has tried to help.

INNOCENTS ABROAD

There are signs of the arrogance of power in the way Americans act when they go to foreign countries. Foreigners frequently comment on the contrast between the behavior of Americans at home and abroad: in our own country, they say, we are hospitable and considerate, but as soon as we get outside our own borders something seems to get into us and wherever we are we become noisy and demanding and we strut around as if we owned the place. The British used to say during the war that the trouble with the Yanks was that they were "overpaid, oversexed, and over here." During a recent vacation in Mexico, I noticed in a small-town airport two groups of students on holiday, one group Japanese, the other American. The Japanese were neatly dressed and were talking and laughing in a manner that neither annoyed anybody nor particularly called attention to themselves. The Americans, on the other hand, were disporting themselves in a conspicuous and offensive manner, stamping around the waiting room in sloppy clothes, drinking beer, and shouting to each other as if no one else were there.

This kind of scene, unfortunately, has become familiar in many parts of the world. I do not wish to exaggerate its significance, but I have the feeling that just as there was once something special about being a Roman or a Spaniard or an Englishman, there is now something about the consciousness of being an American abroad, something about the consciousness of belonging to the biggest, richest country in the world, that encourages people who are perfectly well behaved at home to become boorish when they are in somebody else's country and to treat the local citizens as if they were not really there.

One reason Americans abroad may act as though they "own the place" is that in many places they very nearly do: American companies may dominate large segments of a country's economy; American products are advertised on billboards and displayed in shop windows; American hotels and snack bars are available to protect American tourists from foreign influence; American soldiers may be stationed in the country, and even if they are not, the population are probably well aware that their very survival depends on the wisdom with which America uses her immense military power.

I think that when any American goes abroad, he carries an unconscious knowledge of all this power with him and it affects his behavior, just as it once affected the behavior of Greeks and Romans, of Spaniards, Germans, and Englishmen, in the brief high noons of their respective ascendancies. It was the arrogance of their power that led nineteenth-century Englishmen to suppose that if they shouted at a foreigner loud enough in English he was bound to understand, or that now leads Americans to behave like Mark Twain's "innocents abroad," who reported on their travels in Europe that

> The people of those foreign countries are very, very ignorant. They looked curiously at the costumes we had brought from the wilds of America. They observed that we talked loudly at table sometimes. . . . In Paris they just simply opened their eyes and stared when we spoke to them in French! We never did succeed in making these idiots understand their own language.[6]

THE FATAL IMPACT

Reflecting on his voyages to Polynesia in the late eighteenth century, Captain Cook later wrote that "It would have been better for these people never to have known us." In a book on European explorations of the South Pacific, Alan Moorehead relates how the Tahitians and the Australian aborigines were corrupted by the white man's diseases, alcohol, firearms, laws, and concepts of morality, by what Moorehead calls "the long downslide into Western civilization." The first missionaries to Tahiti, says Moorehead, were "determined to recreate the island in the image of lower-middle-class Protestant England. . . . They kept hammering away at the Tahitian way of life until it crumbled before them, and within two decades they had achieved precisely what they set out to do."[7] It is said that the first missionaries to Hawaii went for the purpose of explaining to the Polynesians that it was sinful to work on Sunday, only to discover that in those bountiful islands nobody worked on any day.

Even when acting with the best of intentions, Americans, like other Western peoples who have carried their civilizations abroad, have had something of the same "fatal impact" on smaller nations that European explorers had on the Tahitians and the native Australians. We have not

---

[6] Mark Twain, *The Innocents Abroad* (New York: The Thistle Press, 1962), p. 494.
[7] Alan Moorehead, *The Fatal Impact* (New York: Harper & Row, Publishers, 1966), pp. 61, 80–81.

harmed people because we wished to; on the contrary, more often than not we have wanted to help people and, in some very important respects, we have helped them. Americans have brought medicine and education, manufactures and modern techniques to many places in the world; but they have also brought themselves and the condescending attitudes of a people whose very success breeds disdain for other cultures. Bringing power without understanding, Americans as well as Europeans have had a devastating effect in less advanced areas of the world; without knowing they were doing it, they have shattered traditional societies, disrupted fragile economies and undermined peoples' self-confidence by the invidious example of their own power and efficiency. They have done this in many instances simply by being big and strong, by giving good advice, by intruding on people who have not wanted them but could not resist them.

The missionary instinct seems to run deep in human nature, and the bigger and stronger and richer we are, the more we feel suited to the missionary task, the more indeed we consider it our duty. Dr. Chisholm relates the story of an eminent cleric who had been proselyting the Eskimos and said: "You know, for years we couldn't do anything with those Eskimos at all; they didn't have any sin. We had to teach them sin for years before we could do anything with them."[8] I am reminded of the three Boy Scouts who reported to their scoutmaster that as their good deed for the day they had helped an old lady to cross the street.

"That's fine," said the scoutmaster, "but why did it take three of you?"

"Well," they explained, "she didn't want to go."

The good deed above all others that Americans feel qualified to perform is the teaching of democracy. Let us consider the results of some American good deeds in various parts of the world.

Over the years since President Monroe proclaimed his doctrine, Latin Americans have had the advantages of United States tutelage in fiscal responsibility, in collective security, and in the techniques of democracy. If they have fallen short in any of these fields, the thought presents itself that the fault may lie as much with the teacher as with the pupils.

When President Theodore Roosevelt announced his "corollary" to the Monroe Doctrine in 1905, he solemnly declared that he regarded the future interventions thus sanctified as a "burden" and a "responsibility" and an obligation to "international equity." Not once, so far as I know, has the United States regarded itself as intervening in a Latin American country for selfish or unworthy motives—a view not necessarily shared, however, by the beneficiaries. Whatever reassurance the purity of our motives may give must be shaken a little by the thought that probably no

[8] Chisholm, *Prescription,* pp. 55–56.

country in human history has ever intervened in another except for motives it regarded as excellent.

For all our noble intentions, the countries which have had most of the tutelage in democracy by United States Marines have not been particularly democratic. These include Haiti, which is under a brutal and superstitious dictatorship; the Dominican Republic, which languished under the brutal Trujillo dictatorship for thirty years and whose second elected government since the overthrow of Trujillo is threatened, like the first, by the power of a military oligarchy; and of course Cuba, which, as no one needs to be reminded, has replaced its traditional right-wing dictatorships with a communist dictatorship.

Maybe, in the light of this extraordinary record of accomplishment, it is time for us to reconsider our teaching methods. Maybe we are not really cut out for the job of spreading the gospel of democracy. Maybe it would profit us to concentrate on our own democracy instead of trying to inflict our particular version of it on all those ungrateful Latin Americans who stubbornly oppose their North American benefactors instead of the "real" enemies whom we have so graciously chosen for them. And maybe —just maybe—if we left our neighbors to make their own judgments and their own mistakes, and confined our assistance to matters of economics and technology instead of philosophy, maybe then they would begin to find the democracy and the dignity that have largely eluded them, and we in turn might begin to find the love and gratitude that we seem to crave.

Korea is another example. We went to war in 1950 to defend South Korea against the Russian-inspired aggression of North Korea. I think that American intervention was justified and necessary; we were defending a country that clearly wanted to be defended, whose army was willing to fight and fought well, and whose government, though dictatorial, was patriotic and commanded the support of the people. Throughout the war, however, the United States emphasized as one of its war aims the survival of the Republic of Korea as a "free society," something which it was not then and is not now. We lost 33,629 American lives in that war and have since spent $5.61 billion on direct military and economic aid and a great deal more on indirect aid to South Korea. The country, nonetheless, remained until recently in a condition of virtual economic stagnation and political instability. Only now is economic progress being made, but the truly surprising fact is that having fought a war for three years to defend the freedom of South Korea, most Americans quickly lost interest in the state of the ward for whom they had sacrificed so much. It is doubtful that more than a handful of Americans now know or care whether South Korea is a "free society."

We are engaged in a war to "defend freedom" in South Vietnam.

Unlike the Republic of Korea, South Vietnam has an army which fights without notable success and a weak, dictatorial government which does not command the loyalty of the South Vietnamese people. The official war aims of the United States government, as I understand them, are to defeat what is regarded as North Vietnamese aggression, to demonstrate the futility of what the communists call "wars of national liberation," and to create conditions under which the South Vietnamese people will be able freely to determine their own future.

I have not the slightest doubt of the sincerity of the President and the Vice-President and the Secretaries of State and Defense in propounding these aims. What I do doubt, and doubt very much, is the ability of the United States to achieve these aims by the means being used. I do not question the power of our weapons and the efficiency of our logistics; I cannot say these things delight me as they seem to delight some of our officials, but they are certainly impressive. What I do question is the ability of the United States or any other Western nation to go into a small, alien, undeveloped Asian nation and create stability where there is chaos, the will to fight where there is defeatism, democracy where there is no tradition of it, and honest government where corruption is almost a way of life.

In the spring of 1966 demonstrators in Saigon burned American jeeps, tried to assault American soldiers, and marched through the streets shouting "Down with American imperialists," while a Buddhist leader made a speech equating the United States with the communists as a threat to South Vietnamese independence. Most Americans are understandably shocked and angered to encounter expressions of hostility from people who would long since have been under the rule of the Viet Cong but for the sacrifice of American lives and money. Why, we may ask, are they so shockingly ungrateful? Surely they must know that their very right to parade and protest and demonstrate depends on the Americans who are defending them.

The answer, I think, is that "fatal impact" of the rich and strong on the poor and weak. Dependent on it though the Vietnamese are, American strength is a reproach to their weakness, American wealth a mockery of their poverty, American success a reminder of their failures. What they resent is the disruptive effect of our strong culture upon their fragile one, an effect which we can no more avoid having than a man can help being bigger than a child. What they fear, I think rightly, is that traditional Vietnamese society cannot survive the American economic and cultural impact.

The evidence of that "fatal impact" is seen in the daily life of Saigon. A *New York Times* correspondent reported—and his information matches that of other observers on the scene—that many Vietnamese find it necessary to put their wives or daughters to work as bar girls or to peddle them to American soldiers as mistresses; that it is not unusual to hear a report that a Vietnamese soldier has committed suicide out of shame because his wife has been working as a bar girl; that Vietnamese have trouble getting taxicabs because drivers will not stop for them, preferring to pick up American soldiers who will pay outrageous fares without complaint; that as a result of the American influx bar girls, prostitutes, pimps, bar owners, and taxi drivers have risen to the higher levels of the economic pyramid; that middle-class Vietnamese families have difficulty renting homes because Americans have driven the rents beyond their reach, and some Vietnamese families have actually been evicted from houses and apartments by landlords who prefer to rent to the affluent Americans; that Vietnamese civil servants, junior army officers, and enlisted men are unable to support their families because of the inflation generated by American spending and the purchasing power of the G.I.'s. One Vietnamese explained to the *New York Times* reporter that "Any time legions of prosperous white men descend on a rudimentary Asian society, you are bound to have trouble." Another said: "We Vietnamese are somewhat xenophobe. We don't like foreigners, any kind of foreigners, so that you shouldn't be surprised that we don't like you."[9]

Sincere though it is, the American effort to build the foundations of freedom in South Vietnam is thus having an effect quite different from the one intended. "All this struggling and striving to make the world better is a great mistake," said George Bernard Shaw, "not because it isn't a good thing to improve the world if you know how to do it, but because striving and struggling is the worst way you could set about doing anything."[10]

One wonders how much the American commitment to Vietnamese freedom is also a commitment to American pride—the two seem to have become part of the same package. When we talk about the freedom of South Vietnam, we may be thinking about how disagreeable it would be to accept a solution short of victory; we may be thinking about how our pride would be injured if we settled for less than we set out to achieve; we may be thinking about our reputation as a great power, fearing that a compromise settlement would shame us before the world, marking us as a second-rate people with flagging courage and determination.

Such fears are as nonsensical as their opposite, the presumption of a universal mission. They are simply unworthy of the richest, most powerful, most productive, and best educated people in the world. One can

[9] Neil Sheehan, "Anti-Americanism Grows in Vietnam," *New York Times*, Apr. 24, 1966, p. 3.
[10] George Bernard Shaw, *Cashel Byron's Profession* (1886), chap. 5.

understand an uncompromising attitude on the part of such countries as China or France: both have been struck low in this century and a certain amount of arrogance may be helpful to them in recovering their pride. It is much less comprehensible on the part of the United States—a nation whose modern history has been an almost uninterrupted chronicle of success, a nation which by now should be so sure of its own power as to be capable of magnanimity, a nation which by now should be able to act on the proposition that, as George Kennan said, "there is more respect to be won in the opinion of the world by a resolute and courageous liquidation of unsound positions than in the most stubborn pursuit of extravagant or unpromising objectives."[11]

The cause of our difficulties in Southeast Asia is not a deficiency of power but an excess of the wrong kind of power, which results in a feeling of impotence when it fails to achieve its desired ends. We are still acting like Boy Scouts dragging reluctant old ladies across streets they do not want to cross. We are trying to remake Vietnamese society, a task which certainly cannot be accomplished by force and which probably cannot be accomplished by any means available to outsiders. The objective may be desirable, but it is not feasible. As Shaw said: "Religion is a great force—the only real motive force in the world; but what you fellows don't understand is that you must get a man through his own religion and not through yours."[12]

With the best intentions in the world the United States has involved itself deeply in the affairs of developing nations in Asia and Latin America, practicing what has been called a kind of "welfare imperialism." Our honest purpose is the advancement of development and democracy, to which end it has been thought necessary to destroy ancient and unproductive modes of life. In this latter function we have been successful, perhaps more successful than we know. Bringing skills and knowledge, money and resources in amounts hitherto unknown in traditional societies, the Americans have overcome indigenous groups and interests and become the dominant force in a number of countries. Far from being bumbling, wasteful, and incompetent, as critics have charged, American government officials, technicians, and economists have been strikingly successful in breaking down the barriers to change in ancient but fragile cultures.

Here, however, our success ends. Traditional rulers, institutions, and

[11] George F. Kennan, "Supplemental Foreign Assistance Fiscal Year 1966—Vietnam," *Hearings Before the Committee on Foreign Relations*, U.S. Senate, 89th Cong., 2nd sess. on S. 2793, Part I (Washington, D.C.: Government Printing Office, 1966), p. 335.
[12] George Bernard Shaw, *Getting Married* (1911).

ways of life have crumbled under the fatal impact of American wealth and power but they have not been replaced by new institutions and new ways of life, nor has their breakdown ushered in an era of democracy and development. It has rather ushered in an era of disorder and demoralization because in the course of destroying old ways of doing things, we have also destroyed the self-confidence and self-reliance without which no society can build indigenous institutions. Inspiring as we have such great awe of our efficiency and wealth, we have reduced some of the intended beneficiaries of our generosity to a condition of dependency and self-denigration. We have done this for the most part inadvertently: with every good intention we have intruded on fragile societies, and our intrusion, though successful in uprooting traditional ways of life, has been strikingly unsuccessful in implanting the democracy and advancing the development which are the honest aims of our "welfare imperialism."

AMERICAN EMPIRE OR AMERICAN EXAMPLE?

Despite its dangerous and unproductive consequences, the idea of being responsible for the whole world seems to be flattering to Americans and I am afraid it is turning our heads, just as the sense of universal responsibility turned the heads of ancient Romans and nineteenth-century British.

In 1965 Henry Fairlie, a British political writer for *The Spectator* and *The Daily Telegraph*, wrote what he called "A Cheer for American Imperialism."[13] An empire, he said, "has no justification except its own existence." It must never contract; it "wastes treasure and life"; its commitments "are without rhyme or reason." Nonetheless, according to Fairlie, the "American empire" is uniquely benevolent, devoted as it is to individual liberty and the rule of law, and having performed such services as getting the author released from a Yugoslav jail simply by his threatening to involve the American Consul, a service which he describes as "sublime."

What romantic nonsense this is. And what dangerous nonsense in the age of nuclear weapons. The idea of an "American empire" might be dismissed as the arrant imagining of a British Gunga Din except that it surely strikes a responsive chord in at least a corner of the usually sensible and humane American mind. It calls to mind the slogans of the past about "manifest destiny" and "making the world safe for democracy," and the demand for "unconditional surrender" in World War II. It calls to mind President McKinley taking counsel with the Supreme Being about his duty to the benighted Filipinos.

13 *The New York Times Magazine,* July 11, 1965.

The "Blessings-of-Civilization Trust," as Mark Twain called it, may have been a "Daisy" in its day, uplifting for the soul and good for business besides, but its day is past. It is past because the great majority of the human race is demanding dignity and independence, not the honor of a supine role in an American empire. It is past because whatever claim America may make for the universal domain of her ideas and values is balanced by the communist counter-claim, armed like our own with nuclear weapons. And, most of all, it is past because it never should have begun, because we are not God's chosen saviour of mankind but only one of mankind's more successful and fortunate branches, endowed by our Creator with about the same capacity for good and evil, no more or less, than the rest of humanity.

An excessive preoccupation with foreign relations over a long period of time is more than a manifestation of arrogance; it is a drain on the power that gave rise to it, because it diverts a nation from the sources of its strength, which are in its domestic life. A nation immersed in foreign affairs is expending its capital, human as well as material; sooner or later that capital must be renewed by some diversion of creative energies from foreign to domestic pursuits. I would doubt that any nation has achieved a durable greatness by conducting a "strong" foreign policy, but many have been ruined by expending their energies in foreign adventures while allowing their domestic bases to deteriorate. The United States emerged as a world power in the twentieth century, not because of what it had done in foreign relations but because it had spent the nineteenth century developing the North American continent; by contrast, the Austrian and Turkish empires collapsed in the twentieth century in large part because they had so long neglected their internal development and organization.

If America has a service to perform in the world—and I believe she has—it is in large part the service of her own example. In our excessive involvement in the affairs of other countries we are not only living off our assets and denying our own people the proper enjoyment of their resources, we are also denying the world the example of a free society enjoying its freedom to the fullest. This is regrettable indeed for a nation that aspires to teach democracy to other nations, because, as Edmund Burke said, "Example is the school of mankind, and they will learn at no other."[14,15]

The missionary instinct in foreign affairs may, in a curious way, reflect a deficiency rather than an excess of national self-confidence. In

14 Edmund Burke, "On a Regicide Peace" (1796).
15 The services America can perform in the world—other than that of her own example—are discussed in Chapter 11. [In that chapter, Fulbright proposes a foreign aid program to replace bilateral foreign aid and its philanthropic orientation. Economic aid would be "conducted as a community enterprise, that is, through such international channels as the United Nations, the International Development Association of the World Bank, and the regional development banks."—EDITOR]

America's case the evidence of a lack of self-confidence is our apparent need for constant proof and reassurance, our nagging desire for popularity, our bitterness and confusion when foreigners fail to appreciate our generosity and good intentions. Lacking an appreciation of the dimensions of our own power, we fail to understand our enormous and disruptive impact on the world; we fail to understand that no matter how good our intentions—and they are, in most cases, decent enough—other nations are alarmed by the very existence of such great power, which, whatever its benevolence, cannot help but remind them of their own helplessness before it.

Those who lack self-assurance are also likely to lack magnanimity, because the one is the condition of the other. Only a nation at peace with itself, with its transgressions as well as its achievements, is capable of a generous understanding of others. Only when we Americans can acknowledge our own past aggressive behavior—in such instances, for example, as the Indian wars and the wars against Mexico and Spain—will we acquire some perspective on the aggressive behavior of others; only when we can understand the human implications of the chasm between American affluence and the poverty of most of the rest of mankind will we be able to understand why the American "way of life" which is so dear to us has few lessons and limited appeal to the poverty-stricken majority of the human race.

It is a curiosity of human nature that lack of self-assurance seems to breed an exaggerated sense of power and mission. When a nation is very powerful but lacking in self-confidence, it is likely to behave in a manner dangerous to itself and to others. Feeling the need to prove what is obvious to everyone else, it begins to confuse great power with unlimited power and great responsibility with total responsibility: it can admit of no error; it must win every argument, no matter how trivial. For lack of an appreciation of how truly powerful it is, the nation begins to lose wisdom and perspective and, with them, the strength and understanding that it takes to be magnanimous to smaller and weaker nations.

Gradually but unmistakably America is showing signs of that arrogance of power which has afflicted, weakened, and in some cases destroyed great nations in the past. In so doing we are not living up to our capacity and promise as a civilized example for the world. The measure of our falling short is the measure of the patriot's duty of dissent.

The Black American

MARTIN LUTHER KING, JR.

Letter From
Birmingham Jail

April 16, 1963

My Dear Fellow Clergymen:

While confined here in the Birmingham city jail, I came across your recent statement calling my present activities "unwise and untimely." Seldom do I pause to answer criticism of my work and ideas. If I sought to answer all the criticisms that cross my desk, my secretaries would have little time for anything other than such correspondence in the course of the day, and I would have no time for constructive work. But since I feel that you are men of genuine good will and that your criticisms are sincerely set forth, I want to try to answer your statement in what I hope will be patient and reasonable terms.

I think I should indicate why I am here in Birmingham, since you have been influenced by the view which argues against "outsiders coming in." I have the honor of serving as president of the Southern Christian

AUTHOR'S NOTE: This response to a published statement by eight fellow clergymen from Alabama (Bishop C. C. J. Carpenter, Bishop Joseph A. Durick, Rabbi Hilton L. Grafman, Bishop Paul Hardin, Bishop Holan B. Harmon, the Reverend George M. Murray, the Reverend Edward V. Ramage and the Reverend Earl Stallings) was composed under somewhat constricting circumstances. Begun on the margins of the newspaper in which the statement appeared while I was in jail, the letter was continued on scraps of writing paper supplied by a friendly Negro trusty, and concluded on a pad my attorneys were eventually permitted to leave me. Although the text remains in substance unaltered, I have indulged in the author's prerogative of polishing it for publication.
"Letter from Birmingham Jail"—April 16, 1963 from *Why We Can't Wait* by Martin Luther King, Jr. Copyright © 1963 by Martin Luther King, Jr. Reprinted by permission of Harper & Row, Publishers.

Leadership Conference, an organization operating in every southern state, with headquarters in Atlanta, Georgia. We have some eighty-five affiliated organizations across the South, and one of them is the Alabama Christian Movement for Human Rights. Frequently we share staff, educational and financial resources with our affiliates. Several months ago the affiliate here in Birmingham asked us to be on call to engage in a nonviolent direct-action program if such were deemed necessary. We readily consented, and when the hour came we lived up to our promise. So I, along with several members of my staff, am here because I have organizational ties here.

But more basically, I am in Birmingham because injustice is here. Just as the prophets of the eighth century B.C. left their villages and carried their "thus saith the Lord" far beyond the boundaries of their home towns, and just as the Apostle Paul left his village of Tarsus and carried the gospel of Jesus Christ to the far corners of the Greco-Roman world, so am I compelled to carry the gospel of freedom beyond my own home town. Like Paul, I must constantly respond to the Macedonian call for aid.

Moreover, I am cognizant of the interrelatedness of all communities and states. I cannot sit idly by in Atlanta and not be concerned about what happens in Birmingham. Injustice anywhere is a threat to justice everywhere. We are caught in an inescapable network of mutuality, tied in a single garment of destiny. Whatever affects one directly, affects all indirectly. Never again can we afford to live with the narrow, provincial "outside agitator" idea. Anyone who lives inside the United States can never be considered an outsider anywhere within its bounds.

You deplore the demonstrations taking place in Birmingham. But your statement, I am sorry to say, fails to express a similar concern for the conditions that brought about the demonstrations. I am sure that none of you would want to rest content with the superficial kind of social analysis that deals merely with effects and does not grapple with underlying causes. It is unfortunate that demonstrations are taking place in Birmingham, but it is even more unfortunate that the city's white power structure left the Negro community with no alternative.

In any nonviolent campaign there are four basic steps: collection of the facts to determine whether injustices exist; negotiation; self-purification; and direct action. We have gone through all these steps in Birmingham. There can be no gainsaying the fact that racial injustice engulfs this community. Birmingham is probably the most thoroughly segregated city in the United States. Its ugly record of brutality is widely known. Negroes have experienced grossly unjust treatment in the courts. There have been more unsolved bombings of Negro homes and churches in Birmingham than in any other city in the nation. These are the hard, brutal facts of the case. On the basis of these conditions, Negro leaders sought to negotiate with the city fathers. But the latter consistently refused to engage in good-faith negotiation.

Then, last September, came the opportunity to talk with leaders of Birmingham's economic community. In the course of the negotiations, certain promises were made by the merchants—for example, to remove the stores' humiliating racial signs. On the basis of these promises, the Reverend Fred Shuttlesworth and the leaders of the Alabama Christian Movement for Human Rights agreed to a moratorium on all demonstrations. As the weeks and months went by, we realized that we were the victims of a broken promise. A few signs, briefly removed, returned; the others remained.

As in so many past experiences, our hopes had been blasted, and the shadow of deep disappointment settled upon us. We had no alternative except to prepare for direct action, whereby we would present our very bodies as a means of laying our case before the conscience of the local and the national community. Mindful of the difficulties involved, we decided to undertake a process of self-purification. We began a series of workshops on nonviolence, and we repeatedly asked ourselves: "Are you able to accept blows without retaliating?" "Are you able to endure the ordeal of jail?" We decided to schedule our direct-action program for the Easter season, realizing that except for Christmas, this is the main shopping period of the year. Knowing that a strong economic-withdrawal program would be the by-product of direct action, we felt that this would be the best time to bring pressure to bear on the merchants for the needed change.

Then it occurred to us that Birmingham's mayoralty election was coming up in March, and we speedily decided to postpone action until after election day. When we discovered that the Commissioner of Public Safety, Eugene "Bull" Connor, had piled up enough votes to be in the run-off, we decided again to postpone action until the day after the run-off so that the demonstrations could not be used to cloud the issues. Like many others, we waited to see Mr. Connor defeated, and to this end we endured postponement after postponement. Having aided in this community need, we felt that our direct-action program could be delayed no longer.

You may well ask: "Why direct action? Why sit-ins, marches and so forth? Isn't negotiation a better path?" You are quite right in calling for negotiation. Indeed, this is the very purpose of direct action. Nonviolent direct action seeks to create such a crisis and foster such a tension that a community which has constantly refused to negotiate is forced to confront the issue. It seeks so to dramatize the issue that it can no longer be ignored. My citing the creation of tension as part of the work of the nonviolent-resister may sound rather shocking. But I must confess that I am not afraid of the word "tension." I have earnestly opposed violent tension, but there is a type of constructive, nonviolent tension which is necessary for growth. Just as Socrates felt that it was necessary to create tension in the mind so that individuals could rise from the bondage of myths and half-truths to the unfettered realm of creative analysis and objective appraisal, so must we see the need for nonviolent gadflies to create the kind of tension in society that will help men rise from the dark depths of prejudice and racism to the majestic heights of understanding and brotherhood.

The purpose of our direct-action program is to create a situation so crisis-packed that it will inevitably open the door to negotiation. I therefore concur with you in your call for negotiation. Too long has our beloved Southland been bogged down in a tragic effort to live in monologue rather than dialogue.

One of the basic points in your statement is that the action that I and my associates have taken in Birmingham is untimely. Some have asked: "Why didn't you give the new city administration time to act?" The only answer that I can give to this query is that the new Birmingham administration must be prodded about as much as the outgoing one, before it will act. We are sadly mistaken if we feel that the election of Albert Boutwell as mayor will bring the millennium to Birmingham. While Mr. Boutwell is a much more gentle person than Mr. Connor, they are both segregationists, dedicated to maintenance of the status quo. I have hope that Mr. Boutwell will be reasonable enough to see the futility of massive resistance to desegregation. But he will not see this without pressure from devotees of civil rights. My friends, I must say to you that we have not made a single gain in civil rights without determined legal and nonviolent pressure. Lamentably, it is an historical fact that privileged groups seldom give up their privileges voluntarily. Individuals may see the moral light and voluntarily give up their unjust posture; but, as Reinhold Niebuhr has reminded us, groups tend to be more immoral than individuals.

We know through painful experience that freedom is never voluntarily given by the oppressor; it must be demanded by the oppressed. Frankly, I have yet to engage in a direct-action campaign that was "well-timed" in the view of those who have not suffered unduly from the disease of segregation. For years now I have heard the word "Wait!" It rings in the ear of every Negro with piercing familiarity. This "Wait" has almost always meant "Never." We must come to see, with one of our distinguished jurists, that "justice too long delayed is justice denied."

We have waited for more than 340 years for our constitutional and God-given rights. The nations of Asia and Africa are moving with jetlike speed toward gaining political independence, but we still creep at horse-

and-buggy pace toward gaining a cup of coffee at a lunch counter. Perhaps it is easy for those who have never felt the stinging darts of segregation to say, "Wait." But when you have seen vicious mobs lynch your mothers and fathers at will and drown your sisters and brothers at whim; when you have seen hate-filled policemen curse, kick and even kill your black brothers and sisters; when you see the vast majority of your twenty million Negro brothers smothering in an airtight cage of poverty in the midst of an affluent society; when you suddenly find your tongue twisted and your speech stammering as you seek to explain to your six-year-old daughter why she can't go to the public amusement park that has just been advertised on television, and see tears welling up in her eyes when she is told that Funtown is closed to colored children, and see ominous clouds of inferiority beginning to form in her little mental sky, and see her beginning to distort her personality by developing an unconscious bitterness toward white people; when you have to concoct an answer for a five-year-old son who is asking: "Daddy, why do white people treat colored people so mean?"; when you take a cross-country drive and find it necessary to sleep night after night in the uncomfortable corners of your automobile because no motel will accept you; when you are humiliated day in and day out by nagging signs reading "white" and "colored"; when your first name becomes "nigger," your middle name becomes "boy" (however old you are) and your last name becomes "John," and your wife and mother are never given the respected title "Mrs."; when you are harried by day and haunted by night by the fact that you are a Negro, living constantly at tiptoe stance, never quite knowing what to expect next, and are plagued with inner fears and outer resentments; when you are forever fighting a degenerating sense of "nobodiness"—then you will understand why we find it difficult to wait. There comes a time when the cup of endurance runs over, and men are no longer willing to be plunged into the abyss of despair. I hope, sirs, you can understand our legitimate and unavoidable impatience.

You express a great deal of anxiety over our willingness to break laws. This is certainly a legitimate concern. Since we so diligently urge people to obey the Supreme Court's decision of 1954 outlawing segregation in the public schools, at first glance it may seem rather paradoxical for us consciously to break laws. One may well ask: "How can you advocate breaking some laws and obeying others?" The answer lies in the fact that there are two types of laws: just and unjust. I would be the first to advocate obeying just laws. One has not only a legal but a moral responsibility to obey just laws. Conversely, one has a moral responsibility to disobey unjust laws. I would agree with St. Augustine that "an unjust law is no law at all."

Now, what is the difference between the two? How does one determine whether a law is just or unjust? A just law is a man-made code that squares with the moral law or the law of God. An unjust law is a code that is out of harmony with the moral law. To put it in the terms of St. Thomas Aquinas: An unjust law is a human law that is not rooted in eternal law and natural law. Any law that uplifts human personality is just. Any law that degrades human personality is unjust. All segregation statutes are unjust because segregation distorts the soul and damages the personality. It gives the segregator a false sense of superiority and the segregated a false sense of inferiority. Segregation, to use the terminology of the Jewish philosopher Martin Buber, substitutes an "I-it" relationship for an "I-thou" relationship and ends up relegating persons to the status of things. Hence segregation is not only politically, economically and sociologically unsound, it is morally wrong and sinful. Paul Tillich has said that sin is separation. Is not segregation an existential expression of man's tragic separation, his awful estrangement, his terrible sinfulness? Thus it is that I can urge men to obey the 1954 decision of the Supreme Court, for it is morally right; and I can urge them to disobey segregation ordinances, for they are morally wrong.

Let us consider a more concrete example of just and unjust laws. An unjust law is a code that a numerical or power majority group compels a minority group to obey but does not make binding on itself. This is *difference* made legal. By the same token, a just law is a code that a majority compels a minority to follow and that it is willing to follow itself. This is *sameness* made legal.

. . . .

I hope you are able to see the distinction I am trying to point out. In no sense do I advocate evading or defying the law, as would the rabid segregationist. That would lead to anarchy. One who breaks an unjust law must do so openly, lovingly, and with a willingness to accept the penalty. I submit that an individual who breaks a law that conscience tells him is unjust, and who willingly accepts the penalty of imprisonment in order to arouse the conscience of the community over its injustice, is in reality expressing the highest respect for law.

. . . .

I must make two honest confessions to you, my Christian and Jewish brothers. First, I must confess that over the past few years I have been gravely disappointed with the white moderate. I have almost reached the regrettable conclusion that the Negro's great stumbling block in his stride toward freedom is not the White Citizen's Counciler or the Ku Klux Klanner, but the white moderate, who is more devoted to "order" than to justice; who prefers a negative peace which is the absence of tension to a positive peace which is the presence of justice; who constantly says: "I agree with you in the goal you seek, but I cannot agree with your methods of direct action"; who paternalistically believes he can set the timetable for another man's freedom; who lives by a mythical concept of time and who constantly advises the Negro to wait for a "more convenient season." Shallow understanding from people of good will is more frustrating than absolute misunderstanding from people of ill will. Lukewarm acceptance is much more bewildering than outright rejection.

. . . .

In your statement you assert that our actions, even though peaceful, must be condemned because they precipitate violence. But is this a logical assertion? Isn't this like condemning a robbed man because his possession of money precipitated the evil act of robbery? Isn't this like condemning Socrates because his unswerving commitment to truth and his philosophical inquiries precipitated the act by the misguided populace in which they made him drink hemlock? Isn't this like condemning Jesus because his unique God-consciousness and never-ceasing devotion to God's will precipitated the evil act of crucifixion? We must come to see that, as the federal courts have consistently affirmed, it is wrong to urge an individual to cease his efforts to gain his basic constitutional rights because the quest may precipitate violence. Society must protect the robbed and punish the robber.

I had also hoped that the white moderate would reject the myth concerning time in relation to the struggle for freedom. I have just received a letter from a white brother in Texas. He writes: "All Christians know that the colored people will receive equal rights eventually, but it is possible that you are in too great a religious hurry. It has taken Christianity almost two thousand years to accomplish what it has. The teachings of Christ take time to come to earth." Such an attitude stems from a tragic misconception that there is something in the very flow of time that will inevitably cure all ills. Actually, time itself is neutral; it can be used either destructively or constructively. More and more I feel that the people of ill will have used time much more effectively than have the people of good will. We will have to repent in this generation not merely for the hateful words and actions of the bad people but for the appalling silence of the good people. Human progress never rolls in on wheels of inevitability; it comes through the tireless efforts of men willing to be co-workers with God, and without this hard work, time itself becomes an ally of the forces of social stagnation. We must use time creatively, in the knowledge that the time is always ripe to do right. Now is the time to make real the promise of democracy and transform our pending national elegy into a creative psalm of brotherhood. Now is the time to lift our national policy from the quicksand of racial injustice to the solid rock of human dignity.

You speak of our activity in Birmingham as extreme. At first I was rather disappointed that fellow clergymen would see my nonviolent efforts as those of an extremist. I began thinking about the fact that I stand in the middle of two opposing forces in the Negro community. One is a force of complacency, made up in part of Negroes who, as a result of long years of oppression, are so drained of self-respect and a sense of "somebodiness" that they have adjusted to segregation; and in part of a few middle-class Negroes who, because of a degree of academic and economic security and because in some ways they profit by segregation, have become insensitive to the problems of the masses. The other force is one of bitterness and hatred, and it comes perilously close to advocating violence. It is expressed in the various black nationalist groups that are springing up across the nation, the largest and best-known being Elijah Muhammad's Muslim movement. Nourished by the Negro's frustration over the continued existence of racial discrimination, this movement is made up of people who have lost faith in America, who have absolutely repudiated Christianity, and who have concluded that the white man is an incorrigible "devil."

I have tried to stand between these two forces, saying that we need emulate neither the "do-nothingism" of the complacent nor the hatred and despair of the black nationalist. For there is the more excellent way of love and nonviolent protest. I am grateful to God that, through the influence of the Negro church, the way of nonviolence became an integral part of our struggle.

If this philosophy had not emerged, by now many streets of the South would, I am convinced, be flowing with blood. And I am further convinced that if our white brothers dismiss as "rabble-rousers" and "outside agitators" those of us who employ nonviolent direct action, and if they refuse to support our nonviolent efforts, millions of Negroes will, out of frustration and despair, seek solace and security in black-nationalist ideologies—a development that would inevitably lead to a frightening racial nightmare.

Oppressed people cannot remain oppressed forever. The yearning for freedom eventually manifests itself, and that is what has happened to the American Negro. Something within has reminded him of his birthright of freedom, and something without has reminded him that it can be gained. Consciously or unconsciously, he has been caught up by the *Zeitgeist*, and with his black brothers of Africa and his brown and yellow brothers of Asia, South America and the Caribbean, the United States Negro is moving with a sense of great urgency toward the promised land of racial justice. If one recognizes this vital urge that has engulfed the Negro community, one should readily understand why public demonstrations are taking place. The Negro has many pent-up resentments and latent frustrations, and he must release them. So let him march; let him make prayer pilgrimages to the city hall; let him go on freedom rides—and try to understand why he must do so. If his repressed emotions are not released in nonviolent ways, they will seek expression through violence; this is not a threat but a fact of history. So I have not said to my people: "Get rid of your discontent." Rather, I have tried to say that this normal and healthy discontent can be channeled into the creative outlet of nonviolent direct action. And now this approach is being termed extremist.

But though I was initially disappointed at being categorized as an extremist, as I continued to think about the matter I gradually gained a measure of satisfaction from the label. Was not Jesus an extremist for love: "Love your enemies, bless them that curse you, do good to them that hate you, and pray for them which despitefully use you, and persecute you." Was not Amos an extremist for justice: "Let justice roll down like waters and righteousness like an ever-flowing stream." Was not Martin Luther an extremist: "Here I stand; I cannot do otherwise, so help me God." And John Bunyan: "I will stay in jail to the end of my days before I make a butchery of my conscience." And Abraham Lincoln: "This nation cannot survive half slave and half free." And Thomas Jefferson: "We hold these truths to be self-evident, that all men are created equal. . . ." So the question is not whether we will be extremists, but what kind of extremists we will be. Will we be extremists for hate or for love? Will we be extremists for the preservation of injustice or for the extension of justice? In that dramatic scene on Calvary's hill three men were crucified. We must never forget that all three were crucified for the same crime—the crime of extremism. Two were extremists for immorality, and thus fell below their environment. The other, Jesus Christ, was an extremist for love, truth and goodness, and thereby rose above his environment. Perhaps the South, the nation and the world are in dire need of creative extremists.

I had hoped that the white moderate would see this need. Perhaps I was too optimistic; perhaps I expected too much. I suppose I should have realized that few members of the oppressor race can understand the deep groans and passionate yearnings of the oppressed race, and still fewer have the vision to see that injustice must be rooted out by strong, persistent and determined action. I am thankful, however, that some of our white brothers in the South have grasped the meaning of this social revolution and committed themselves to it. They are still too few in quantity, but they are big in quality. Some—such as Ralph McGill, Lillian Smith, Harry Golden, James McBride Dabbs, Ann Braden and Sarah Patton Boyle—have written about our struggle in eloquent and prophetic terms. Others have marched with us down nameless streets of the South. They have languished in filthy, roach-infested jails, suffering the abuse and brutality of policemen who view them as "dirty nigger-lovers." Unlike so many of their moderate brothers and sisters, they have recognized the urgency of the moment and sensed the need for powerful "action" antidotes to combat the disease of segregation.

Let me take note of my other major disappointment. I have been so greatly disappointed with the white church and its leadership. Of course, there are some notable exceptions. I am not unmindful of the fact that each of you has taken some significant stands on this issue. I commend you, Reverend Stallings, for your Christian stand on this past Sunday, in welcoming Negroes to your worship service on a nonsegregated basis. I commend the Catholic leaders of this state for integrating Spring Hill College several years ago.

But despite these notable exceptions, I must honestly reiterate that I have been disappointed with the church. I do not say this as one of those negative critics who can always find something wrong with the church. I say this as a minister of the gospel, who loves the church; who was nurtured in its bosom; who has been sustained by its spiritual blessings and who will remain true to it as long as the cord of life shall lengthen.

When I was suddenly catapulted into the leadership of the bus protest in Montgomery, Alabama, a few years ago, I felt we would be supported by the white church. I felt that the white ministers, priests and rabbis of the South would be among our strongest allies. Instead, some have been outright opponents, refusing to understand the freedom movement and misrepresenting its leaders; all too many others have been more cautious than courageous and have remained silent behind the anaesthetizing security of stained-glass windows.

In spite of my shattered dreams, I came to Birmingham with the hope that the white religious leadership of this community would see the justice of our cause and, with deep moral concern, would serve as the channel through which our just grievances could reach the power structure. I had hoped that each of you would understand. But again I have been disappointed.

I have heard numerous southern religious leaders admonish their worshipers to comply with a desegregation decision because it is the law, but I have longed to hear white ministers declare: "Follow this decree because integration is morally right and because the Negro is your brother." In the midst of blatant injustices inflicted upon the Negro, I have watched white churchmen stand on the sideline and mouth pious irrelevancies and sanctimonious trivialities. In the midst of a mighty struggle to rid our nation of racial and economic injustice, I have heard many ministers say: "Those are social issues, with which the gospel has no real concern." And I have watched many churches commit themselves to a completely otherworldly religion which makes a strange, un-Biblical distinction between body and soul, between the sacred and the secular.

I have traveled the length and breadth of Alabama, Mississippi and all the other southern states. On sweltering summer days and crisp autumn mornings I have looked at the South's beautiful churches with their lofty spires pointing heavenward. I have beheld the impressive outlines of her massive religious-education buildings. Over and over I have found myself asking: "What kind of people worship here? Who is their God? Where were their voices when the lips of Governor Barnett dripped with words of interposition and nullification? Where were they when Governor Wallace gave a clarion call for defiance and hatred? Where were their voices of support when bruised and weary Negro men and women decided to rise from the dark dungeons of complacency to the bright hills of creative protest?"

Yes, these questions are still in my mind. In deep disappointment I have wept over the laxity of the church. But be assured that my tears have been tears of love. There can be no deep disappointment where there is not deep love. Yes, I love the church. How could I do otherwise? I am in the rather unique position of being the son, the grandson and the great-grandson of preachers. Yes, I see the church as the body of Christ. But, oh! How we have blemished and scarred that body through social neglect and through fear of being nonconformists.

There was a time when the church was very powerful—in the time when the early Christians rejoiced at being deemed worthy to suffer for what they believed. In those days the church was not merely a thermometer that recorded the ideas and principles of popular opinion; it was a thermostat that transformed the mores of society. Whenever the early Christians entered a town, the people in power became disturbed and immediately sought to convict the Christians for being "disturbers of the peace" and "outside agitators." But the Christians pressed on, in the conviction that they were "a colony of heaven," called to obey God rather than man. Small in number, they were big in commitment. They were too God-intoxicated to be "astronomically intimidated." By their effort and example they brought an end to such ancient evils as infanticide and gladiatorial contests.

Things are different now. So often the contemporary church is a weak, ineffectual voice with an uncertain sound. So often it is an arch-defender of the status quo. Far from being disturbed by the presence of the church, the power structure of the average community is consoled by the church's silent—and often even vocal—sanction of things as they are.

But the judgment of God is upon the church as never before. If today's church does not recapture the sacrificial spirit of the early church, it will lose its authenticity, forfeit the loyalty of millions, and be dismissed as an irrelevant social club with no meaning for the twentieth century. Every day I meet young people whose disappointment with the church has turned into outright disgust.

Perhaps I have once again been too optimistic. Is organized religion too inextricably bound to the status quo to save our nation and the world? Perhaps I must turn my faith to the inner spiritual church, the church within the church, as the true *ekklesia* and the hope of the world. But again I am thankful to God that some noble souls from the ranks of organized religion have broken loose from the paralyzing chains of conformity and joined us as active partners in the struggle for freedom. They have left their secure congregations and walked the streets of Albany, Georgia, with us. They have gone down the highways of the South on tortuous rides for freedom. Yes, they have gone to jail with us. Some have been dismissed from their churches, have lost the support of their bishops and fellow ministers. But they have acted in the faith that right defeated is stronger than evil triumphant. Their witness has been the spiritual salt that has preserved the true meaning of the gospel in these troubled times. They have carved a tunnel of hope through the dark mountain of disappointment.

I hope the church as a whole will meet the challenge of this decisive hour. But even if the church does not come to the aid of justice, I have no despair about the future. I have no fear about the outcome of our struggle in Birmingham, even if our motives are at present misunderstood. We will reach the goal of freedom in Birmingham and all over the nation, because the goal of America is freedom. Abused and scorned though we may be, our destiny is tied up with America's destiny. Before the pilgrims landed at Plymouth, we were here. Before the pen of Jefferson etched the majestic words of the Declaration of Independence across the pages of history, we were here. For more than two centuries our forebears labored in this country without wages; they made cotton king; they built the homes of their masters while suffering gross injustice and shameful humiliation—and yet out of a bottomless vitality they continued to thrive and develop. If the inexpressible cruelties of slavery could not stop us, the opposition we now face will surely fail. We will win our freedom because the sacred heritage of our nation and the eternal will of God are embodied in our echoing demands.

Before closing I feel impelled to mention one other point in your statement that has troubled me profoundly. You warmly commended the Birmingham police force for keeping "order" and "preventing violence." I doubt that you would have so warmly commended the policemen if you were to observe their ugly and inhumane treatment of Negroes here in the city jail; if you were to watch them push and curse old Negro women and young Negro girls; if you were to see them slap and kick old Negro

men and young boys; if you were to observe them, as they did on two
occasions, refuse to give us food because we wanted to sing our grace
together. I cannot join you in your praise of the Birmingham police
department.

It is true that the police have exercised a degree of discipline in
handling the demonstrators. In this sense they have conducted themselves
rather "nonviolently" in public. But for what purpose? To preserve the
evil system of segregation. . . .

I wish you had commended the Negro sit-inners and demonstrators
of Birmingham for their sublime courage, their willingness to suffer and
their amazing discipline in the midst of great provocation. One day the
South will recognize its real heroes. They will be the James Merediths,
with the noble sense of purpose that enables them to face jeering and
hostile mobs, and with the agonizing loneliness that characterizes the life
of the pioneer. They will be old, oppressed, battered Negro women, symbolized in a seventy-two-year-old woman in Montgomery, Alabama, who
rose up with a sense of dignity and with her people decided not to ride
segregated buses, and who responded with ungrammatical profundity to
one who inquired about her weariness: "My feets is tired, but my soul is
at rest." They will be the young high school and college students, the
young ministers of the gospel and a host of their elders, courageously and
nonviolently sitting in at lunch counters and willingly going to jail for
conscience' sake. One day the South will know that when these disin-
herited children of God sat down at lunch counters, they were in reality
standing up for what is best in the American dream and for the most
sacred values in our Judaeo-Christian heritage, thereby bringing our
nation back to those great wells of democracy which were dug deep by
the founding fathers in their formulation of the Constitution and the
Declaration of Independence.

Never before have I written so long a letter. I'm afraid it is much
too long to take your precious time. I can assure you that it would have
been much shorter if I had been writing from a comfortable desk, but
what else can one do when he is alone in a narrow jail cell, other than
write long letters, think long thoughts and pray long prayers?

If I have said anything in this letter that overstates the truth and
indicates an unreasonable impatience, I beg you to forgive me. If I have
said anything that understates the truth and indicates my having a
patience that allows me to settle for anything less than brotherhood, I beg
God to forgive me.

I hope this letter finds you strong in the faith. I also hope that circumstances will soon make it possible for me to meet each of you, not as
an integrationist or a civil-rights leader but as a fellow clergyman and a
Christian brother. Let us all hope that the dark clouds of racial prejudice

will soon pass away and the deep fog of misunderstanding will be lifted from our fear-drenched communities, and in some not too distant tomorrow the radiant stars of love and brotherhood will shine over our great nation with all their scintillating beauty.

Yours for the cause of Peace and Brotherhood,
MARTIN LUTHER KING, JR.

ELIJAH MUHAMMAD

An Independent Black Nation And America's Downfall

The poor slave. After his masters let him go free, his first problem to solve was securing a home of his own for the first time. He must now do for self. Master is no longer responsible for him, he must solve his own problems.

He must now realize that he must work hard to be equal of other nations. He must also remember that justice and righteousness is his defense and wickedness his enemy and the downfall of his government and his people.

He must learn to make friends and to protect himself against enemies. He must dig into the earth for her rich treasures. He must now seek the friendship of other nations to do business with them and trade product for product.

But if the slave is lazy, he will always be the slave for another. No nation respects a beggar.

We, the members of the original Black Nation of the earth, who were once lost from our own kind, are supposed to be free. It absolutely does not make sense for us to be seeking integration with our slave-masters' children instead of seeking unity among our own kind.

There is not any EARTH offered to us in integrating—how can we and our children build an independent nation of this earth without some of it that we call our own.

Do not we look ignorant begging white America to accept us as equal members of their society without having one square foot of earth that we can call our own?

We are like hunter dogs whom the hunter is tired of and wishes that they would go and hunt food for themselves. But the poor, foolish dog is

From Elijah Muhammad, *Message to the Blackman in America* (Chicago: Muhammad Mosque of Islam No. 2, 1965), pp. 229–30, 269–75. Reprinted by permission of Elijah Muhammad.

there whenever his master sits down to eat, standing in the door begging with his tongue hanging out and wagging his tail, while at the same time, had he gone into the woods looking for a meal, he would not have had to suffer the hatred, kicks and curses of his master.

Without some of this earth for a home that we can call our own, rest assured we will forever be 22 million begging slaves at the door of some nation. We, the black people of America, should be ashamed of ourselves to go sit in the white businesses to force them to serve us.

Let us unite and serve ourselves! If the spiritual leaders could understand the Bible's prophecy, they would see how foolish they are in doing the things they are now doing.

We should seek a permanent home for our nation—not by begging others for what is theirs—and stop acting foolish and unite. Do for self before you will have it to do!

The white race's days are drawing to a close; their rule over the darker nations must end, according to Allah (God) and His prophets. This wicked world must give way for a world of righteousness.

. . . .

Allah manifests the fall of America. He desires to make America fall as a warning to her brothers in Europe. White Americans and Germans— Allah has taught me—are the most wicked of the white race. The wicked deeds that have been performed and are still being performed by white Americans upon the so-called Negroes (their slaves) are the worst in the annals of history.

They have been clever enough in their wickedness to make the so-called Negro slaves love them, though they are their open enemies and murderers. Allah in the person of Master Fard Muhammad, to whom be praised forever, now judges the American whites and is causing America's fall and total destruction. Egypt under Pharaoh is an example. It fulfills the signs and other prophecies of the doom of this people as foretold by the prophets from Noah to Jesus.

Moses and Jesus are the most outstanding prophets in the history of the Caucasian race for the past 4,000 years. There are several other contemporaries, but Moses and Jesus are the major prophets of the white race's history. The whole of the civilized world today, as prophesied in Isaiah, is against the white man of America. Allah hates the wicked American whites and threatens to remove them from the face of the earth.

Since white Americans and the white race in general have deceived the entire world of black people and their brethren (brown, red and yellow), Allah now is causing these people to wake up and see the white race as it really is, the created enemy of the darker people. As we see today, there is a general awakening of the darker people into the knowledge of self and the knowledge of their age-old (6,000 years) enemies all over the earth. The American white race cannot sincerely give the so-called Negroes (their slaves) a square deal. She only desires to deceive them.

Today, America is trying, against her will, to give the so-called Negro civil rights (which is against the very nature and will of the white race) for the first time since the black man has been here. America falsely offers him social equality in certain parts of the country. This social equality consists mostly of permitting the American black race to mix openly with the white man and his women (the devils). The actual idea, however, is to grant the so-called Negro social equality among the lower class of whites. This is done so that the scriptures, wherein the prophecy that the white man tempts and corrupts the so-called Negroes with his women, might be fulfilled.

God has taught me that the white race was grafted unalike, and, being unalike, it is able to attract the black man and black woman, getting them to do all the evil and indecency known to the white race.

The years 1965 and 1966 are going to be fateful for America, bringing in the "Fall of America." As one of the prophets of the Bible prophesied in regard to her, "As the morning spreads abroad upon the mountains a great and strong people set in battle array" (Joel 2:2). This is the setting of the nations for a showdown to determine who will live on earth. The survivor is to build a nation of peace to rule the people of the earth forever under the guidance of Almighty God, Allah. With the nations setting forth for a final war at this time, God pleads for His people (the inheritors of the earth, the so-called Negroes).

The so-called Negro is the prey of the white man of America, being held firmly in the white man's power, along with 2 million Indians who must be redeemed at this time and will be, if the so-called Negro turns to His Redeemer. The problem of the American black man is his unwillingness to be separated from his 400-year-old enemies. The problem, therefore, is harder to solve, especially with the enemy trying to fascinate the Negro with his lower class girls and women arraying them partly nude before the Negroes in every public news medium (cheap daily newspapers and magazines, radio and TV) and the Negro is quick to imitate.

The problem between these two people, separating and dignifying the so-called Negroes so they may be accepted and respected as equals or superiors to other nations, must be solved. This is God's promise to the so-called Negro (the lost and found members of the original Black Nation of the earth). This promise was made through the mouths of His prophets (Bible and Qur-an), that He would separate us from our enemies, dignify us and make us the masters after this wicked race has been judged and destroyed for its own evil.

But, as I said, the solving of this problem, which means the redemption of the Negro, is hard to do, since he loves his enemies. (See Bible;

Deut. 18:15, 18; Psalms; Isaiah; Matthew 25:32; and Revelations, Chapter 14.)

The manifestation of Allah and judgment between the so-called Negro and the enemy of God and Nation of Islam will make the so-called Negro see and know his enemy and himself, his people, his God and his religion.

We hear the statements of black educational, political and Christian classes, which express their love for the white man, publicly asking to be his brothers, if not his brothers-in-law. Now, this class wants to make it clear to the world that they really love the white race and not the black race. This means they want to be white instead of black. The devils have made them hate black. They reject the thought of black ever being the ruler or equal with the ruler. They ask boldly for inferiority, not only for themselves, but for their people.

They want to absorb themselves and their kind (especially the so-called American Negro) into the race of white people, thus ending the black race. It is just the opposite with Allah (God), myself and my followers. We "want out completely." We want no claim to kinship with a people who, by nature, are not our kin. Read from Genesis to the Revelation in the Bible and from Sura 2 to Sura 114 of the Holy Qur-an.

By no means are the so-called Negroes and the whites kin. God did not create them to ever become brothers. One is created an enemy against the other, and since the righteous are more powerful than the wicked, Allah, the God of righteous, set a time of reckoning for the enemy (the white man) of the righteous.

We want separation. We want a home on this earth we can call our own. We want to go for self and leave the enemy who has been sentenced to death by Allah (Rev. 20:10-14) from the day he was created. (See this subject in the Bible and Qur-an). No one, white, black, brown, yellow or red can prove to me by any scriptures of Allah (God) sent by one of the prophets of Allah (God) that we should not be separated from the white race, that we should believe and follow the religion dictated, shaped and formed by the theologians of the white race.

The coming Allah and the judgment of the wicked world is made clear by the prophetic sayings of the Prophets. The so-called reverends and the proud intellectual class are doomed to destruction with the enemy, if they remain with him instead of joining onto Allah, Who loves them and Who will deliver them and the Nation of Islam.

The so-called Negro masses must be warned of the grave mistake they make in following the leadership of those who love and befriend their murderers. This will not get them freedom or civil rights.

America is falling. Her doom has come, and none said the prophets shall help her in the day of her downfall. In the Bible, God pleads with you to fly out of her (America) and seek refuge in Him (Rev. 18:4). What is going to happen in 1965 and 1966? It certainly will change your minds about following a doomed people, a people who hate you and your kind and who call one who teaches the truth about them a hater. They are the producers of hatred of us. We are with God and the righteous.

I compare the fall of America with the fall of ancient Babylon. Her wickedness (sins), is the same as history shows of ancient Babylon. "Babylon is suddenly fallen and the destroyed howl for her; take balm for her pains, if so she may be healed" (Jer. 51:81). What were the sins of ancient Babylon? According to history she was rich; she was proud and her riches increased her corruption. She had every merchandise that the nations wanted or demanded; her ships carried her mechandise to the ports of every nation.

She was a drunkard; wine and strong drinks were in her daily practice. She was filled with adultery and murder; she persecuted and killed the people of God. She killed the saints and prophets of Allah (God). Hate and filthiness, gambling, sports of every evil as you practice in America were practiced in Babylon. Only America is modern and much worse. Ancient Babylon was destroyed by her neighboring nations.

I warn you to let their destruction serve as a warning for America. This people has gone to the limit in doing evil; as God dealt with ancient people, so will He deal with the modern Babylon (America). As God says: "Son of Man, when the land (people) sinneth against Me by trespassing grievously, then will I stretch out Mine hand upon it, and will break the staff of bread thereof, and will send famine upon it, and will cut off man and beast from it" (Ezekiel 14:13).

We see with our own eyes—but, the wicked Americans are too proud to confess that they see the bread of America gradually being cut off. Take a look into the Southwest and Middle West, see the hand of Allah (God) at work against modern Babylon—to break the whole staff of her bread for her evils done against His people (the so-called Negroes).

Texas and Kansas were once two of the nation's proudest states. Kansas, known for its wheat and Texas, for its cattle, cotton, corn and many other vegetables and fruits. They are today in the grip of a drought, continuous raging dust storms; their river beds lie bare, their fish stinking on the banks in dry parched mud. When the rain comes, it brings very little relief and does more damage than good. Snow comes—it brings not joy, but death and destruction. After the snow comes more dust storms. With the rain come hail stones, very large stones. America has not seen the large hail stones; she will see hail stones the size of small blocks of ice breaking down crops, trees, the roofs of homes, killing cattle and fowl. Behind this terrific earthquake, the people—frightened, killed, much sickness, and death will be widespread. You are getting a token of it now. On the outside, a threat of an atomic war between the nations of the earth. Yet you have your eyes closed at the manifest judgment of Allah (God), going on in your midst to bring this country to naught.

Allah (God) has found His people (the so-called Negroes), and is angry with the slave-masters for the evil done by them to His people (the so-called Negroes). Allah (God) is going to repay them according to their doings.

My poor people who have turned to their own God and religion (Allah and Islam), are being tracked down and watched as though they are about to rob a bank. This is done to try and put fear in them—so that they might stay away from God (Allah) and His true religion (Islam), as the devil knows—their salvation and defense.

They (the devils) watch the steps of the righteous (the Negroes) and seek to slay them (Psalms 37:32). The so-called Negroes live under the very shadow of death in America. There is no justice for them in the courts of their slave-masters. Why should not America be chastised for her evils done to the so-called Negroes? If God destroyed ancient Babylon for the mockery made of the sacred vessels taken from the Temple in Jerusalem, what do you think Allah (God) should do for America's mockery of the so-called Negroes—that she took from their native land and people and filled them with wine and whiskey.

Now she (America) puts on a show of temptation with their women (white women) in newspapers, magazines, in the streets half nude, and posing in the so-called Negroes' faces in the most indecent manner that is known to mankind—to trick them (so-called Negroes) to death and hell along with them. Be wise, my people, and shut your eyes to them—do not look at them in such an indecent way. Clean your homes of white people's pictures—put your own on the walls. The only so-called Negroes' pictures you will see in their homes are one they have lynched, one they want to kill, or one who has betrayed his own people for them.

America is falling; she is a habitation of devils and every uncleanness and hateful people of the righteous. Forsake her and fly to your own before it is too late.

NATHAN WRIGHT, JR.

Black Power:
Self-Development And
Self-Respect

What is said here concerning self-development and self-respect is designed chiefly as an in-group discussion for black people. It may have significance for others who listen in on this family discussion, as well.

Perhaps the central concern of the current issue of Black Power—for the good of the Negro and for the larger good of this whole nation and of our world today—is the self-development and the growth into maturity of the black people of America.

Black people have been the sleeping giants of this land. Among all Americans, their power, insights and experience, potentially ready to enrich this nation, have been least developed. In words of cosmic import which speak to black people in uniquely immediate terms, "we have not yet become what we shall be."

The black people of America are this nation's most rich and ready asset—its greatest raw material—as once the unmined earth and its untouched forests, fields and rivers were. In former years this nation built its greatness upon the utilization, not unmixed with wastefulness, of the vast physical resources which had lain untapped. Today, the new frontier of this nation's destiny lies in the development and utilization to the full of its infinitely greater human resources. What greater and potentially more useful reservoir of undeveloped and unutilized human resources does this nation have than in the black people of this land?

From the book *Black Power and Urban Unrest* by Nathan Wright, Jr. Copyright © 1967 by Nathan Wright, Jr. Published by Hawthorn Books, Inc. 70 Fifth Avenue, New York, N.Y. (The substance of this article was originally delivered as an address at the Abyssinian Church in Harlem, New York, on October 23, 1966.)

367

THE NEED FOR SELF-DEVELOPMENT

The great difficulty which we have had in coming into our own in America has only, in these recent days of impetus toward Black Power, begun to be made plain. We have operated, for at least the last crucial period of thirty years, on the assumption that Negroes needed to be led into their wanted place of maturity in American life.

This assumption should perhaps have been seen to be fictitious on its face. It is simply naive to believe that any person or any group of people may grow into maturity save in terms of their own self-development. Human growth cannot be produced from without: it must always be developed from within. Thus, thanks to the undoubtedly divine accident of the current focus on Black Power, black boys and girls, and black men and women—long lulled into a feeling of functionlessness and little worth —are awaking to realize that only through self-development can they become the people of power and of majesty and of might which their bearing of the image of their Creator has destined them to be.

There is, on the part of the Negro, a manifest need for self-development. Yet, of recent years, we as black people have assumed that a slave mentality of dependence upon others, as we had in former years, was appropriate for the twentieth-century destiny to which we are called. This crippling dependence upon others has hung like an albatross on our necks. It has led us to the state of stagnation and bewildered consternation which we find, with a few notable exceptions, pervading the life of the black people of America today.

The experience of all rising ethnic groups in this our beloved land has been that each rising group in American life must do for itself that which no other group may do for it. Each rising group has had to devise, to engineer, and to control in its own way its own plan, however crude or inept it may seem to have been, for its own particular growth into freedom, into self-development, and into self-sufficiency and into self-respect.

This path of self-development has been—since the well-known rejection by the American people in 1776 of the King George Plan for Colonial Development—the one and only truly American way. There has never been in the American experience a German-American plan for Jewish development. Nor has there been in the American experience a Polish plan for Italian development. Yet the black people of America have been led in these recent decades to believe that their due inheritance in America could come best, or even only, from a white American plan for black freedom. This is incongruous on its very face. The issue of Black Power for black people—and for the good of American life as a whole—speaks to the need for black people to move from the stance of humble and dependent and impotent beggars to the stature of men who will take again into their own hands, as all men must, the fashioning of their own destiny for their own growth into self-development and self-respect. Now herein precisely lies the singular difference between the impetus toward Black Power on the one hand and what we have known as the civil rights movement on the other.

While the civil rights movement has emphasized what black people have been due, the emphasis of black self-development is on what black people may give to America. The thrust of Black Power is toward national fulfillment through the utilization of the potentialities and latent gifts of all. Both Black Power and the civil rights movement must have their vital and necessary places. The civil rights movement has in its own invaluable way emphasized what the American Negro has been due as an American from the day of each black man's birth. Without the efforts of the civil rights movement, particularly over these past thirty and more years, it would be difficult to speculate on where we, and this nation as a whole, might be. The civil rights movement, with its interracial dialogue, needs to grow and to flourish. We must never indulge in the vain luxury of criticizing what our leaders—with the aid of others—have done for us in the past.

What we must do, however, for the days ahead in the light of newly perceived conditions is to establish new and more realistic priorities in terms of the business of self-development. While pushing and participating in the absolutely worthwhile interracial program in the field of civil rights, the black people of America ought long ago to have been addressing themselves to the far more basic business of the development by black people of black people for the growth into self-sufficiency and self-respect of black people. This is the main and previously neglected business to which we must address ourselves. It is to this top priority concern of self-development that the issue of Black Power calls the black people of America today.

In the past, we've needed help; and we have received it. But we lacked even more the fundamental necessity of self-help, and self-initiative. It is by this alone we as a people may grow into that self-direction and self-sufficiency which is incumbent upon all who would claim the respect due to responsible and mature men. It is by black self-development that this nation may come most fully into its own. The absence of black self-development has taxed the resources of the nation and limited the national destiny.

Now what, exactly, do we mean by self-development? We mean, for one thing, that we as black people must put behind us the "Hand me something" philosophy. In Philadelphia, we are told, they sang a song which said that:

"Jesus Christ will lead me and F. D. R. will feed me."
And they asked, "What need have we, then, to fear?" Now such a philosophy, in part, may be said to be good for any time. But a part of it also is appropriate only on a limited and temporary basis. It is said that if you give a man a fish, you feed him for a day. But if you teach him to fish and then *let him fish in the stream,* you feed that man for a lifetime.

Black Power in terms of self-development means that we want to fish as all Americans should do together in the main stream of American life. It means that we must reject the assumption that long-term relief is a reasonable option for any man. This assumption must no longer be allowed. It is a minimum moral imperative for men to be thrust into and sustained in substantial jobs. At this point, we as black people must not equivocate. We must make it clear that long-term relief is weakening and damaging to all poor people, and especially so to us as a racial group. We must demand the abolition of its use in such a way. When people ask us about what substitute we would offer, we must tell them that this involves a second step, which we shall get to next. In principle, the welfare system presently is an effective curse upon the poor. Once this is clearly and unequivocally established, we may then address ourselves to the need to devise ways for human rehabilitation. This will call, understandably, for resourcefulness. Finding ways for bringing all America's human potential to its flower is a basic moral imperative for our nation and is a duty which must be met by all of us.

Black Power means black development into self-sufficiency for the good of Negroes and for the good of the whole nation. We want—as others must want—to replace the helping hand which now aids us with our *own* hand—to sustain ourselves and not be burdens on all others.

Black self-development means something more, as well. It means that we want to put into glorious use the latent resources that we have for devising new ways of bringing fulfillment to all of life. From our position of powerlessness we have learned that only through an immediate and equitable extension of power can the black and white poor of our land be transformed from crippling liabilities into tangible assets. Poverty will begin to be abated most effectively when the particular and precious insights of black people are used in devising anti-poverty efforts.

Black self-development also means that we as black people must take the initiative—using the brainpower and the other resources of all, under our own leadership—in building black unity, black pride and black self-confidence for the larger good of this whole nation. A strong, independent press oriented to the needs of black people will help us to achieve this.

Black people have much to give to America. But it is only as black people first have confidence, pride and self-respect that they can give to America the rich gifts which it needs and must demand of us.

SELF-RESPECT AND RESPECT BY OTHERS

Undoubtedly the most crucial part of black self-development is the building of black men's self-respect.

Of all Americans, the black people of this land are by far the most intensely loyal. No one has ever questioned this. We are the unique products of this our native land; and in every respect—for good *and* for ill—we have sought to emulate and to fulfill all that is American.

In this endeavor, we have even gone so far as to adopt the white American disdain for all that pertains to blackness. The sad fact is that in America black people have been taught that to be like other Americans they must come to hate themselves. And this we all too often do with tragic vengeance. Doubtless many Negroes decry Black Power because of a cultural perception of incongruity between "power" and "blackness." Negroes are culturally conditioned to see themselves as childlike, immature and powerless. But the Scriptures tell us that we must love God with all our hearts and our neighbors *as ourselves.* How can we love our neighbors when we do not love and respect ourselves?

An eminent young Negro psychiatrist, from whom we shall be hearing increasingly in the days ahead because of his aggressive professional advocacy of the philosophy of Black Power, reminds us of the therapeutic need for the development of black men's self-respect. He writes: "The Negro 'community's high rate of crimes of violence, illegitimacy and broken homes can be traced in part to the Negro's learned self-hatred as well as to his poverty."[1] He believes that the kind of so-called integration which white people have offered to the black community "may have negative effects upon the Negro and may undermine his obvious need for strong positive group identification."

No man can instill pride and self-respect in another man. The same is true with ethnic groups. Every ethnic group, like every family, devises means of instilling group pride. Each idealizes its past and glorifies its ventures. So must the black people of America do. Instead of hating ourselves—as any group which dwells on its weakness might do—we must accentuate the positive aspects of who and what we are. Every Negro in America must come to grow each day in self-esteem and self-respect. This must be encouraged at every hand for the good of ourselves and for the greater good of all.

Not long ago I looked a black man in the face. His complexion was

[1] Dr. Alvin F. Poussaint, senior clinician, Tufts University Medical College Psychiatry Clinic, and southern field director of the National Medical Committee for Human Rights, in "Operation Understanding,' *Our Sunday Visitor,* October 23, 1966, p. 1.

darker than mine. His lips were thicker than mine. His nose was flatter and his hair had a tighter kink. I might add that he was a black man's man in that he stood up for black pride through black self-development and Black Power. And as I looked that black man in the face, I could only smile, for I realized that I was looking at one of the handsomest men on earth! We must have pride in ourselves.

When we look at black women who have dignity and a sense of pride in themselves, can there be any real doubt as to the superlative virtue of Black Power? A black man, who might have been any or all of us, recently said this: "When I was a child I was led to understand something of the nature of my heritage. I came to understand that from my relatively recent ancestral past the blood of black kings and princes flowed through my proud black veins. I knew also that the blood of proud Indian chieftains was mixed therewith. This to me was a source of undiluted pride. Then I came to know that in a more recent past the blood of white aristocracy, the very flower of white manhood, made its somewhat mixed contribution to the determinants of my life. This latter fact gave me, understandably, no greater sense of pride. But from my youth up," he concluded, "I have grown in the recognition that black men, and women and young people needed to appropriate the proud black heritage which is theirs, perhaps in a sense above all Americans, to have."

Negroes must, then, be proud of the variegated blackness which is theirs. When once we have come to have pride in what we are, and have been and must come to be, then—and only then—will others come to respect us for what we signify first and foremost to ourselves.

We hear all kinds of economic and political and psychological theories about the nature of racial prejudice. But the more I read and reflect upon them, the more I tend to believe that fundamentally they are straining at a relatively commonplace mechanism. When so-called racial prejudice is looked at in the context of Black Power as self-development, it may be explained in an elementary and far more creative way in terms of the dynamics of family life.

Look, for example, at the well-known story of the Prodigal Son. The brother in that classic story could not forgive an apparent blemish in his brother's life. Whether the defects we see in those close to us are imaginary or real, the family or in-group rejects with an irrational vengeance those who fail to measure up to the family's patterns or its agreed-upon purposes or goals.

In this light, the American black man's failure to stand securely by himself, however difficult the task, may provide sufficient explanation for his rejection by the American national family. In this sense, the black American may be perceived as a permanent and potentially significant part of the American household, with so-called racial prejudice being the family's intensive reaction to the failure of one whom they wish to uphold the basic and continuing family tradition of self-development. To carry the parable further, we may have squandered a generation's treasure of time seeking after the elusive fruits of some degree of integration when we had not first developed sufficient pride in what we are to integrate as equals.

We need to have pride in ourselves. No one may give this to us. It is a matter of self-development.

THE REDEMPTION OF AMERICAN LIFE

Self-development, as I have said, may bring about the fulfillment of American life through the nation's answer to the Negro's incessant pleas.

The Negro people of America want far more desperately than any other Americans for this nation to come into its own. This means that the black people of this land are, like the Jews of old, a people peculiarly elected to transmit and to perform no less than a sacred trust.

It is for us as black people to take the initiative in calling this nation as a whole to growth into maturity. The past and present apparent immaturity of the Negro is part and parcel of a wholesale national immaturity. Immaturity has begotton immaturity. Neither a nation nor a family may become what it should be without an equitable extension of relationships of power. Fail to encourage growth into self-sufficiency, and the family suffers as a whole. So it is with us.

We who are black people want this nation to grow up into the fulness of mature wisdom and power and might. This can come to the nation as a whole only as it comes to its each and every part.

It is for us who are black people to take the initiative in saving the nation of which we are an inextricable part. We must take the initiative to save the nation from the path of economic self-destruction, as it spirals its staggering costs for a kind of welfare system which we must reject in favor of far less costly and more fulfillment-laden efforts at genuine rehabilitation.

Black Power speaks—by its insistence upon equitable power relationships—to the precarious and perilous plight of those who are too powerful and to the needs of all in America of every color and every condition who are destined to become less than they should be by a debilitating absence of power.

In some sense of the word, all channels for the operation of cosmic purposes are woefully unworthy of their task. This is said in this instance of a young man whom we shall not name but who might be described as rash and wonderful, erratic and magnificent, as perhaps demagogue and perhaps also prophet and who in his own seemingly immature and yet undoubtedly brilliant way has raised for our generation an issue which may hold the key to the resolution of so many problems in almost every area of our corporate and personal life. If the devil himself had raised in these recent months the issue of *power,* it could hardly be less grace-laden for us and for our world.

Not long ago I sat with a group of men who to me were as great as they were serious and perplexed. They were alarmed at the recent turn of events, in which people long working together, apparently in unity for the good of all in America, had turned their backs or retreated in the area of civil rights. Some of these men spoke in terms of gloom and of dismay. We all listened attentively, and then one clergyman present suggested that there was at least one person in the room who did not accept the spirit of the conversation. He was asked the reason why. His answer came in a way that should give our hearts cause for rejoicing.

He said that for years he had hoped that somehow and in some way the issues in the area of civil rights and of race relations and of every form of inequity for any and all people could be made far more clear than they had been. People with so many mixed and different motives were working together for apparently good and noble purposes in an effectively neutralizing way. Yet there were no sharp and plain criteria for finding out just exactly where the battle lines could be clearly drawn. Then came the issue of power, and for him light came suddenly out of darkness. Those, he said, who worked for the immediate and equitable extension of power were on the side of a God who sought to be revealed in the here and now as a God of power, of majesty and of might. Those who would withhold or make light of the need for the equitable extension of power were, whatever their verbal protestations, fundamentally on the other side.

He went on to explain that whether the backlash grew or diminished, from the day of that revelation, it mattered very little. For to him, nothing short of the long-awaited day of the Lord had come, where the sheep might be separated from the goats. If those who are for more equitable power, he said, were only few in number, as they might appear at this hour to be, then with the battle lines clearly and unmistakably drawn we might—with the prophet Elisha—at last look up into the heavens and recognize as we see the host of heaven and the chariots of fire that "They that are with us are more than they who are against us."

We move on to one more brief story before we close. Joseph, in the classic biblical story, was sold by his brothers into Egyptian slavery. Several things happened which are suggestive of the black people's role in terms of both self-development and the moral and social development of this nation. Like Joseph, we as black people have been rejected and enslaved in various ways. In our rejected state, like Joseph we have developed resources which might well have a saving value for those who have rejected us. We have been pushed out to the margins of American life; and from our peculiar vantage point of a kind of dramatic distance we can see more clearly than other Americans what life is like down at the center of the stage. By many signs which need not be named, this nation, like Joseph's brethren who came to him in Egypt seeking succor, may be crying out at this time for the saving gifts which it is the destiny of black men alone at this crucial hour to give.

Doubtless the import of all that we have been saying here has begun in a way to be made plain. The task of self-development is our burden and ours alone as the central task, as the main business which is before us. This we must accept and aggressively and forthrightly implement not only for our needed self-respect but also for the respect and acceptance of others, which must inevitably follow upon our growth into self-esteem and into self-respect.

This nation needs us, as does our world. We must take our hats from our hands, and we must stand on our feet. The old, if we but open our eyes to see it, has passed away. The new day is at hand. We must put away childish things, and assume the proud demeanor of men.

Index

A

Abell, Aaron I., 217
Abrams, Ray H., 276
Adams, John, 65
Alger, Horatio, 214
Allen, Gay Wilson, 115
American Home Missionary Society, 112
Anglican Society for the Propagation of the Gospel, 61
Anglo-Saxon destiny, 303-308
Aron, Raymond, 277
Auden, W. H., 18

B

Bainton, Roland H., 277
Baker, R. S., 274
Baldwin, Alice M., 66
Barnett, Frank R., 318
Beecher, Henry Ward, 113, 155, 156, 162-76, 213, 214, 229-43
Beecher, Lyman, 15, 16, 113, 119-27
Beisner, Robert L., 117
Bellah, Robert, 8, 10, 14, 17
Beveridge, Albert J., 116, 140-53
Bibliographies, 30, 66, 118, 161, 217, 276-77, 318-19
Black American problems, 314-19, 347-75
Black Power, 317-18, 367-75
Blum, John Morton, 271, 277
Boalsburg, Penn., 1-2
Bodo, John R., 118

Boorstin, Daniel, 30, 66
Bridenbaugh, Carl, 66
Bryan, William A., 63
Bryan, William Jennings, 117
Burns, Edward M., 118
Bushnell, Horace, 160, 197-209

C

Carmichael, Stokely, 317, 318
Carnegie, Andrew, 117, 214, 215
China, 313
Churchill, Winston, 275
Civil religion, 8-21
Civil war, 155-209
Cleage, Albert, 318
Clebsch, William A., 160-61
Clemenceau, Georges, 274
Cold war, 277
Colonial period, 25-59
Commager, Henry Steele, 117
Communism, 311
Constitution of the U.S., 61-109
Constitutional convention, 64
Cooke, Terence J., 5, 6
Cousins, Norman, 66
Creel, George, 272
Crowder, Richard, 28
Cuba, 312

D

Dale, Thomas, 26